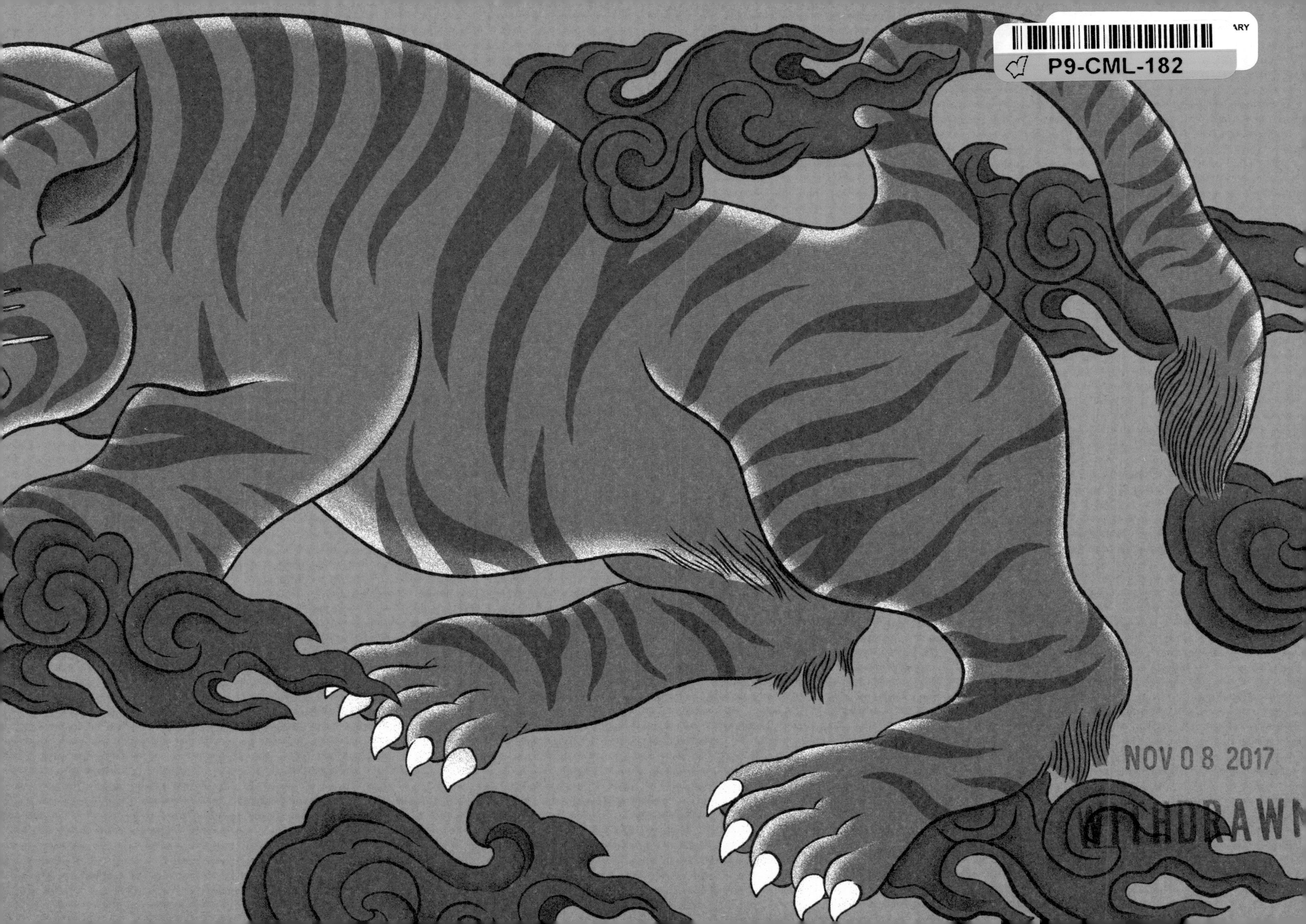

DREAMS in THIN AIR

Experienced and narrated by Michael Magnus Nybrandt

Illustrated by Thomas Engelbrecht Mikkelsen

CONUNDRUM PRESS

FOREWORD
BY HIS HOLINESS THE DALAI LAMA

Right after our arrival as refugees in 1959, with the active encouragement of then Indian Prime Minister Jawaharlal Nehru, we introduced modern education in the Tibetan schools that are spread across India. From the start, sporting activities were introduced as an integral part of the curriculum, to promote both a positive competitive spirit and an awareness of the importance of general physical exercise.

Despite the enthusiasm with which Tibetan children have taken to organized sports they have not had much opportunity to participate in international competition outside India. Nevertheless, some friends and dedicated individuals have made efforts to enable Tibetans to play against international sides. One such friend is Michael Magnus Nybrandt, who in the summer of 2001 arranged for a Tibetan football team formed in our exiled community in India to play a football match in Copenhagen, Denmark. The game received international media attention and in the process drew attention to the plight of the Tibetan people.

Michael was inspired to help the Tibetans take part in such sporting events by a trip he made to Tibet in 1997 on a bicycle. He is now publishing an attractive graphic novel based on the journeys he made in Tibet, which prompted him to organize the 2001 football match. This is a happy story when people from different parts of the world play and enjoy themselves together.

May 26, 2016

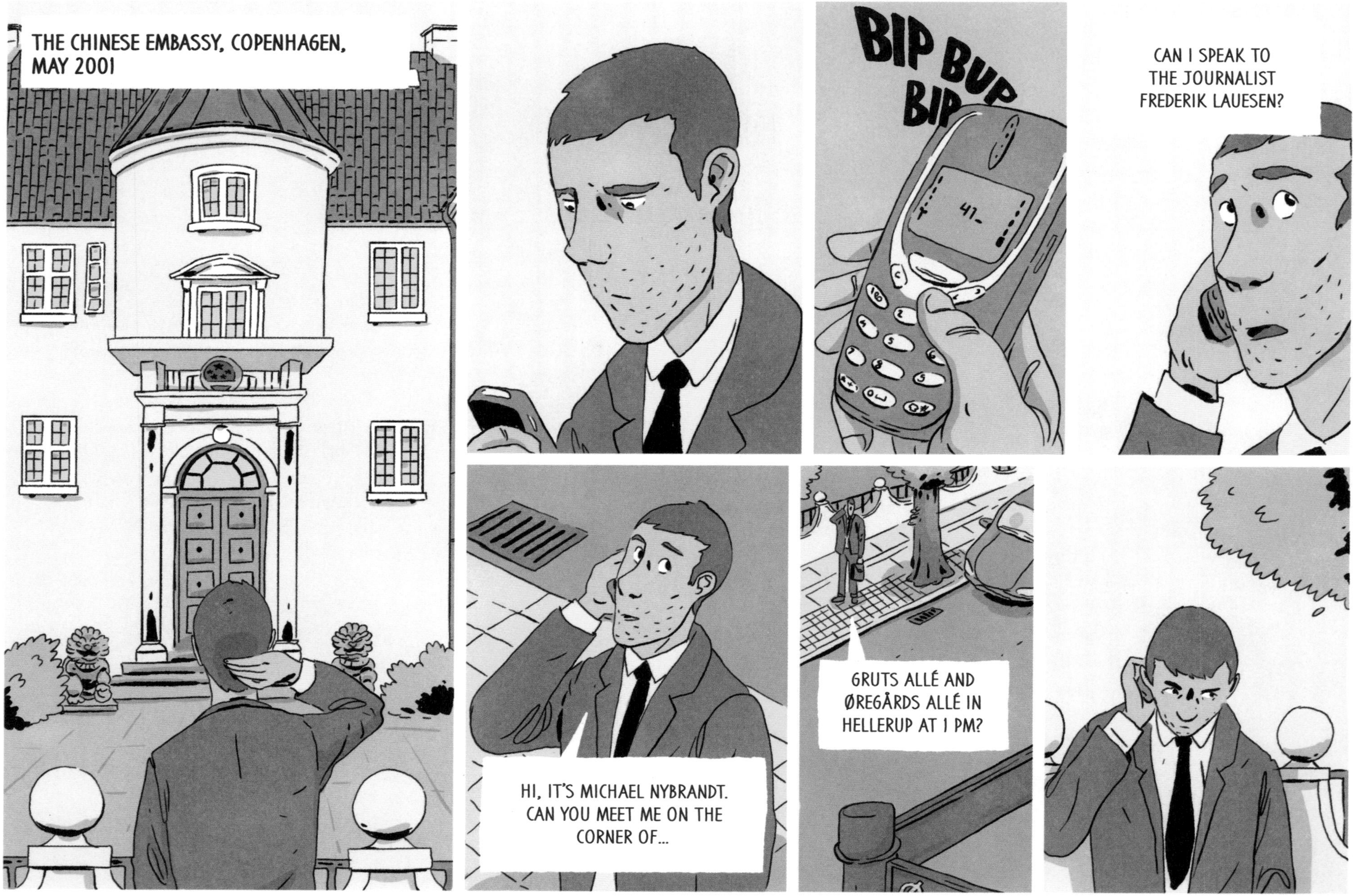
THE CHINESE EMBASSY, COPENHAGEN, MAY 2001
BIP BUP BIP
CAN I SPEAK TO THE JOURNALIST FREDERIK LAUESEN?
HI, IT'S MICHAEL NYBRANDT. CAN YOU MEET ME ON THE CORNER OF...
GRUTS ALLÉ AND ØREGÅRDS ALLÉ IN HELLERUP AT 1 PM?

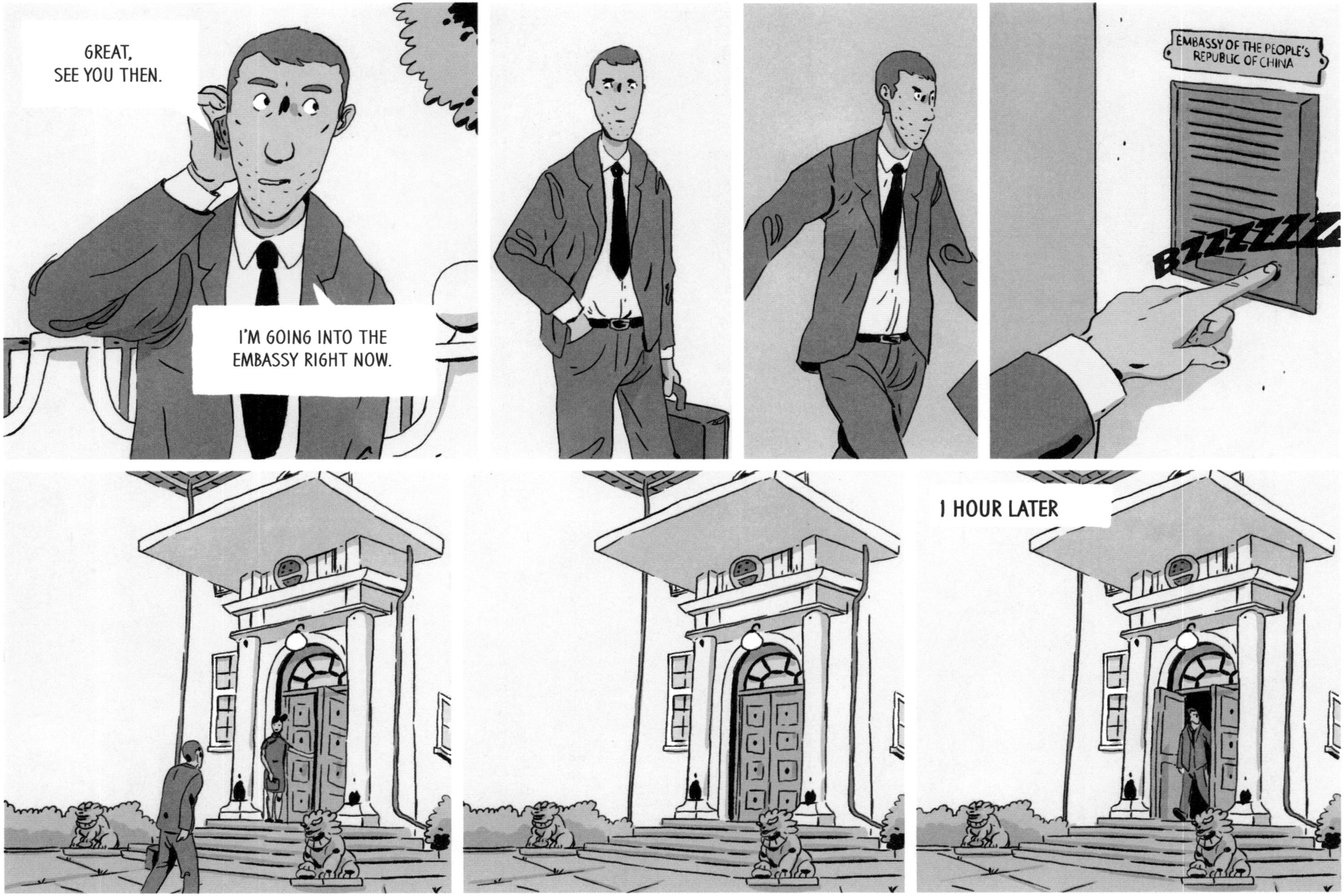
GREAT, SEE YOU THEN.
I'M GOING INTO THE EMBASSY RIGHT NOW.
EMBASSY OF THE PEOPLE'S REPUBLIC OF CHINA
BZZZZZZ
1 HOUR LATER

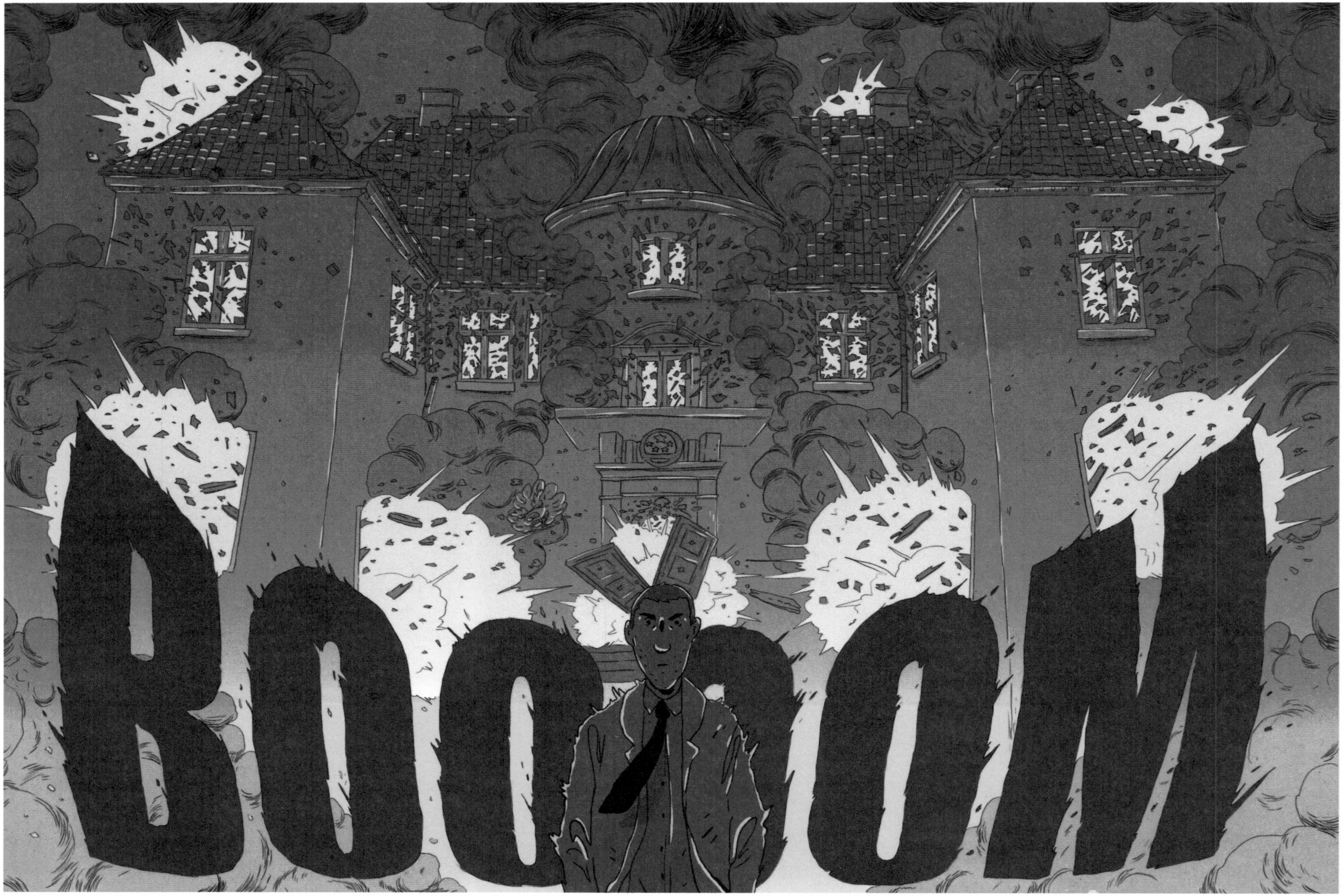
BOOOOM

CHAPTER 1

TOWARDS TIBET

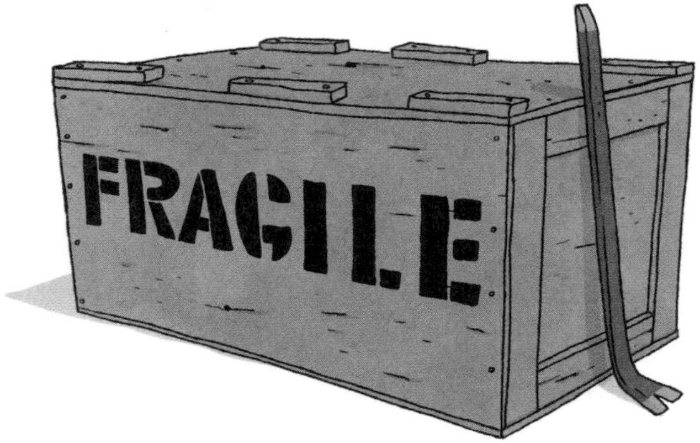
FRAGILE

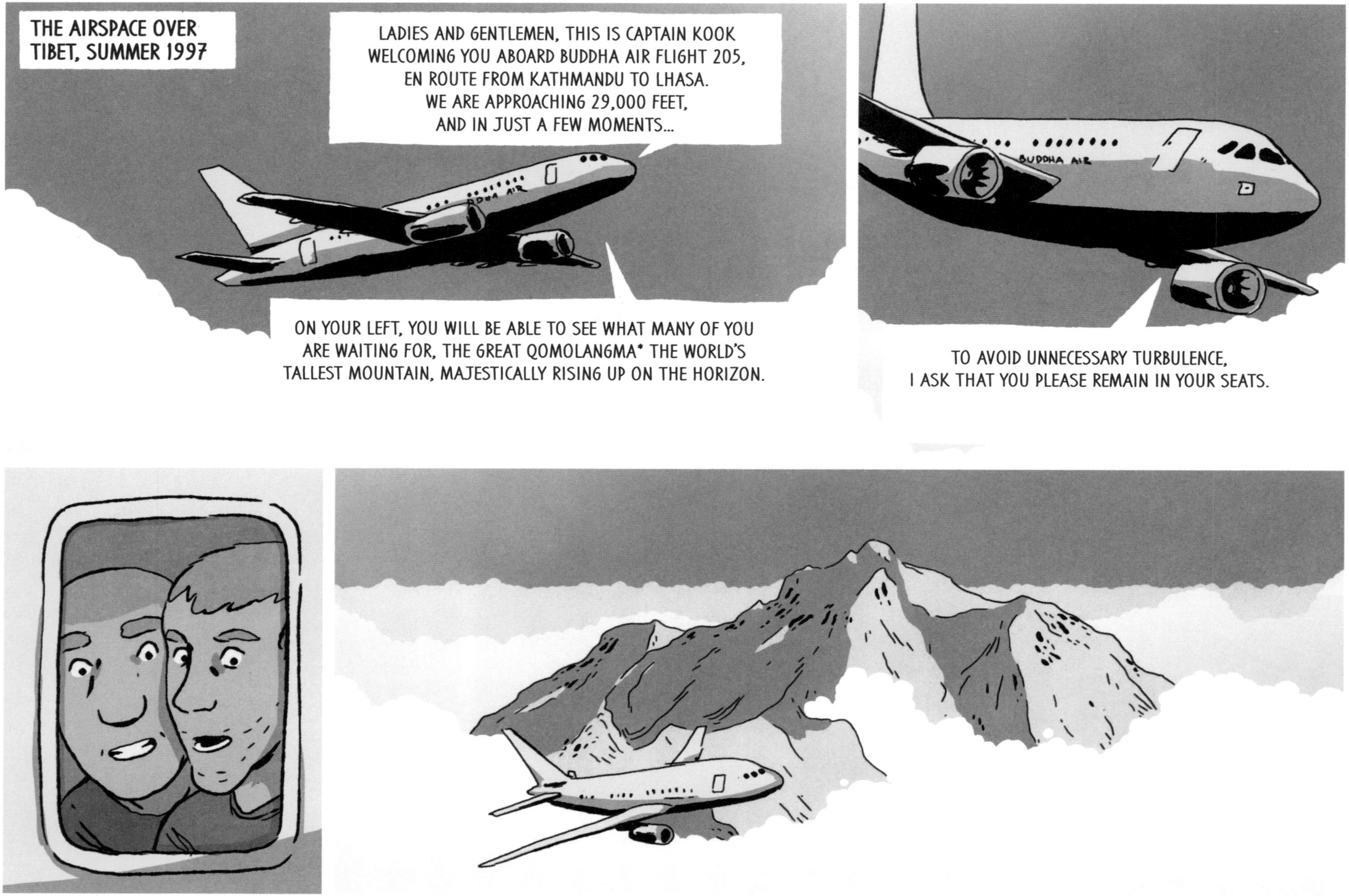
THE AIRSPACE OVER TIBET, SUMMER 1997
LADIES AND GENTLEMEN, THIS IS CAPTAIN KOOK WELCOMING YOU ABOARD BUDDHA AIR FLIGHT 205, EN ROUTE FROM KATHMANDU TO LHASA. WE ARE APPROACHING 29,000 FEET, AND IN JUST A FEW MOMENTS...
ON YOUR LEFT, YOU WILL BE ABLE TO SEE WHAT MANY OF YOU ARE WAITING FOR, THE GREAT QOMOLANGMA* THE WORLD'S TALLEST MOUNTAIN, MAJESTICALLY RISING UP ON THE HORIZON.
BUDDHA AIR
TO AVOID UNNECESSARY TURBULENCE, I ASK THAT YOU PLEASE REMAIN IN YOUR SEATS.

*MOUNT EVEREST, AMONG THE HIMALAYAN POPULATION CALLED QOMOLANGMA, WHICH TRANSLATES AS "HOLY MOTHER".

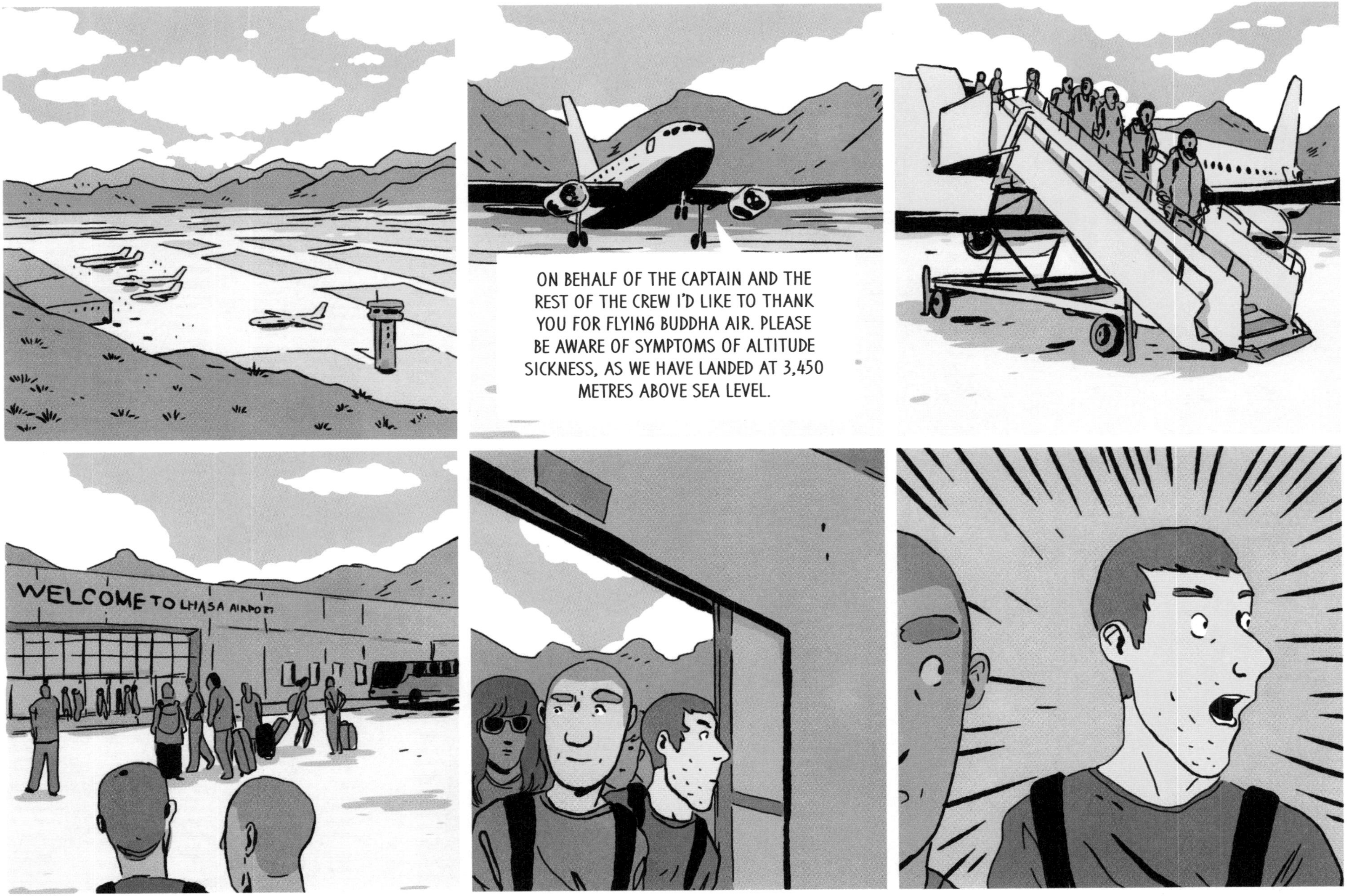
ON BEHALF OF THE CAPTAIN AND THE REST OF THE CREW I'D LIKE TO THANK YOU FOR FLYING BUDDHA AIR. PLEASE BE AWARE OF SYMPTOMS OF ALTITUDE SICKNESS, AS WE HAVE LANDED AT 3,450 METRES ABOVE SEA LEVEL.
WELCOME TO LHASA AIRPORT

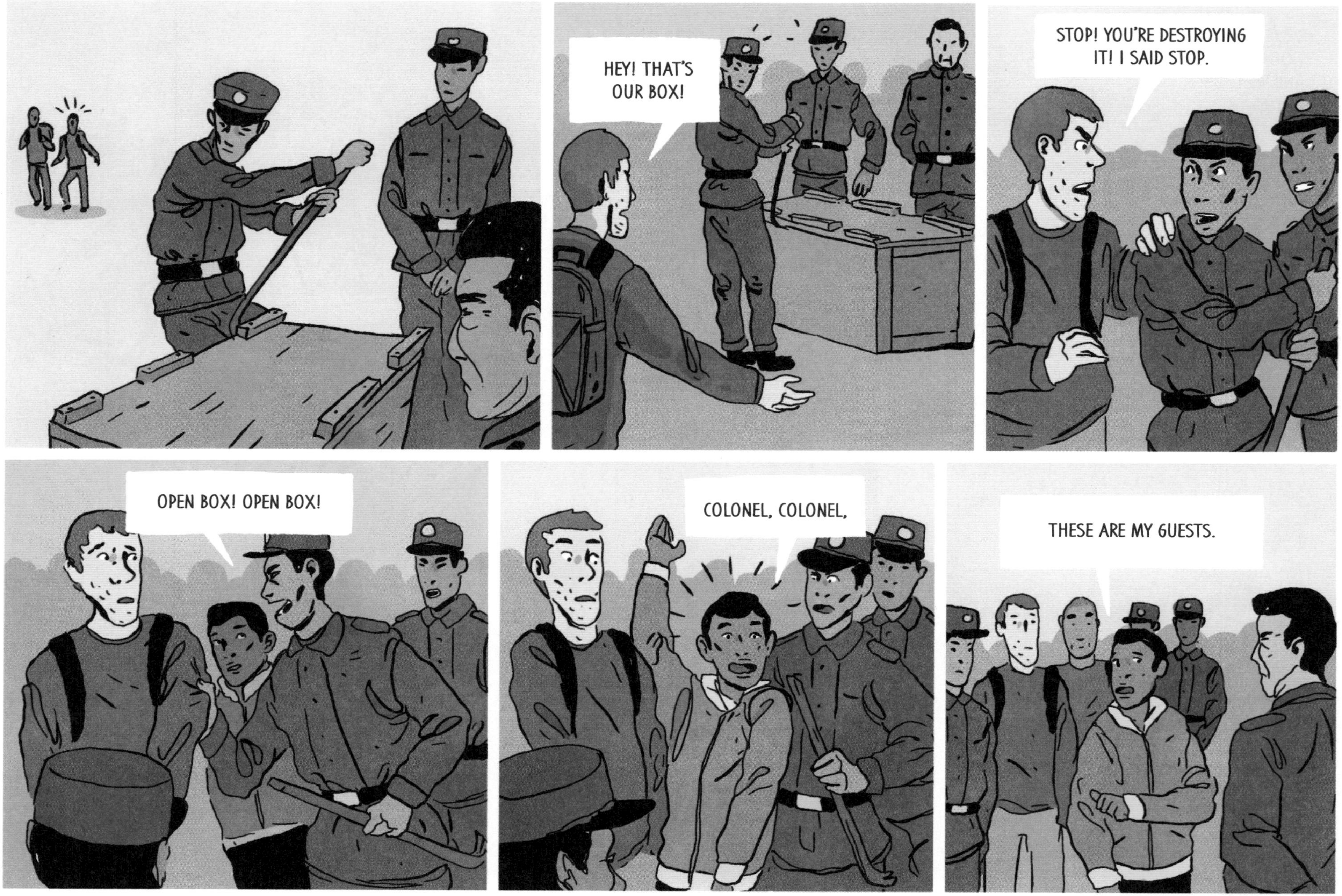
HEY! THAT'S OUR BOX!
STOP! YOU'RE DESTROYING IT! I SAID STOP.
OPEN BOX! OPEN BOX!
COLONEL, COLONEL,
THESE ARE MY GUESTS.

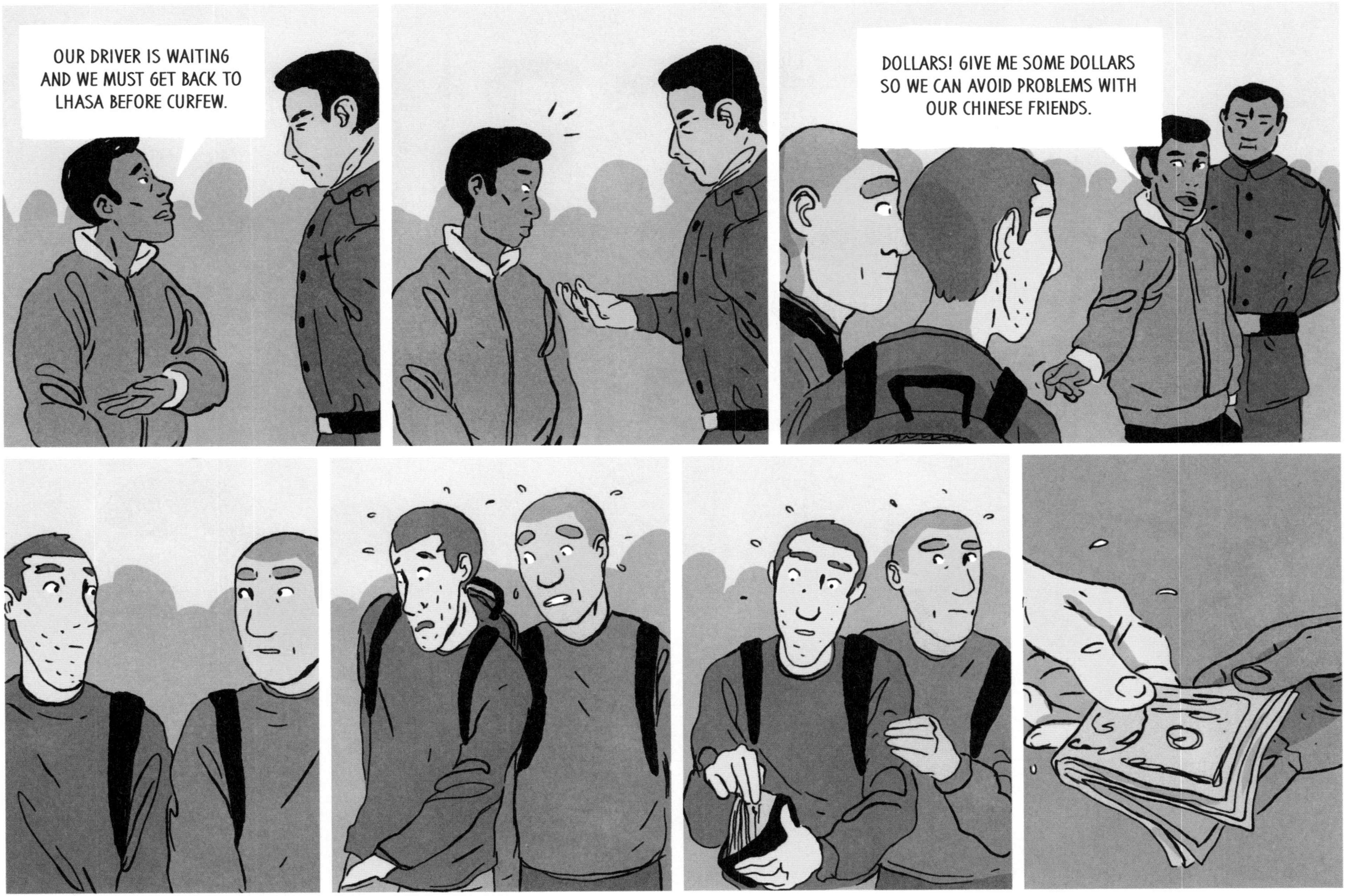
OUR DRIVER IS WAITING AND WE MUST GET BACK TO LHASA BEFORE CURFEW.
DOLLARS! GIVE ME SOME DOLLARS SO WE CAN AVOID PROBLEMS WITH OUR CHINESE FRIENDS.

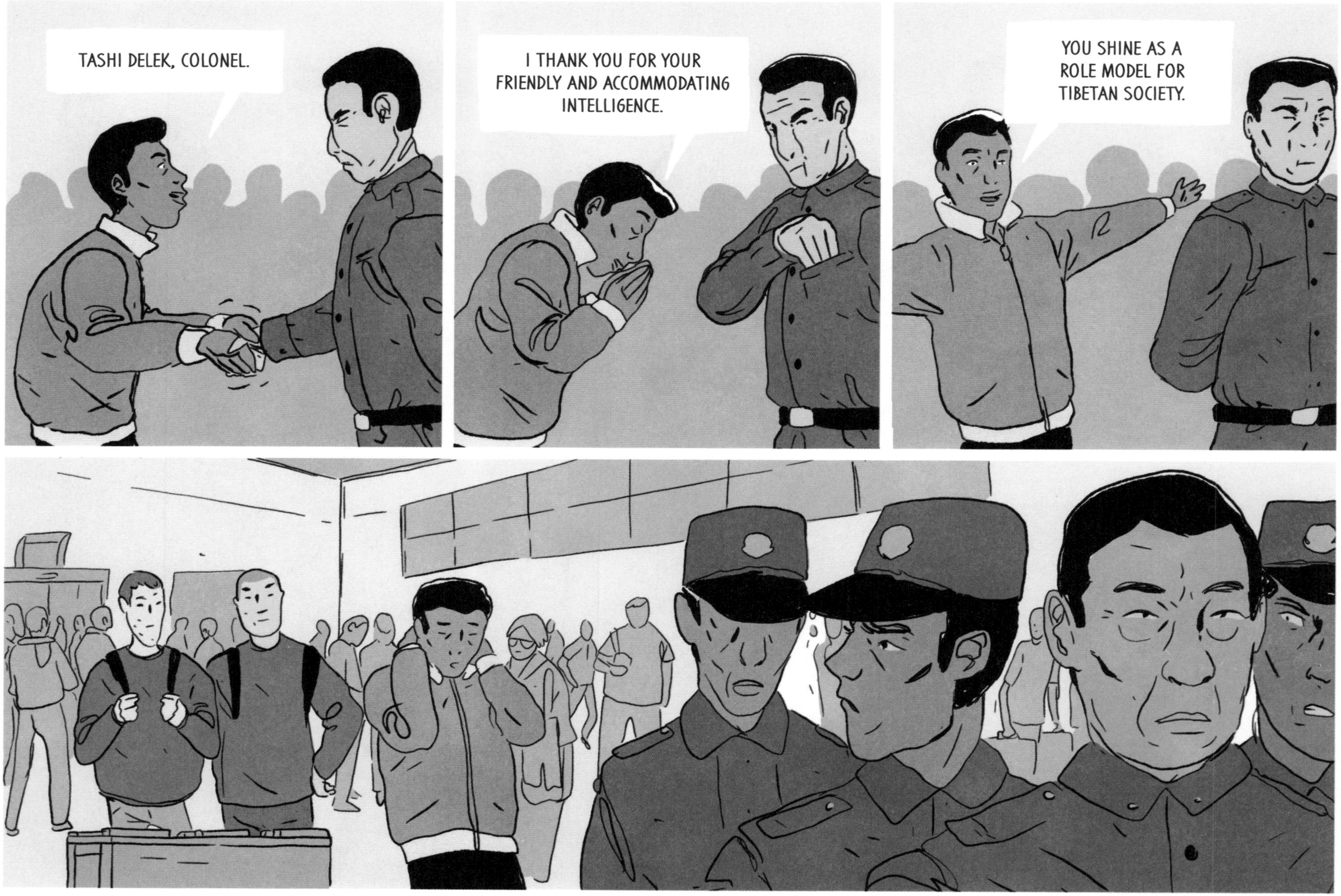
TASHI DELEK, COLONEL.
I THANK YOU FOR YOUR FRIENDLY AND ACCOMMODATING INTELLIGENCE.
YOU SHINE AS A ROLE MODEL FOR TIBETAN SOCIETY.

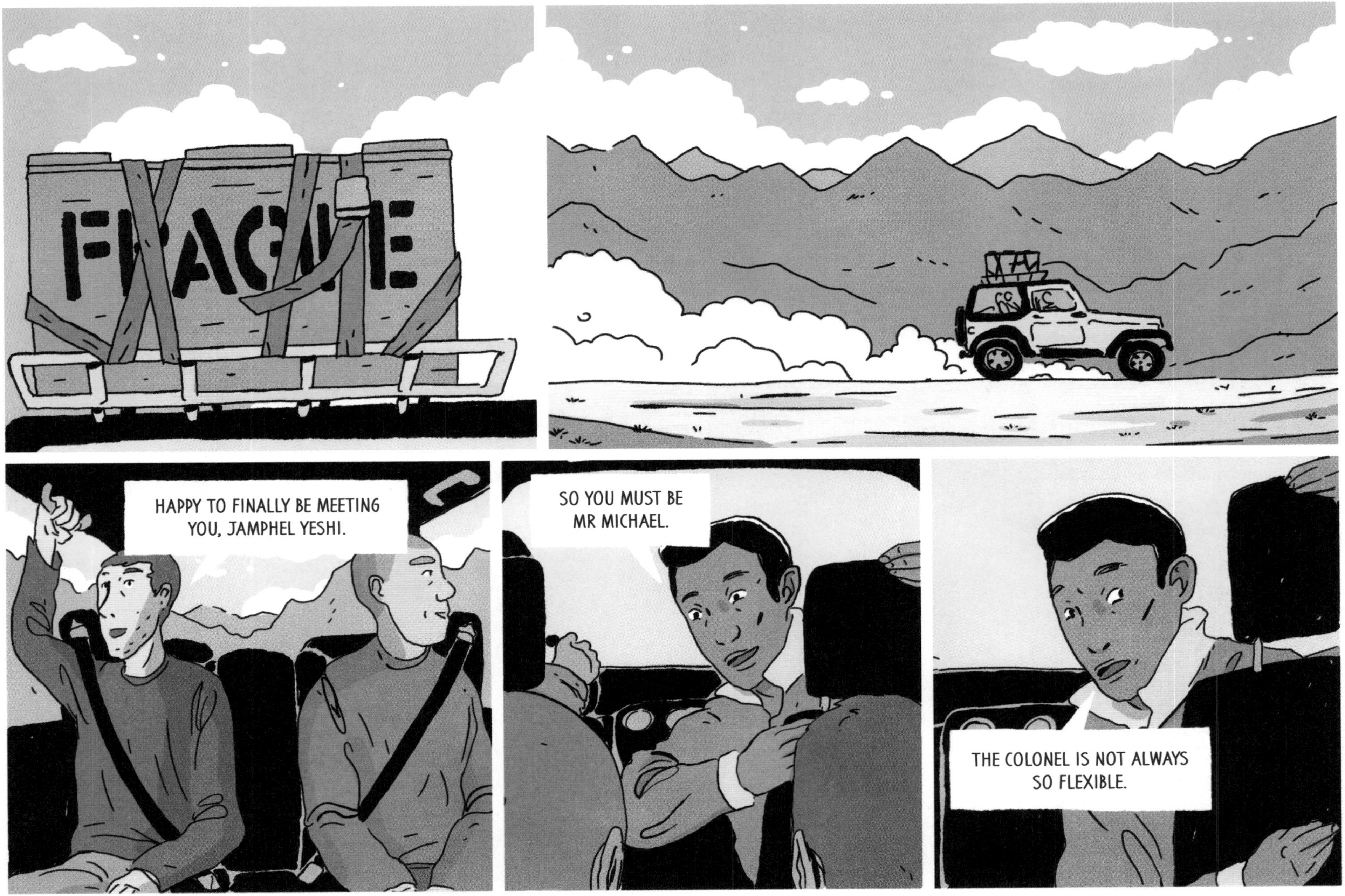
HAPPY TO FINALLY BE MEETING YOU, JAMPHEL YESHI.
SO YOU MUST BE MR MICHAEL.
THE COLONEL IS NOT ALWAYS SO FLEXIBLE.

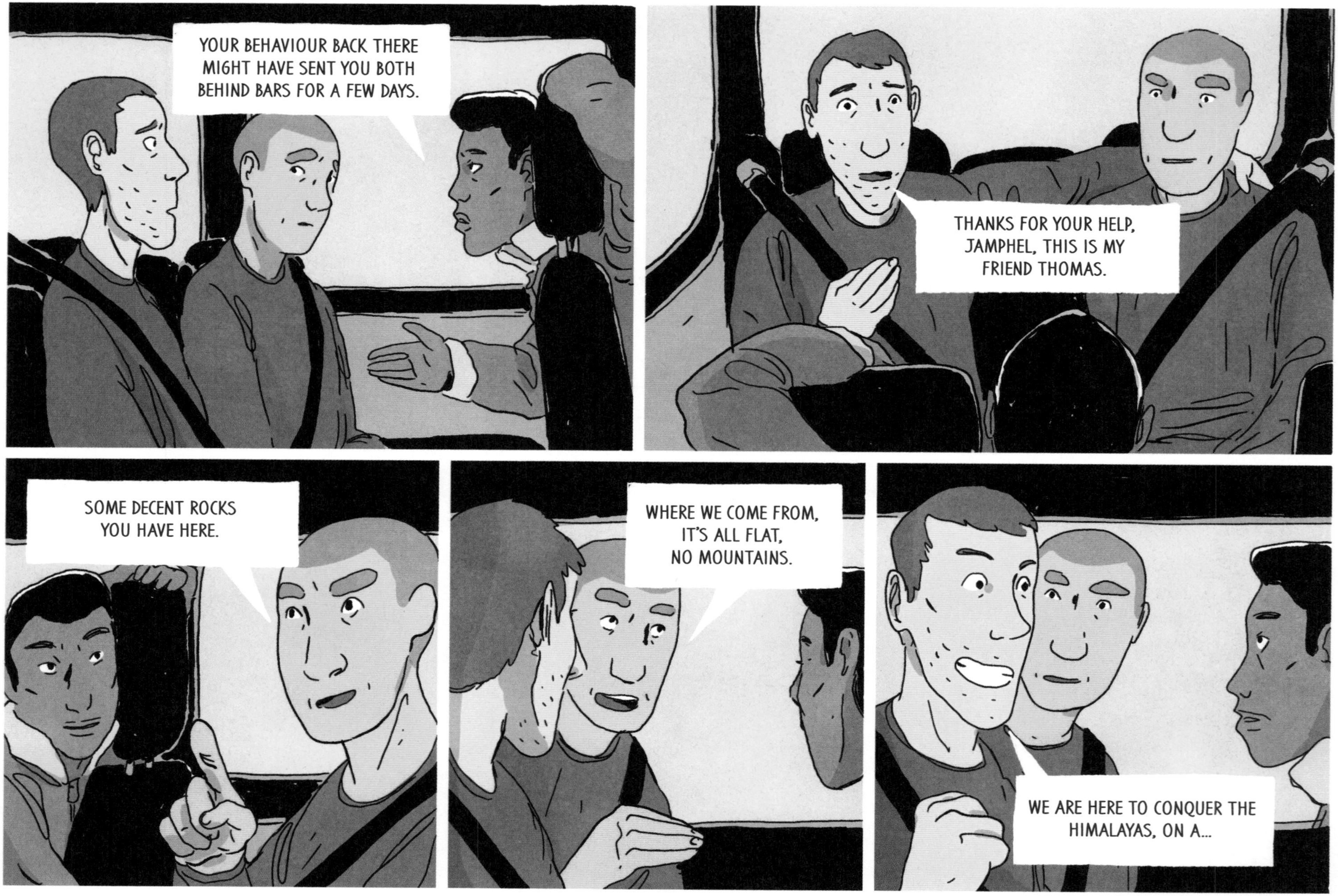
YOUR BEHAVIOUR BACK THERE MIGHT HAVE SENT YOU BOTH BEHIND BARS FOR A FEW DAYS.
THANKS FOR YOUR HELP, JAMPHEL, THIS IS MY FRIEND THOMAS.
SOME DECENT ROCKS YOU HAVE HERE.
WHERE WE COME FROM, IT'S ALL FLAT, NO MOUNTAINS.
WE ARE HERE TO CONQUER THE HIMALAYAS, ON A...

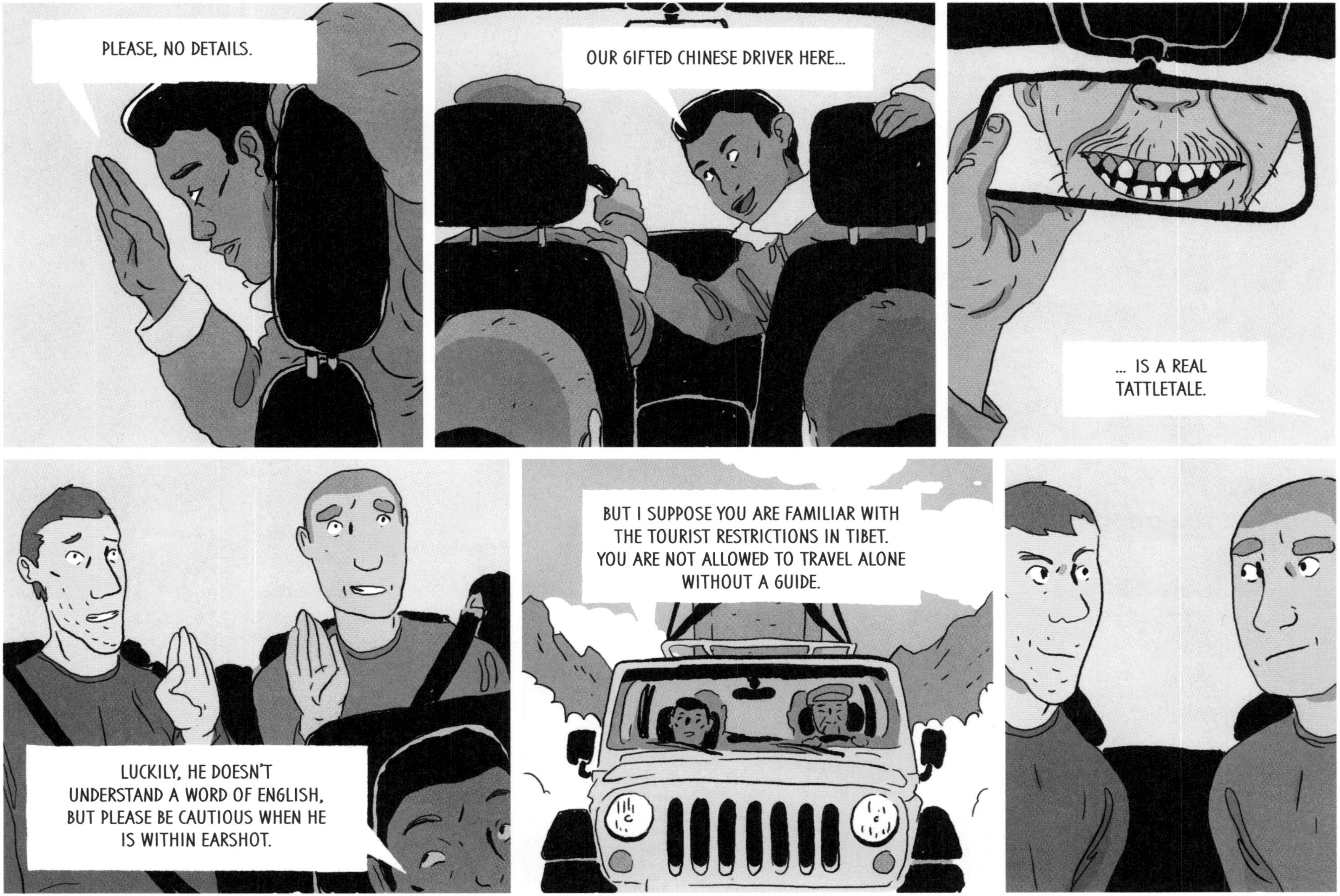
PLEASE, NO DETAILS.
OUR GIFTED CHINESE DRIVER HERE...
... IS A REAL TATTLETALE.
LUCKILY, HE DOESN'T UNDERSTAND A WORD OF ENGLISH, BUT PLEASE BE CAUTIOUS WHEN HE IS WITHIN EARSHOT.
BUT I SUPPOSE YOU ARE FAMILIAR WITH THE TOURIST RESTRICTIONS IN TIBET. YOU ARE NOT ALLOWED TO TRAVEL ALONE WITHOUT A GUIDE.

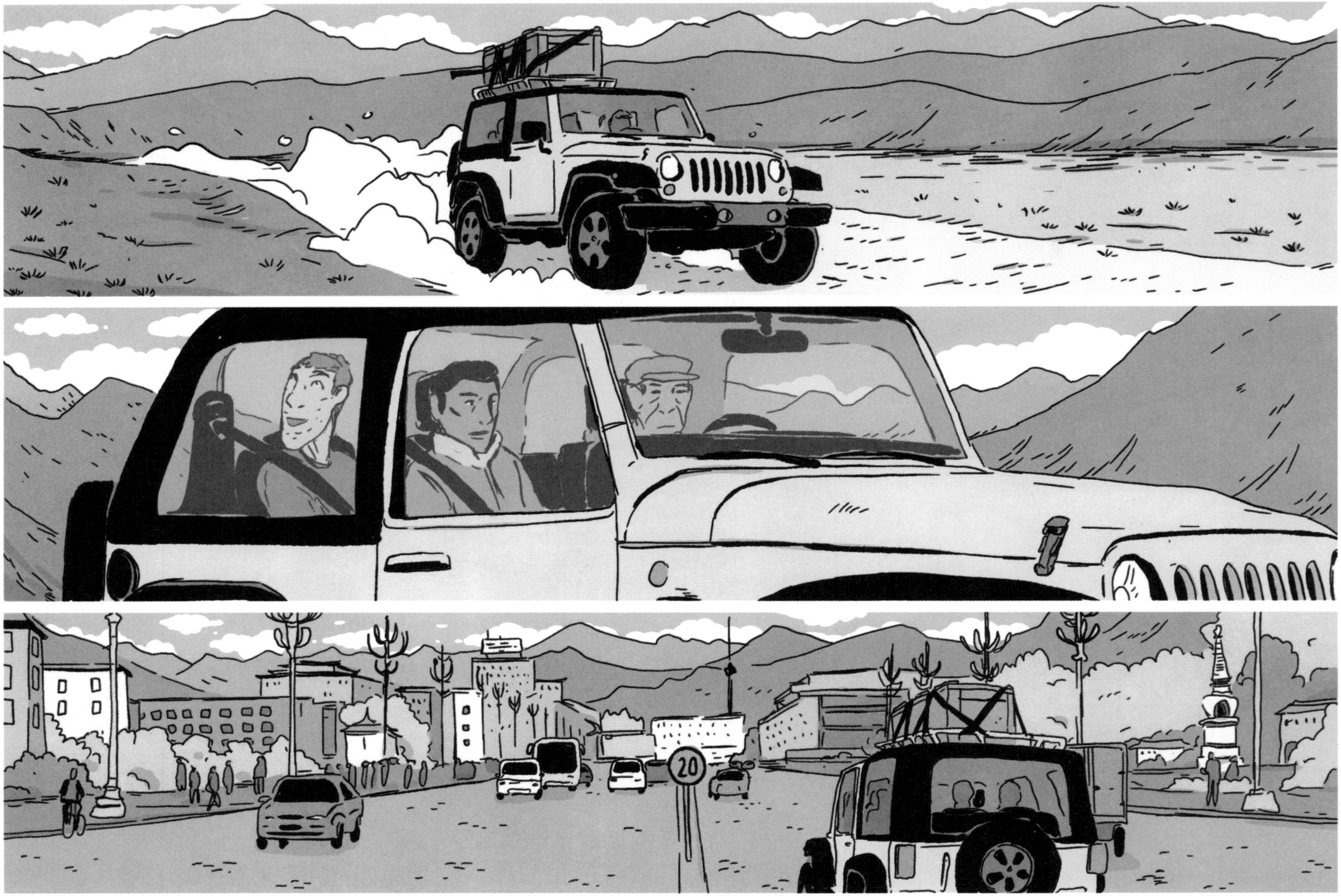
20

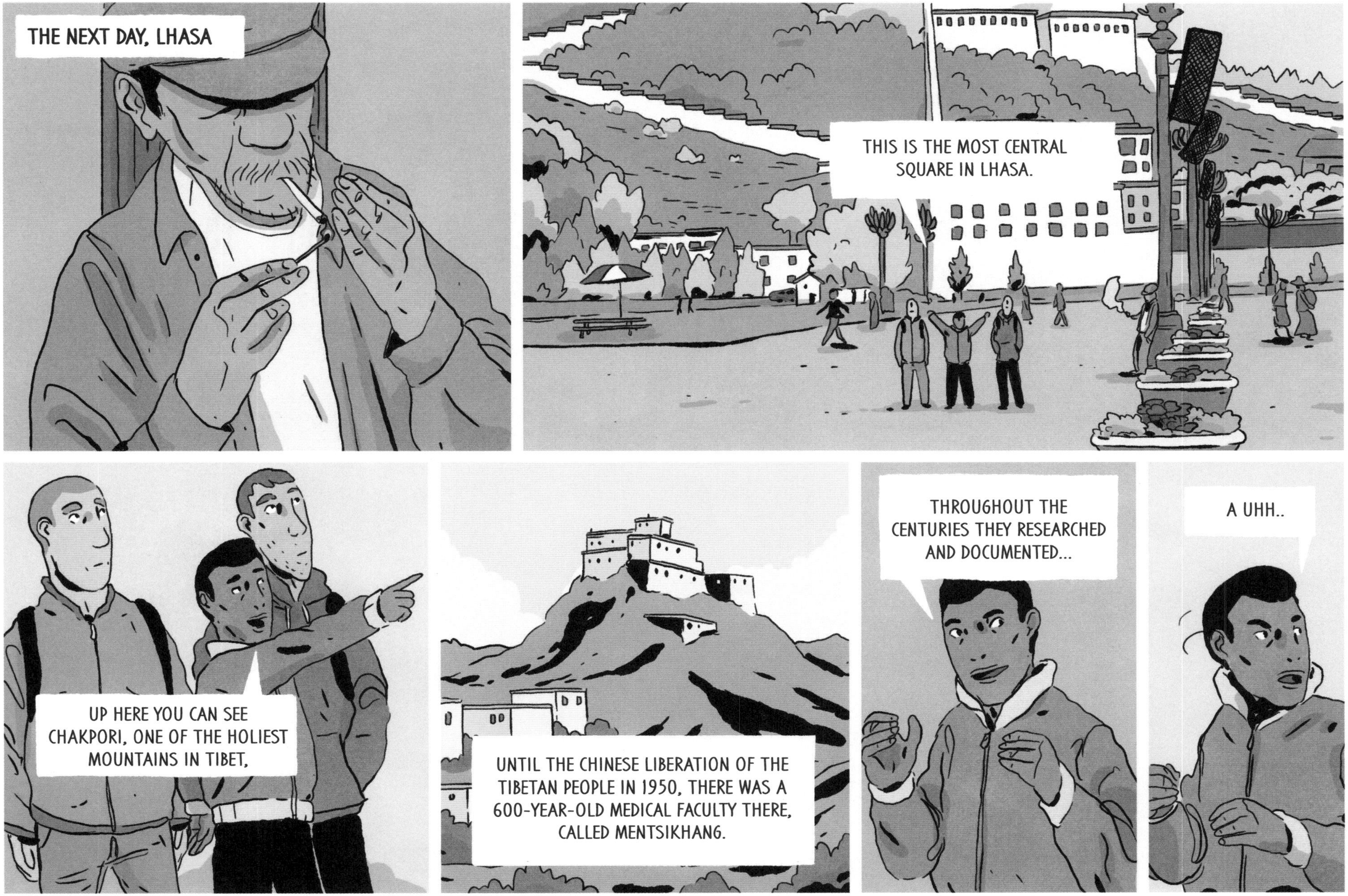
THE NEXT DAY, LHASA
THIS IS THE MOST CENTRAL SQUARE IN LHASA.
UP HERE YOU CAN SEE CHAKPORI, ONE OF THE HOLIEST MOUNTAINS IN TIBET,
UNTIL THE CHINESE LIBERATION OF THE TIBETAN PEOPLE IN 1950, THERE WAS A 600-YEAR-OLD MEDICAL FACULTY THERE, CALLED MENTSIKHANG.
THROUGHOUT THE CENTURIES THEY RESEARCHED AND DOCUMENTED...
A UHH..

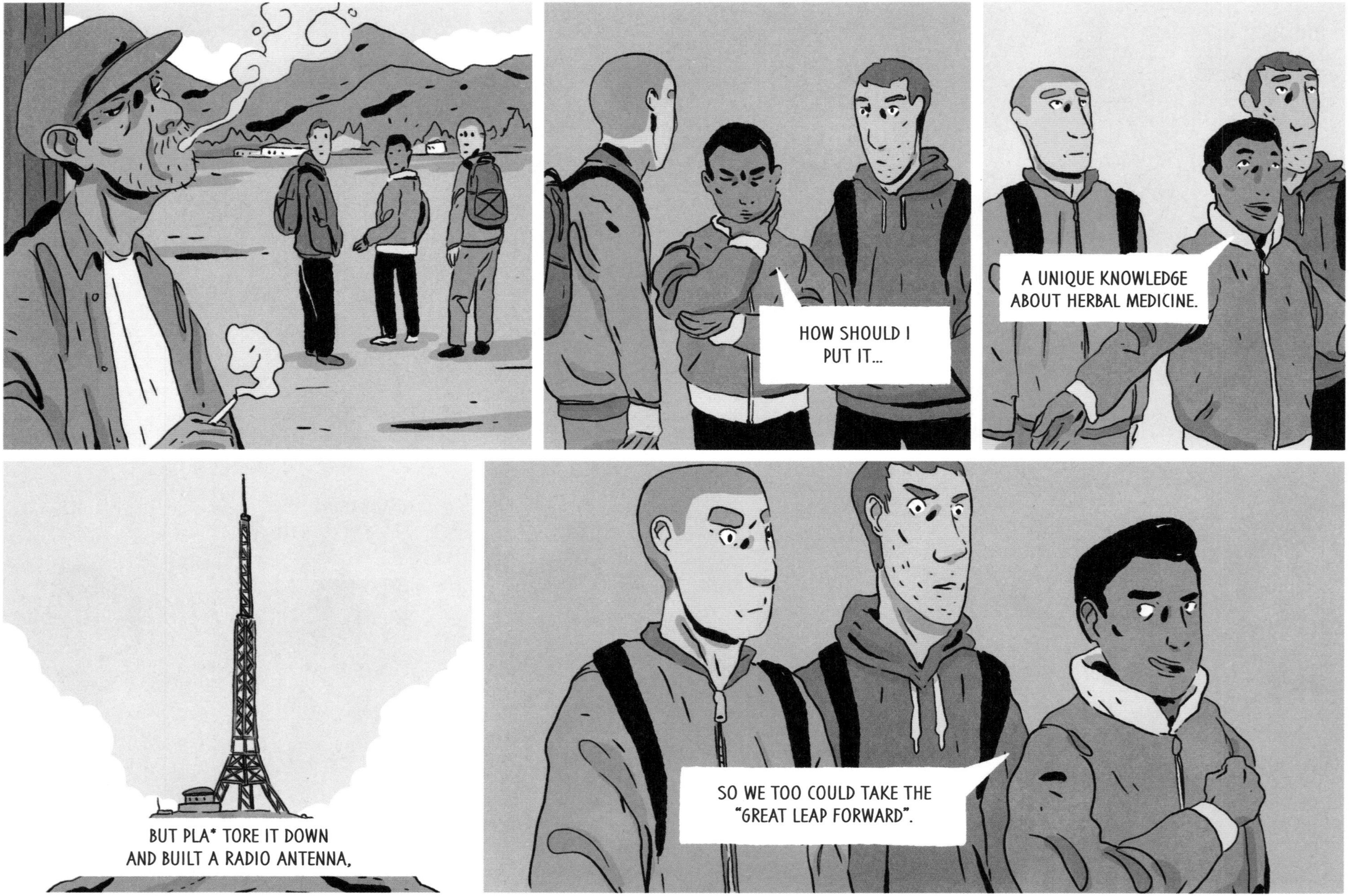
HOW SHOULD I PUT IT...
A UNIQUE KNOWLEDGE ABOUT HERBAL MEDICINE.
BUT PLA* TORE IT DOWN AND BUILT A RADIO ANTENNA,
SO WE TOO COULD TAKE THE "GREAT LEAP FORWARD".

*THE PEOPLE'S LIBERATION ARMY - THE ARMED FORCES OF THE PEOPLE'S REPUBLIC OF CHINA.

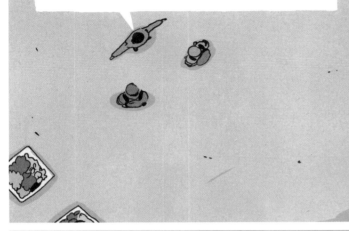

THE SQUARE HERE WAS ONCE A POPULAR OASIS WITH TREES, FLOWERS AND A SMALL PEACEFUL LAKE WHERE PEOPLE OFTEN JUST HUNG OUT AND STROLLED AROUND HAND IN HAND. INSTEAD WE'VE NOW GOT...

... A GREAT CONCRETE SQUARE.

PLOK!

USED FOR PARADES AND OTHER OBSCURE MILITARY FESTIVITIES.

IF YOU TURN AROUND, YOU CAN SEE...

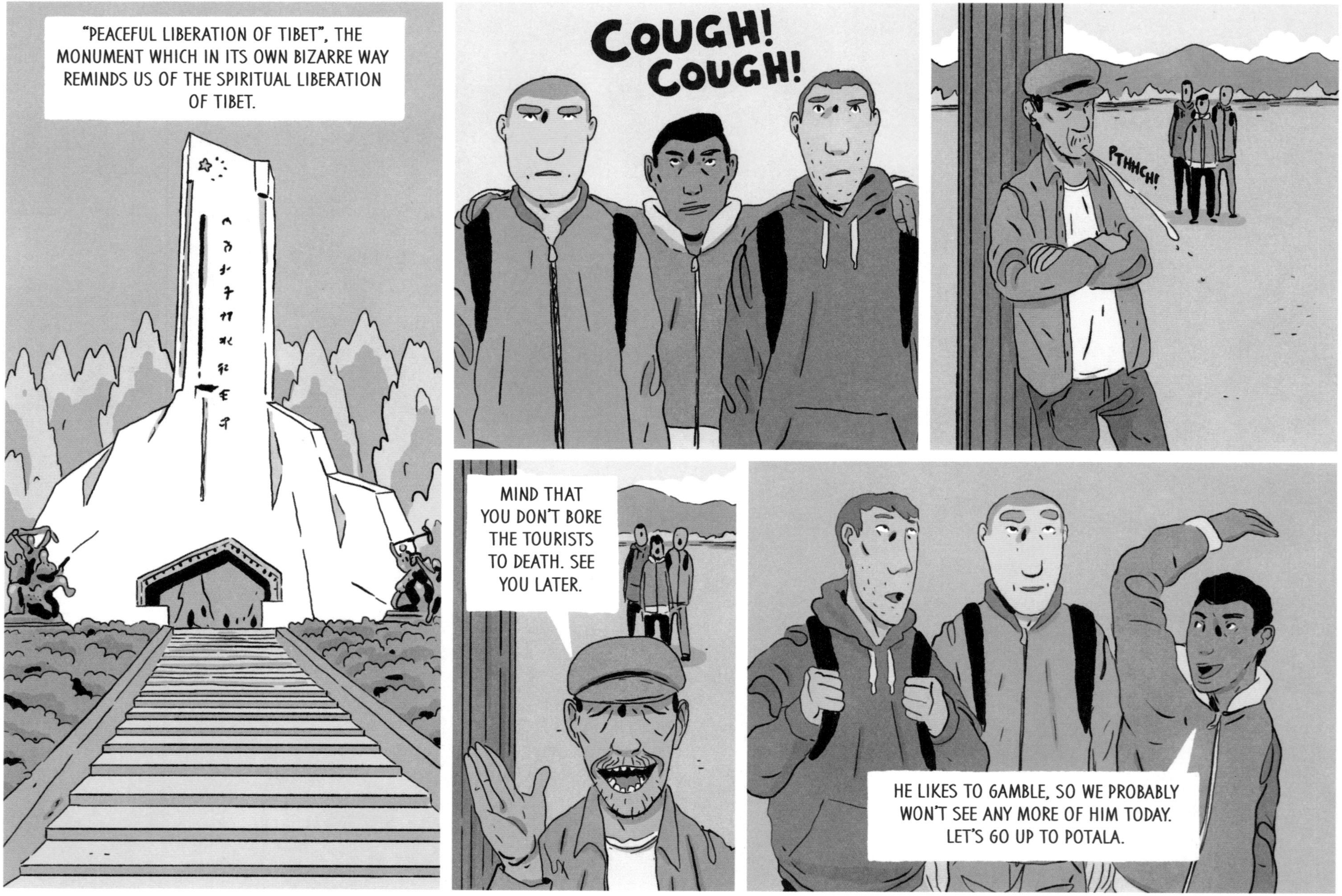
"PEACEFUL LIBERATION OF TIBET", THE MONUMENT WHICH IN ITS OWN BIZARRE WAY REMINDS US OF THE SPIRITUAL LIBERATION OF TIBET.
COUGH! COUGH!
PTHHCH!
MIND THAT YOU DON'T BORE THE TOURISTS TO DEATH. SEE YOU LATER.
HE LIKES TO GAMBLE, SO WE PROBABLY WON'T SEE ANY MORE OF HIM TODAY. LET'S GO UP TO POTALA.

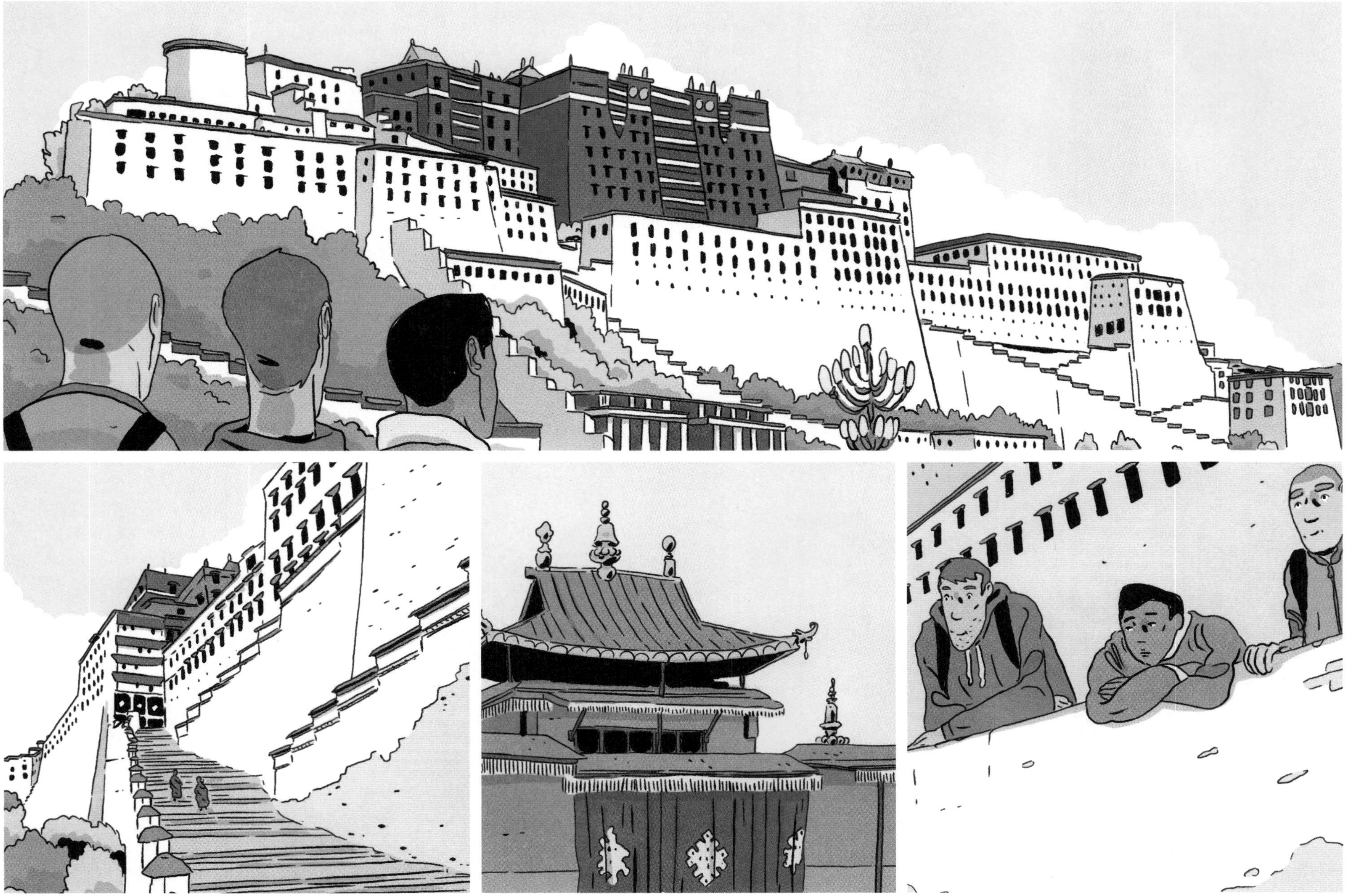

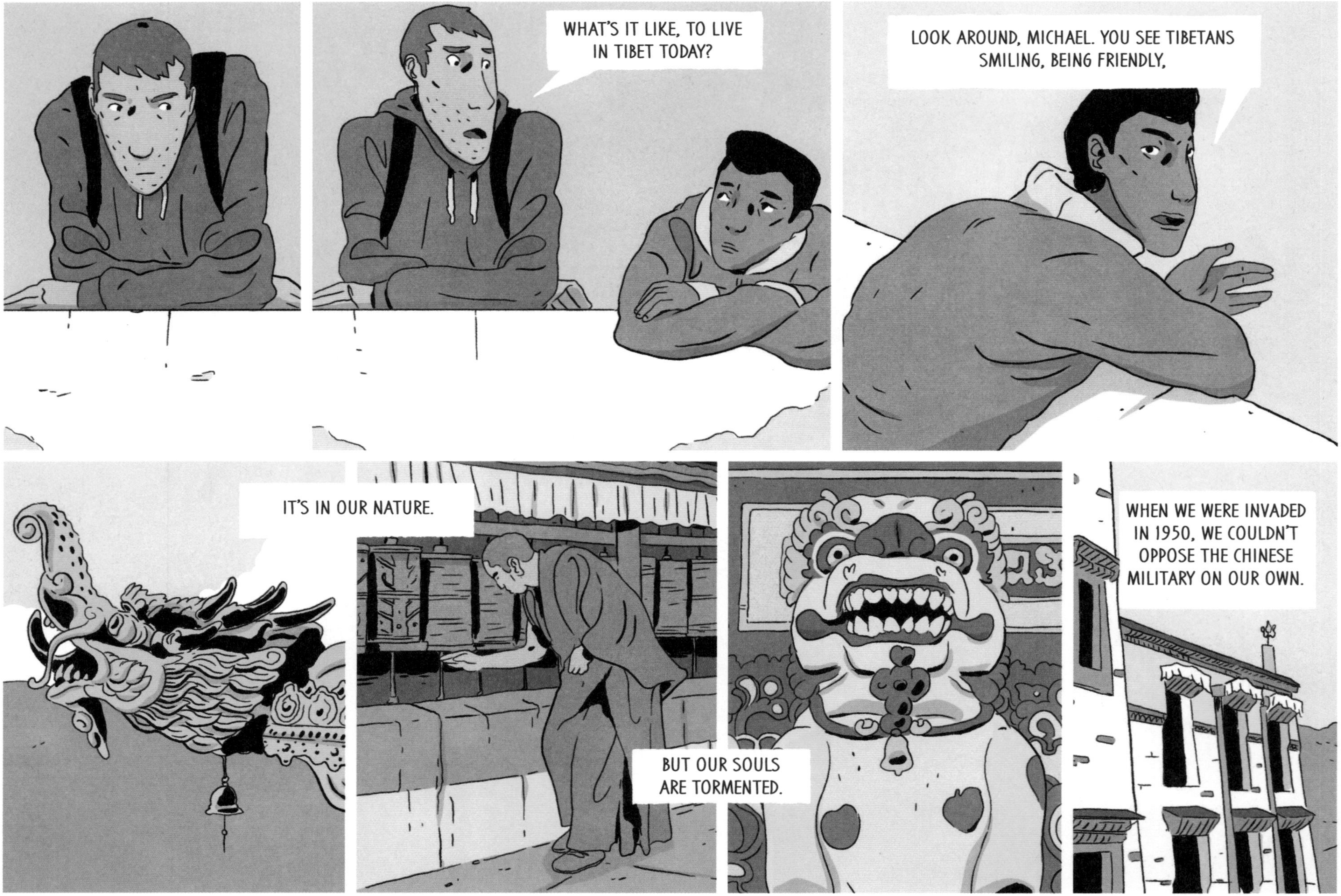
WHAT'S IT LIKE, TO LIVE IN TIBET TODAY?
LOOK AROUND, MICHAEL. YOU SEE TIBETANS SMILING, BEING FRIENDLY,
IT'S IN OUR NATURE.
BUT OUR SOULS ARE TORMENTED.
WHEN WE WERE INVADED IN 1950, WE COULDN'T OPPOSE THE CHINESE MILITARY ON OUR OWN.

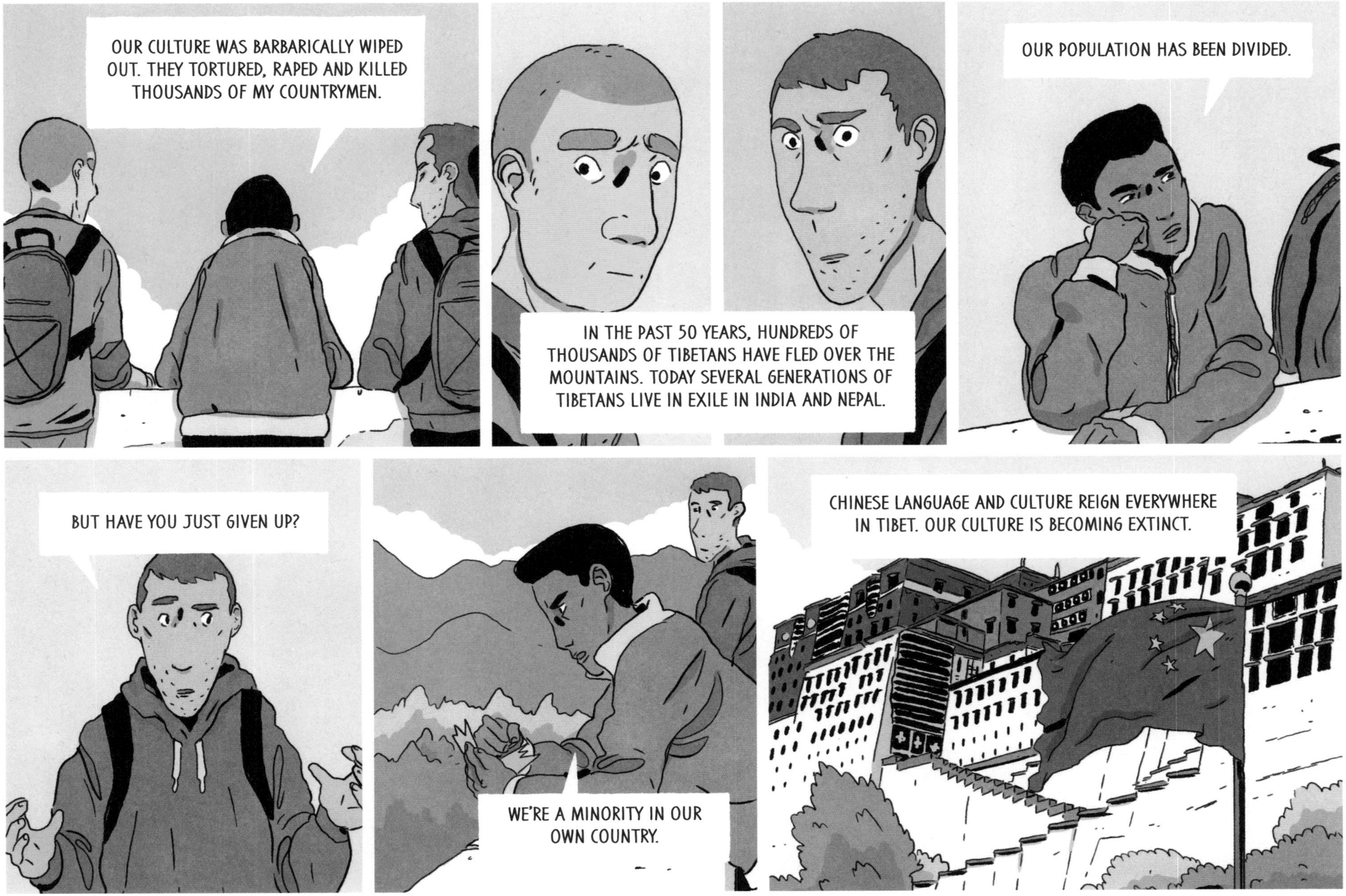
OUR CULTURE WAS BARBARICALLY WIPED OUT. THEY TORTURED, RAPED AND KILLED THOUSANDS OF MY COUNTRYMEN.
IN THE PAST 50 YEARS, HUNDREDS OF THOUSANDS OF TIBETANS HAVE FLED OVER THE MOUNTAINS. TODAY SEVERAL GENERATIONS OF TIBETANS LIVE IN EXILE IN INDIA AND NEPAL.
OUR POPULATION HAS BEEN DIVIDED.
BUT HAVE YOU JUST GIVEN UP?
WE'RE A MINORITY IN OUR OWN COUNTRY.
CHINESE LANGUAGE AND CULTURE REIGN EVERYWHERE IN TIBET. OUR CULTURE IS BECOMING EXTINCT.

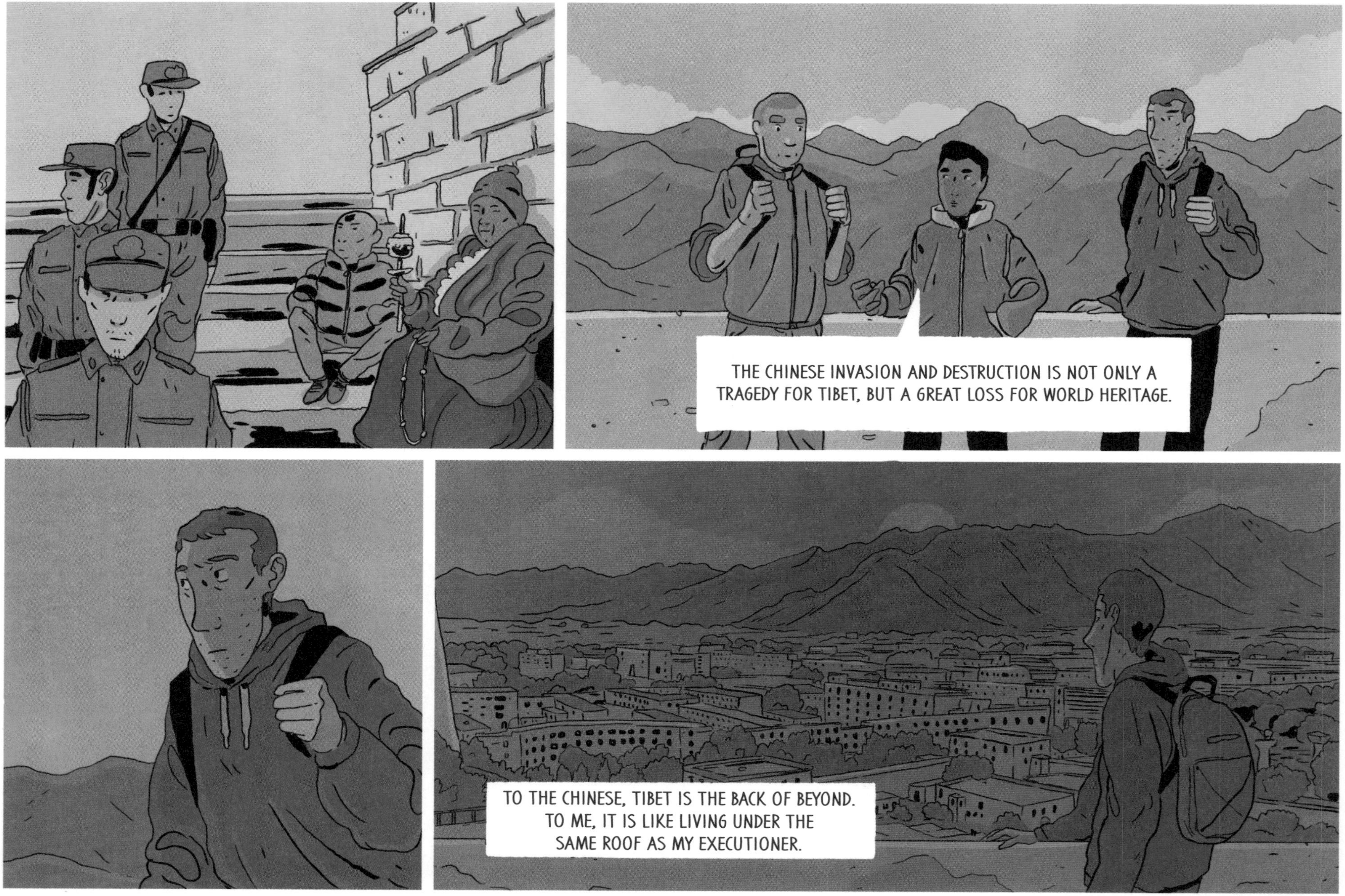
THE CHINESE INVASION AND DESTRUCTION IS NOT ONLY A TRAGEDY FOR TIBET, BUT A GREAT LOSS FOR WORLD HERITAGE.
TO THE CHINESE, TIBET IS THE BACK OF BEYOND. TO ME, IT IS LIKE LIVING UNDER THE SAME ROOF AS MY EXECUTIONER.

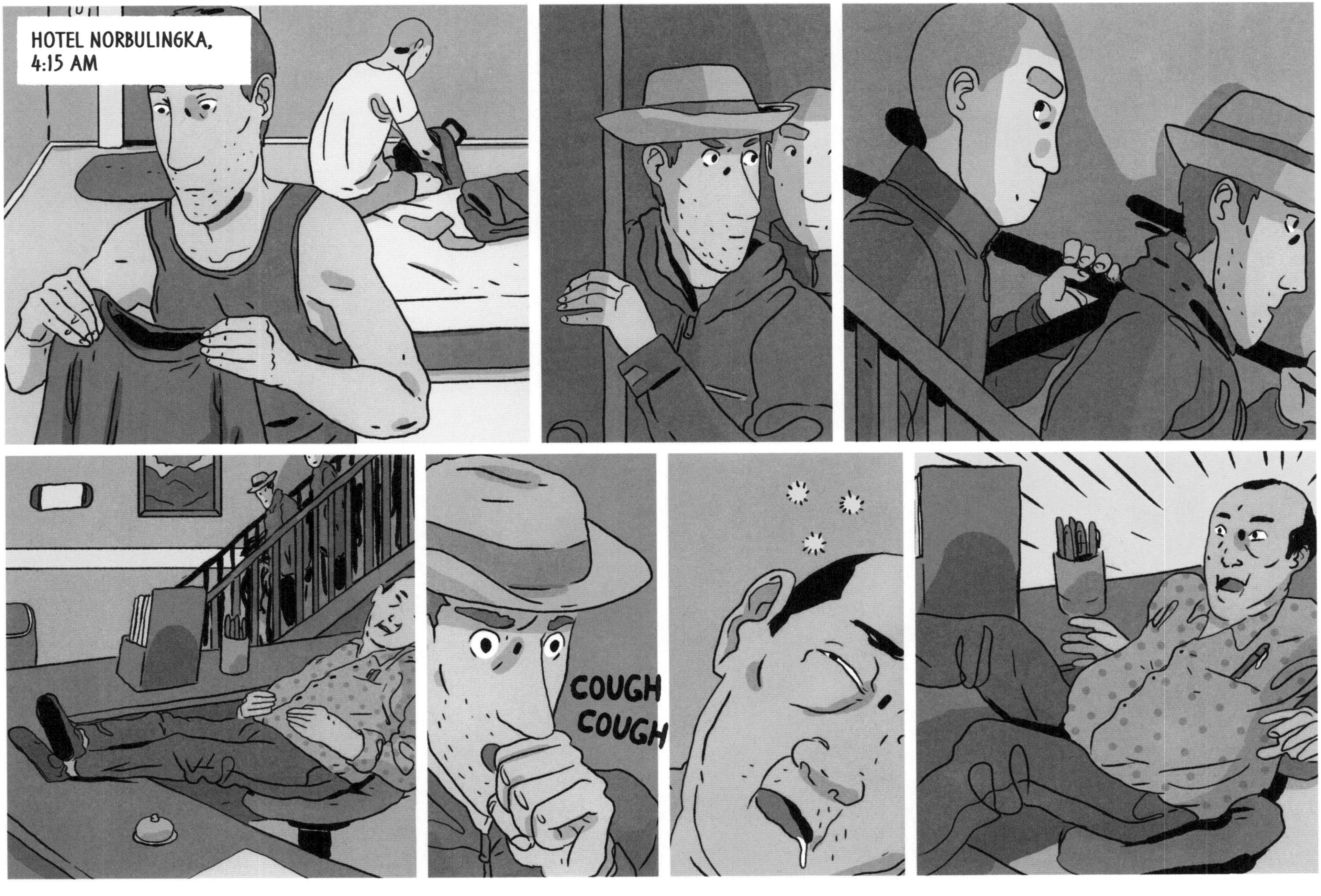
HOTEL NORBULINGKA,
4:15 AM
COUGH
COUGH

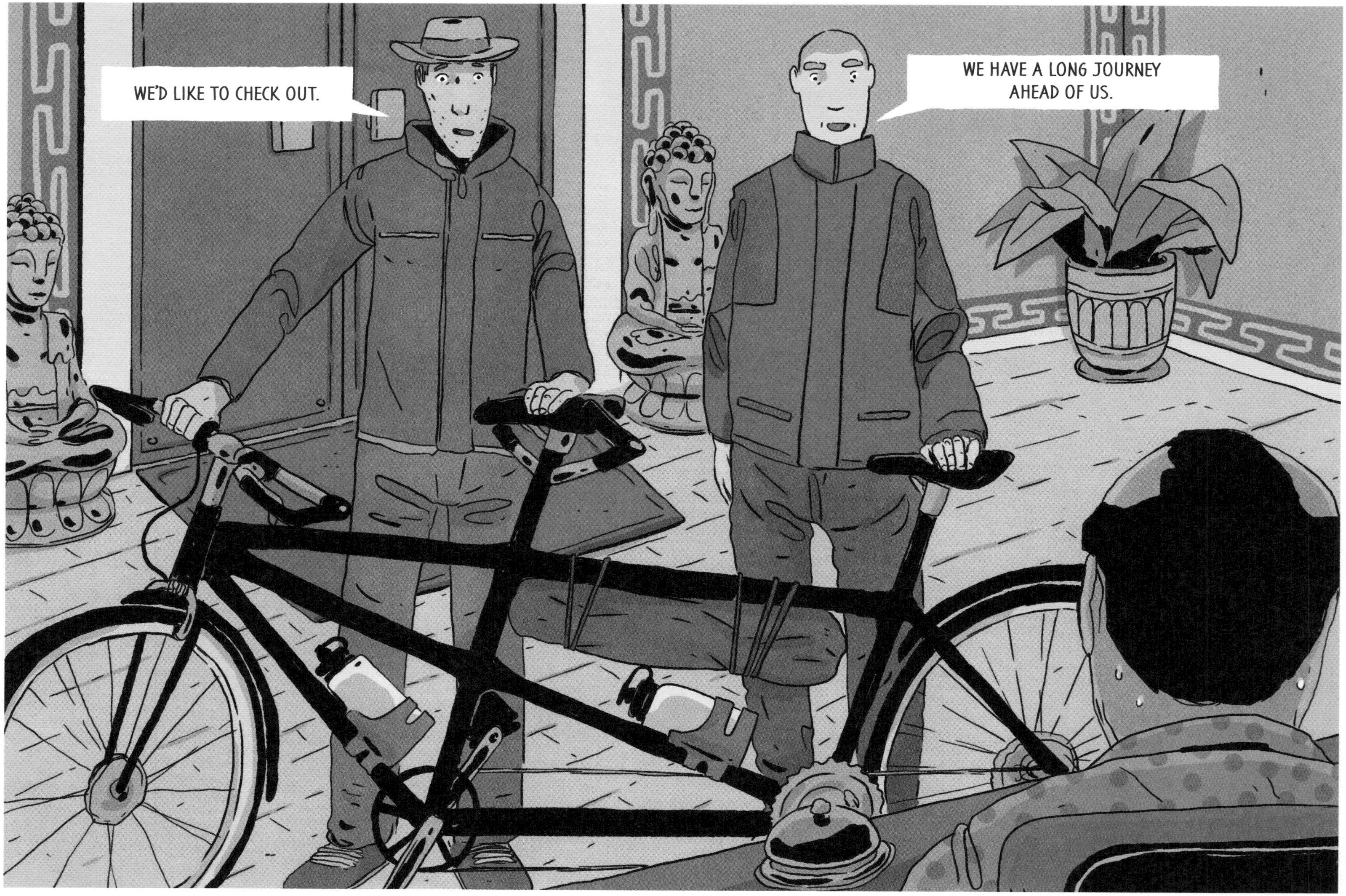
WE'D LIKE TO CHECK OUT.
WE HAVE A LONG JOURNEY AHEAD OF US.

CHAPTER 2
THE EASY WAY

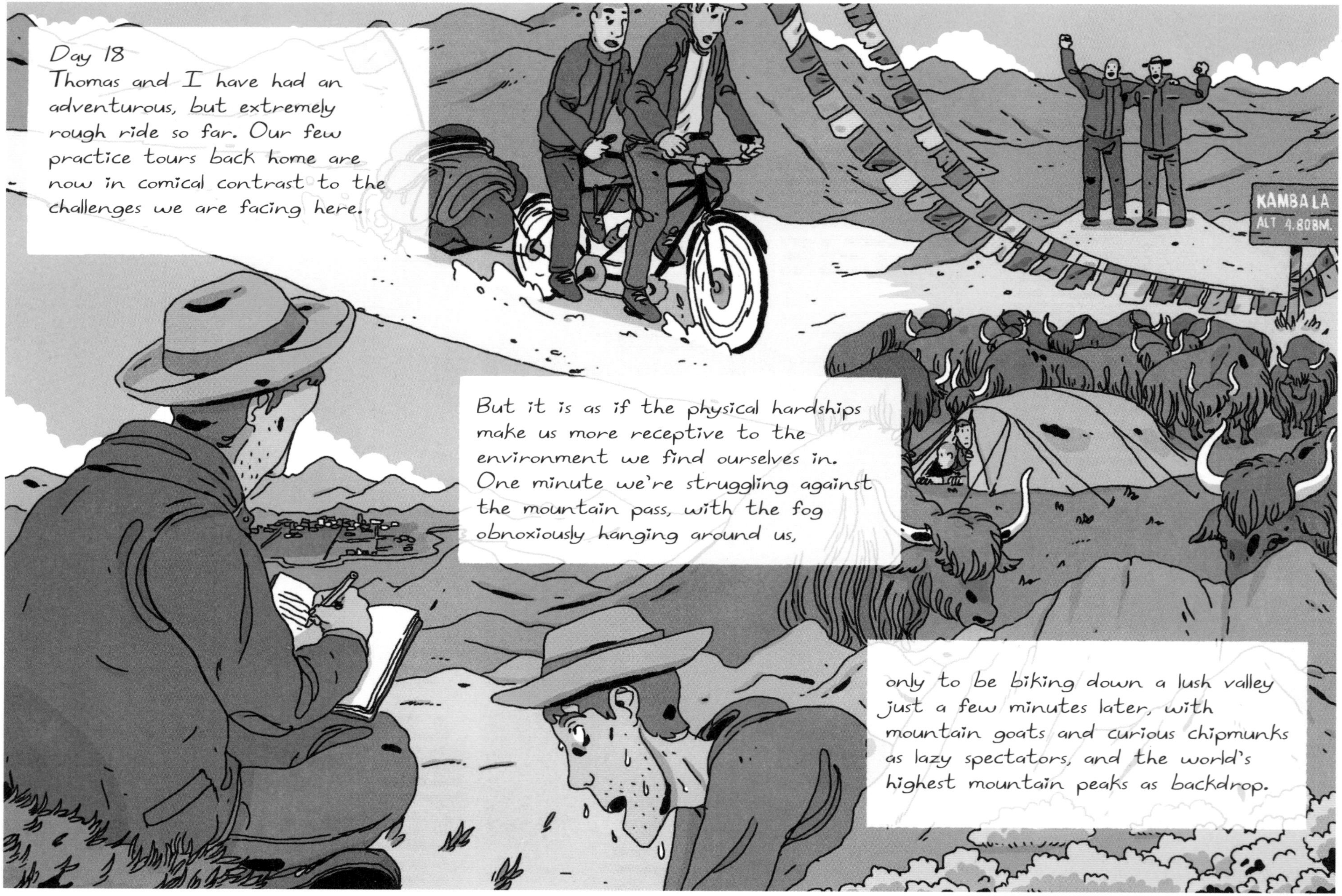
Day 18
Thomas and I have had an adventurous, but extremely rough ride so far. Our few practice tours back home are now in comical contrast to the challenges we are facing here.
KAMBA LA
ALT 4.808M.
But it is as if the physical hardships make us more receptive to the environment we find ourselves in. One minute we're struggling against the mountain pass, with the fog obnoxiously hanging around us,
only to be biking down a lush valley just a few minutes later, with mountain goats and curious chipmunks as lazy spectators, and the world's highest mountain peaks as backdrop.

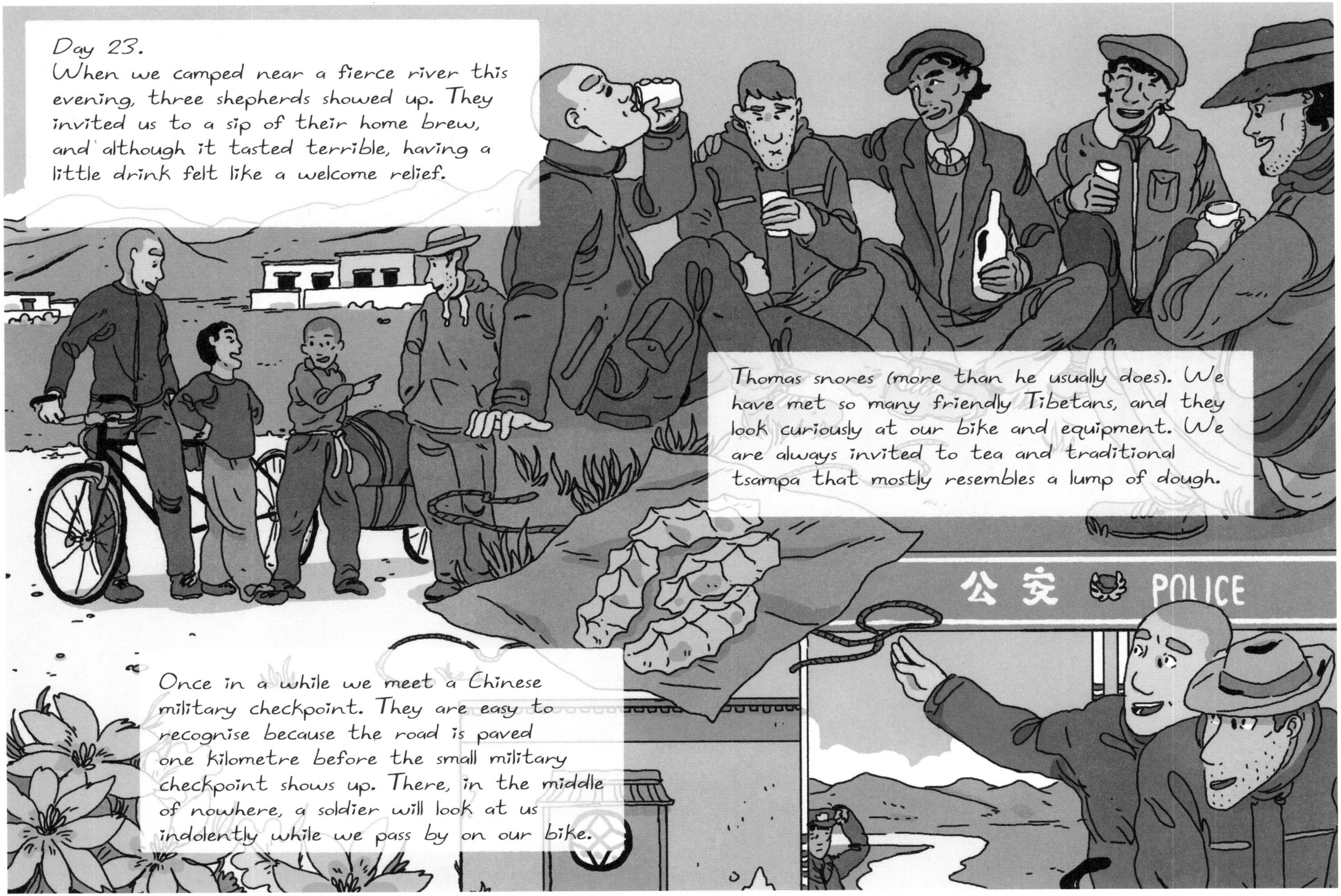

Day 23.
When we camped near a fierce river this evening, three shepherds showed up. They invited us to a sip of their home brew, and although it tasted terrible, having a little drink felt like a welcome relief.
Thomas snores (more than he usually does). We have met so many friendly Tibetans, and they look curiously at our bike and equipment. We are always invited to tea and traditional tsampa that mostly resembles a lump of dough.
公安 POLICE
Once in a while we meet a Chinese military checkpoint. They are easy to recognise because the road is paved one kilometre before the small military checkpoint shows up. There, in the middle of nowhere, a soldier will look at us indolently while we pass by on our bike.

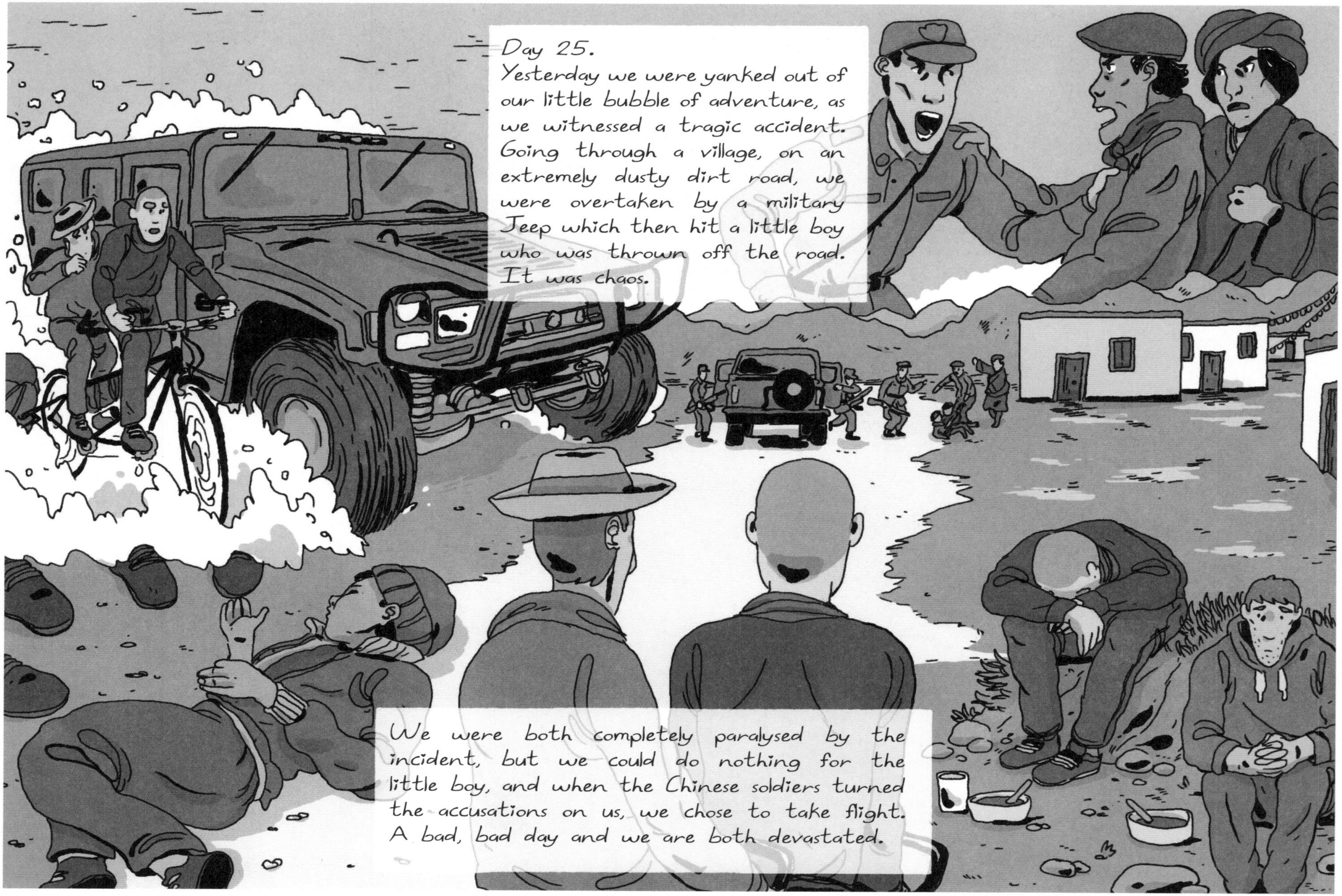
Day 25.
Yesterday we were yanked out of our little bubble of adventure, as we witnessed a tragic accident. Going through a village, on an extremely dusty dirt road, we were overtaken by a military Jeep which then hit a little boy who was thrown off the road. It was chaos.
We were both completely paralysed by the incident, but we could do nothing for the little boy, and when the Chinese soldiers turned the accusations on us, we chose to take flight. A bad, bad day and we are both devastated.

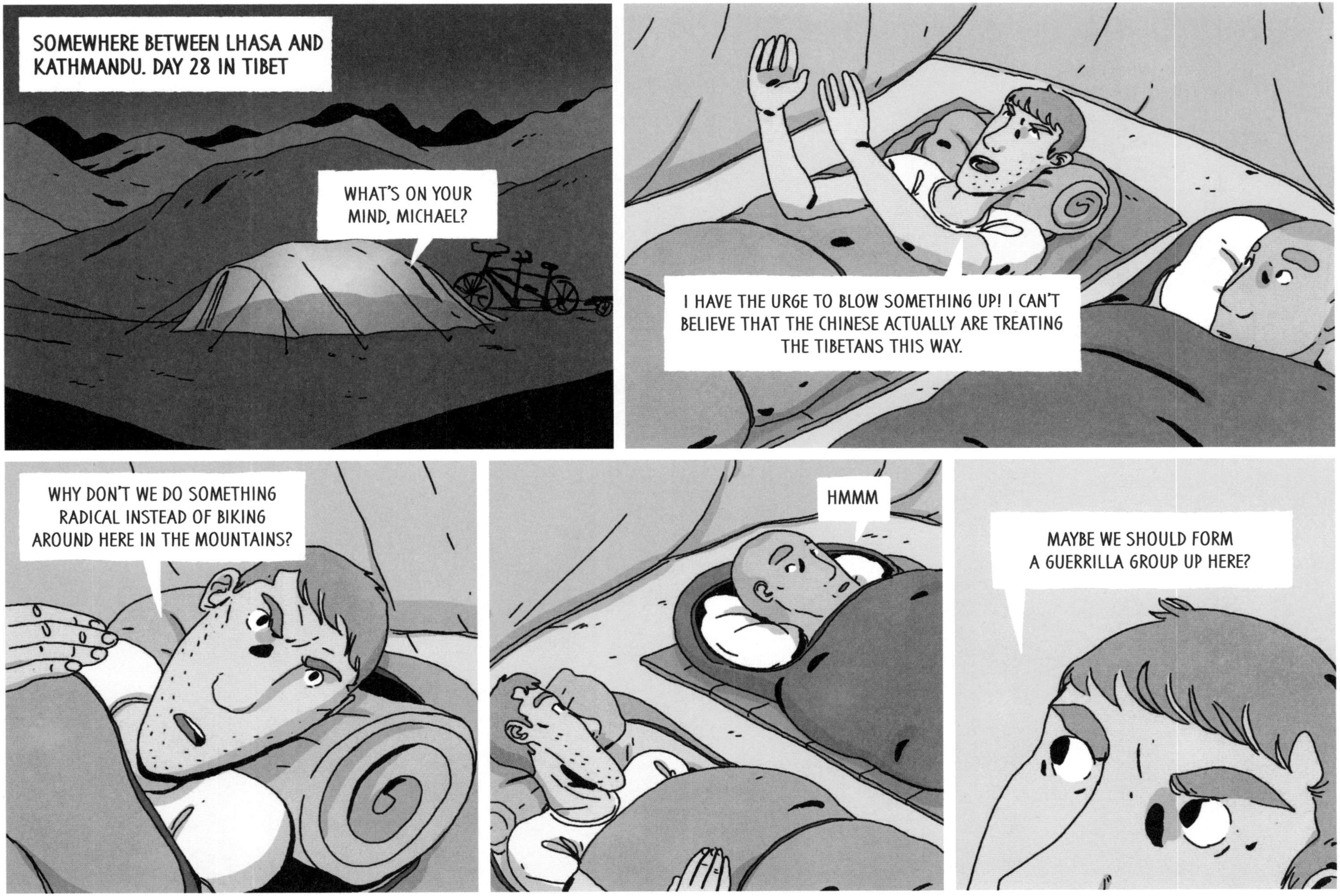

SOMEWHERE BETWEEN LHASA AND KATHMANDU. DAY 28 IN TIBET
WHAT'S ON YOUR MIND, MICHAEL?
I HAVE THE URGE TO BLOW SOMETHING UP! I CAN'T BELIEVE THAT THE CHINESE ACTUALLY ARE TREATING THE TIBETANS THIS WAY.
WHY DON'T WE DO SOMETHING RADICAL INSTEAD OF BIKING AROUND HERE IN THE MOUNTAINS?
HMMM
MAYBE WE SHOULD FORM A GUERRILLA GROUP UP HERE?

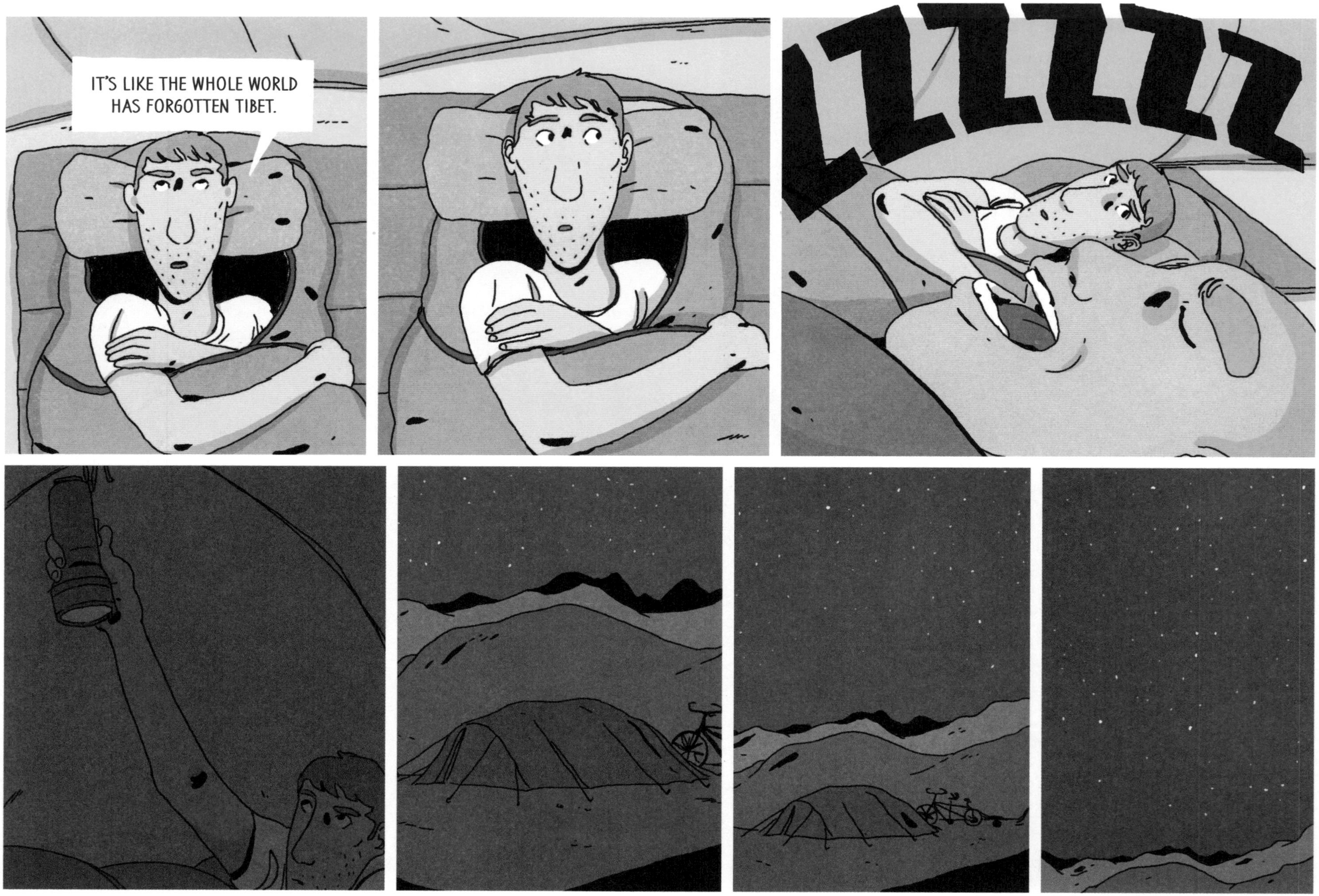
IT'S LIKE THE WHOLE WORLD HAS FORGOTTEN TIBET.
ZZZZZZZ

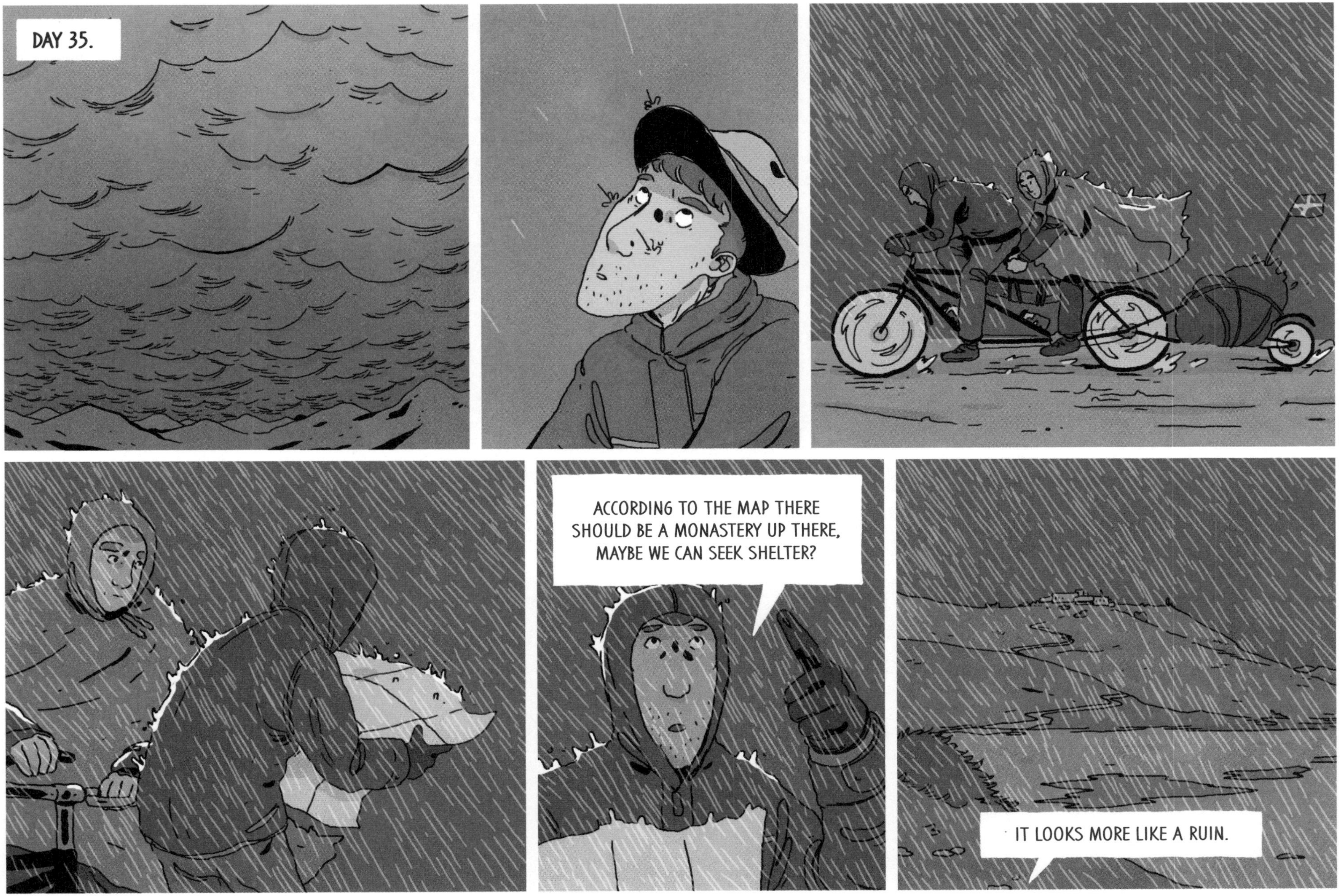
DAY 35.
ACCORDING TO THE MAP THERE SHOULD BE A MONASTERY UP THERE, MAYBE WE CAN SEEK SHELTER?
IT LOOKS MORE LIKE A RUIN.

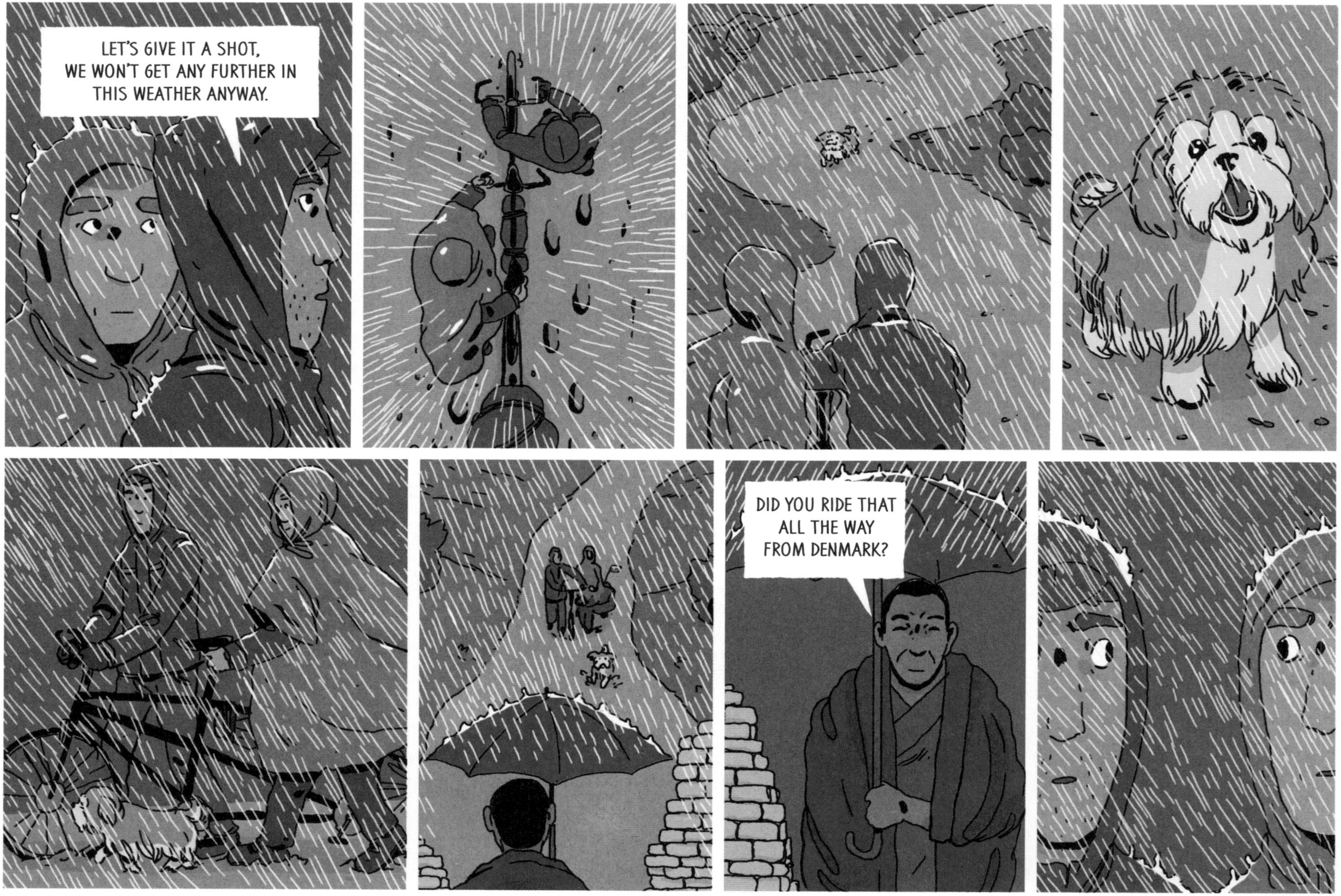
LET'S GIVE IT A SHOT, WE WON'T GET ANY FURTHER IN THIS WEATHER ANYWAY.
DID YOU RIDE THAT ALL THE WAY FROM DENMARK?

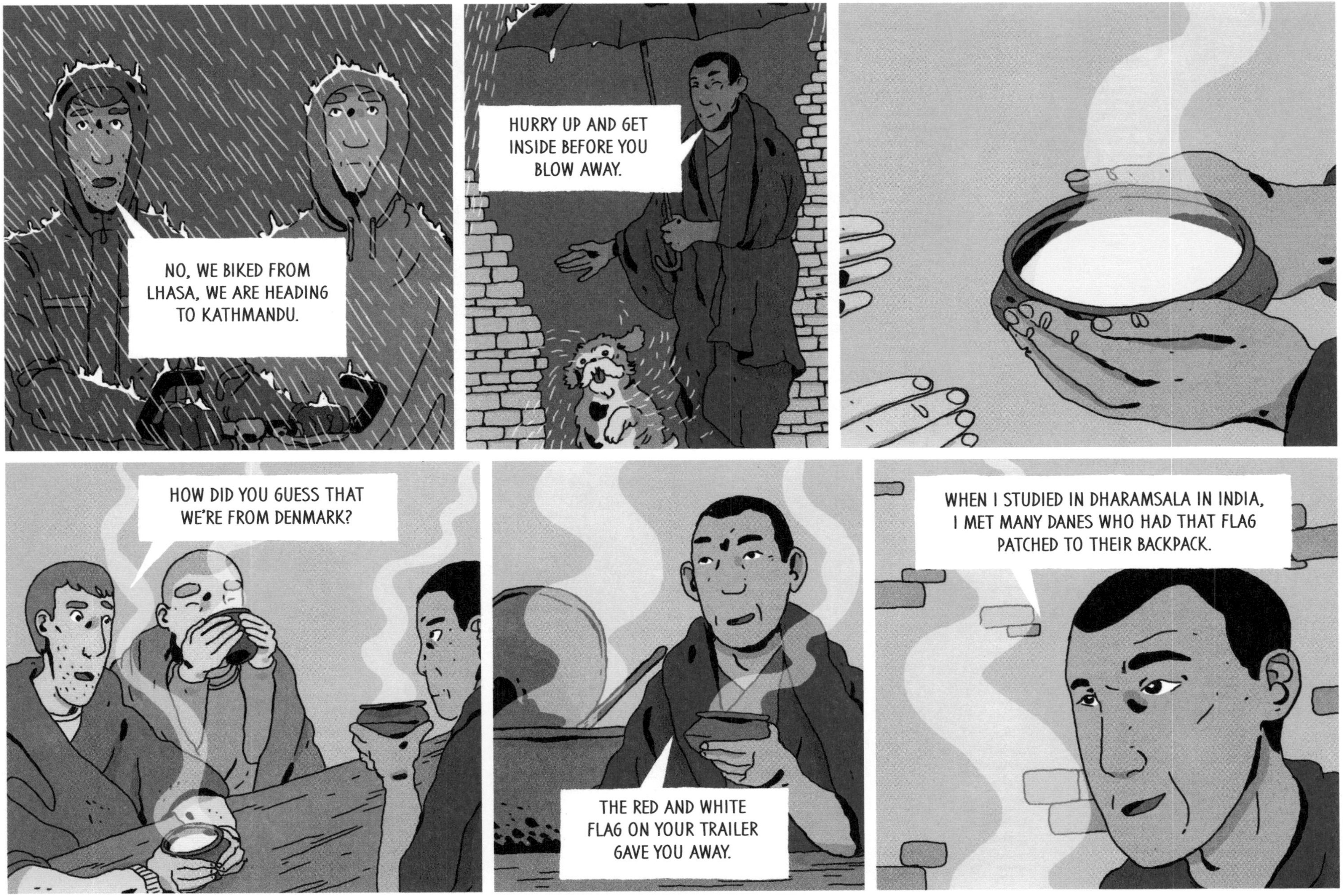
NO, WE BIKED FROM LHASA, WE ARE HEADING TO KATHMANDU.
HURRY UP AND GET INSIDE BEFORE YOU BLOW AWAY.
HOW DID YOU GUESS THAT WE'RE FROM DENMARK?
THE RED AND WHITE FLAG ON YOUR TRAILER GAVE YOU AWAY.
WHEN I STUDIED IN DHARAMSALA IN INDIA, I MET MANY DANES WHO HAD THAT FLAG PATCHED TO THEIR BACKPACK.

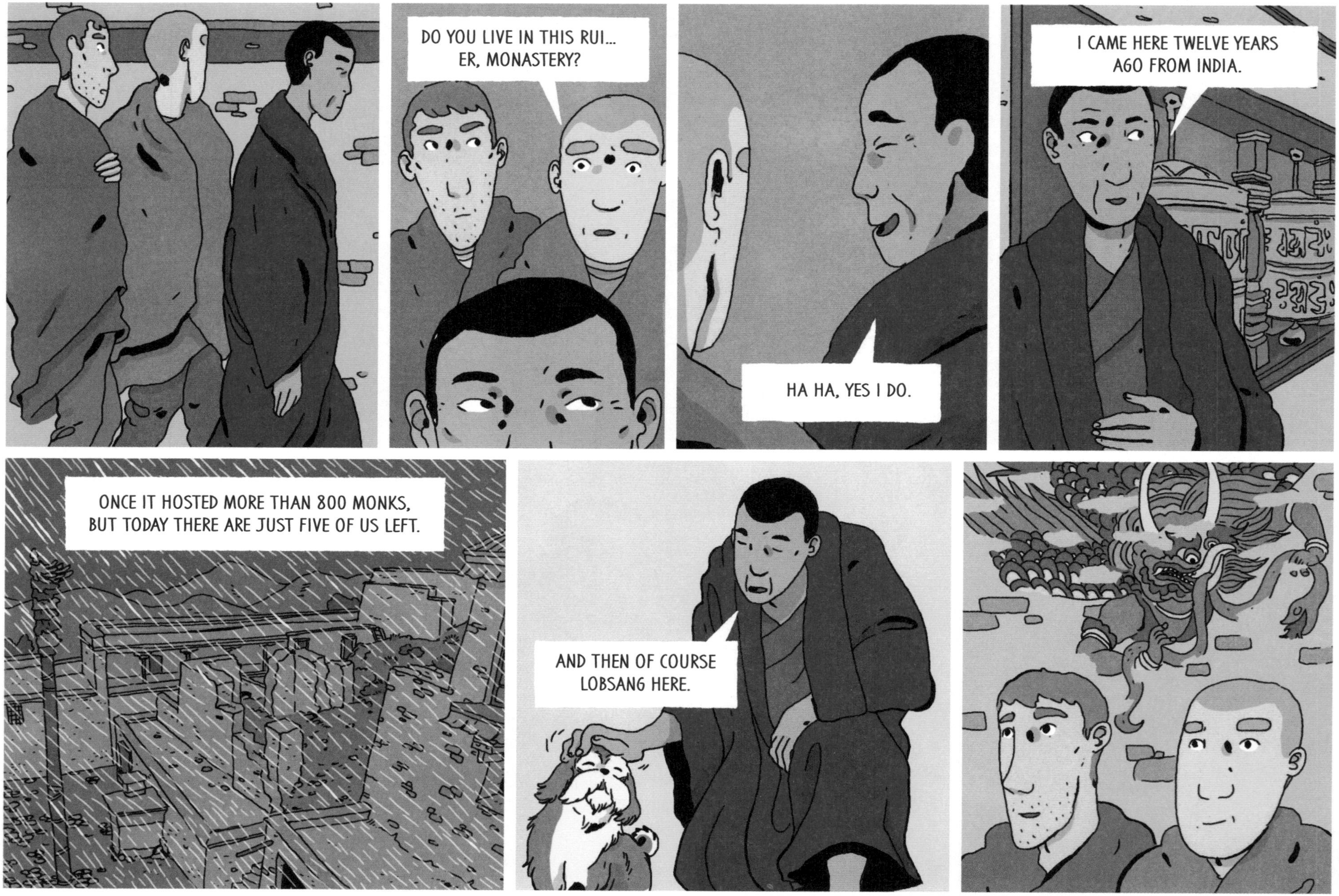
DO YOU LIVE IN THIS RUI... ER, MONASTERY?
HA HA, YES I DO.
I CAME HERE TWELVE YEARS AGO FROM INDIA.
ONCE IT HOSTED MORE THAN 800 MONKS, BUT TODAY THERE ARE JUST FIVE OF US LEFT.
AND THEN OF COURSE LOBSANG HERE.

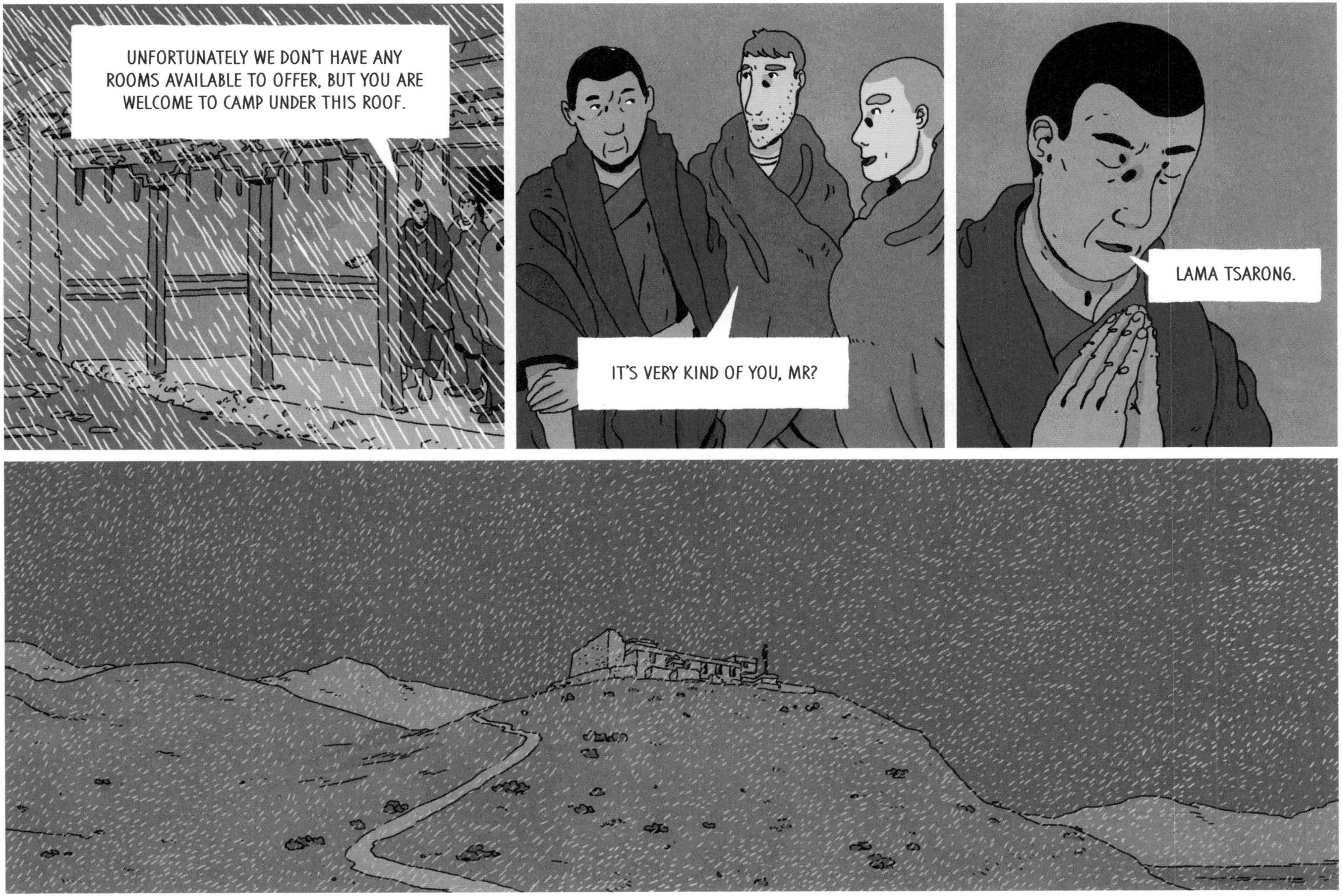
UNFORTUNATELY WE DON'T HAVE ANY ROOMS AVAILABLE TO OFFER, BUT YOU ARE WELCOME TO CAMP UNDER THIS ROOF.
IT'S VERY KIND OF YOU, MR?
LAMA TSARONG.

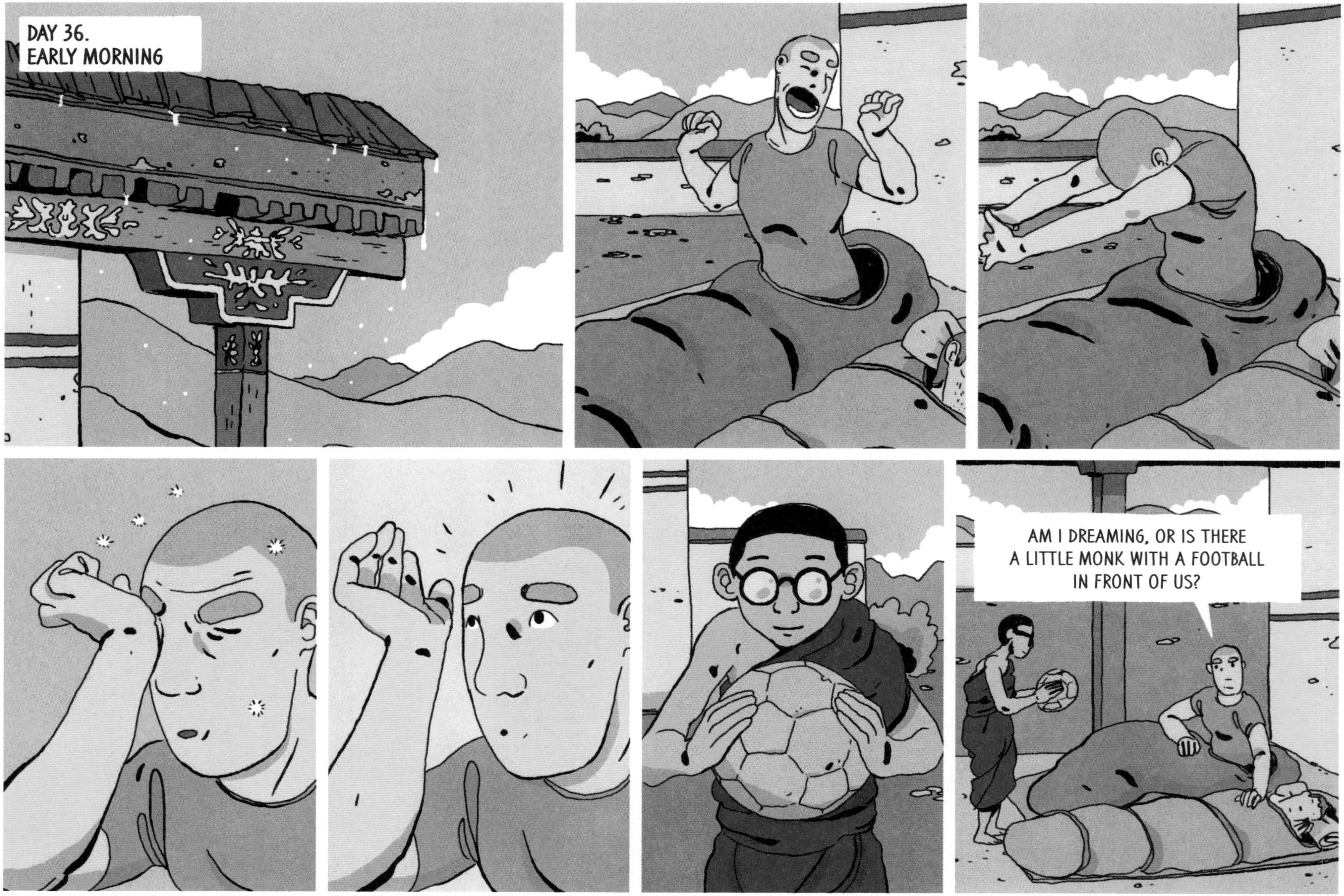
DAY 36.
EARLY MORNING
AM I DREAMING, OR IS THERE A LITTLE MONK WITH A FOOTBALL IN FRONT OF US?

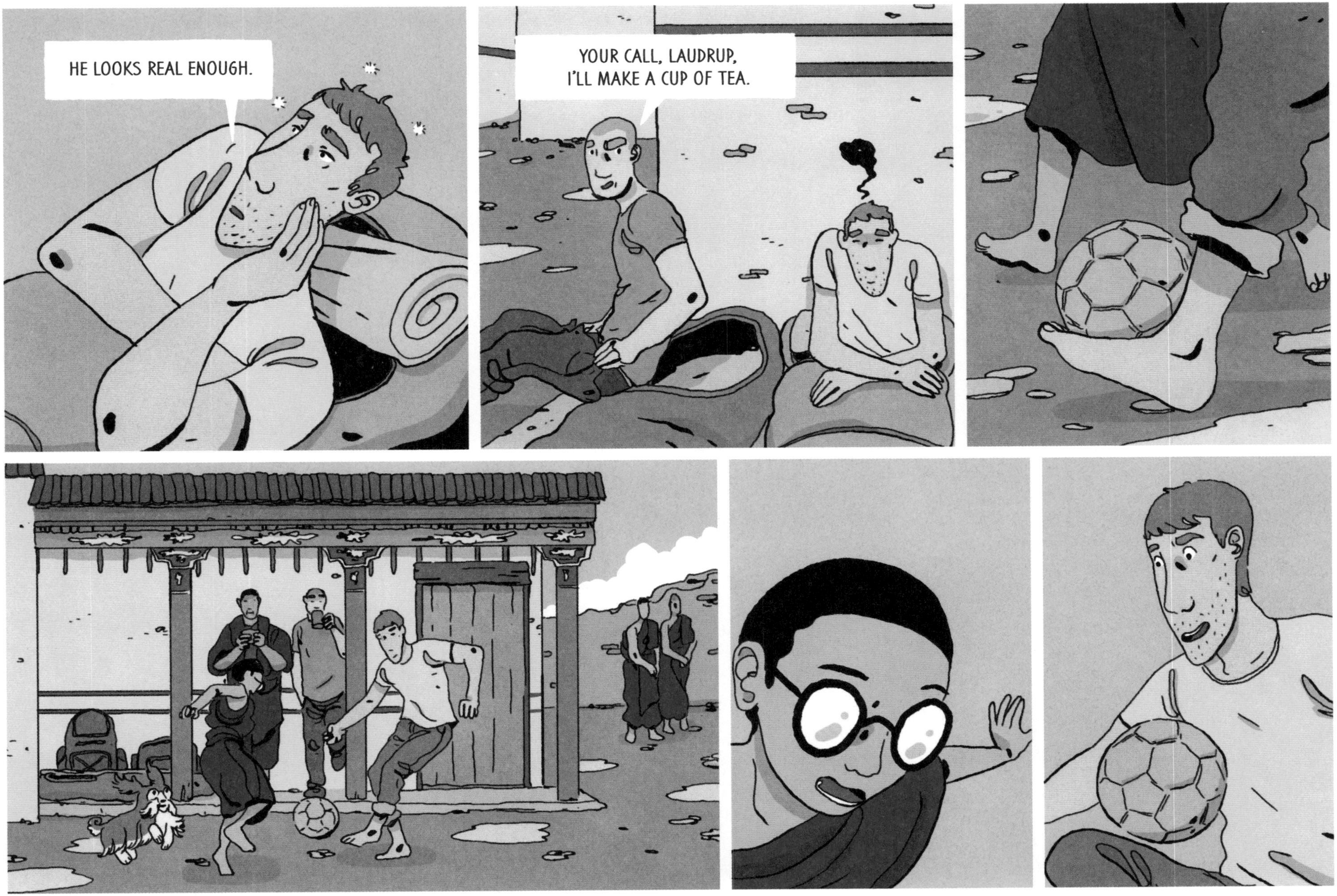
HE LOOKS REAL ENOUGH.
YOUR CALL, LAUDRUP, I'LL MAKE A CUP OF TEA.

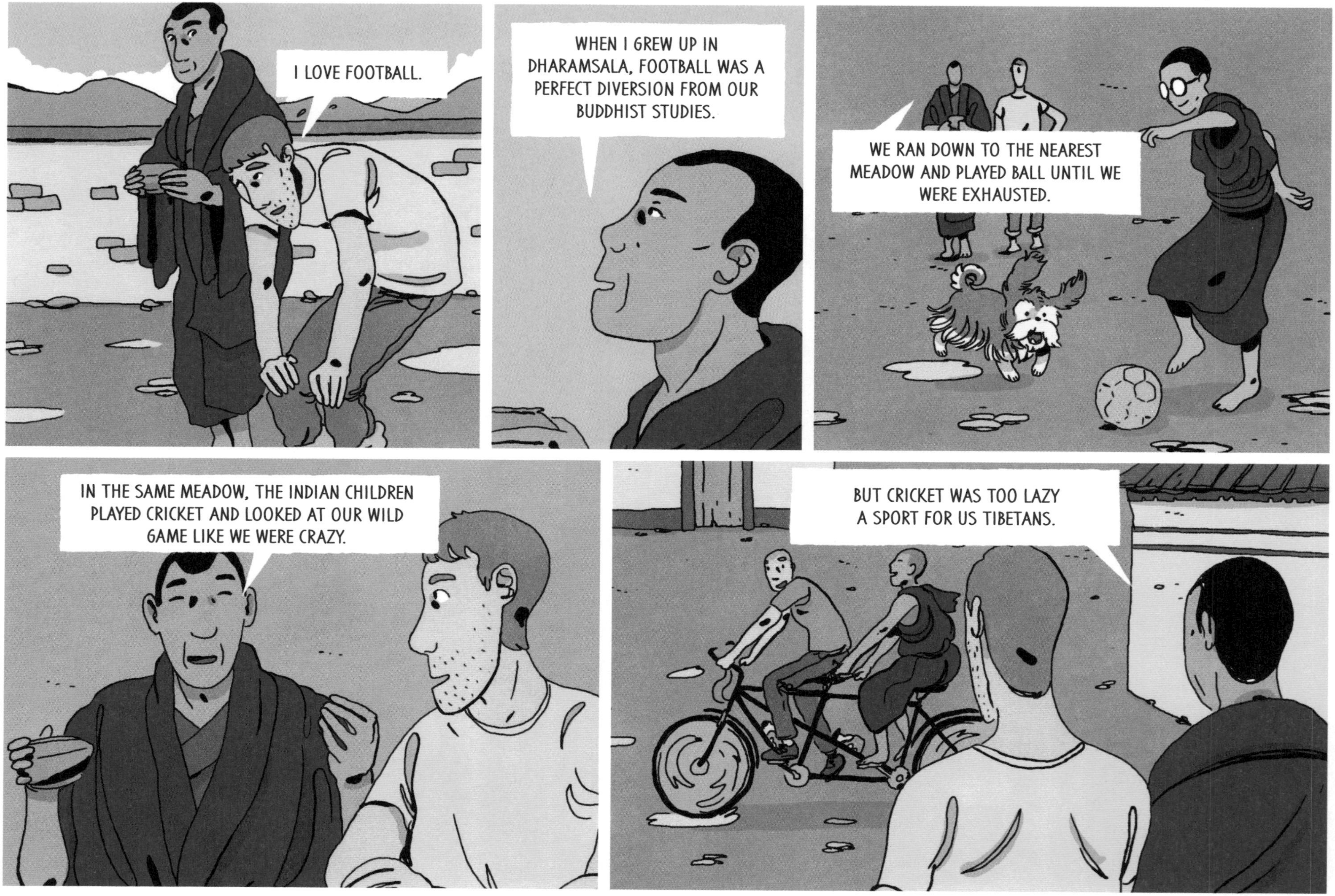

I LOVE FOOTBALL.
WHEN I GREW UP IN DHARAMSALA, FOOTBALL WAS A PERFECT DIVERSION FROM OUR BUDDHIST STUDIES.
WE RAN DOWN TO THE NEAREST MEADOW AND PLAYED BALL UNTIL WE WERE EXHAUSTED.
IN THE SAME MEADOW, THE INDIAN CHILDREN PLAYED CRICKET AND LOOKED AT OUR WILD GAME LIKE WE WERE CRAZY.
BUT CRICKET WAS TOO LAZY A SPORT FOR US TIBETANS.

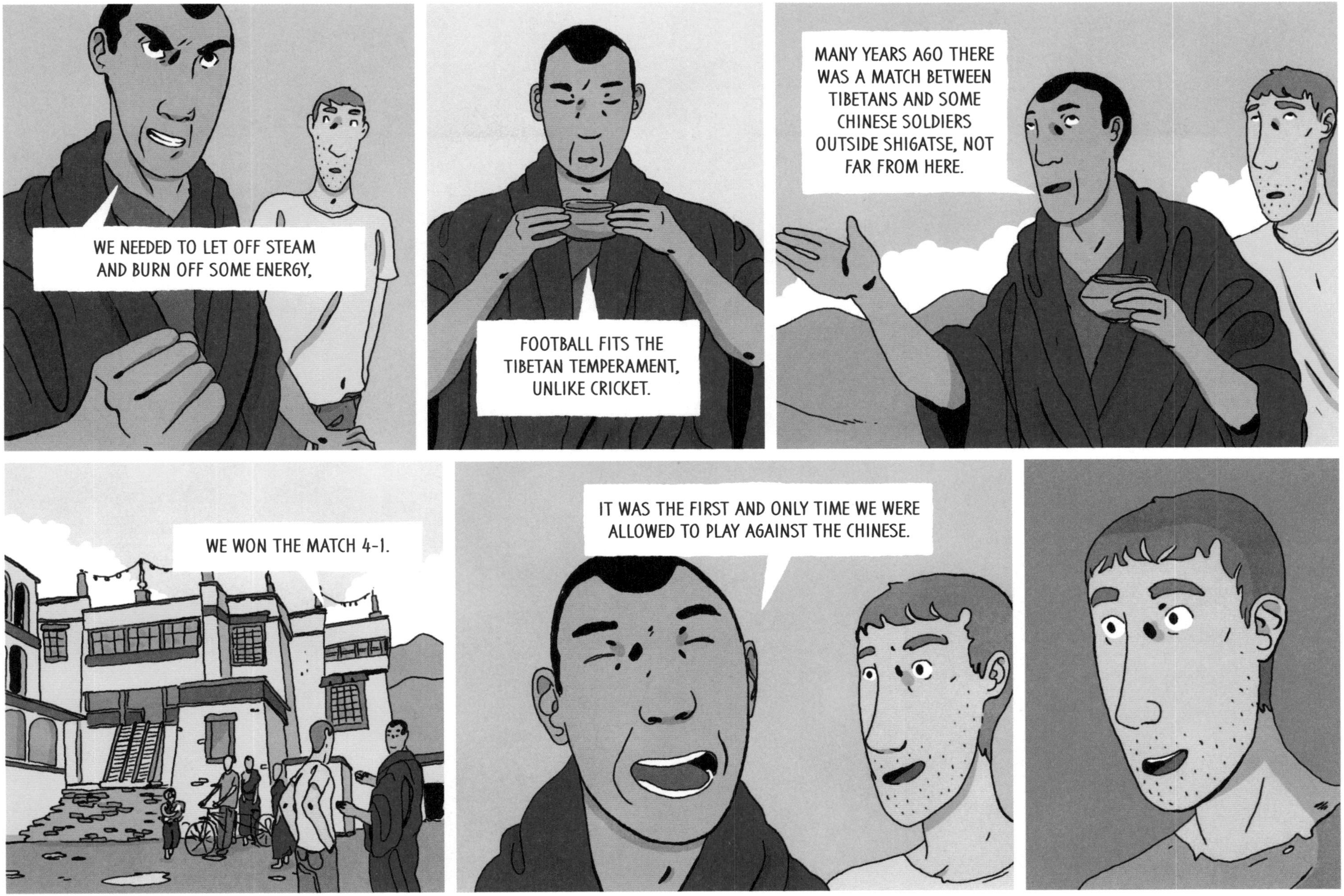
WE NEEDED TO LET OFF STEAM AND BURN OFF SOME ENERGY,
FOOTBALL FITS THE TIBETAN TEMPERAMENT, UNLIKE CRICKET.
MANY YEARS AGO THERE WAS A MATCH BETWEEN TIBETANS AND SOME CHINESE SOLDIERS OUTSIDE SHIGATSE, NOT FAR FROM HERE.
WE WON THE MATCH 4-1.
IT WAS THE FIRST AND ONLY TIME WE WERE ALLOWED TO PLAY AGAINST THE CHINESE.

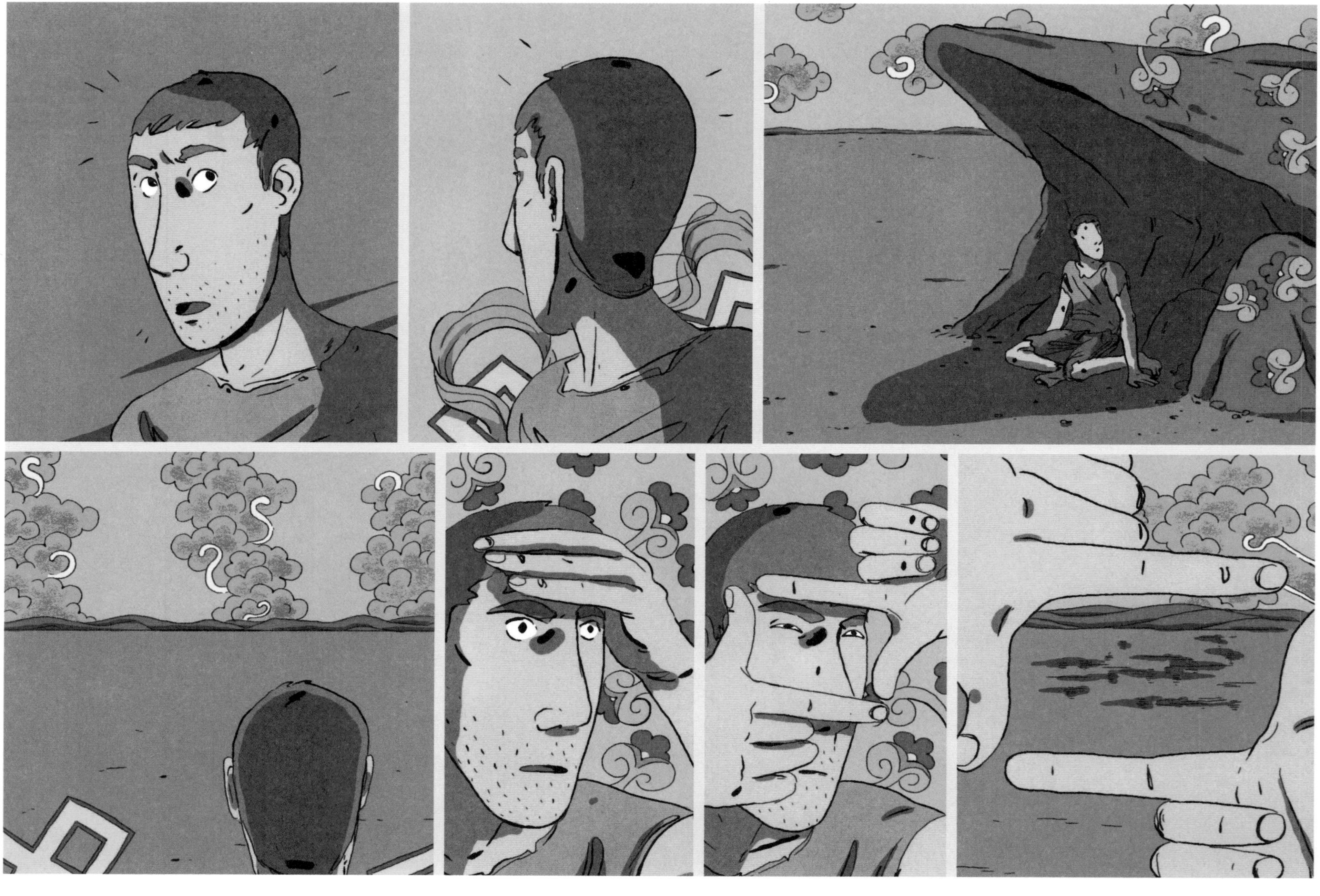

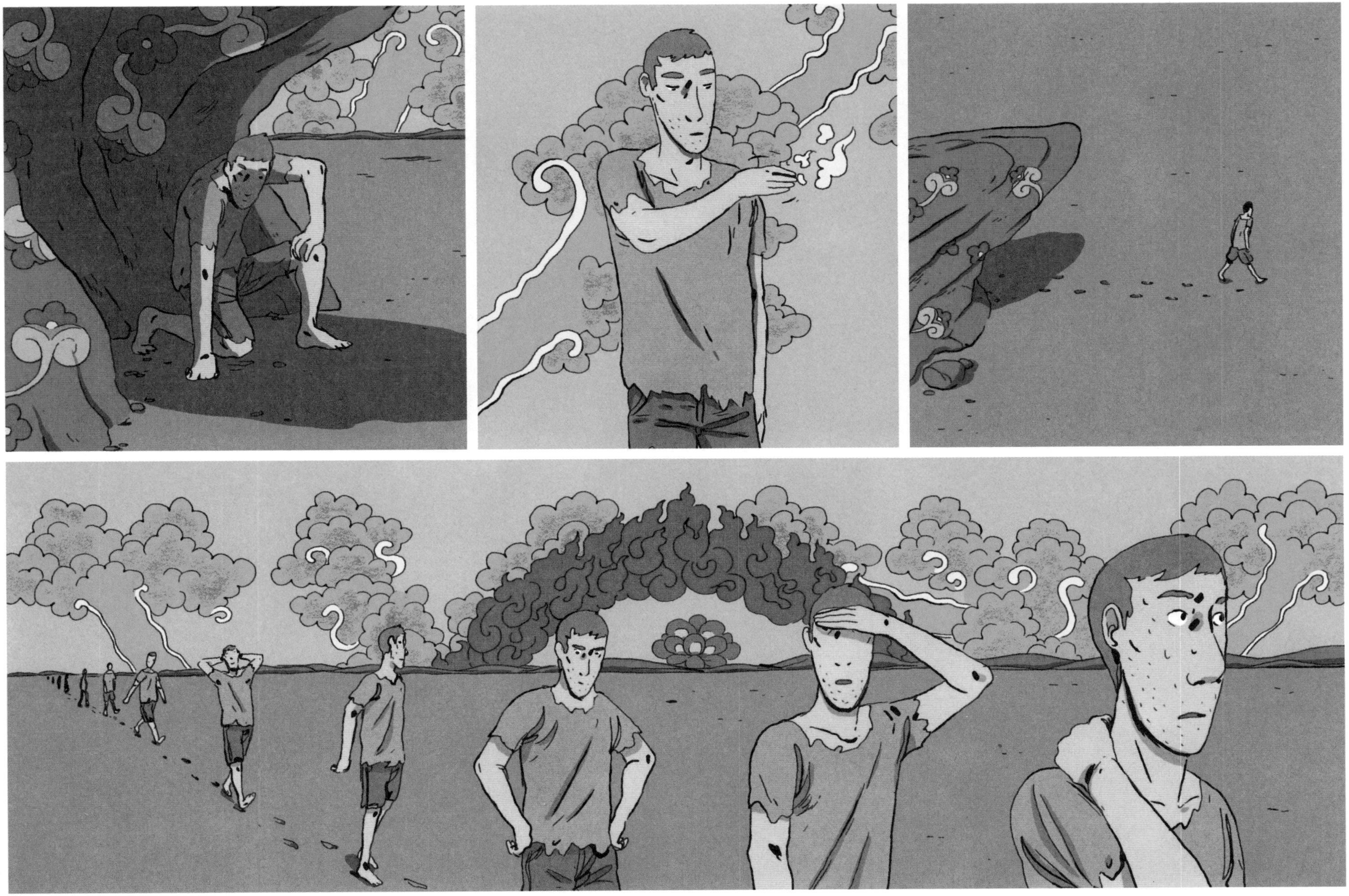

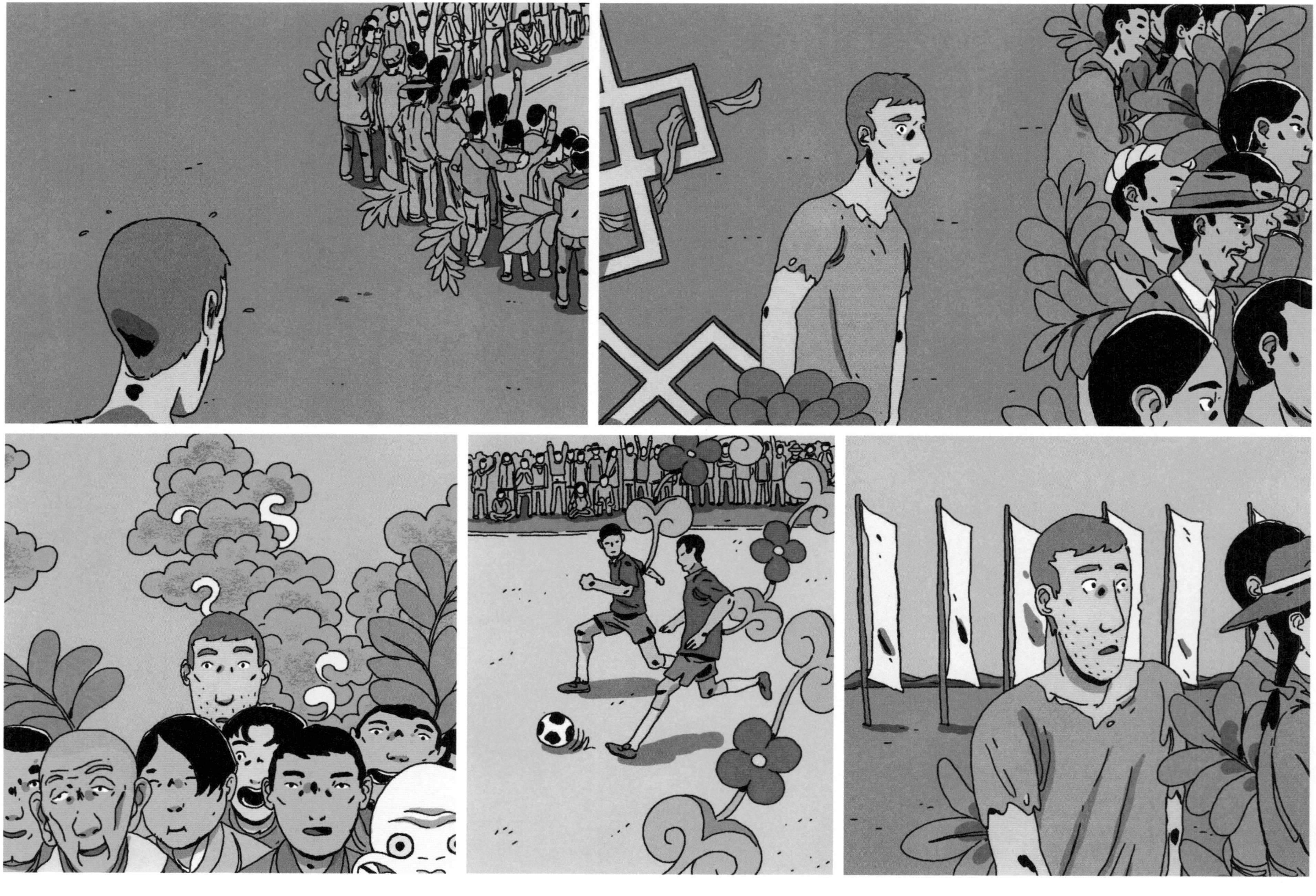

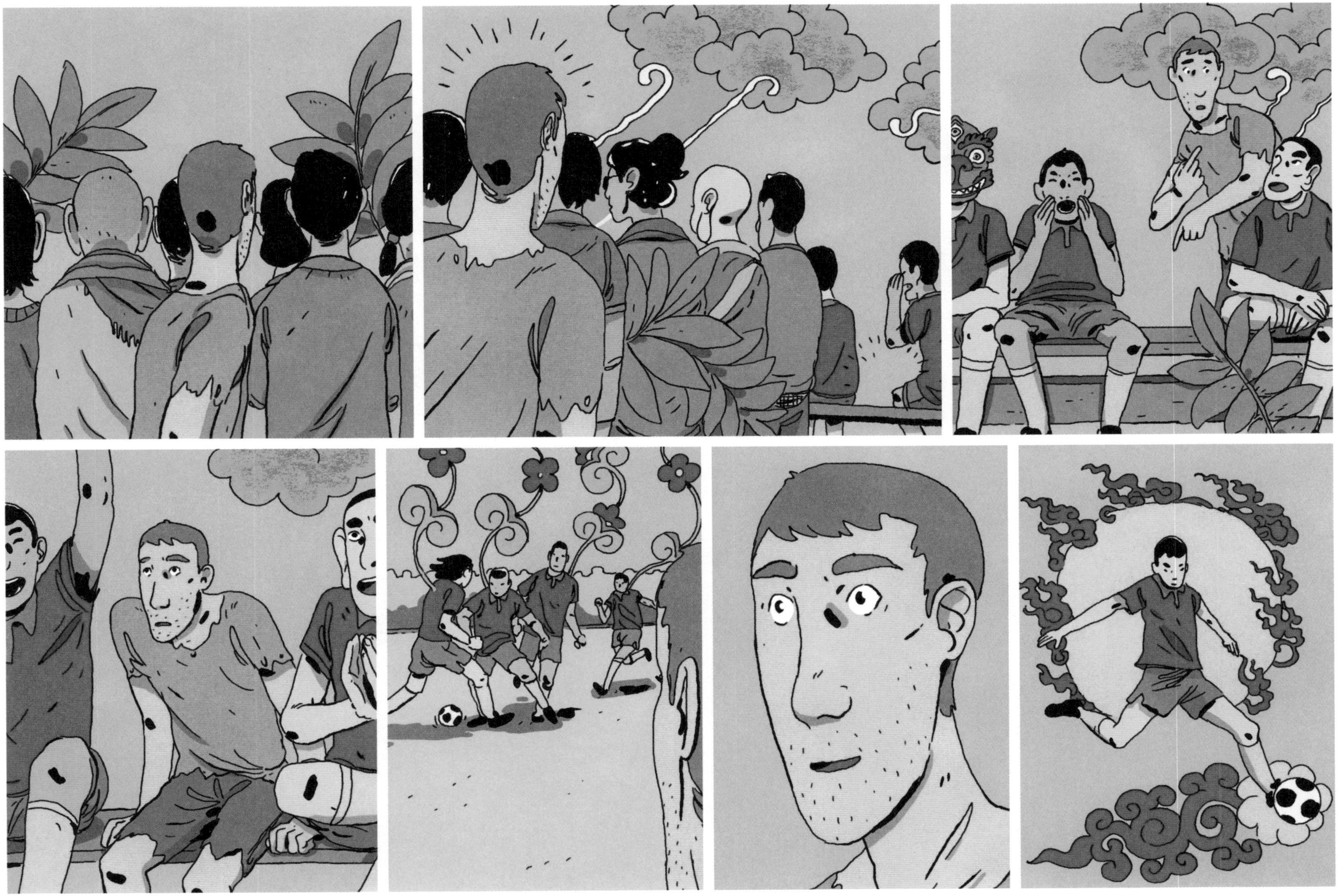

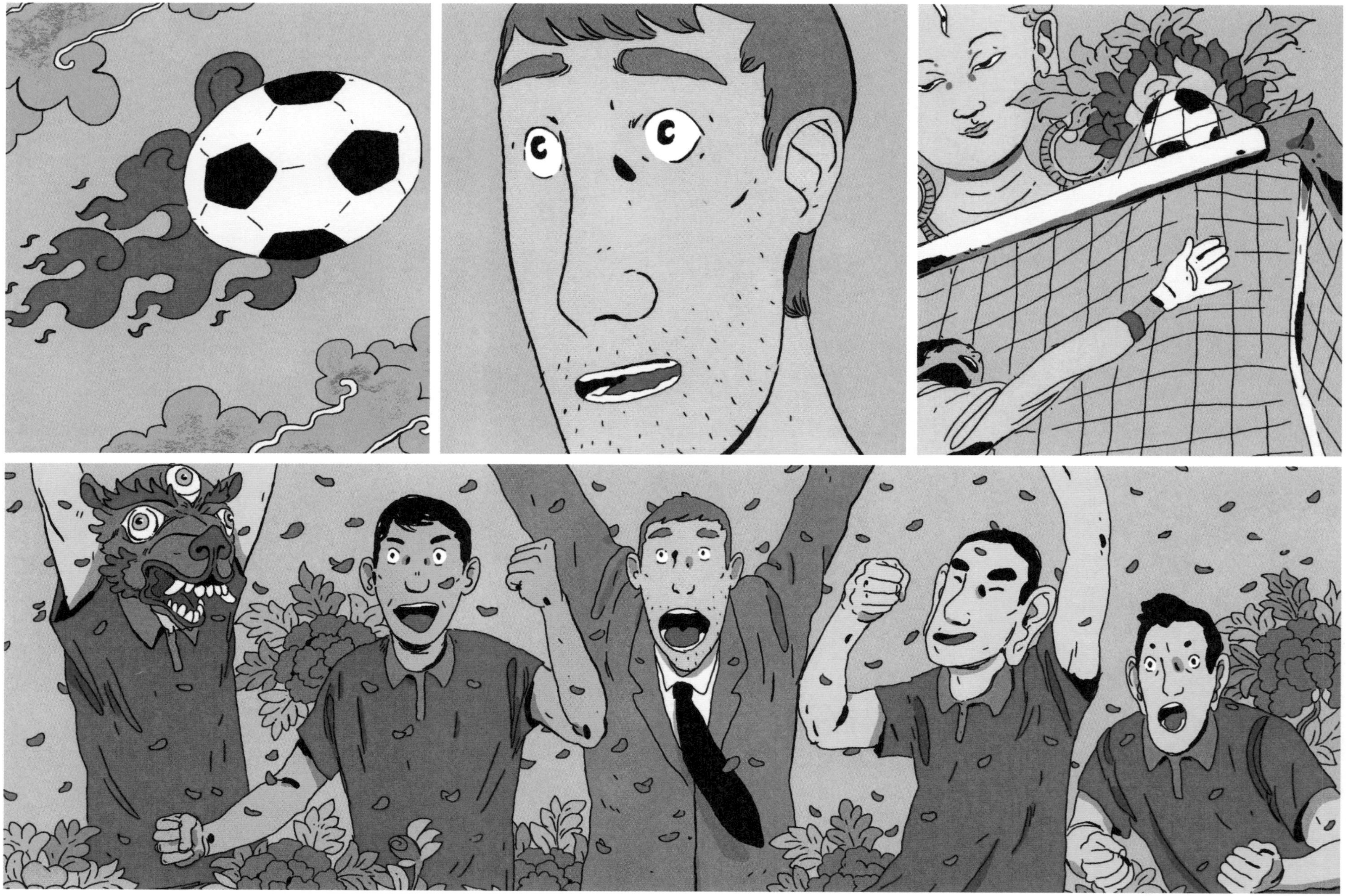

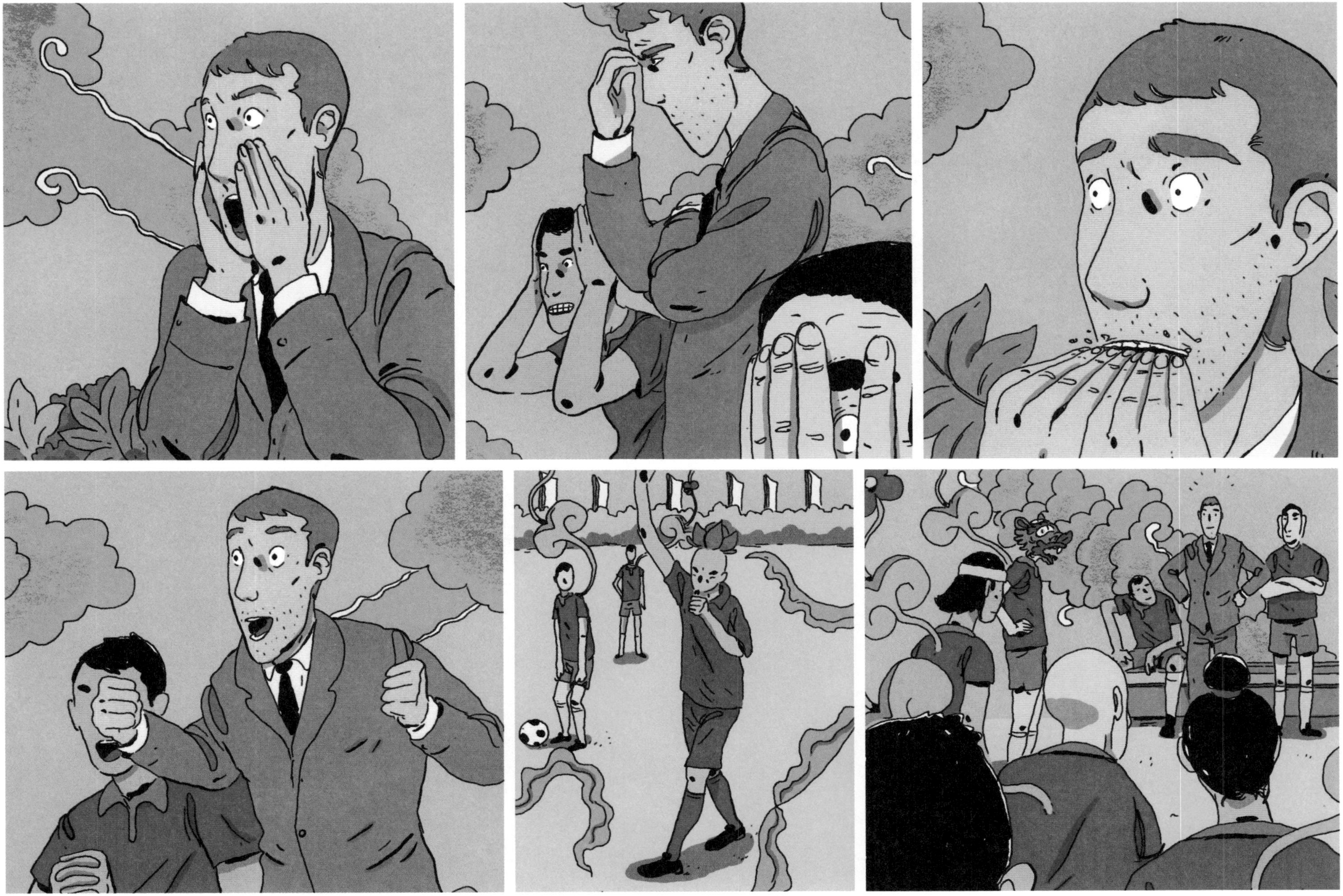

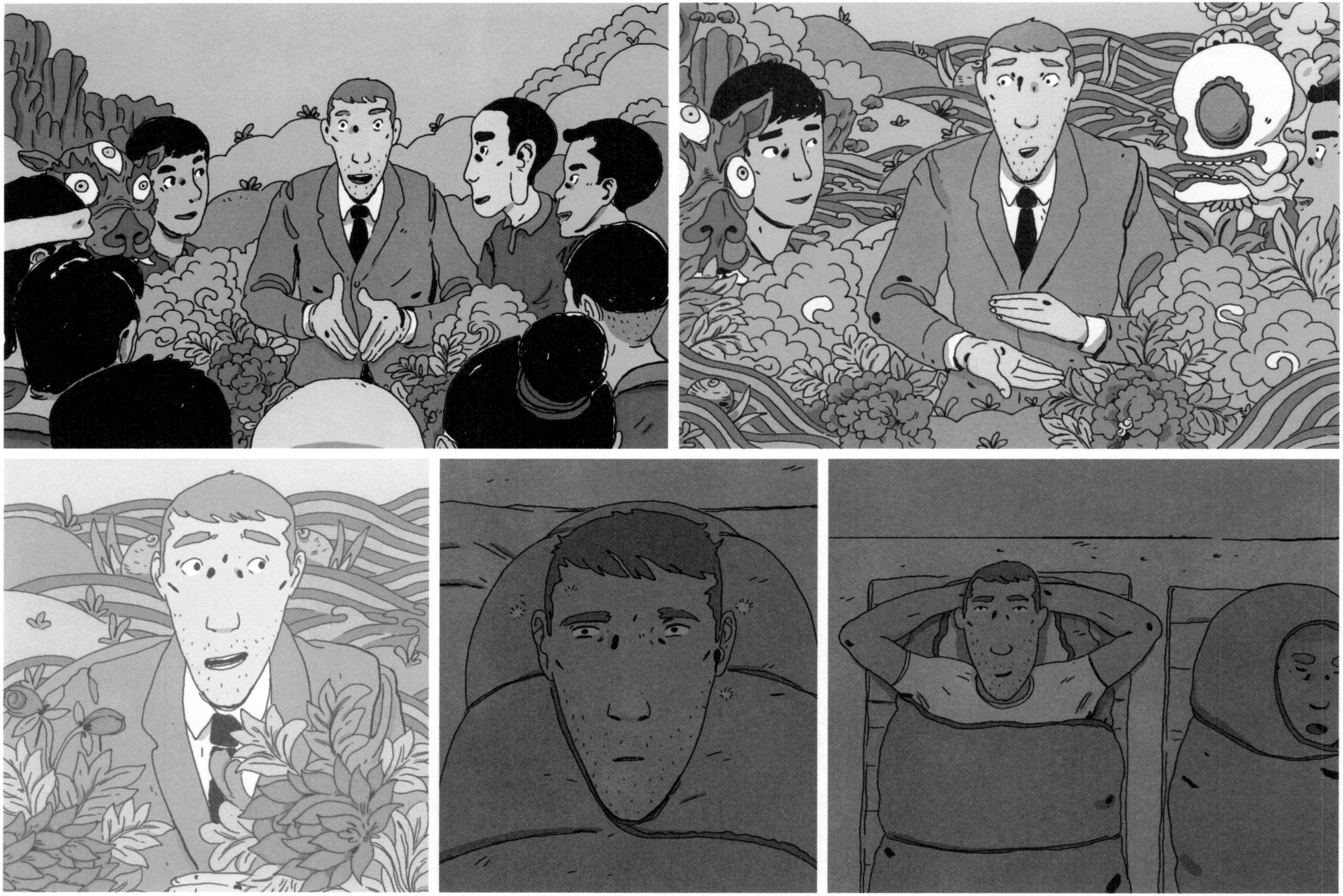

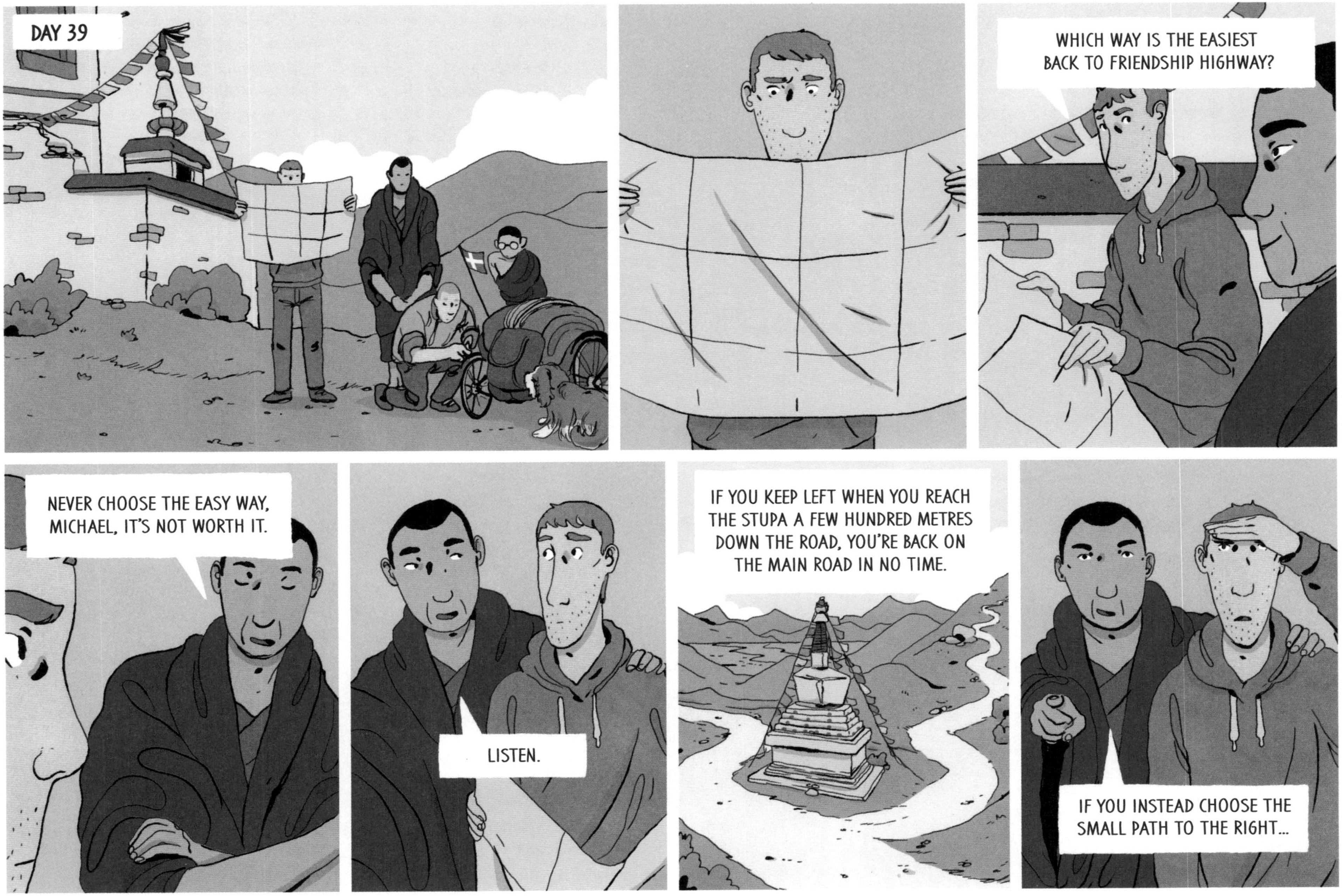
DAY 39
WHICH WAY IS THE EASIEST BACK TO FRIENDSHIP HIGHWAY?
NEVER CHOOSE THE EASY WAY, MICHAEL, IT'S NOT WORTH IT.
LISTEN.
IF YOU KEEP LEFT WHEN YOU REACH THE STUPA A FEW HUNDRED METRES DOWN THE ROAD, YOU'RE BACK ON THE MAIN ROAD IN NO TIME.
IF YOU INSTEAD CHOOSE THE SMALL PATH TO THE RIGHT...

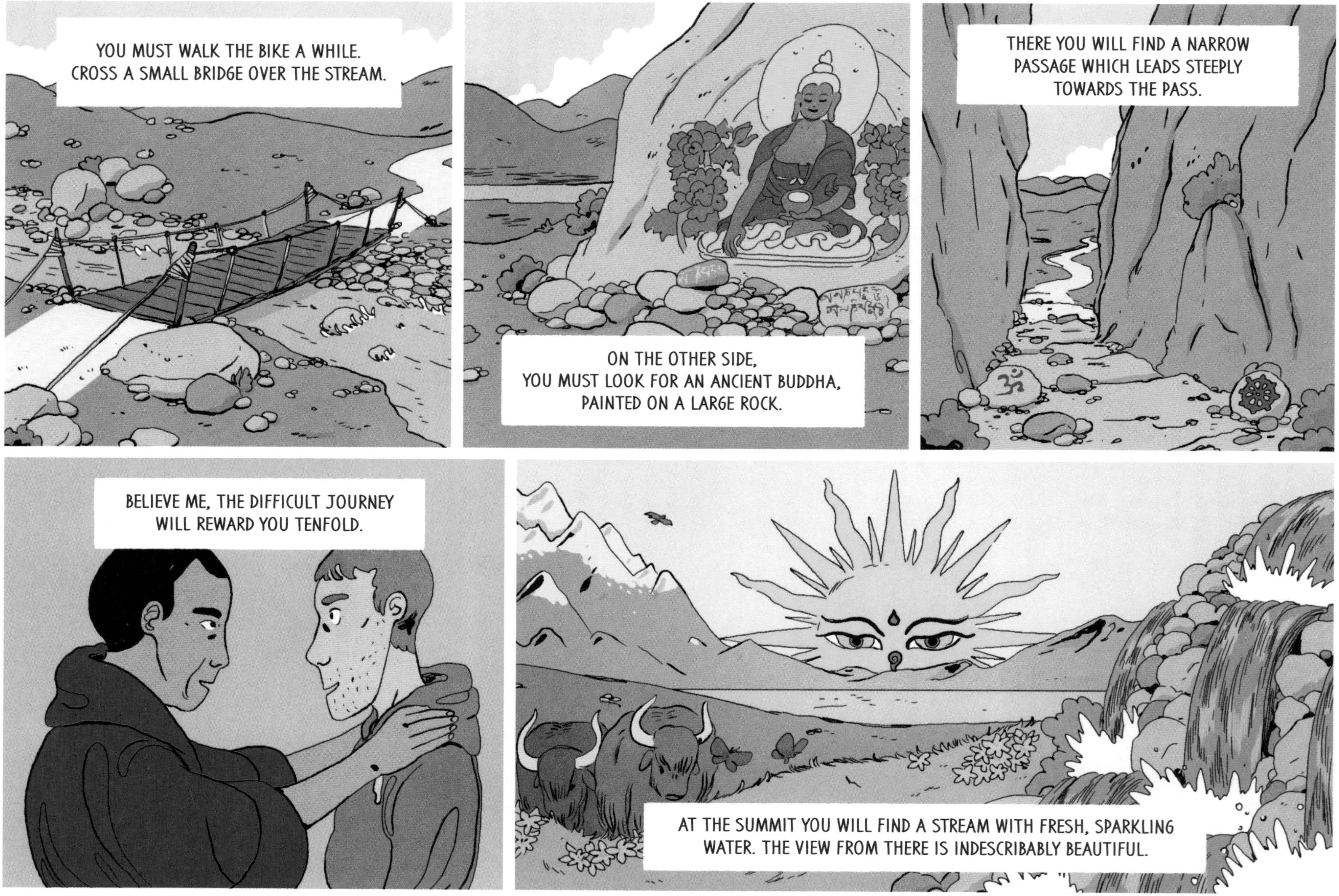
YOU MUST WALK THE BIKE A WHILE.
CROSS A SMALL BRIDGE OVER THE STREAM.
ON THE OTHER SIDE,
YOU MUST LOOK FOR AN ANCIENT BUDDHA,
PAINTED ON A LARGE ROCK.
THERE YOU WILL FIND A NARROW
PASSAGE WHICH LEADS STEEPLY
TOWARDS THE PASS.
BELIEVE ME, THE DIFFICULT JOURNEY
WILL REWARD YOU TENFOLD.
AT THE SUMMIT YOU WILL FIND A STREAM WITH FRESH, SPARKLING
WATER. THE VIEW FROM THERE IS INDESCRIBABLY BEAUTIFUL.

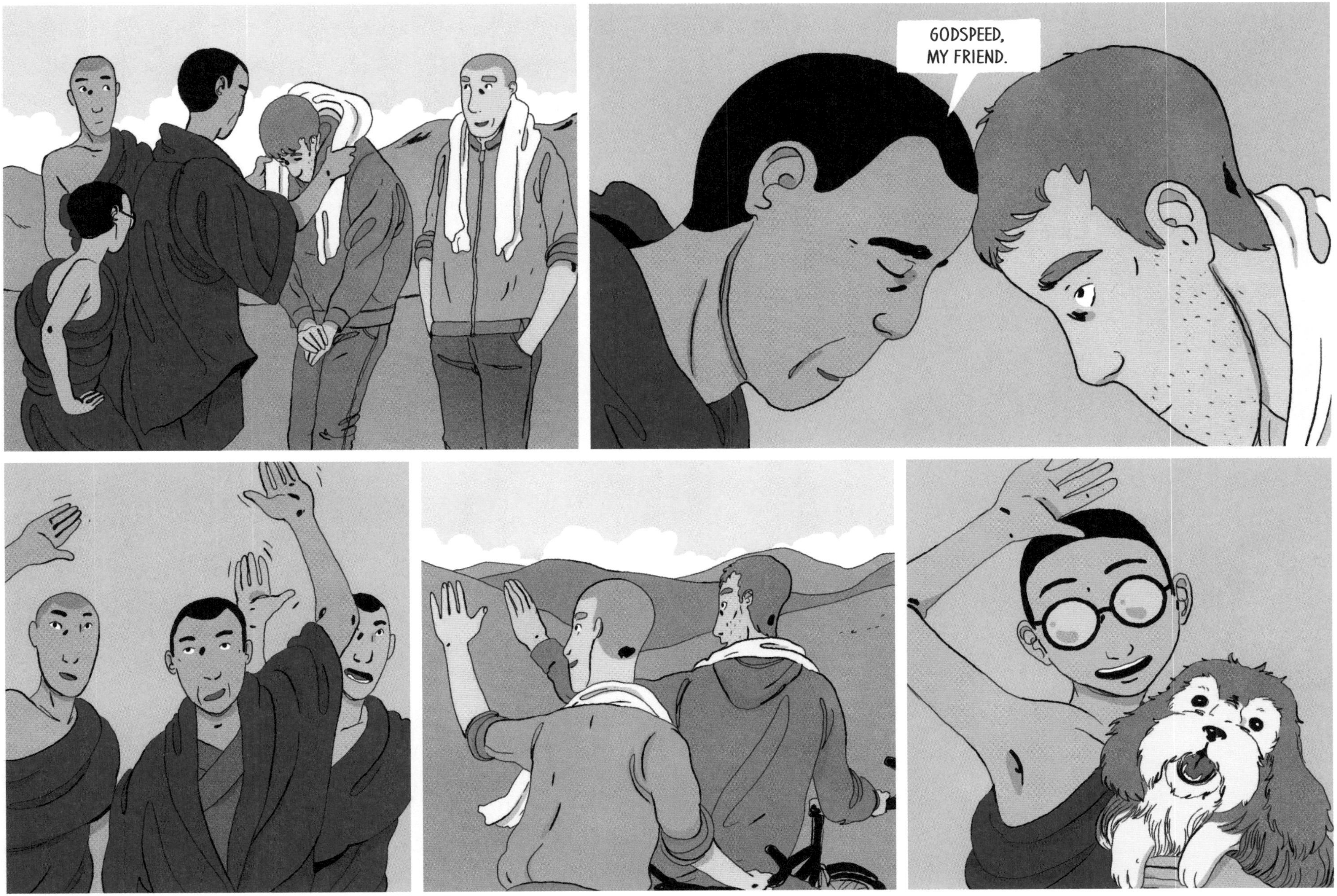
GODSPEED,
MY FRIEND.

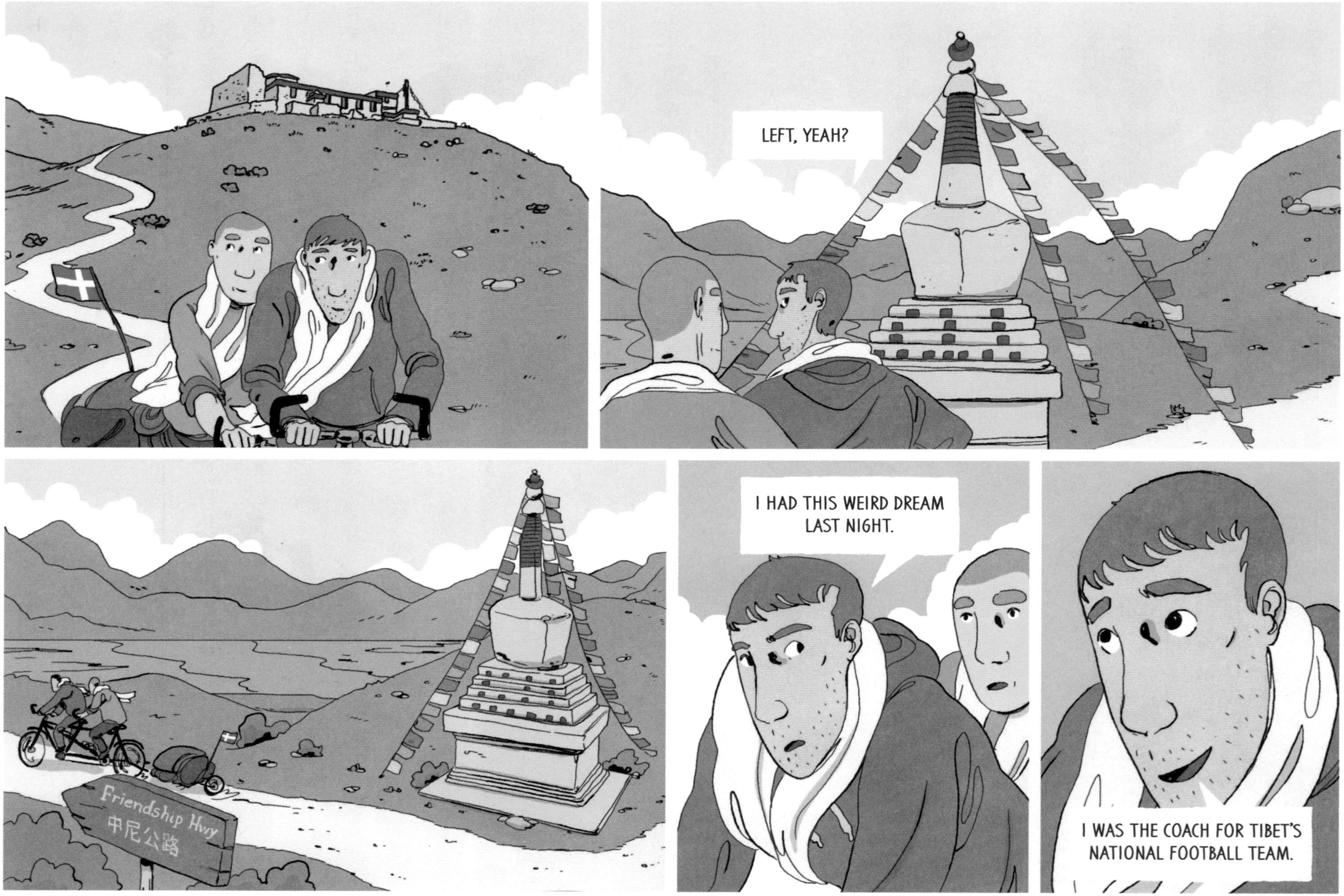
LEFT, YEAH?
Friendship Hwy
中尼公路
I HAD THIS WEIRD DREAM LAST NIGHT.
I WAS THE COACH FOR TIBET'S NATIONAL FOOTBALL TEAM.

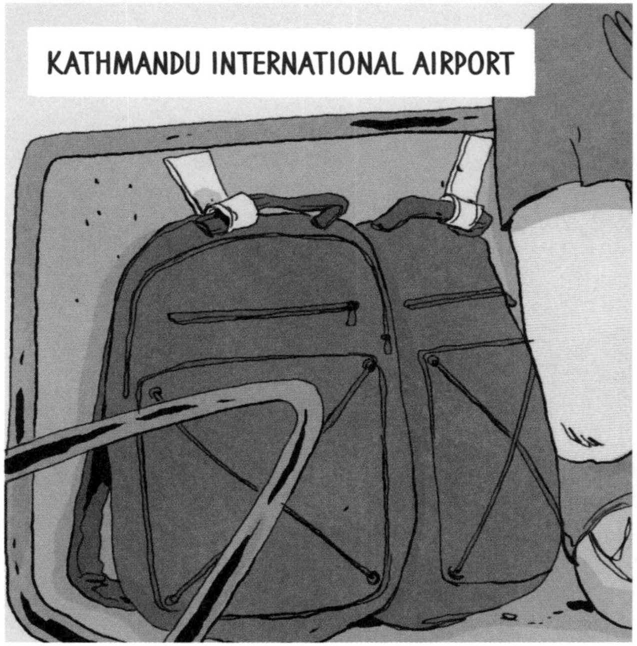
KATHMANDU INTERNATIONAL AIRPORT

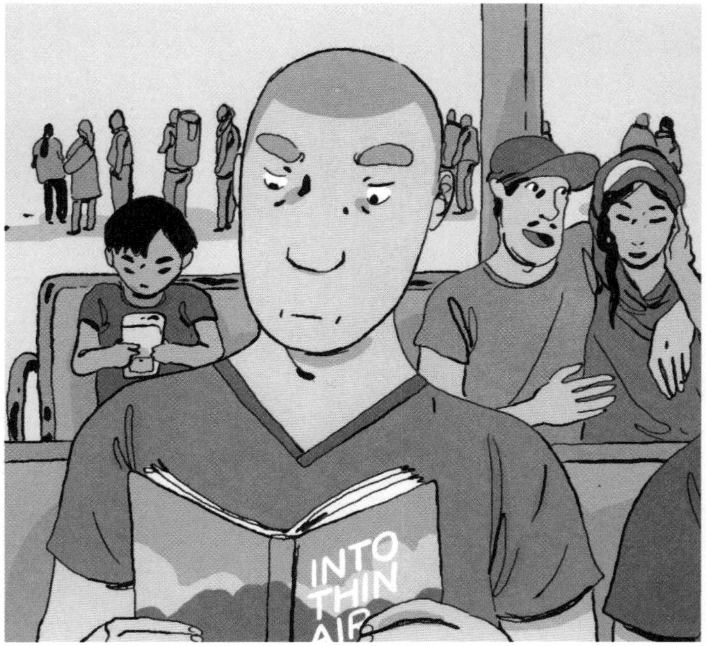
INTO
THIN

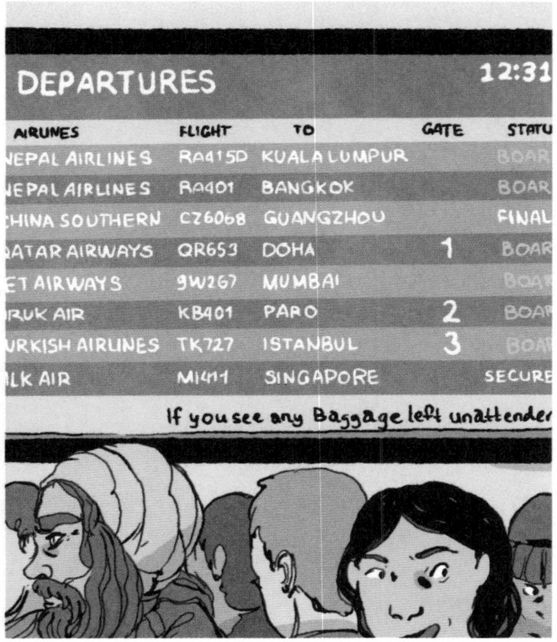
DEPARTURES
12:31
AIRLINES FLIGHT TO GATE
EPAL AIRLINES RA415D KUALA LUMPUR
EPAL AIRLINES RA401 BANGKOK
HINA SOUTHERN CZ6068 GUANGZHOU FINAL
ATAR AIRWAYS QR653 DOHA 1
ET AIRWAYS 9W267 MUMBAI
RUK AIR KB401 PARO 2
URKISH AIRLINES TK727 ISTANBUL 3
LK AIR MI411 SINGAPORE
If you see any Baggage left

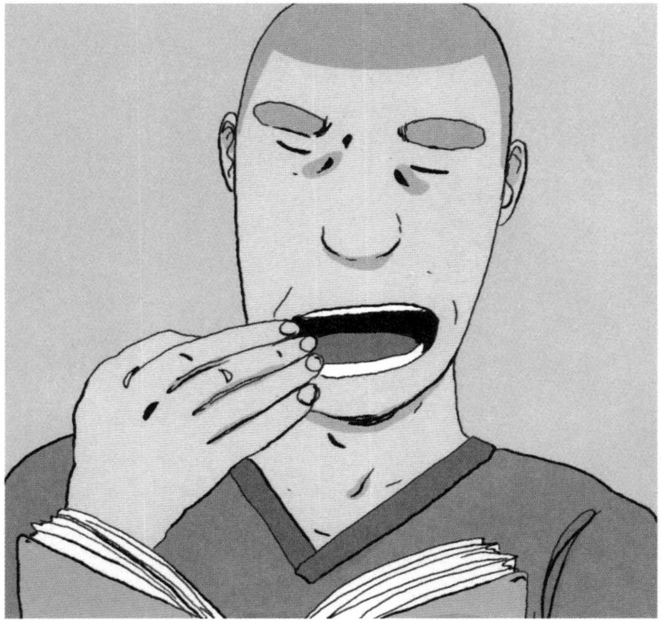

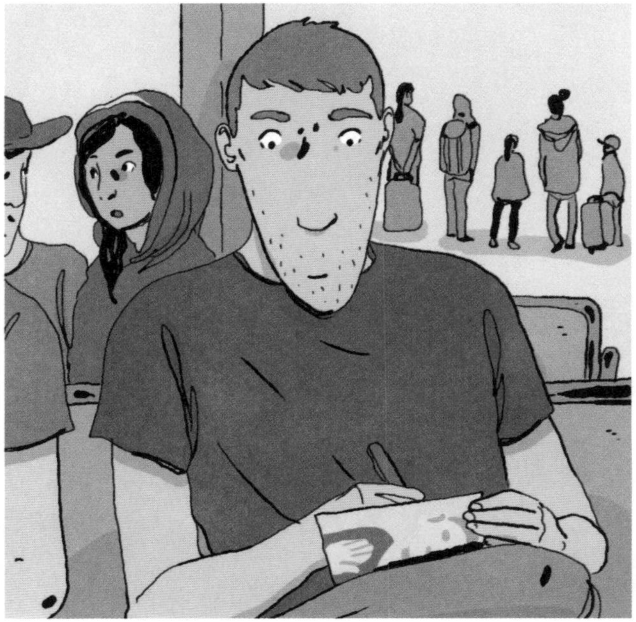

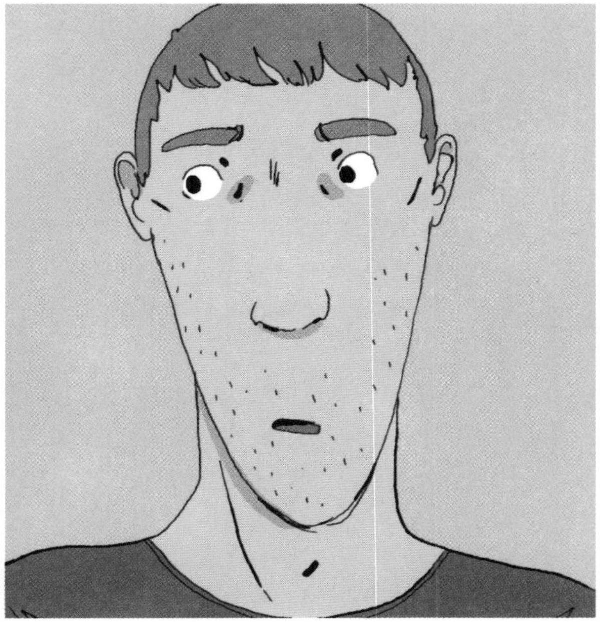

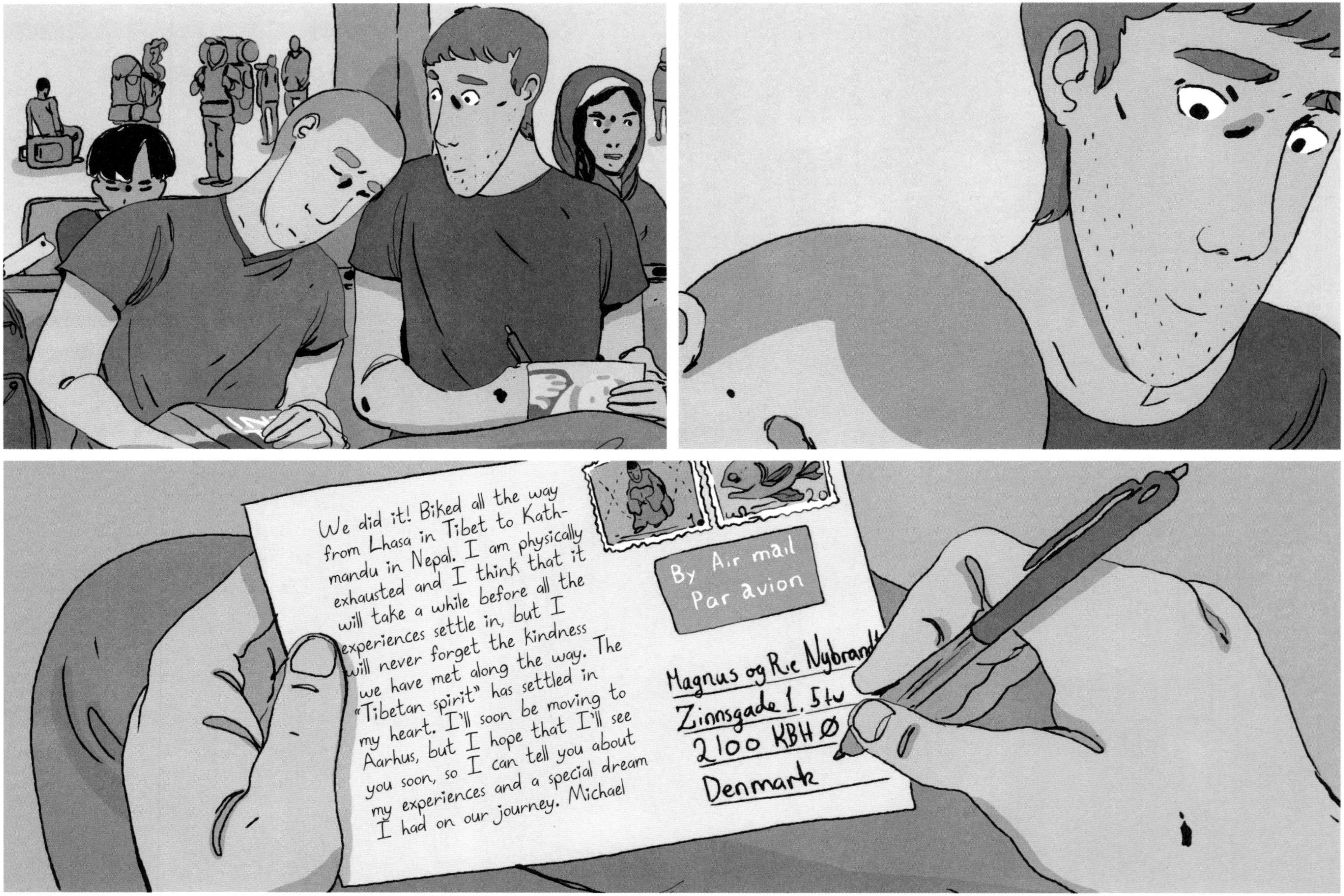
We did it! Biked all the way
from Lhasa in Tibet to Kathmandu in Nepal. I am physically
exhausted and I think that it
will take a while before all the
experiences settle in, but I
will never forget the kindness
we have met along the way. The
"Tibetan spirit" has settled in
my heart. I'll soon be moving to
Aarhus, but I hope that I'll see
you soon, so I can tell you about
my experiences and a special dream
I had on our journey. Michael
By Air mail
Par avion
Magnus og Rie Nybrandt
Zinnsgade 1, 5 tv
2100 KBH Ø
Denmark

CHAPTER 3

KAOSPILOT

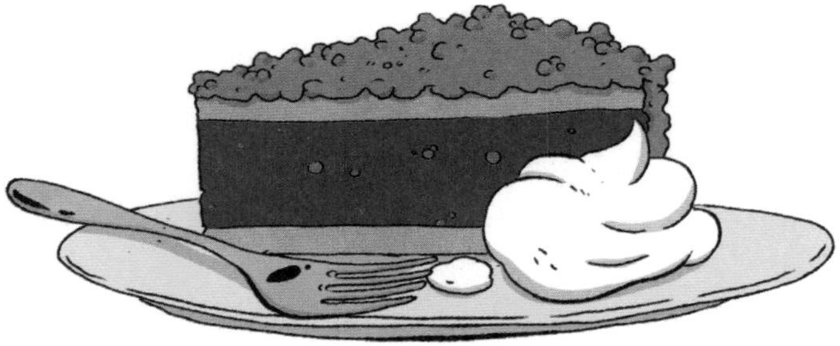

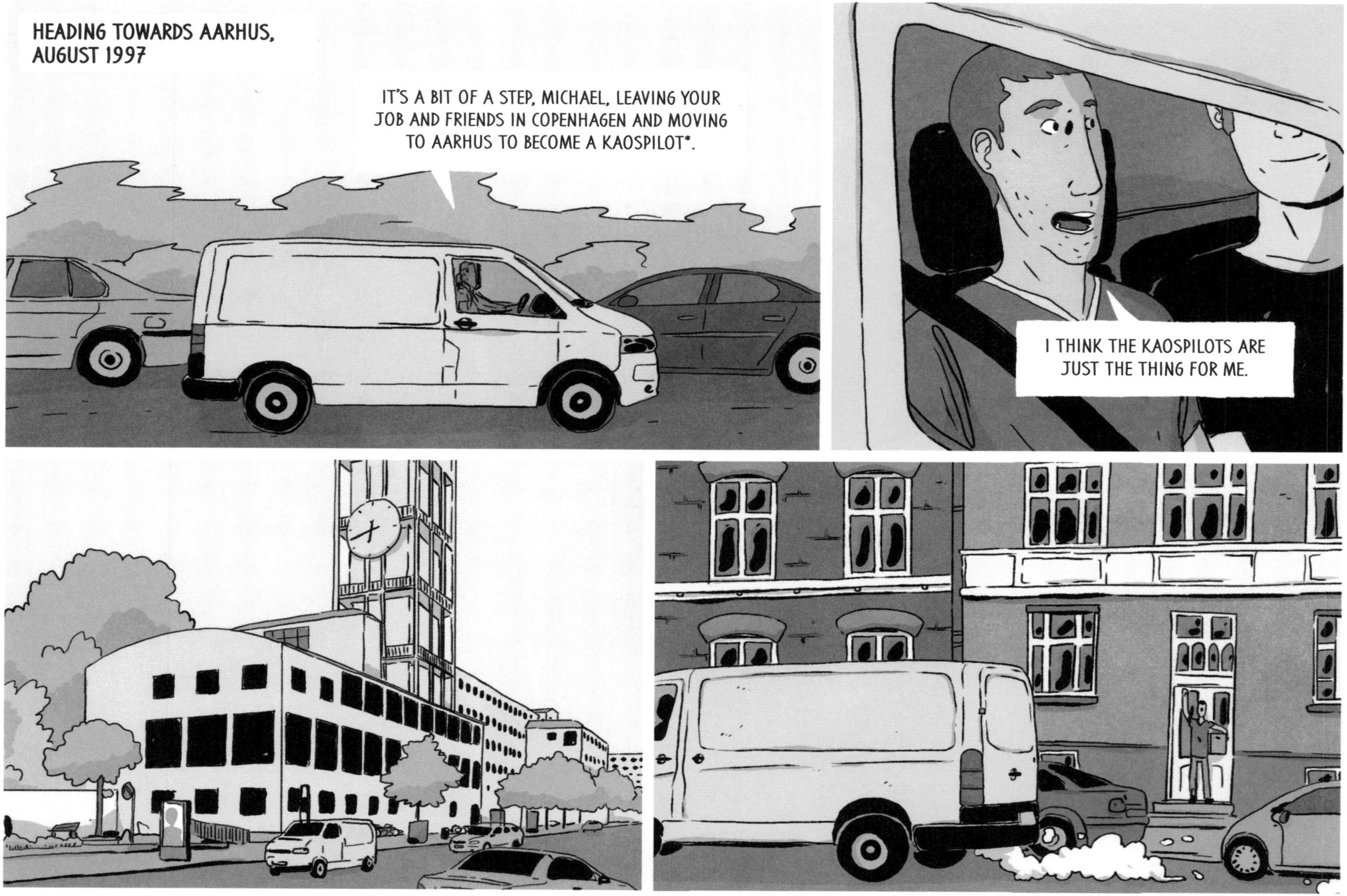
HEADING TOWARDS AARHUS, AUGUST 1997
IT'S A BIT OF A STEP, MICHAEL, LEAVING YOUR JOB AND FRIENDS IN COPENHAGEN AND MOVING TO AARHUS TO BECOME A KAOSPILOT*.
I THINK THE KAOSPILOTS ARE JUST THE THING FOR ME.

*KAOSPILOT - A 3 YEAR PROJECT MANAGEMENT DEGREE IN ENTREPRENEURSHIP AND CULTURAL INNOVATION BASED IN AARHUS, DENMARK.

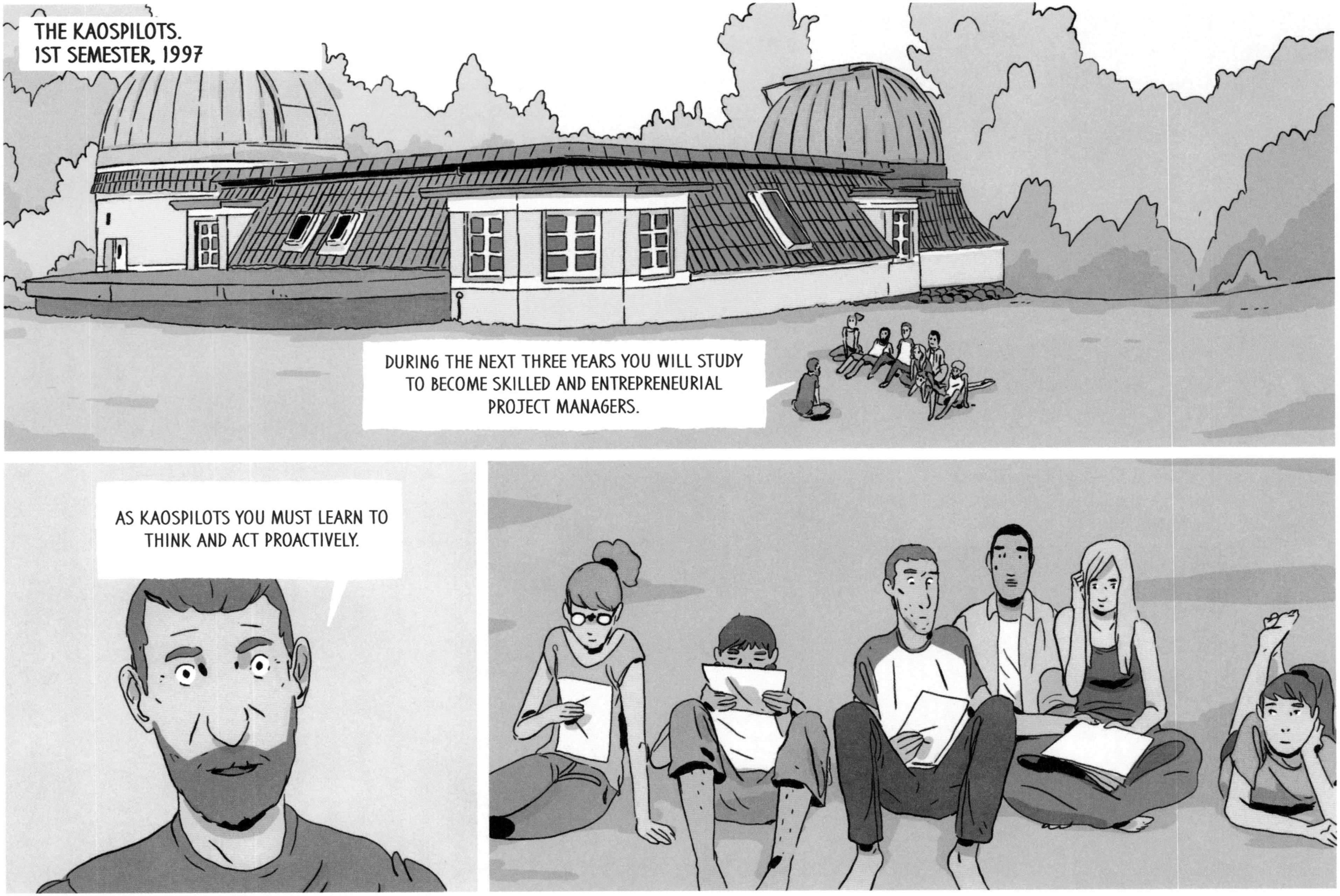
THE KAOSPILOTS.
1ST SEMESTER, 1997
DURING THE NEXT THREE YEARS YOU WILL STUDY TO BECOME SKILLED AND ENTREPRENEURIAL PROJECT MANAGERS.
AS KAOSPILOTS YOU MUST LEARN TO THINK AND ACT PROACTIVELY.

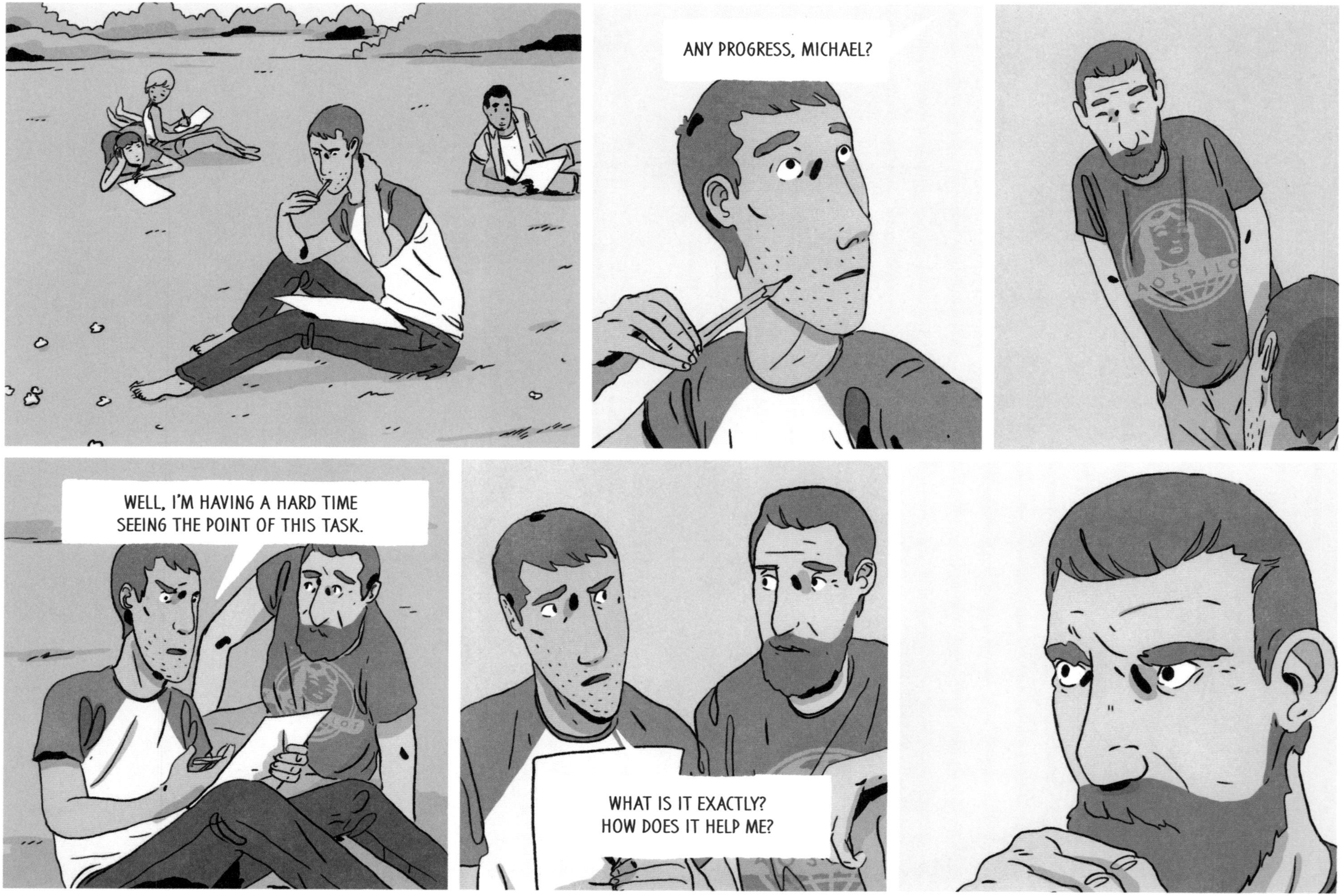
ANY PROGRESS, MICHAEL?
WELL, I'M HAVING A HARD TIME SEEING THE POINT OF THIS TASK.
WHAT IS IT EXACTLY? HOW DOES IT HELP ME?

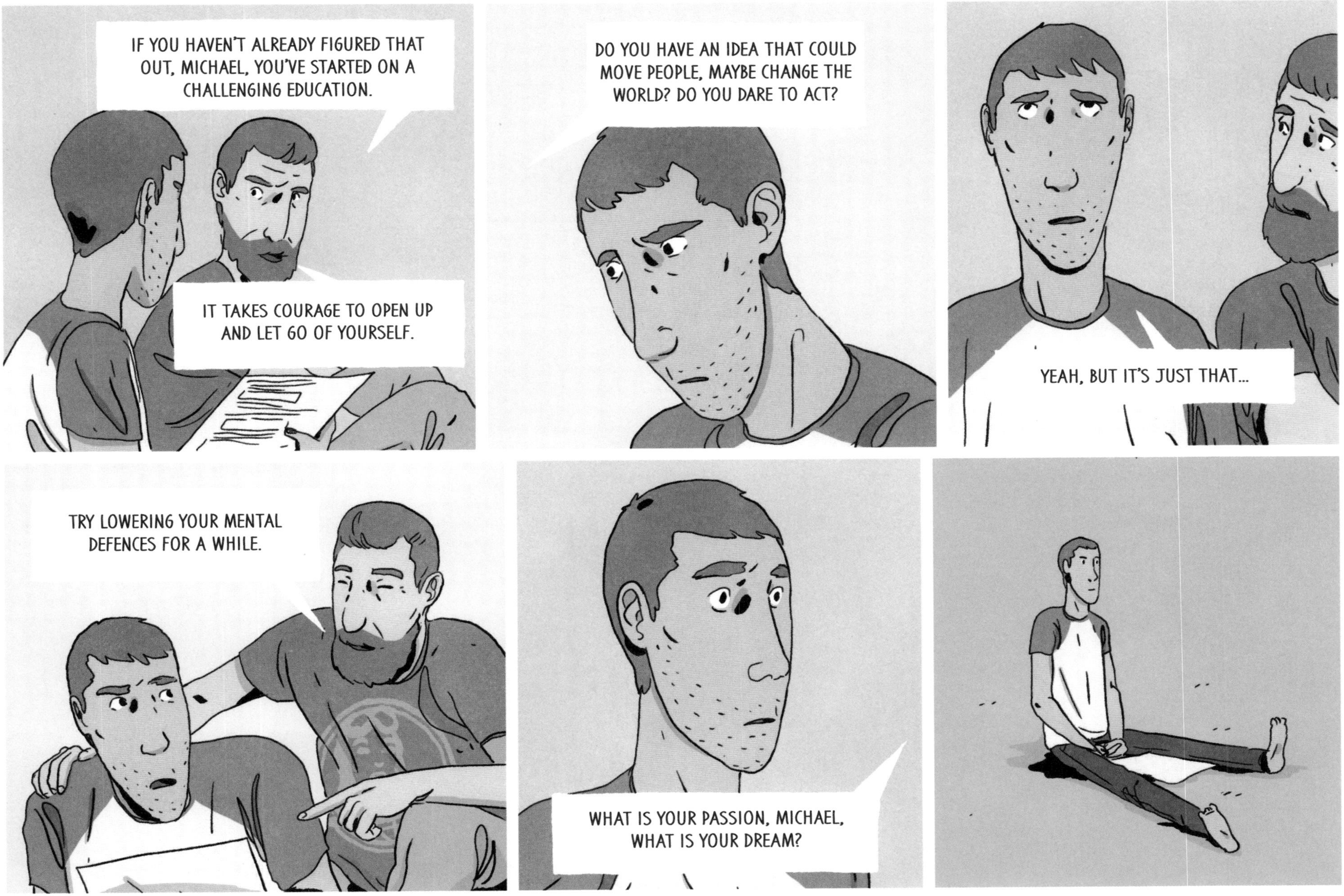
IF YOU HAVEN'T ALREADY FIGURED THAT OUT, MICHAEL, YOU'VE STARTED ON A CHALLENGING EDUCATION.
IT TAKES COURAGE TO OPEN UP AND LET GO OF YOURSELF.
DO YOU HAVE AN IDEA THAT COULD MOVE PEOPLE, MAYBE CHANGE THE WORLD? DO YOU DARE TO ACT?
YEAH, BUT IT'S JUST THAT...
TRY LOWERING YOUR MENTAL DEFENCES FOR A WHILE.
WHAT IS YOUR PASSION, MICHAEL, WHAT IS YOUR DREAM?

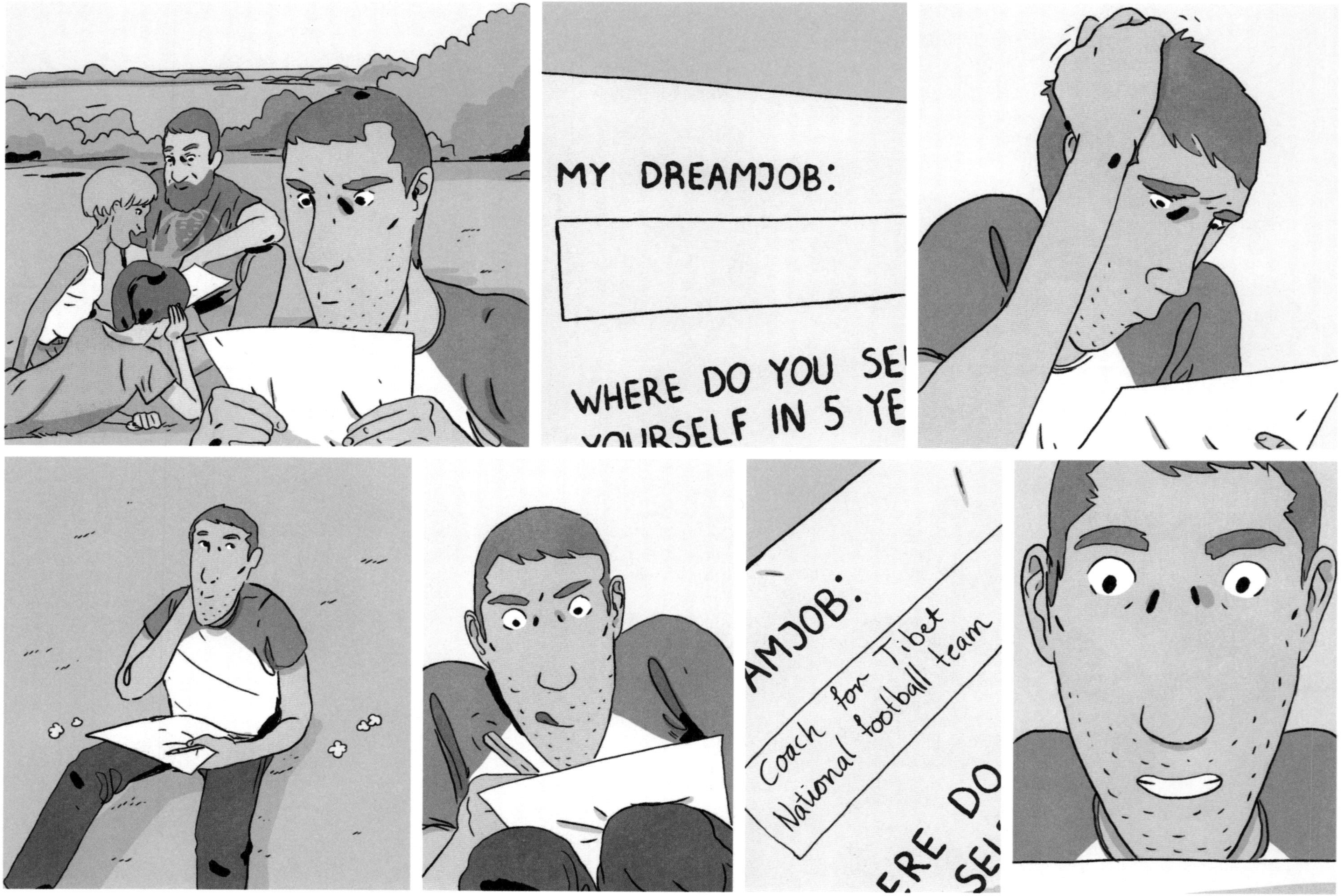

MY DREAMJOB:
WHERE DO YOU SE
YOURSELF IN 5 YE
AMJOB:
Coach for Tibet
National football team
ERE DO

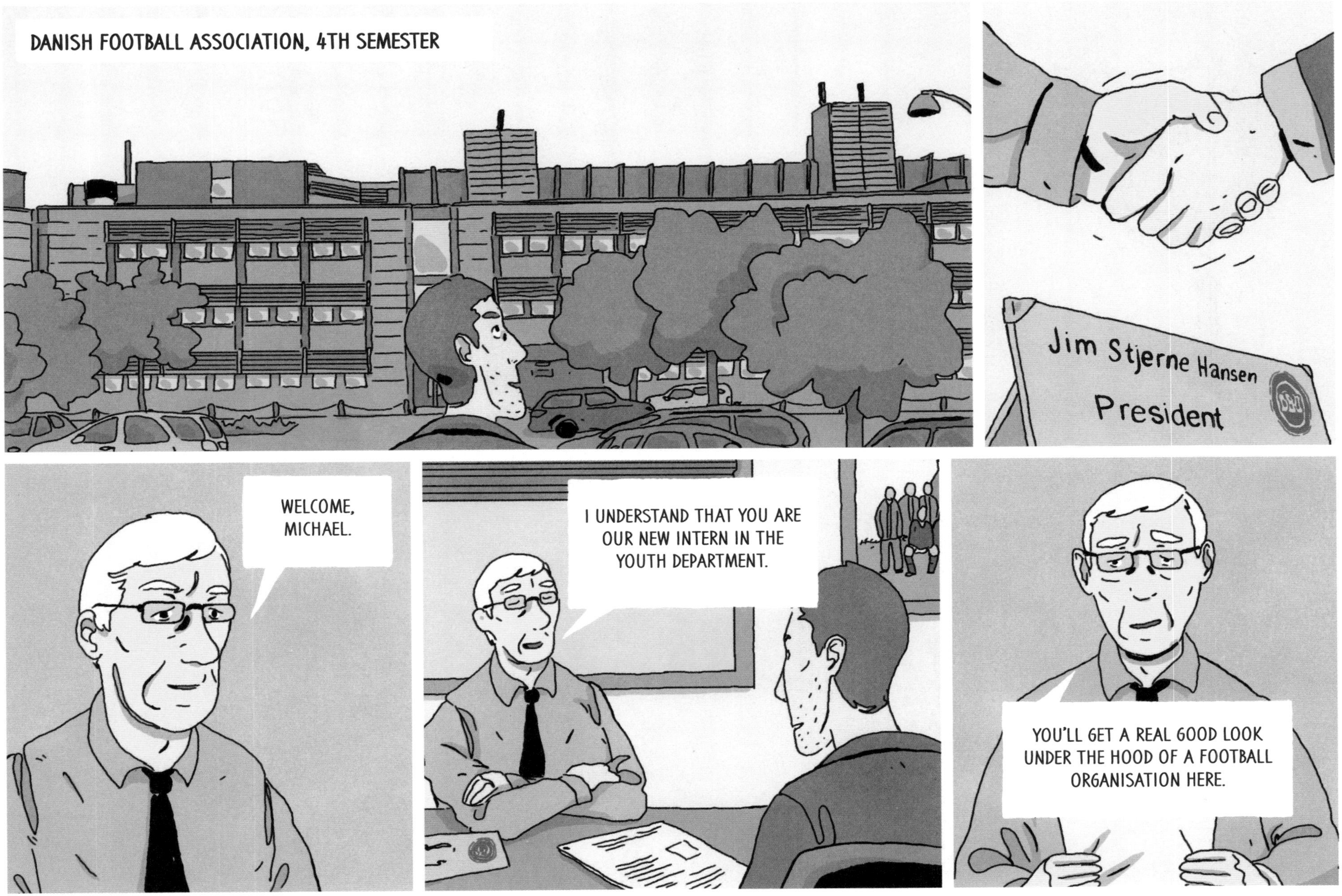
DANISH FOOTBALL ASSOCIATION, 4TH SEMESTER
Jim Stjerne Hansen
President
WELCOME, MICHAEL.
I UNDERSTAND THAT YOU ARE OUR NEW INTERN IN THE YOUTH DEPARTMENT.
YOU'LL GET A REAL GOOD LOOK UNDER THE HOOD OF A FOOTBALL ORGANISATION HERE.

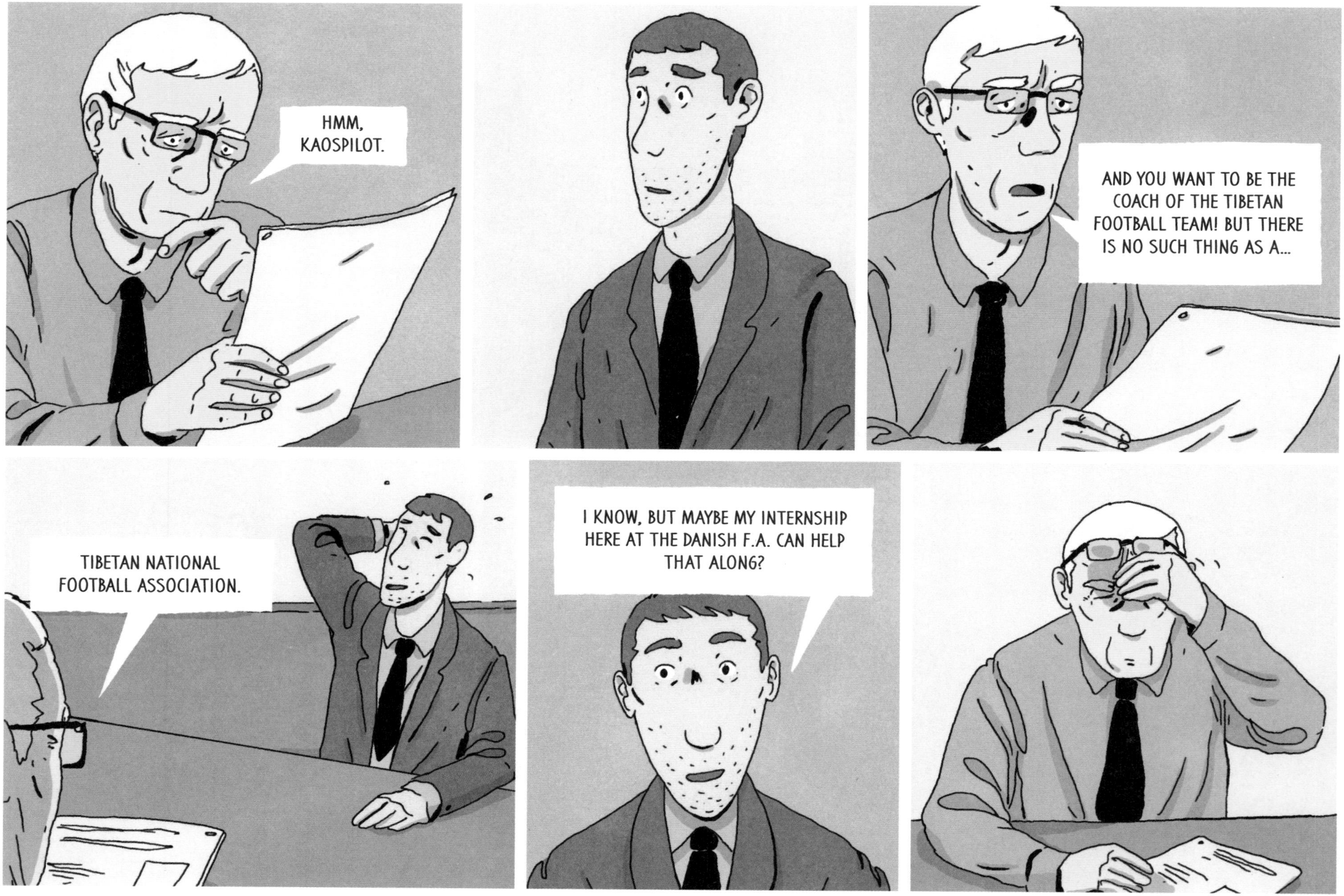
HMM, KAOSPILOT.
AND YOU WANT TO BE THE COACH OF THE TIBETAN FOOTBALL TEAM! BUT THERE IS NO SUCH THING AS A...
TIBETAN NATIONAL FOOTBALL ASSOCIATION.
I KNOW, BUT MAYBE MY INTERNSHIP HERE AT THE DANISH F.A. CAN HELP THAT ALONG?

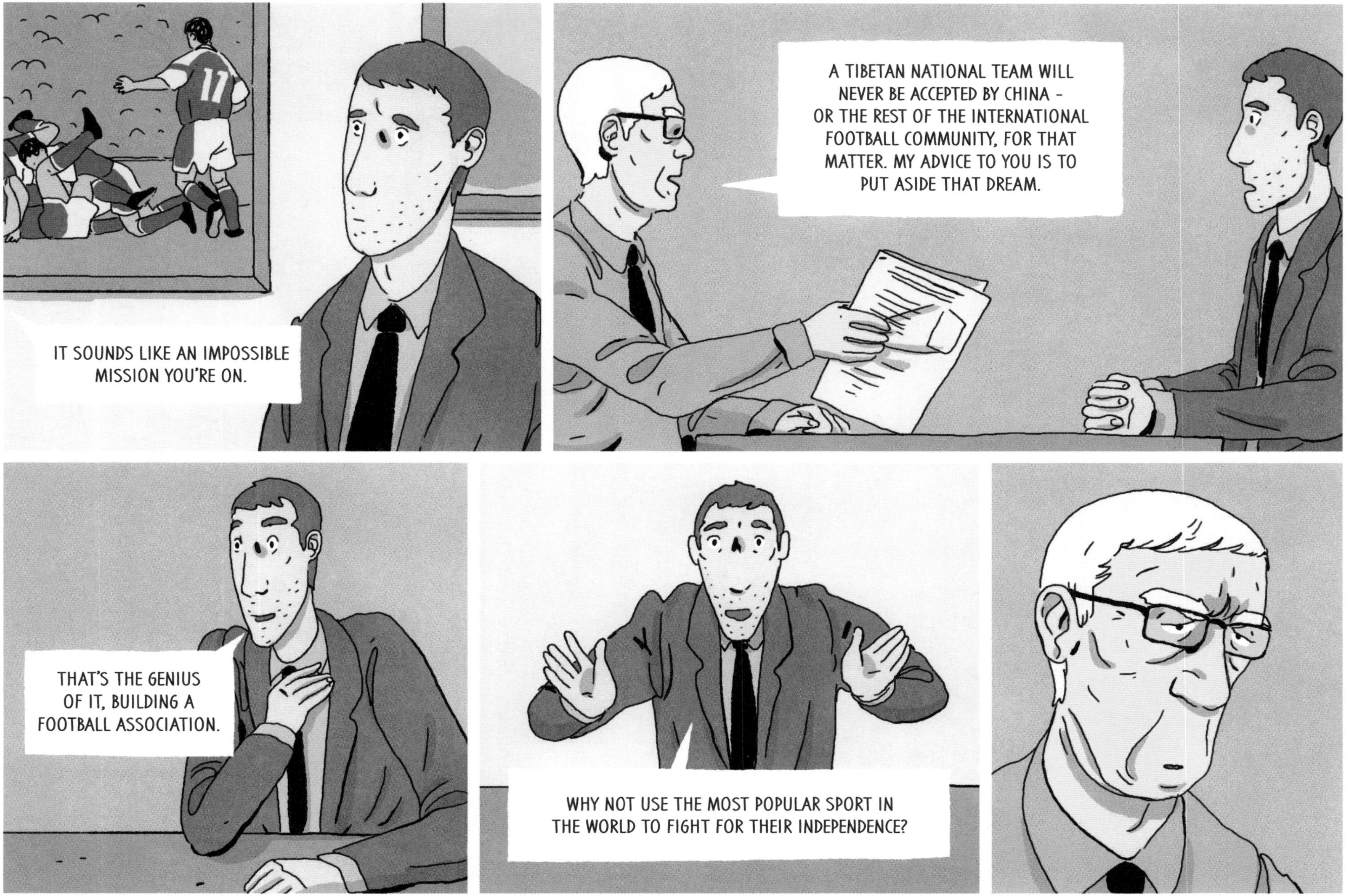
IT SOUNDS LIKE AN IMPOSSIBLE MISSION YOU'RE ON.
A TIBETAN NATIONAL TEAM WILL NEVER BE ACCEPTED BY CHINA - OR THE REST OF THE INTERNATIONAL FOOTBALL COMMUNITY, FOR THAT MATTER. MY ADVICE TO YOU IS TO PUT ASIDE THAT DREAM.
THAT'S THE GENIUS OF IT, BUILDING A FOOTBALL ASSOCIATION.
WHY NOT USE THE MOST POPULAR SPORT IN THE WORLD TO FIGHT FOR THEIR INDEPENDENCE?
11

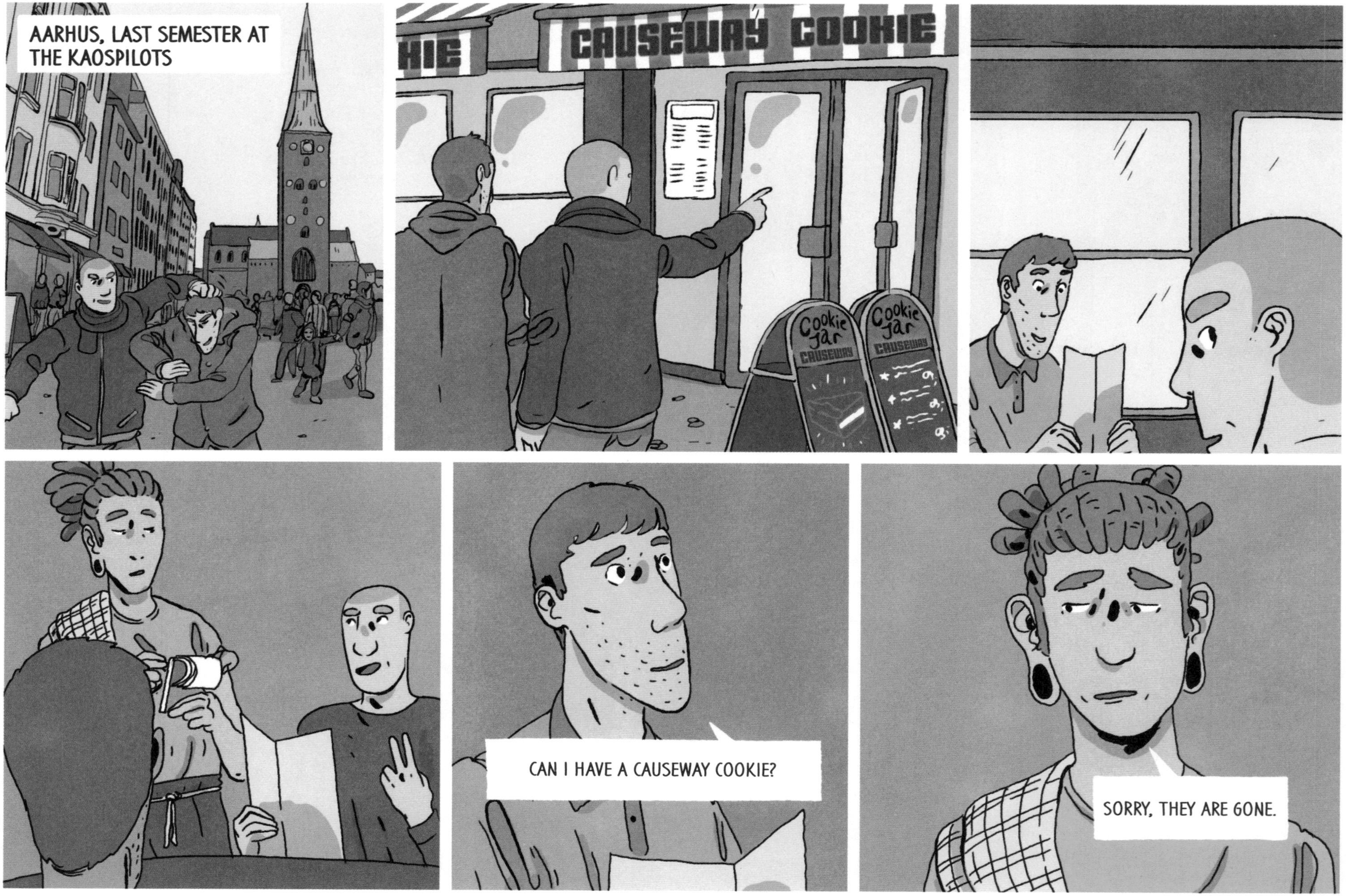
AARHUS, LAST SEMESTER AT THE KAOSPILOTS
CAUSEWAY COOKIE
Cookie Jar
Cookie Jar
CAN I HAVE A CAUSEWAY COOKIE?
SORRY, THEY ARE GONE.

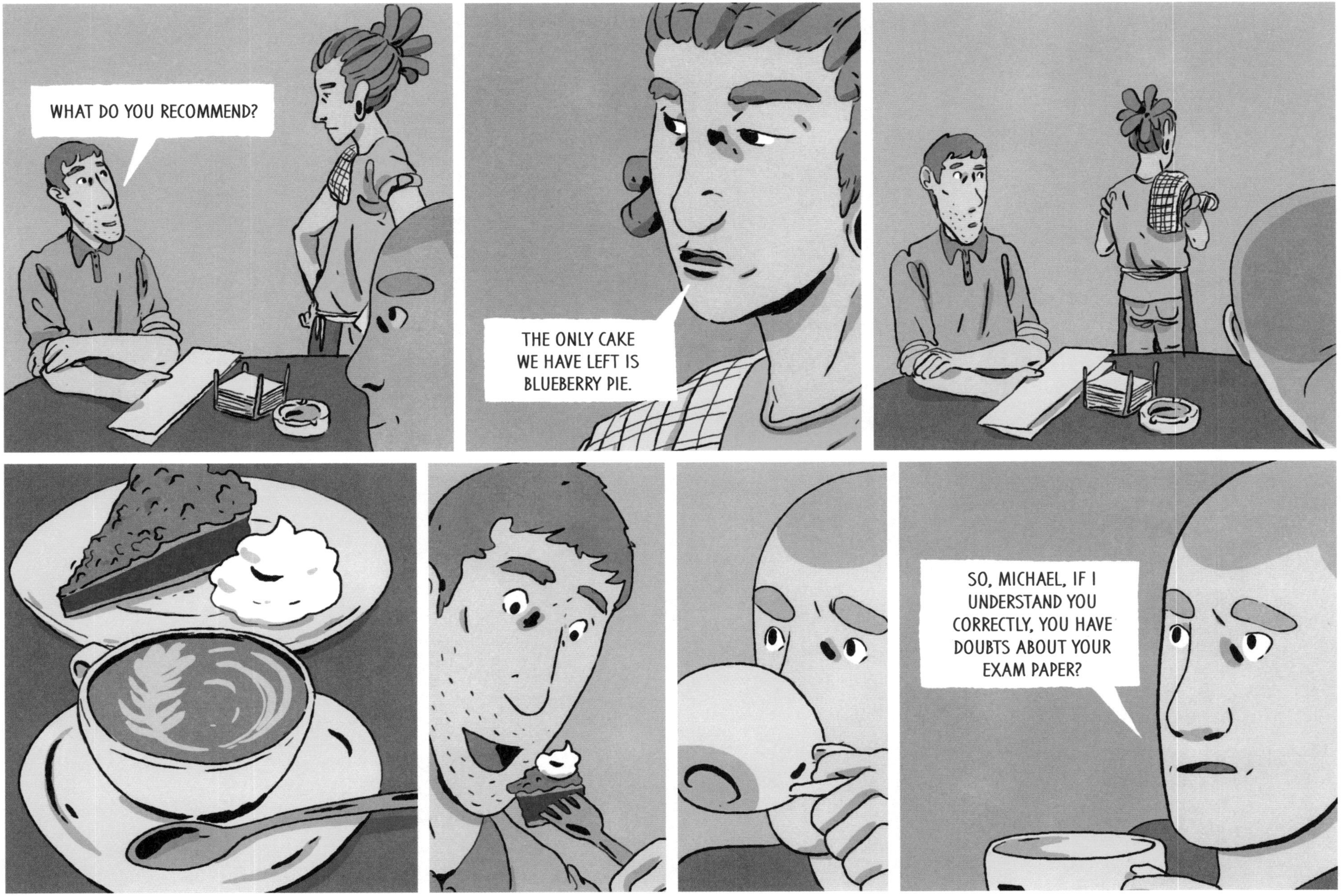
WHAT DO YOU RECOMMEND?
THE ONLY CAKE WE HAVE LEFT IS BLUEBERRY PIE.
SO, MICHAEL, IF I UNDERSTAND YOU CORRECTLY, YOU HAVE DOUBTS ABOUT YOUR EXAM PAPER?

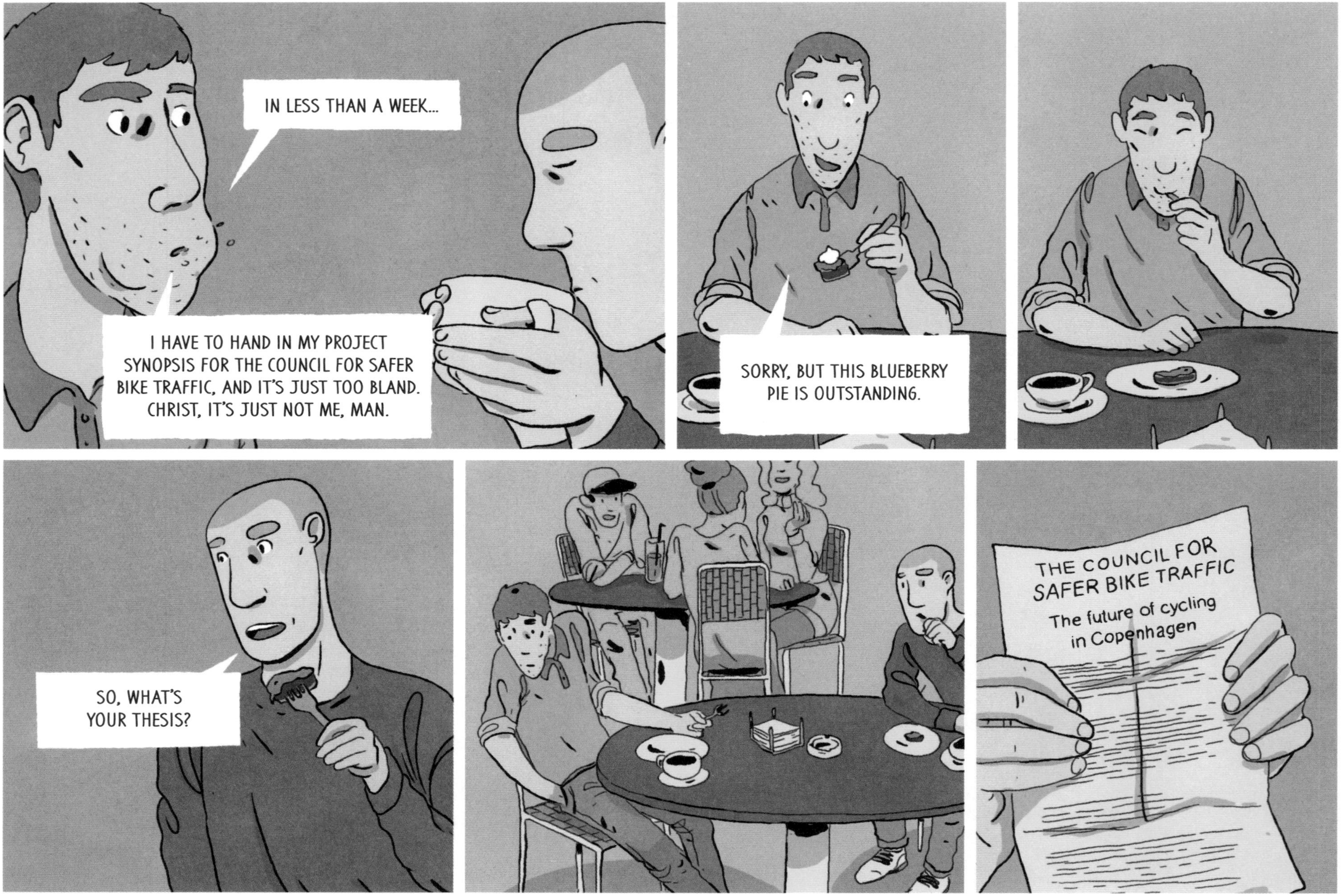
IN LESS THAN A WEEK...
I HAVE TO HAND IN MY PROJECT SYNOPSIS FOR THE COUNCIL FOR SAFER BIKE TRAFFIC, AND IT'S JUST TOO BLAND. CHRIST, IT'S JUST NOT ME, MAN.
SORRY, BUT THIS BLUEBERRY PIE IS OUTSTANDING.
SO, WHAT'S YOUR THESIS?
THE COUNCIL FOR SAFER BIKE TRAFFIC
The future of cycling in Copenhagen

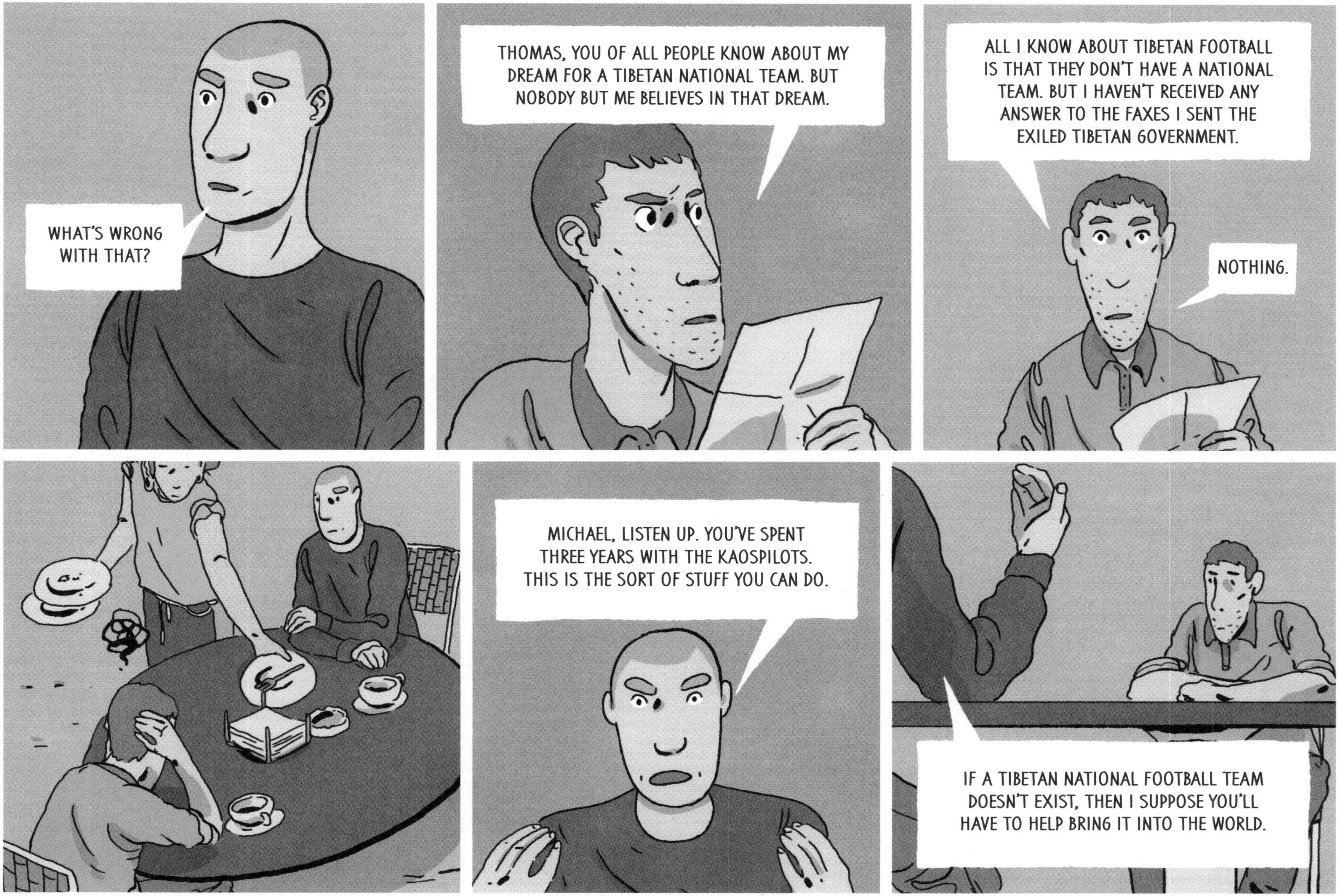
WHAT'S WRONG WITH THAT?
THOMAS, YOU OF ALL PEOPLE KNOW ABOUT MY DREAM FOR A TIBETAN NATIONAL TEAM. BUT NOBODY BUT ME BELIEVES IN THAT DREAM.
ALL I KNOW ABOUT TIBETAN FOOTBALL IS THAT THEY DON'T HAVE A NATIONAL TEAM. BUT I HAVEN'T RECEIVED ANY ANSWER TO THE FAXES I SENT THE EXILED TIBETAN GOVERNMENT.
NOTHING.
MICHAEL, LISTEN UP. YOU'VE SPENT THREE YEARS WITH THE KAOSPILOTS. THIS IS THE SORT OF STUFF YOU CAN DO.
IF A TIBETAN NATIONAL FOOTBALL TEAM DOESN'T EXIST, THEN I SUPPOSE YOU'LL HAVE TO HELP BRING IT INTO THE WORLD.

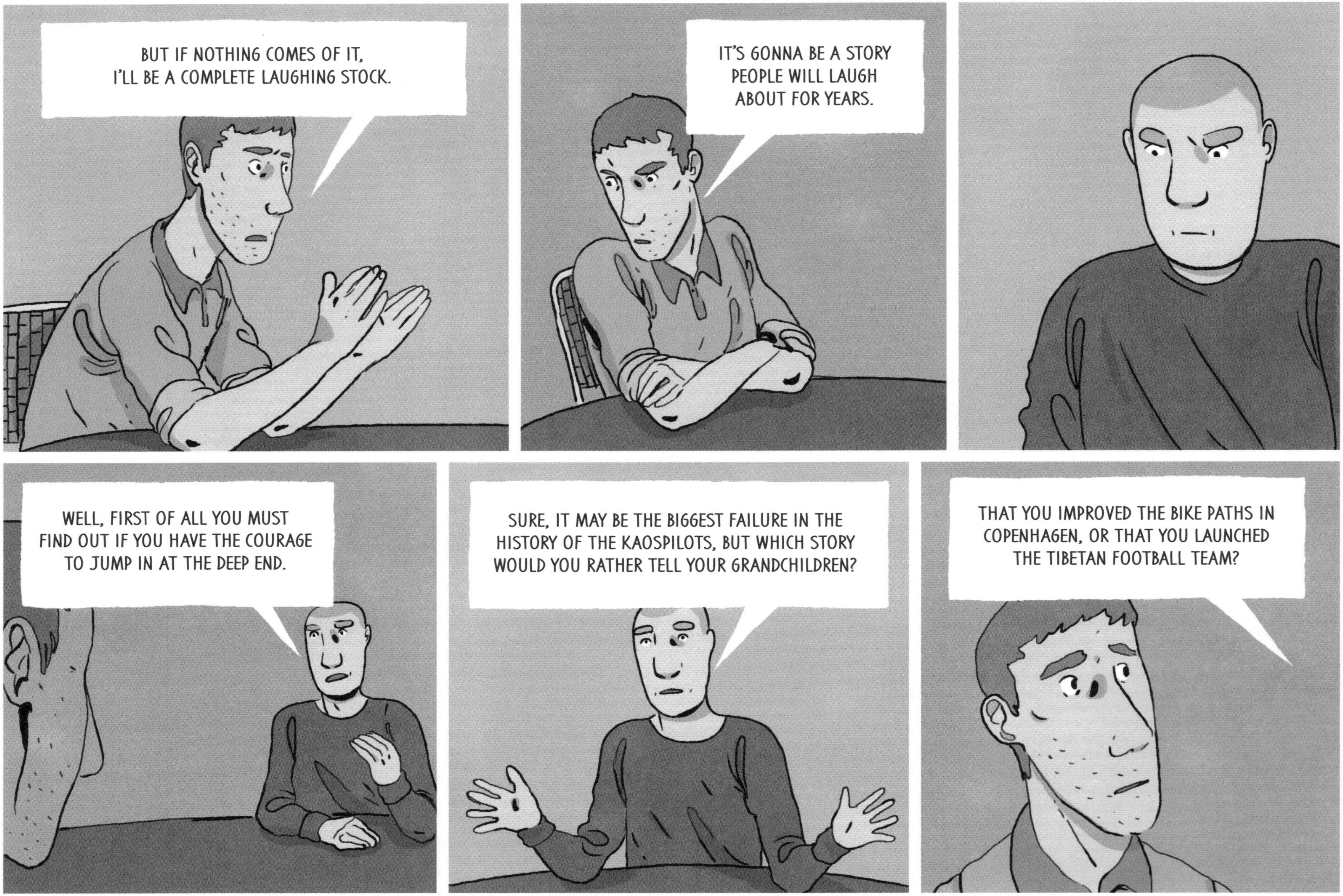
BUT IF NOTHING COMES OF IT, I'LL BE A COMPLETE LAUGHING STOCK.
IT'S GONNA BE A STORY PEOPLE WILL LAUGH ABOUT FOR YEARS.
WELL, FIRST OF ALL YOU MUST FIND OUT IF YOU HAVE THE COURAGE TO JUMP IN AT THE DEEP END.
SURE, IT MAY BE THE BIGGEST FAILURE IN THE HISTORY OF THE KAOSPILOTS, BUT WHICH STORY WOULD YOU RATHER TELL YOUR GRANDCHILDREN?
THAT YOU IMPROVED THE BIKE PATHS IN COPENHAGEN, OR THAT YOU LAUNCHED THE TIBETAN FOOTBALL TEAM?

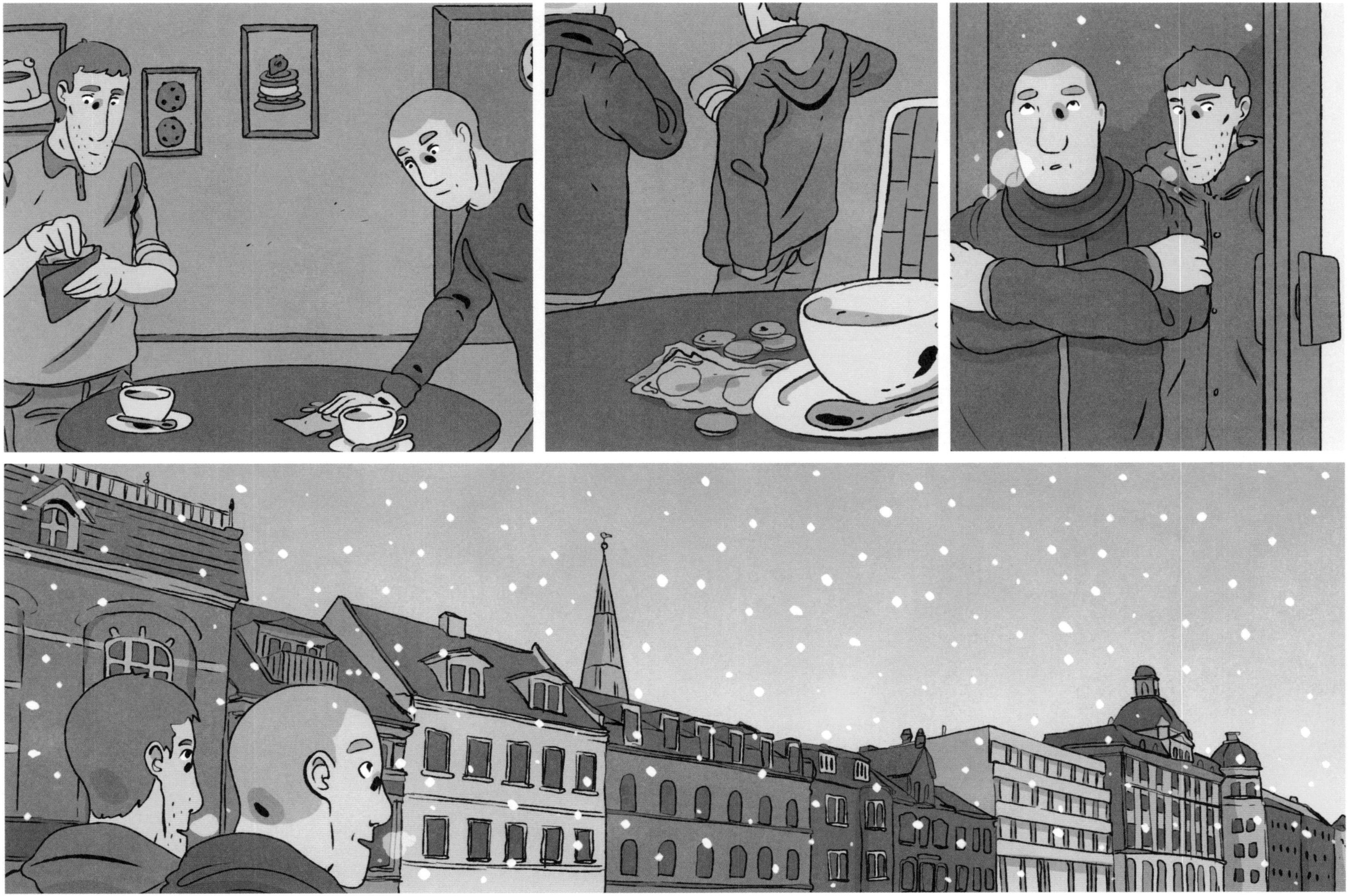

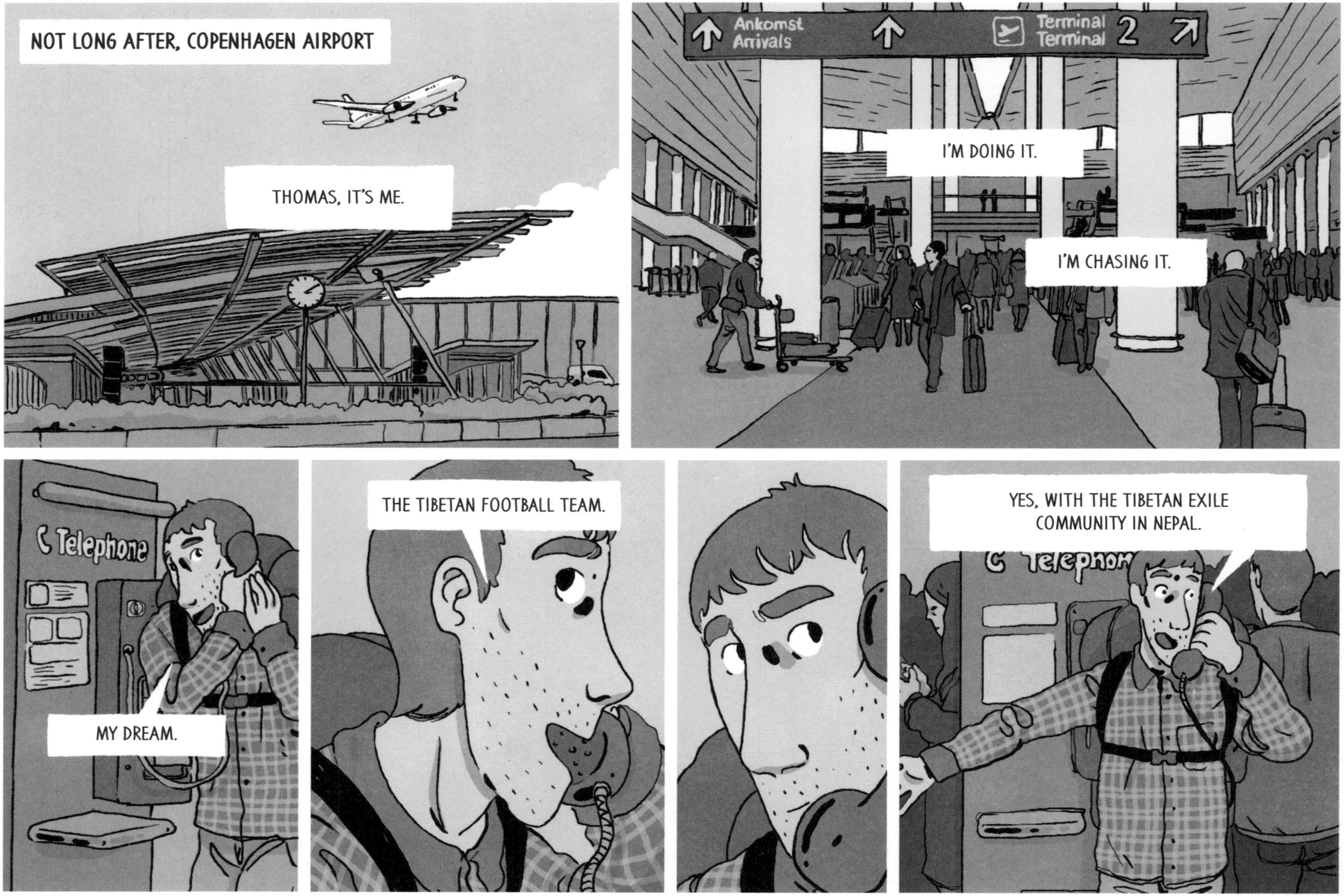

NOT LONG AFTER, COPENHAGEN AIRPORT
THOMAS, IT'S ME.
Ankomst Arrivals
Terminal Terminal 2
I'M DOING IT.
I'M CHASING IT.
Telephone
MY DREAM.
THE TIBETAN FOOTBALL TEAM.
YES, WITH THE TIBETAN EXILE COMMUNITY IN NEPAL.

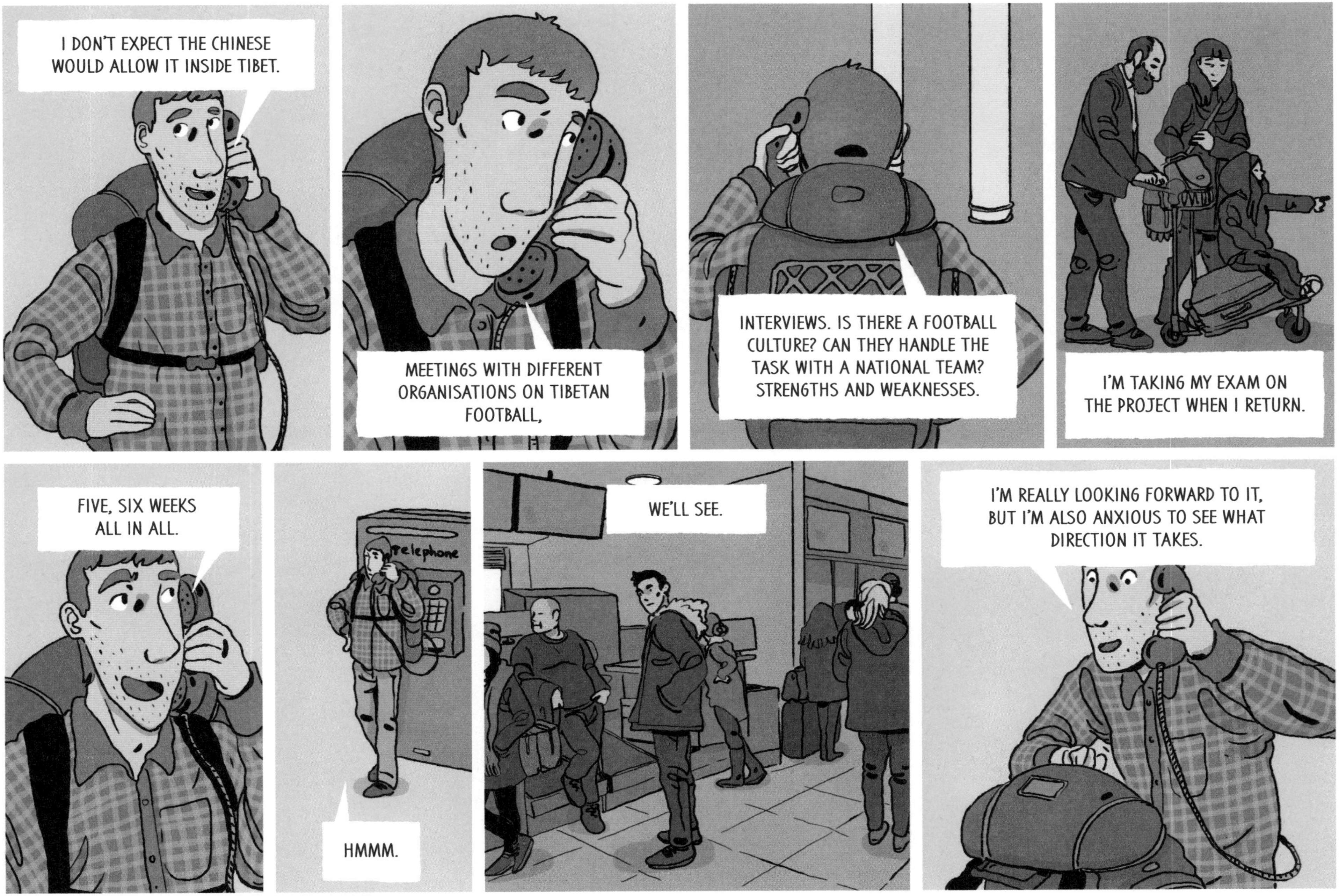
I DON'T EXPECT THE CHINESE WOULD ALLOW IT INSIDE TIBET.
MEETINGS WITH DIFFERENT ORGANISATIONS ON TIBETAN FOOTBALL,
INTERVIEWS. IS THERE A FOOTBALL CULTURE? CAN THEY HANDLE THE TASK WITH A NATIONAL TEAM? STRENGTHS AND WEAKNESSES.
I'M TAKING MY EXAM ON THE PROJECT WHEN I RETURN.
FIVE, SIX WEEKS ALL IN ALL.
Telephone
HMMM.
WE'LL SEE.
I'M REALLY LOOKING FORWARD TO IT, BUT I'M ALSO ANXIOUS TO SEE WHAT DIRECTION IT TAKES.

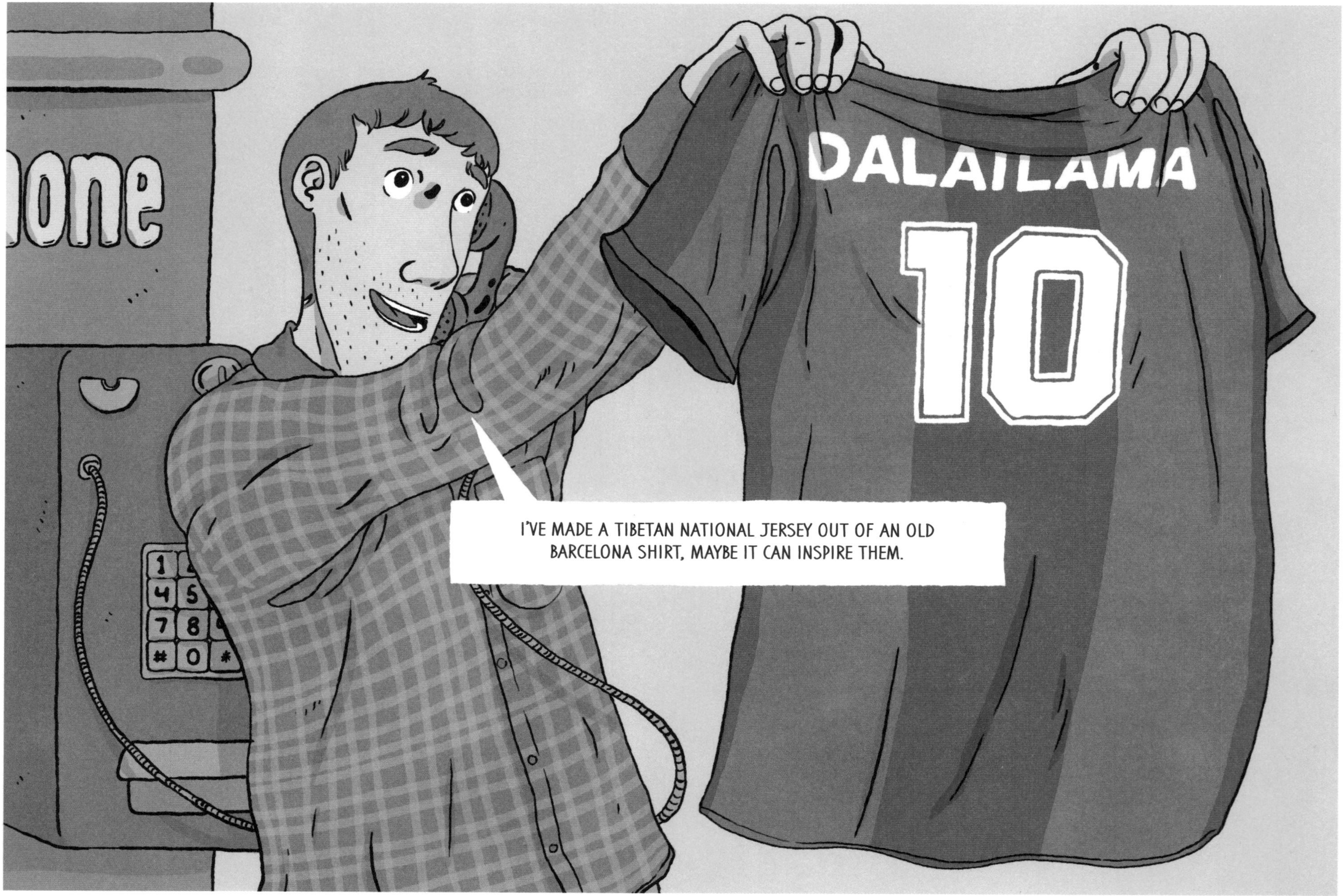
none
DALAILAMA
10
I'VE MADE A TIBETAN NATIONAL JERSEY OUT OF AN OLD BARCELONA SHIRT, MAYBE IT CAN INSPIRE THEM.

CHAPTER 4
DHARAMSALA

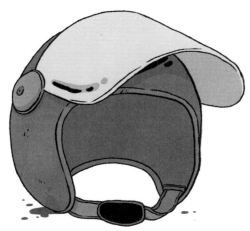

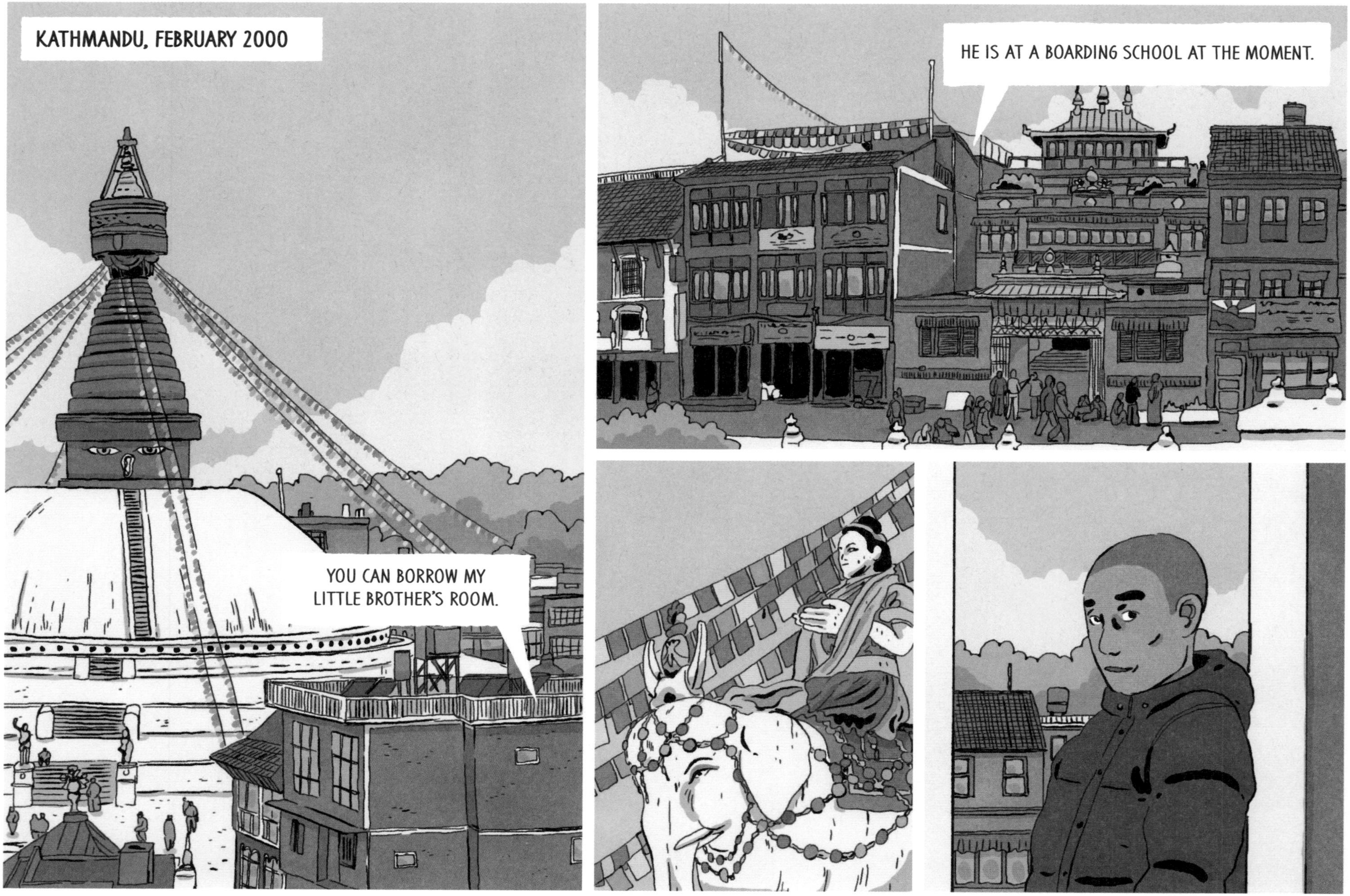
KATHMANDU, FEBRUARY 2000
YOU CAN BORROW MY LITTLE BROTHER'S ROOM.
HE IS AT A BOARDING SCHOOL AT THE MOMENT.

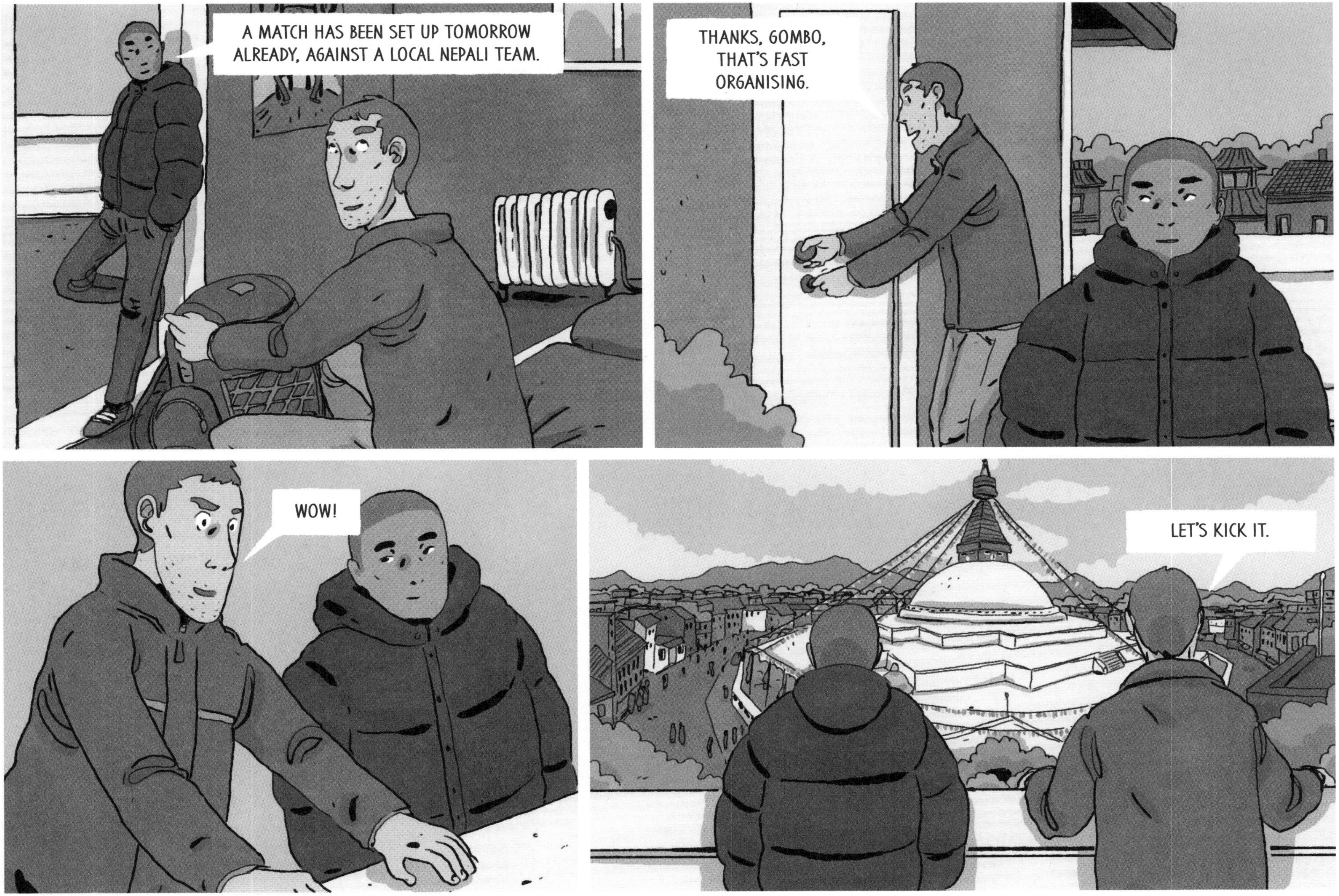
A MATCH HAS BEEN SET UP TOMORROW ALREADY, AGAINST A LOCAL NEPALI TEAM.
THANKS, GOMBO, THAT'S FAST ORGANISING.
WOW!
LET'S KICK IT.

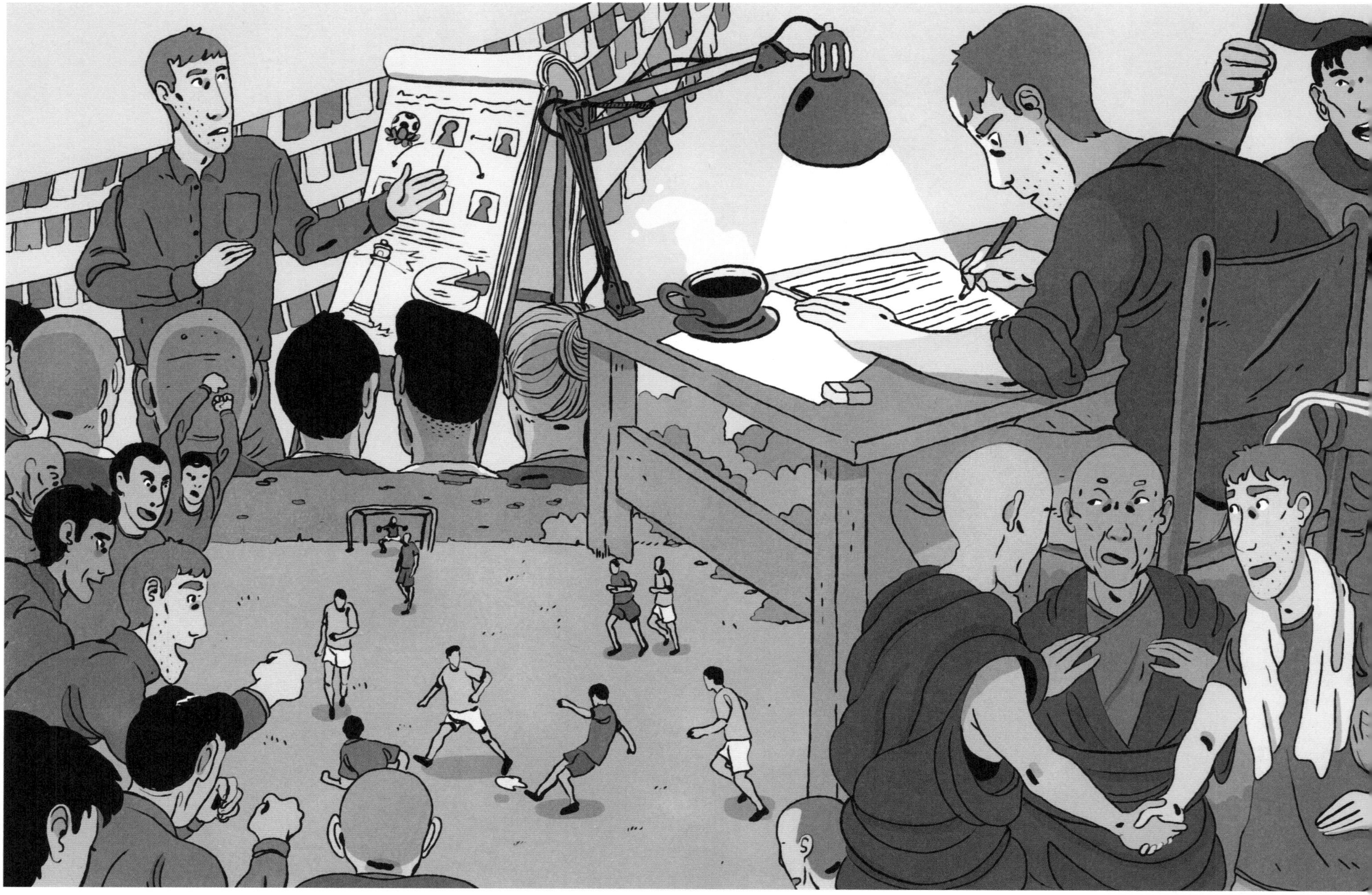

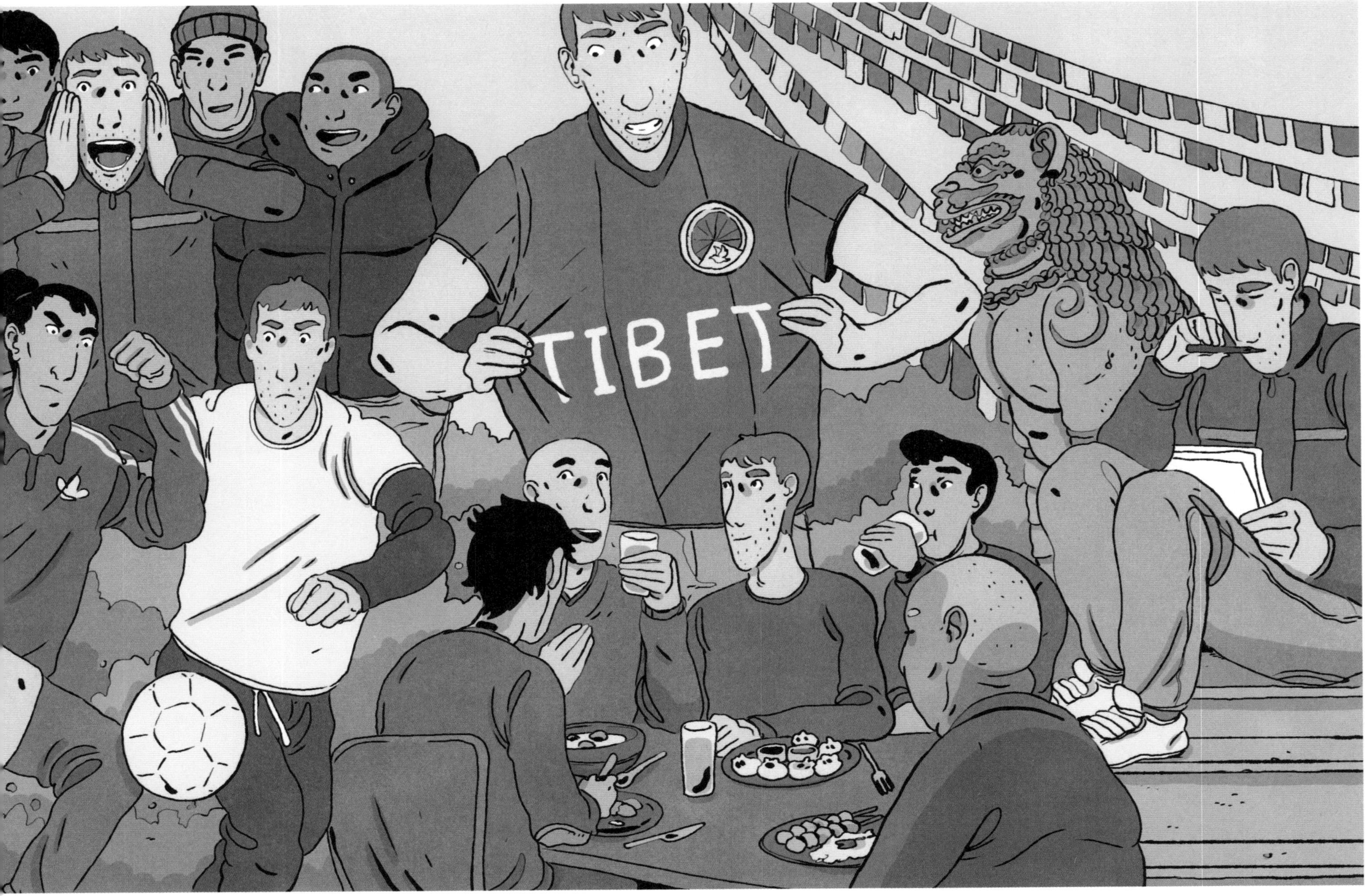
TIBET

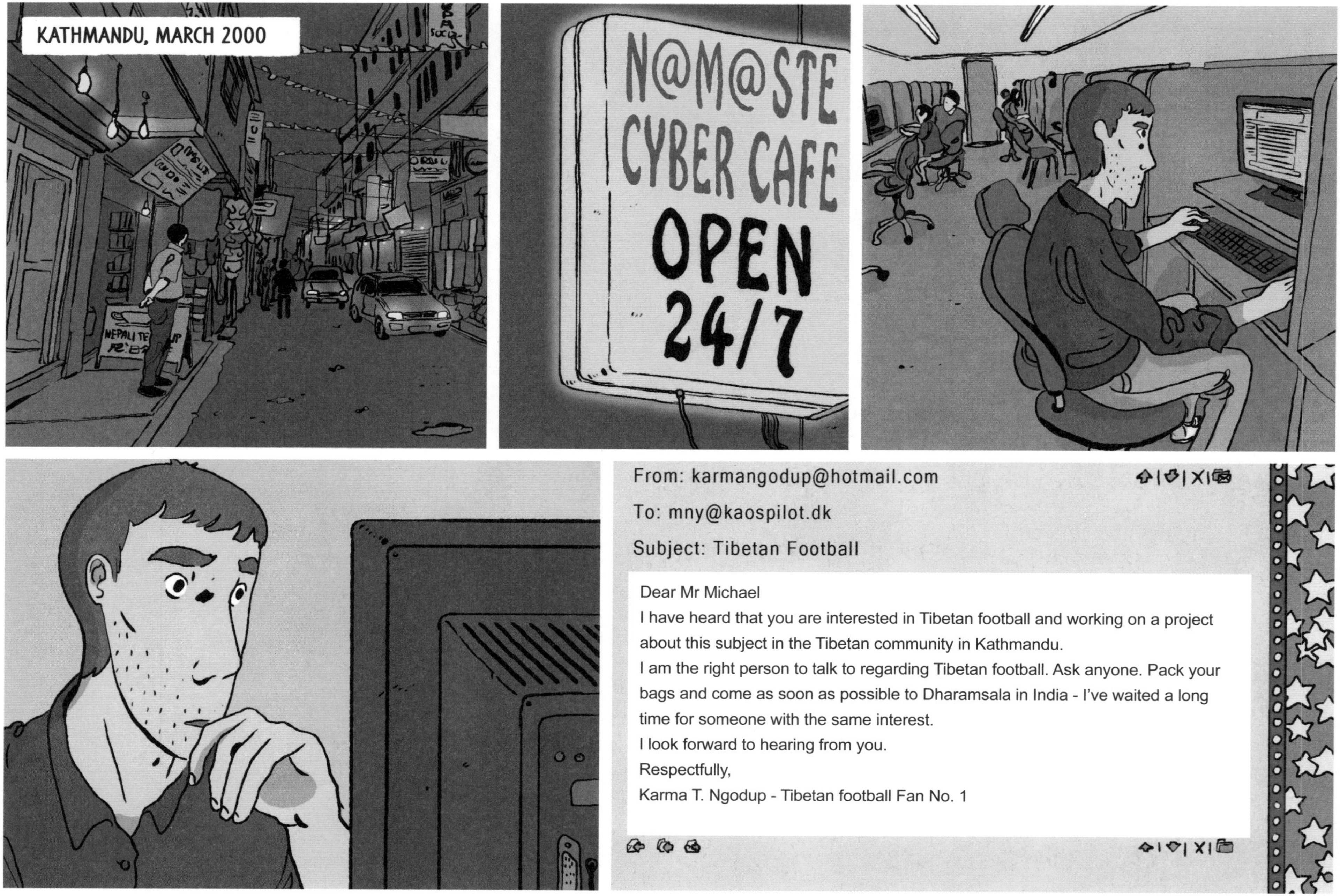
KATHMANDU, MARCH 2000
N@M@STE
CYBER CAFE
OPEN
24/7
From: karmangodup@hotmail.com
To: mny@kaospilot.dk
Subject: Tibetan Football
Dear Mr Michael
I have heard that you are interested in Tibetan football and working on a project about this subject in the Tibetan community in Kathmandu.
I am the right person to talk to regarding Tibetan football. Ask anyone. Pack your bags and come as soon as possible to Dharamsala in India - I've waited a long time for someone with the same interest.
I look forward to hearing from you.
Respectfully,
Karma T. Ngodup - Tibetan football Fan No. 1

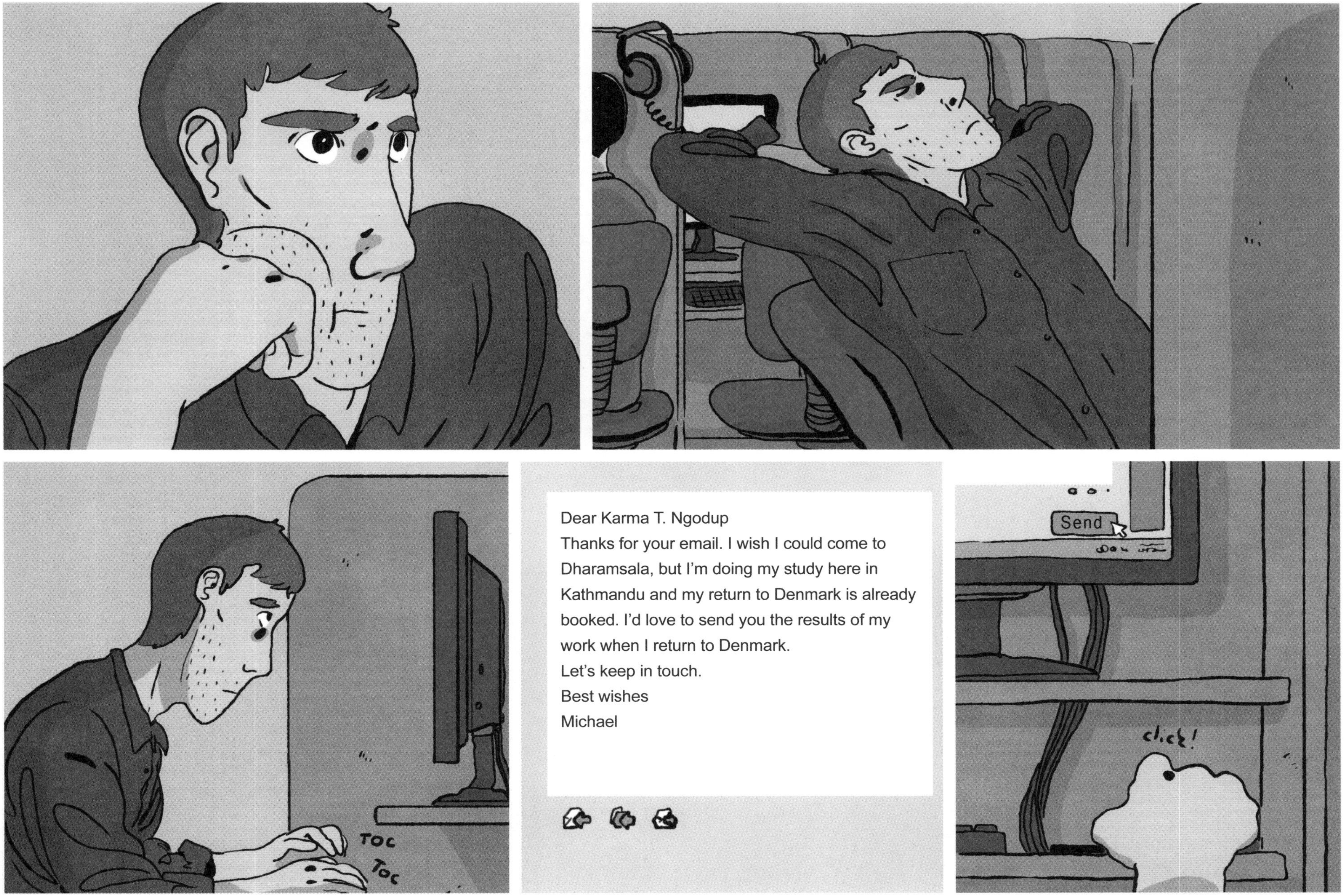
TOC
TOC
Dear Karma T. Ngodup
Thanks for your email. I wish I could come to Dharamsala, but I'm doing my study here in Kathmandu and my return to Denmark is already booked. I'd love to send you the results of my work when I return to Denmark.
Let's keep in touch.
Best wishes
Michael
Send
click!

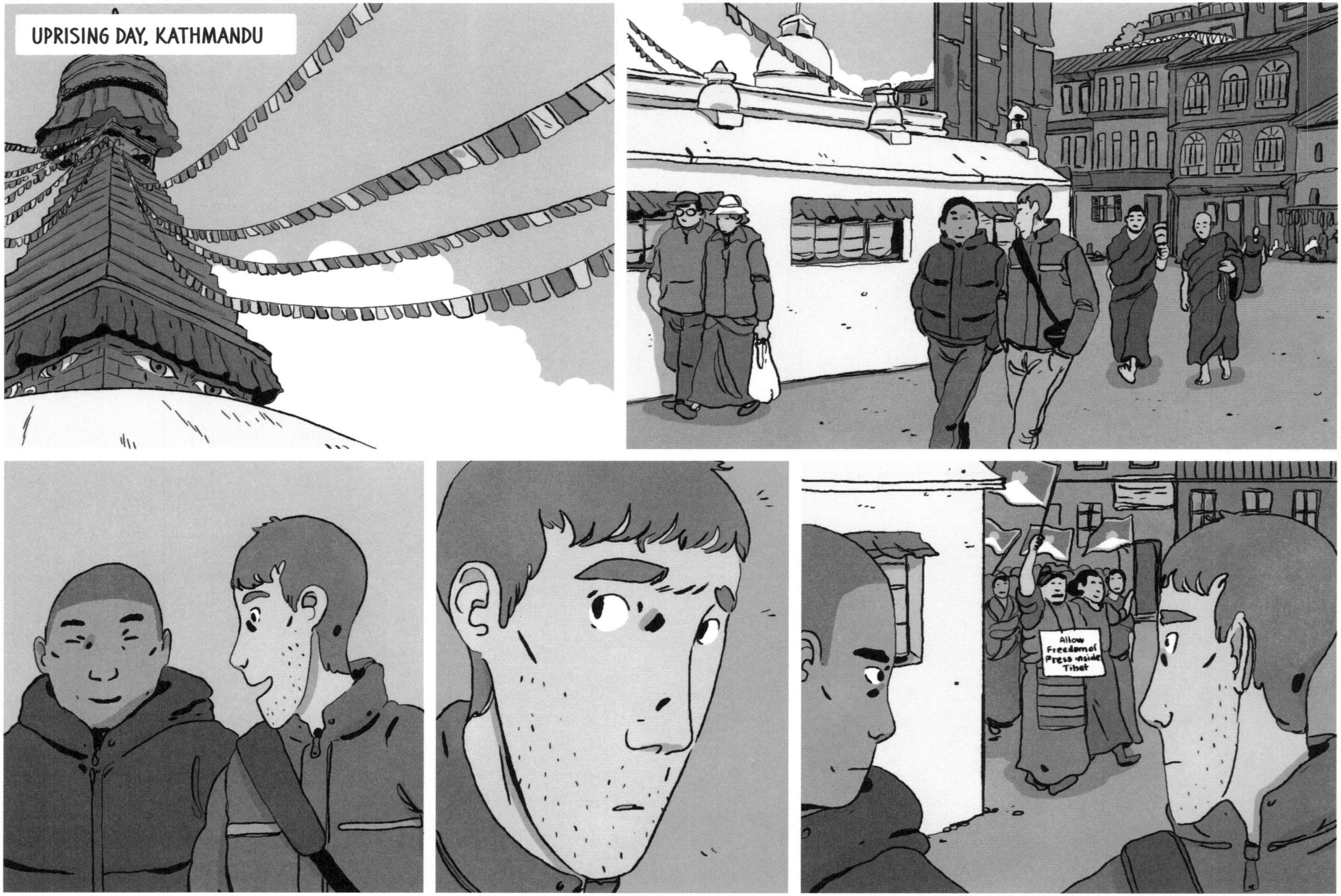
UPRISING DAY, KATHMANDU
Allow Freedom of Press inside Tibet

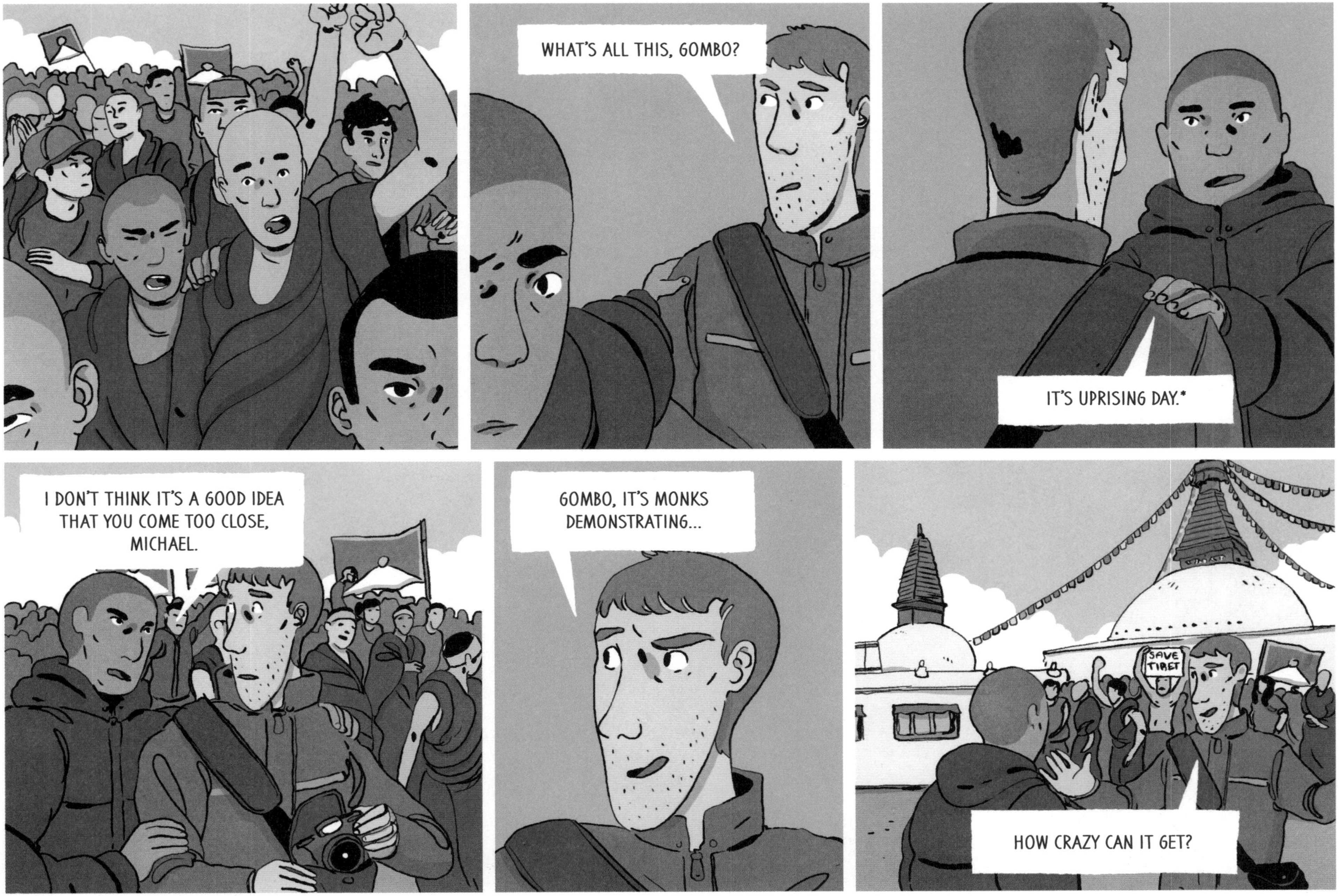
WHAT'S ALL THIS, GOMBO?
IT'S UPRISING DAY.*
I DON'T THINK IT'S A GOOD IDEA THAT YOU COME TOO CLOSE, MICHAEL.
GOMBO, IT'S MONKS DEMONSTRATING...
SAVE TIBET
HOW CRAZY CAN IT GET?

*UPRISING DAY MARKS THE SAD ANNIVERSARY OF THE TIBETAN UPRISING AGAINST THE CHINESE OCCUPIERS ON MARCH 10, 1959 WHEN THOUSANDS OF TIBETANS WERE KILLED.

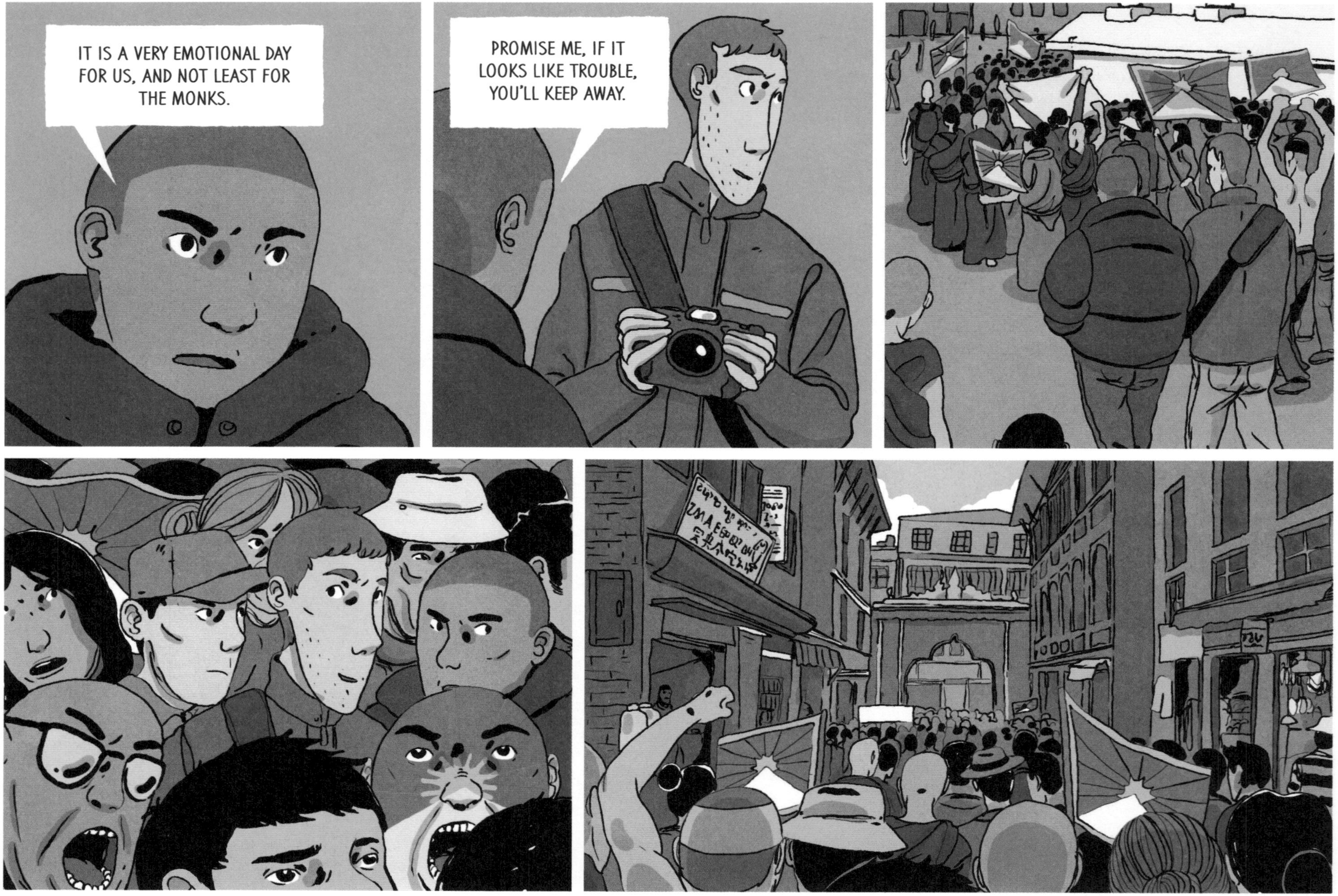
IT IS A VERY EMOTIONAL DAY FOR US, AND NOT LEAST FOR THE MONKS.
PROMISE ME, IF IT LOOKS LIKE TROUBLE, YOU'LL KEEP AWAY.

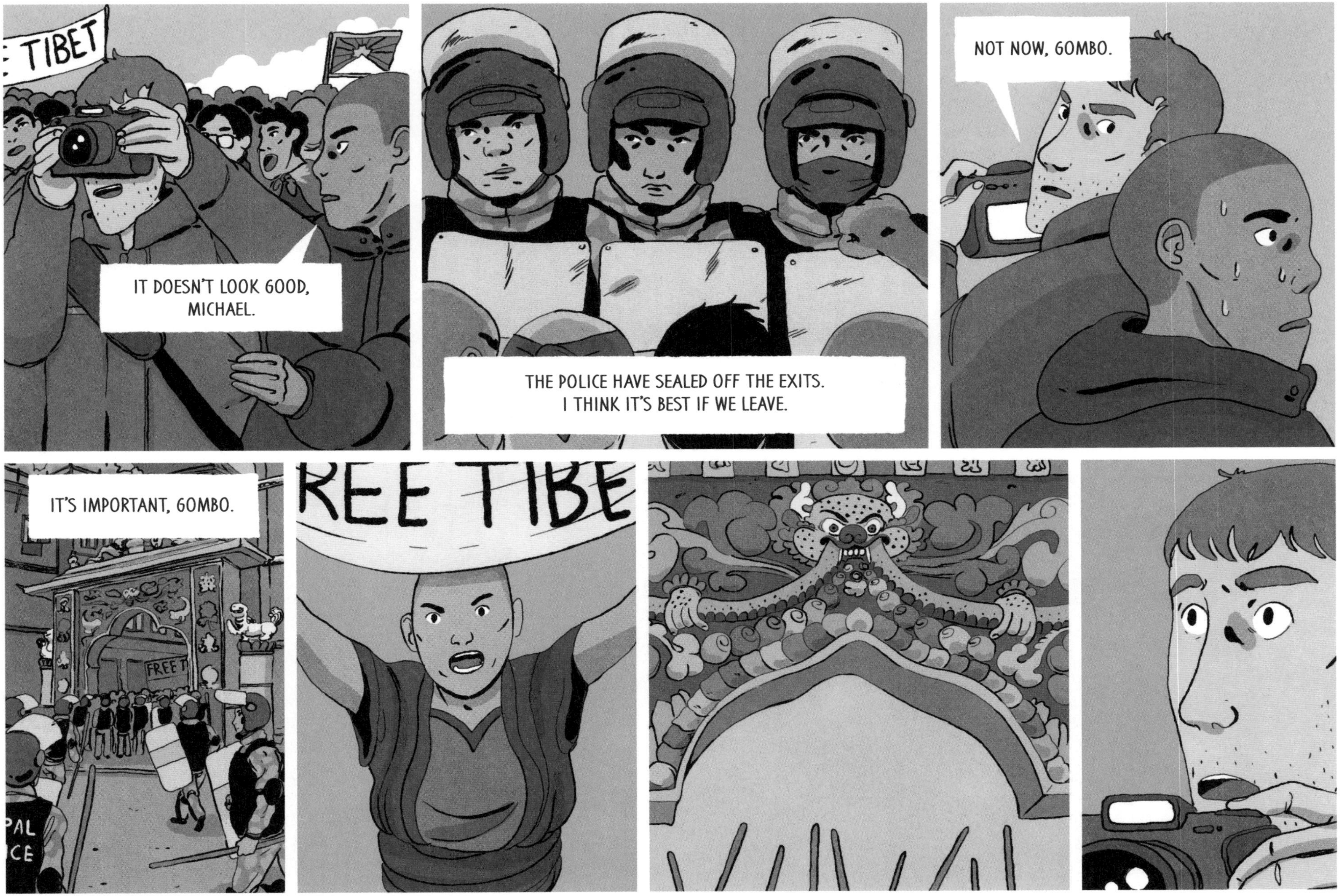
E TIBET
IT DOESN'T LOOK GOOD, MICHAEL.
THE POLICE HAVE SEALED OFF THE EXITS. I THINK IT'S BEST IF WE LEAVE.
NOT NOW, GOMBO.
IT'S IMPORTANT, GOMBO.
FREE T
PAL
CE
REE TIBE

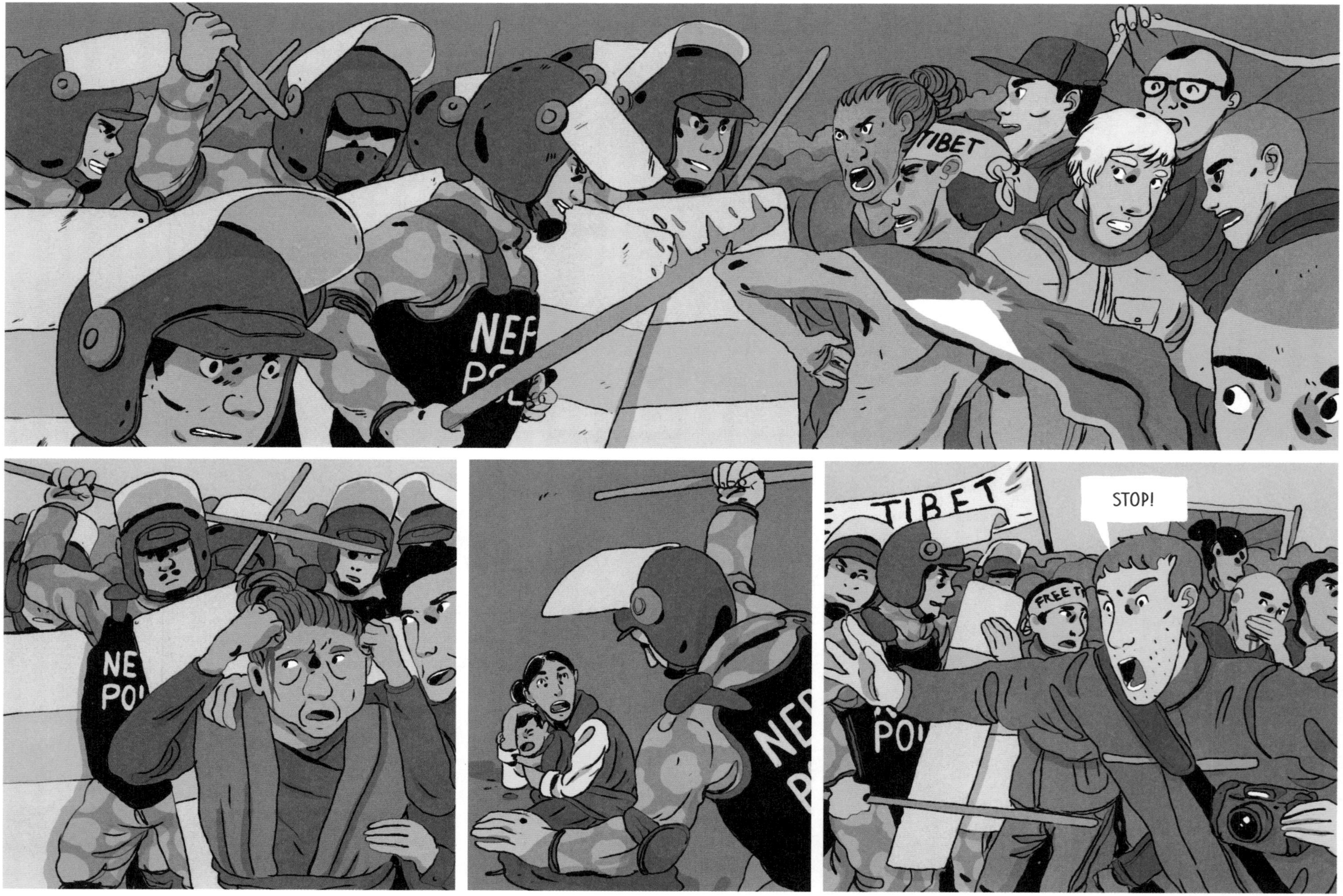
TIBET
TIBET
STOP!

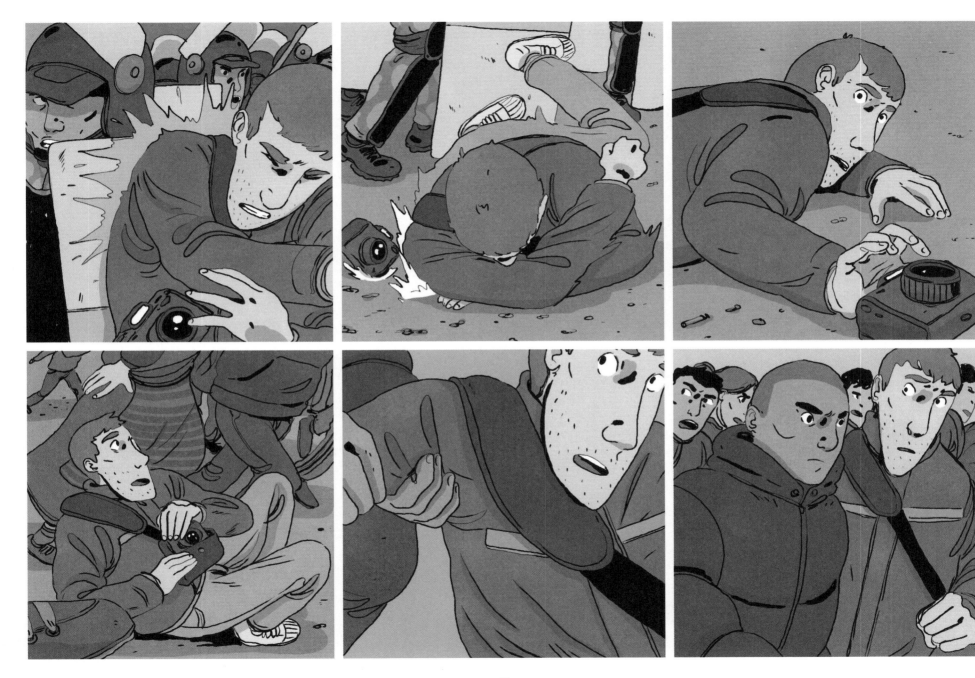

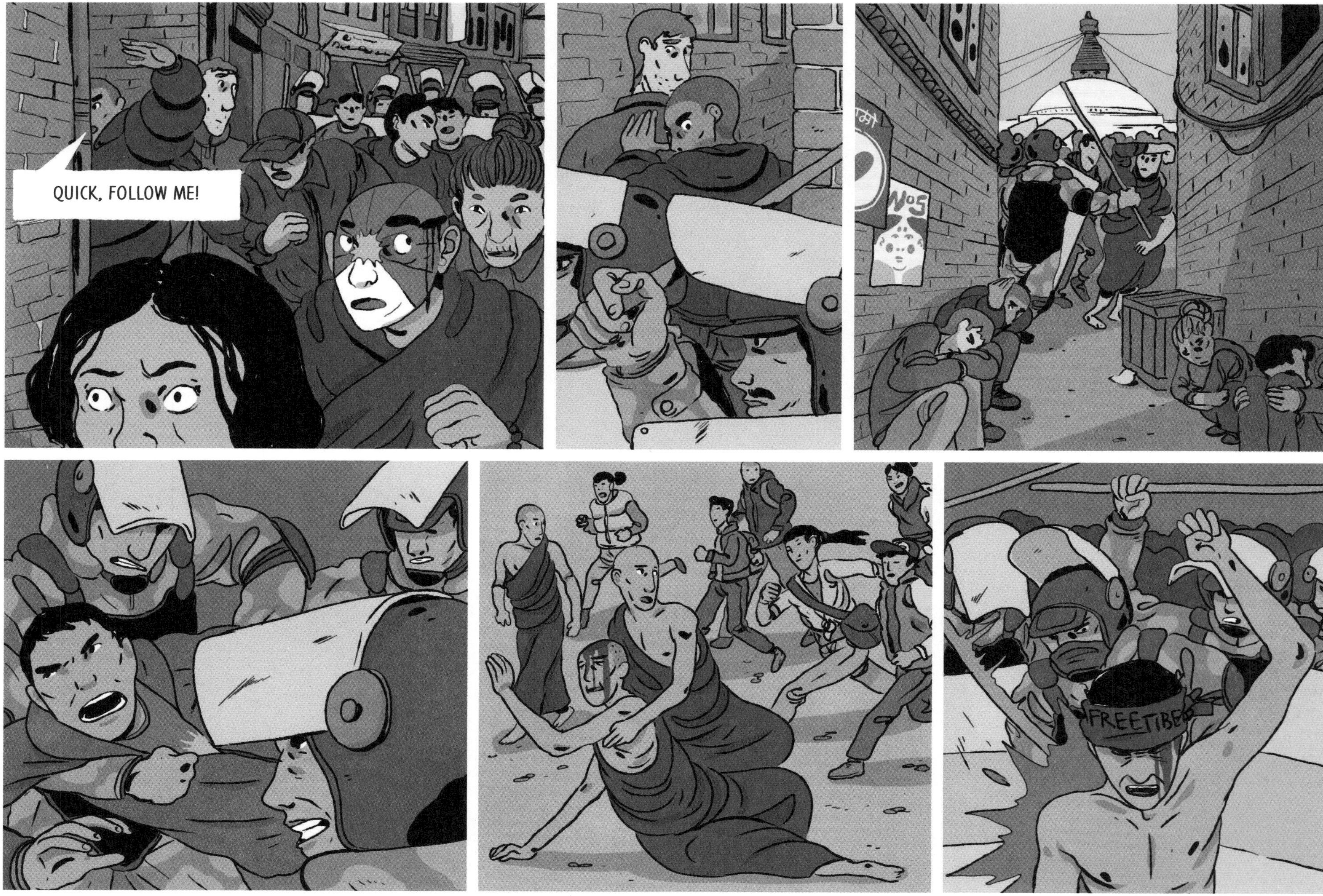
QUICK, FOLLOW ME!
FREETIBE

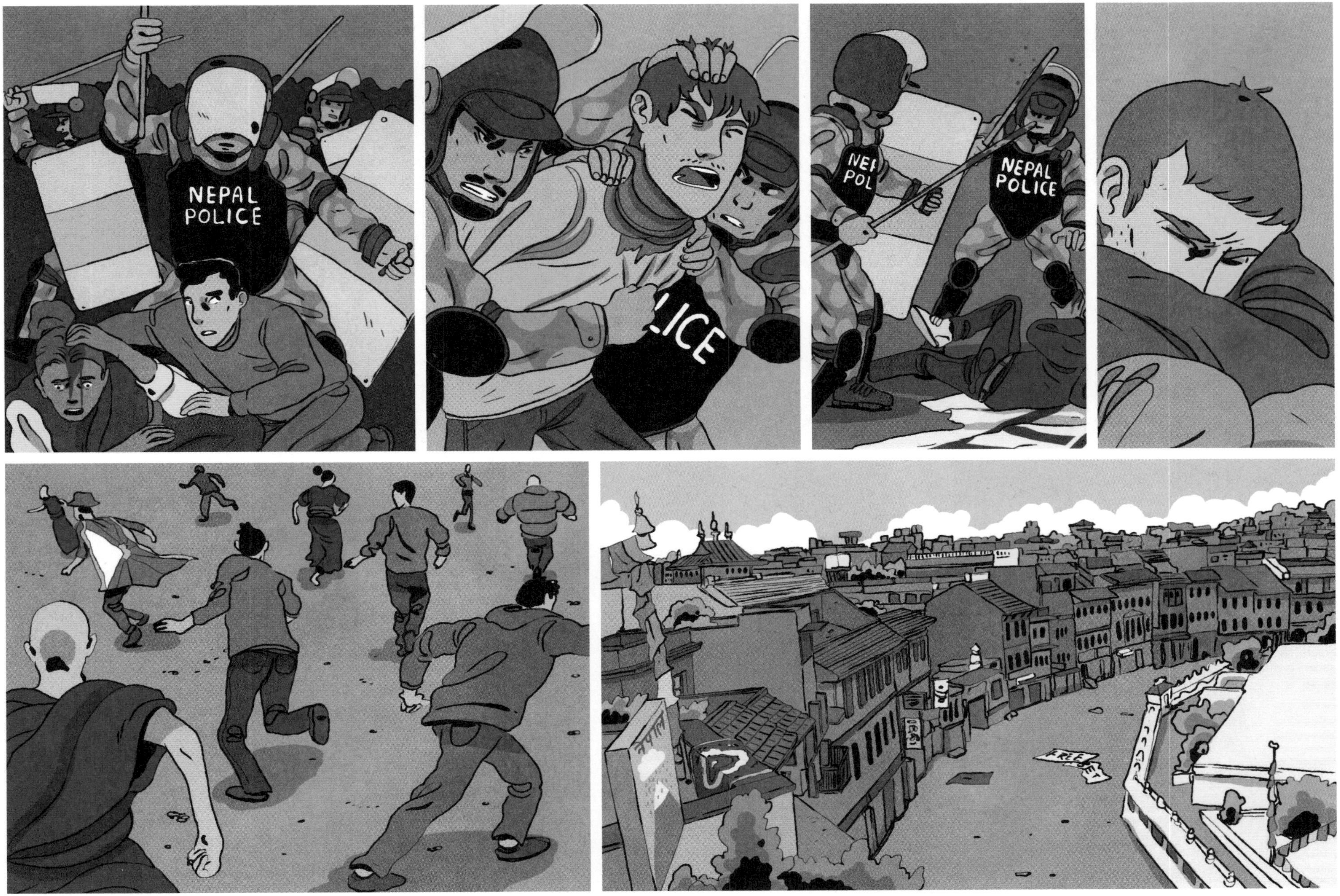
NEPAL POLICE
LICE
NEPA POLI
NEPAL POLICE
नेपाल
FREE

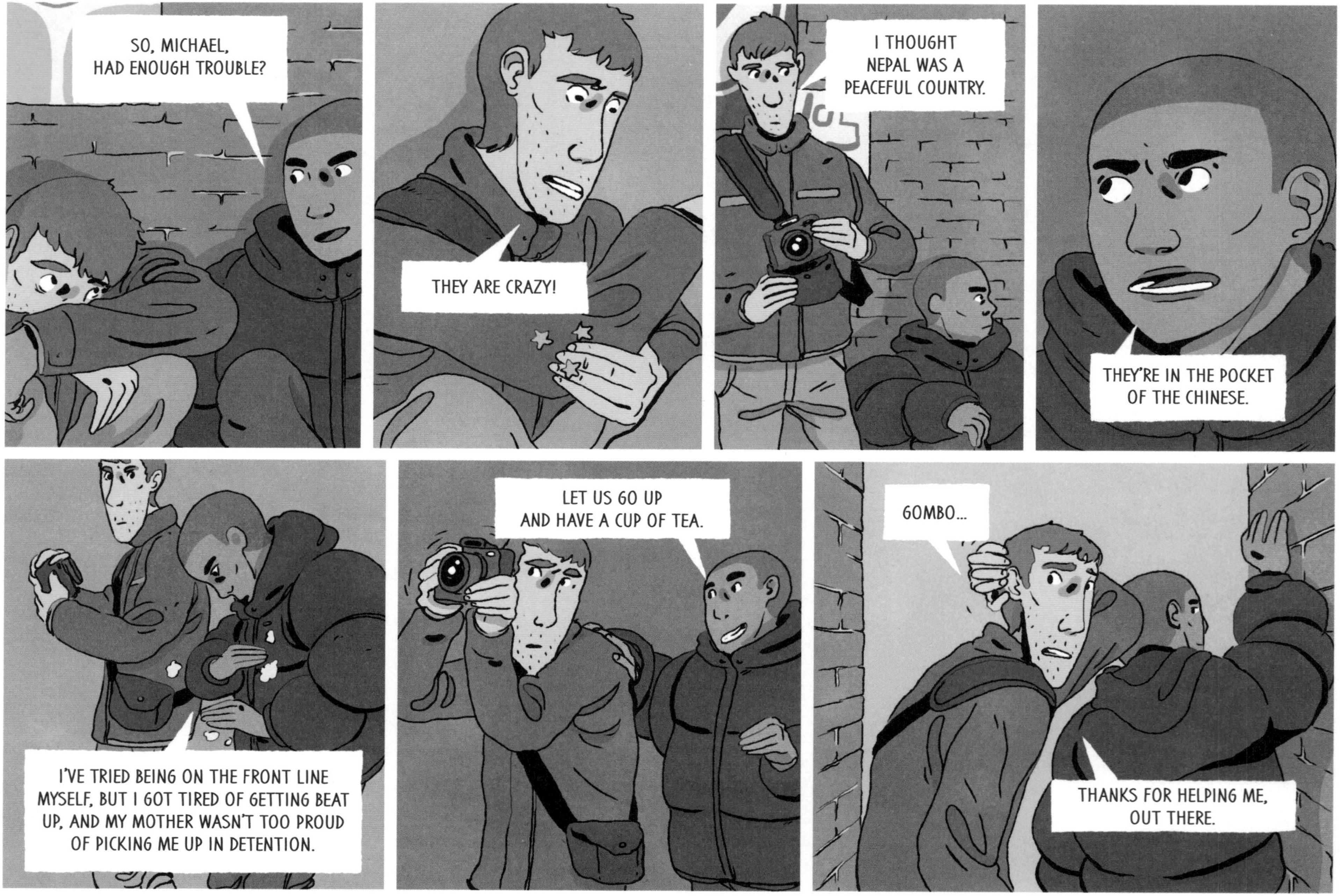
SO, MICHAEL, HAD ENOUGH TROUBLE?
THEY ARE CRAZY!
I THOUGHT NEPAL WAS A PEACEFUL COUNTRY.
THEY'RE IN THE POCKET OF THE CHINESE.
I'VE TRIED BEING ON THE FRONT LINE MYSELF, BUT I GOT TIRED OF GETTING BEAT UP, AND MY MOTHER WASN'T TOO PROUD OF PICKING ME UP IN DETENTION.
LET US GO UP AND HAVE A CUP OF TEA.
GOMBO...
THANKS FOR HELPING ME, OUT THERE.

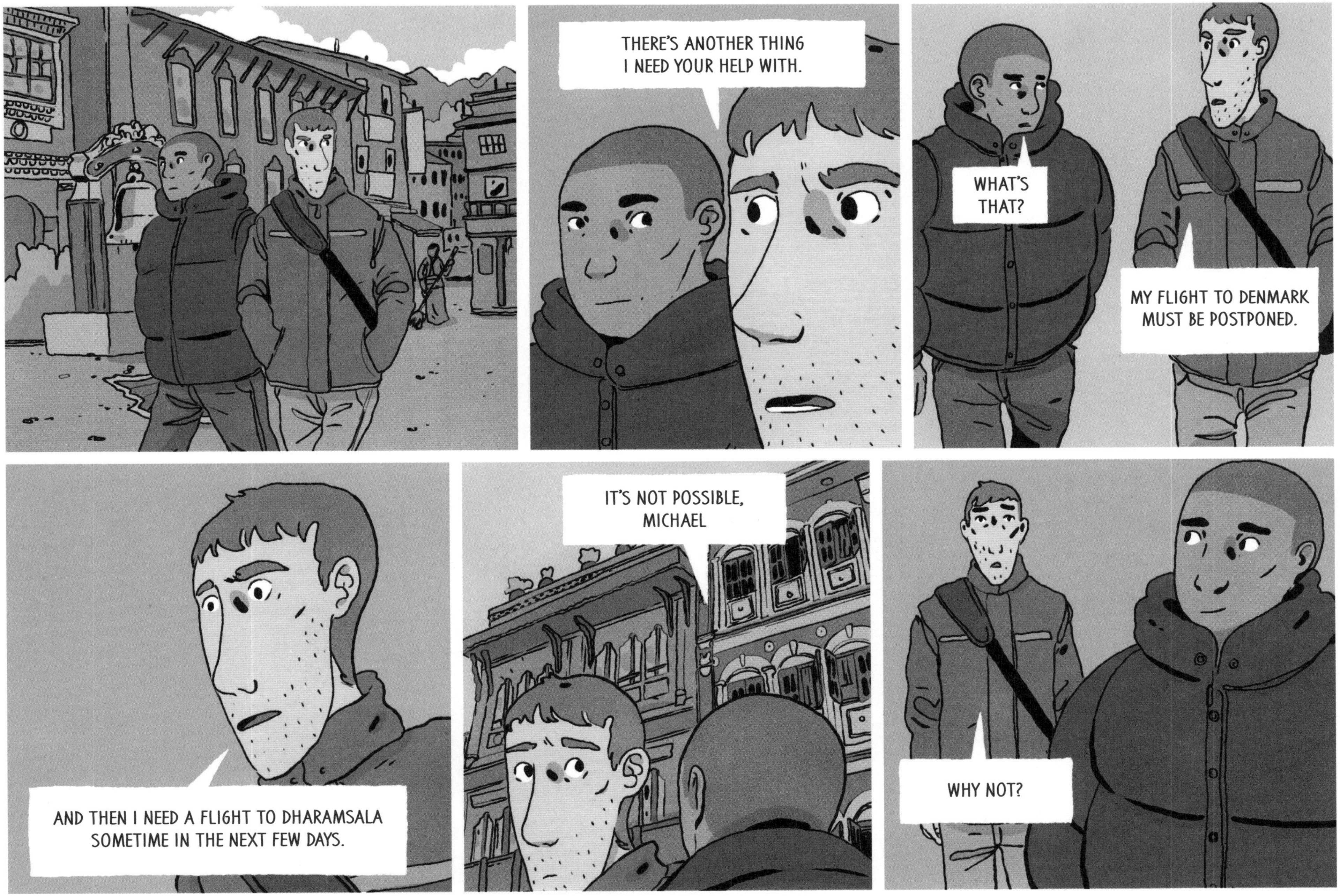
THERE'S ANOTHER THING I NEED YOUR HELP WITH.
WHAT'S THAT?
MY FLIGHT TO DENMARK MUST BE POSTPONED.
AND THEN I NEED A FLIGHT TO DHARAMSALA SOMETIME IN THE NEXT FEW DAYS.
IT'S NOT POSSIBLE, MICHAEL
WHY NOT?

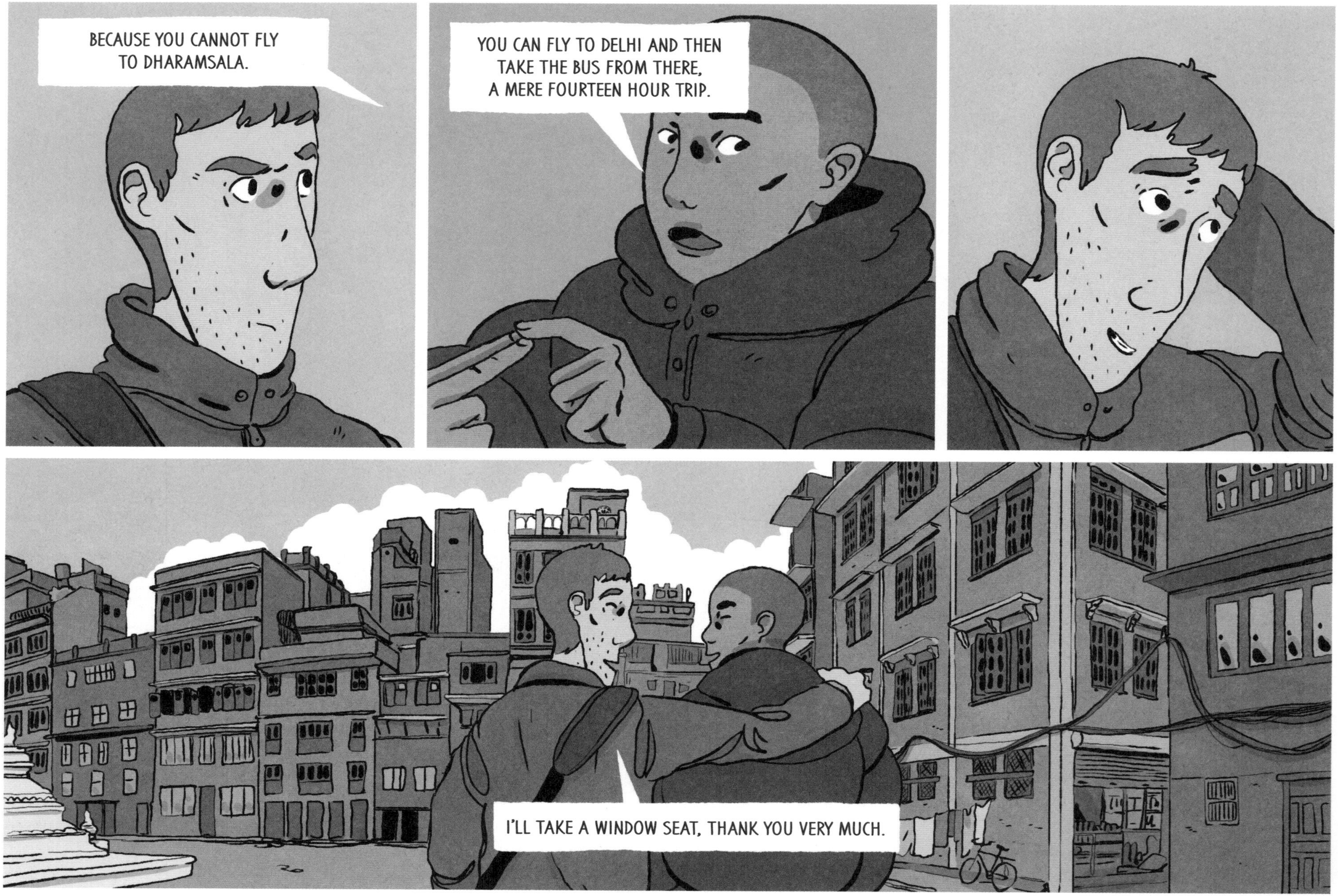
BECAUSE YOU CANNOT FLY TO DHARAMSALA.
YOU CAN FLY TO DELHI AND THEN TAKE THE BUS FROM THERE, A MERE FOURTEEN HOUR TRIP.
I'LL TAKE A WINDOW SEAT, THANK YOU VERY MUCH.

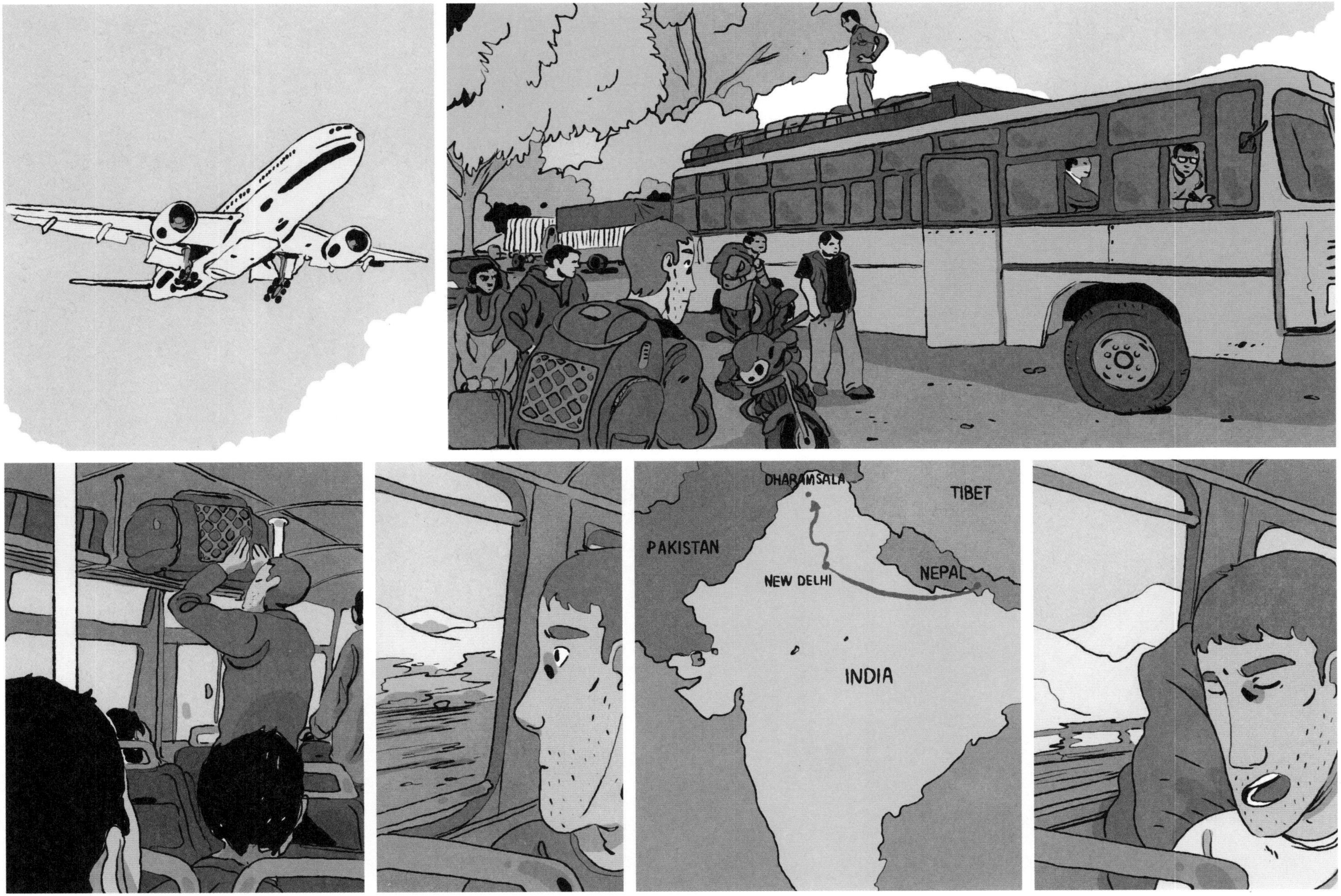
DHARAMSALA
TIBET
PAKISTAN
NEW DELHI
NEPAL
INDIA

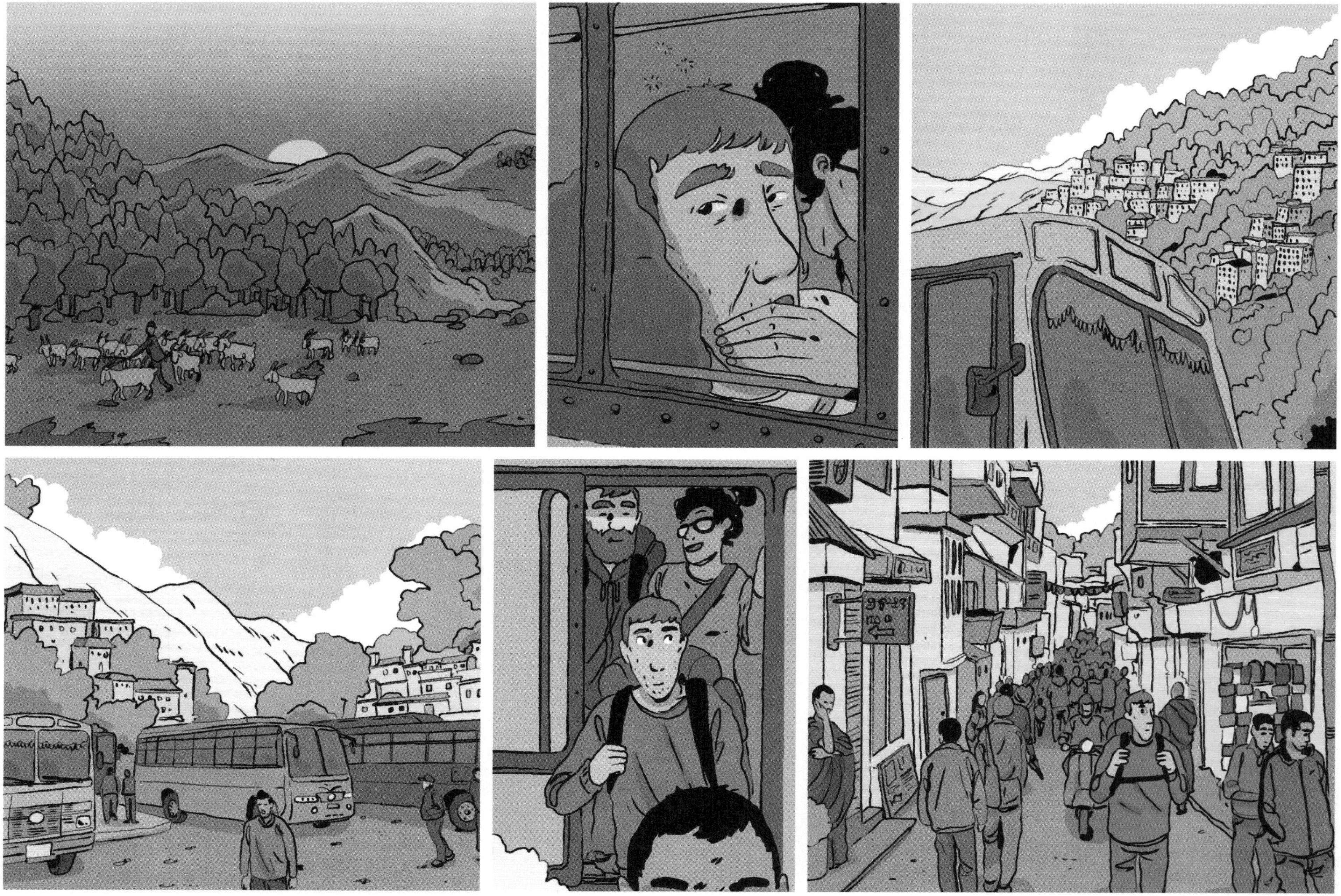

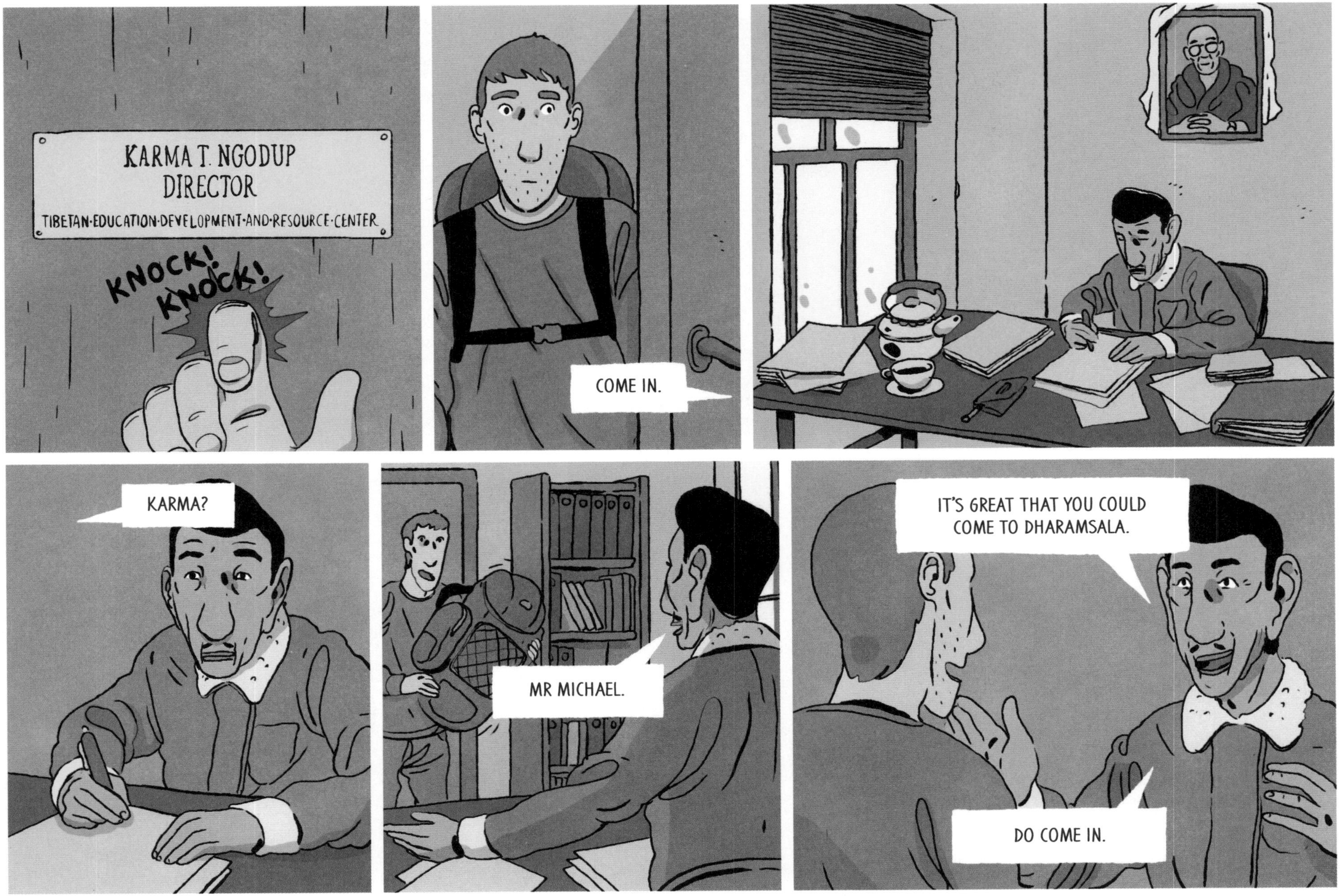
KARMA T. NGODUP
DIRECTOR
TIBETAN·EDUCATION·DEVELOPMENT·AND·RESOURCE·CENTER
KNOCK! KNOCK!
COME IN.
KARMA?
MR MICHAEL.
IT'S GREAT THAT YOU COULD COME TO DHARAMSALA.
DO COME IN.

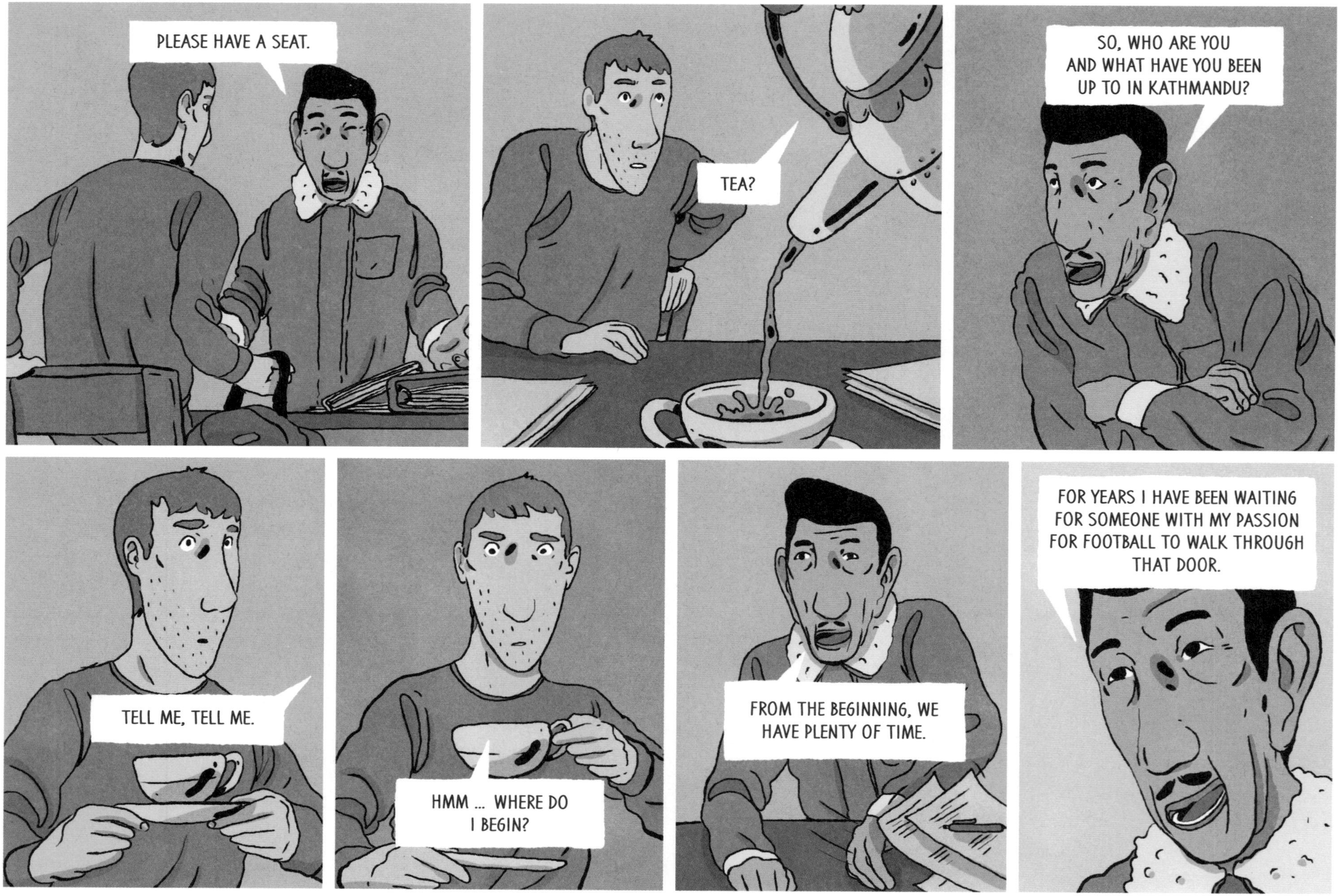
PLEASE HAVE A SEAT.
TEA?
SO, WHO ARE YOU AND WHAT HAVE YOU BEEN UP TO IN KATHMANDU?
TELL ME, TELL ME.
HMM ... WHERE DO I BEGIN?
FROM THE BEGINNING, WE HAVE PLENTY OF TIME.
FOR YEARS I HAVE BEEN WAITING FOR SOMEONE WITH MY PASSION FOR FOOTBALL TO WALK THROUGH THAT DOOR.

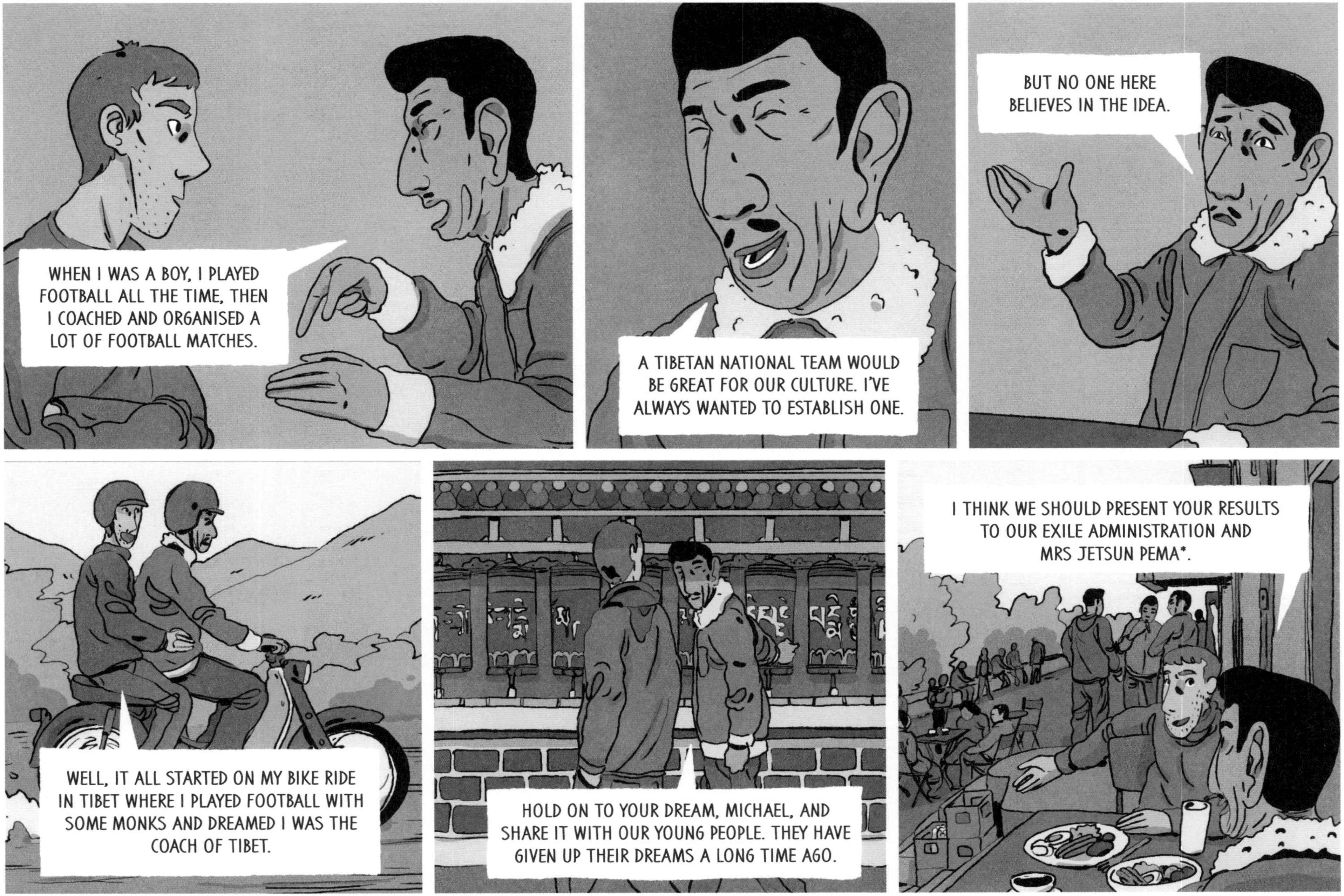
WHEN I WAS A BOY, I PLAYED FOOTBALL ALL THE TIME, THEN I COACHED AND ORGANISED A LOT OF FOOTBALL MATCHES.
A TIBETAN NATIONAL TEAM WOULD BE GREAT FOR OUR CULTURE. I'VE ALWAYS WANTED TO ESTABLISH ONE.
BUT NO ONE HERE BELIEVES IN THE IDEA.
WELL, IT ALL STARTED ON MY BIKE RIDE IN TIBET WHERE I PLAYED FOOTBALL WITH SOME MONKS AND DREAMED I WAS THE COACH OF TIBET.
HOLD ON TO YOUR DREAM, MICHAEL, AND SHARE IT WITH OUR YOUNG PEOPLE. THEY HAVE GIVEN UP THEIR DREAMS A LONG TIME AGO.
I THINK WE SHOULD PRESENT YOUR RESULTS TO OUR EXILE ADMINISTRATION AND MRS JETSUN PEMA*.

*MRS JETSUN PEMA - PRESIDENT OF THE TIBETAN CHILDREN'S VILLAGES - THE SCHOOL SYSTEM FOR TIBETAN REFUGEE STUDENTS - AND THE SISTER OF HIS HOLINESS DALAI LAMA.

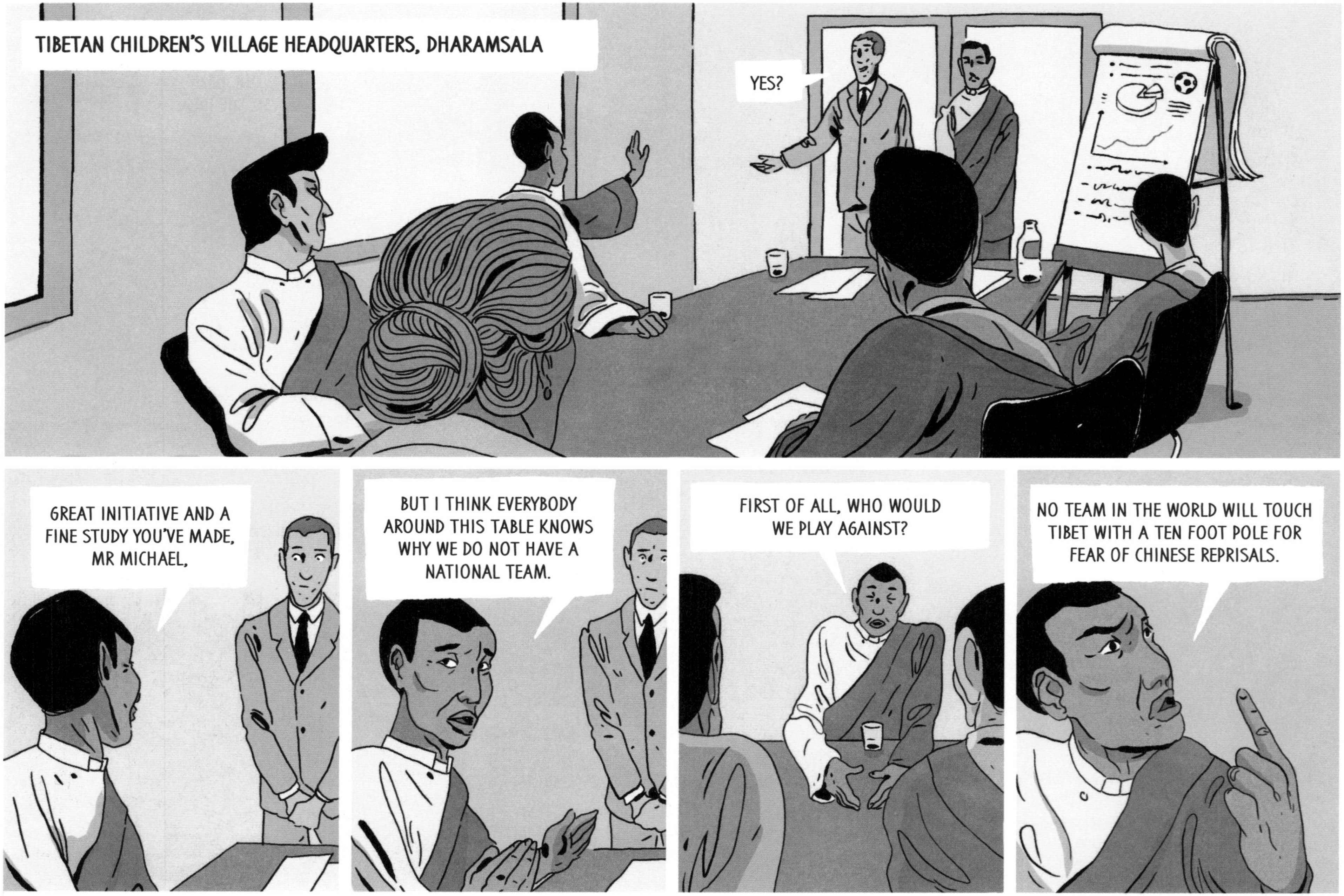
TIBETAN CHILDREN'S VILLAGE HEADQUARTERS, DHARAMSALA
YES?
GREAT INITIATIVE AND A FINE STUDY YOU'VE MADE, MR MICHAEL,
BUT I THINK EVERYBODY AROUND THIS TABLE KNOWS WHY WE DO NOT HAVE A NATIONAL TEAM.
FIRST OF ALL, WHO WOULD WE PLAY AGAINST?
NO TEAM IN THE WORLD WILL TOUCH TIBET WITH A TEN FOOT POLE FOR FEAR OF CHINESE REPRISALS.

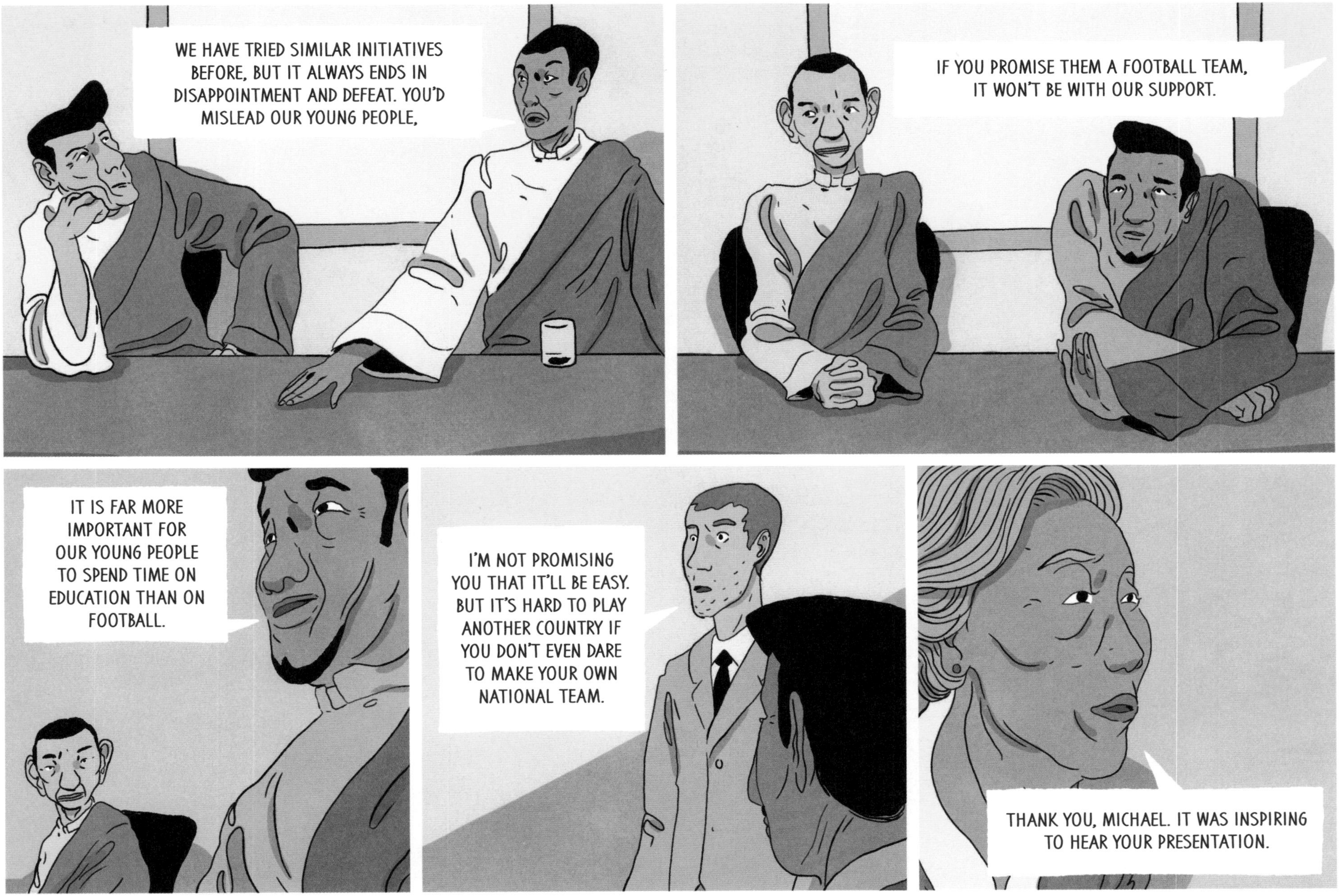
WE HAVE TRIED SIMILAR INITIATIVES BEFORE, BUT IT ALWAYS ENDS IN DISAPPOINTMENT AND DEFEAT. YOU'D MISLEAD OUR YOUNG PEOPLE,
IF YOU PROMISE THEM A FOOTBALL TEAM, IT WON'T BE WITH OUR SUPPORT.
IT IS FAR MORE IMPORTANT FOR OUR YOUNG PEOPLE TO SPEND TIME ON EDUCATION THAN ON FOOTBALL.
I'M NOT PROMISING YOU THAT IT'LL BE EASY. BUT IT'S HARD TO PLAY ANOTHER COUNTRY IF YOU DON'T EVEN DARE TO MAKE YOUR OWN NATIONAL TEAM.
THANK YOU, MICHAEL. IT WAS INSPIRING TO HEAR YOUR PRESENTATION.

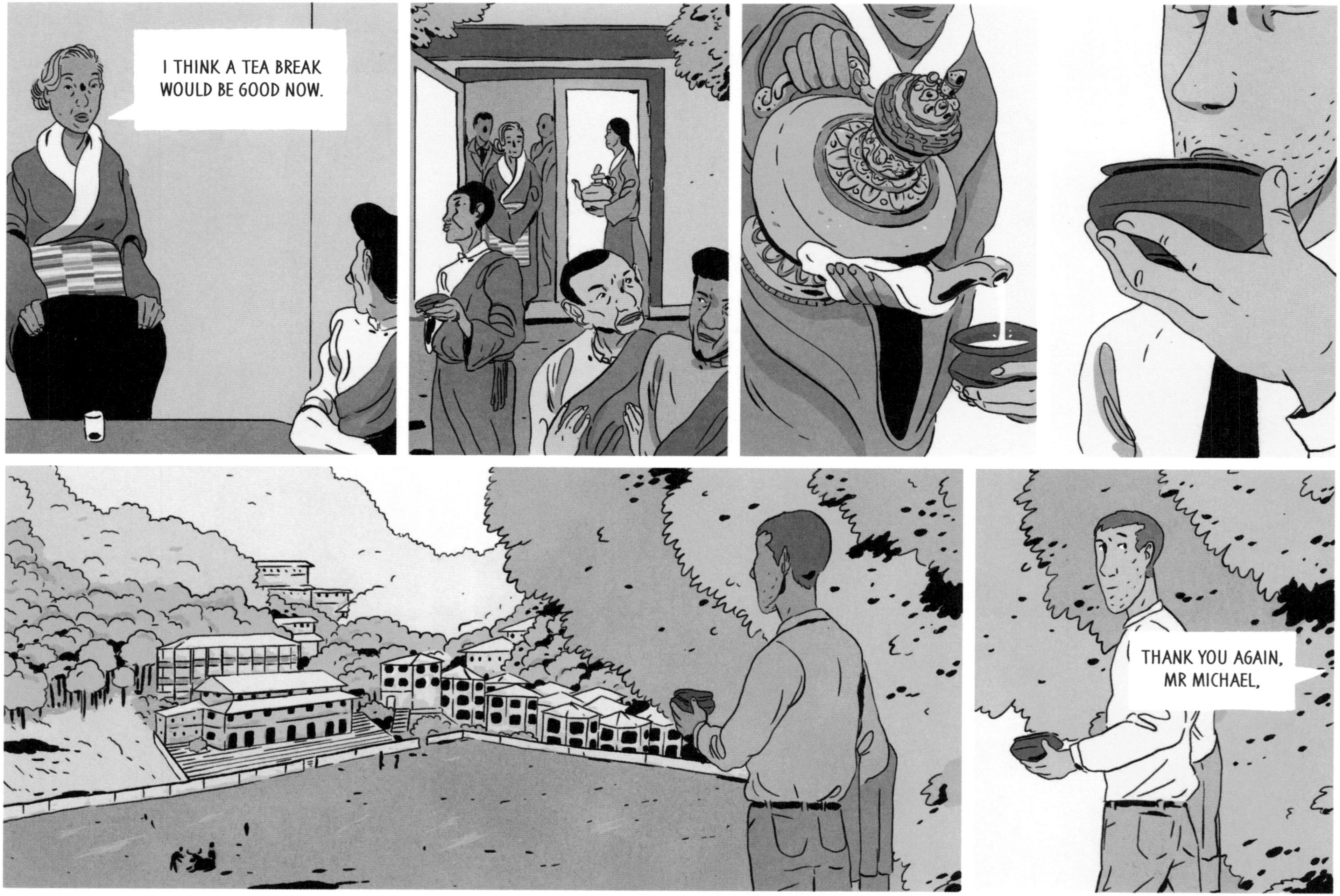
I THINK A TEA BREAK WOULD BE GOOD NOW.
THANK YOU AGAIN, MR MICHAEL,

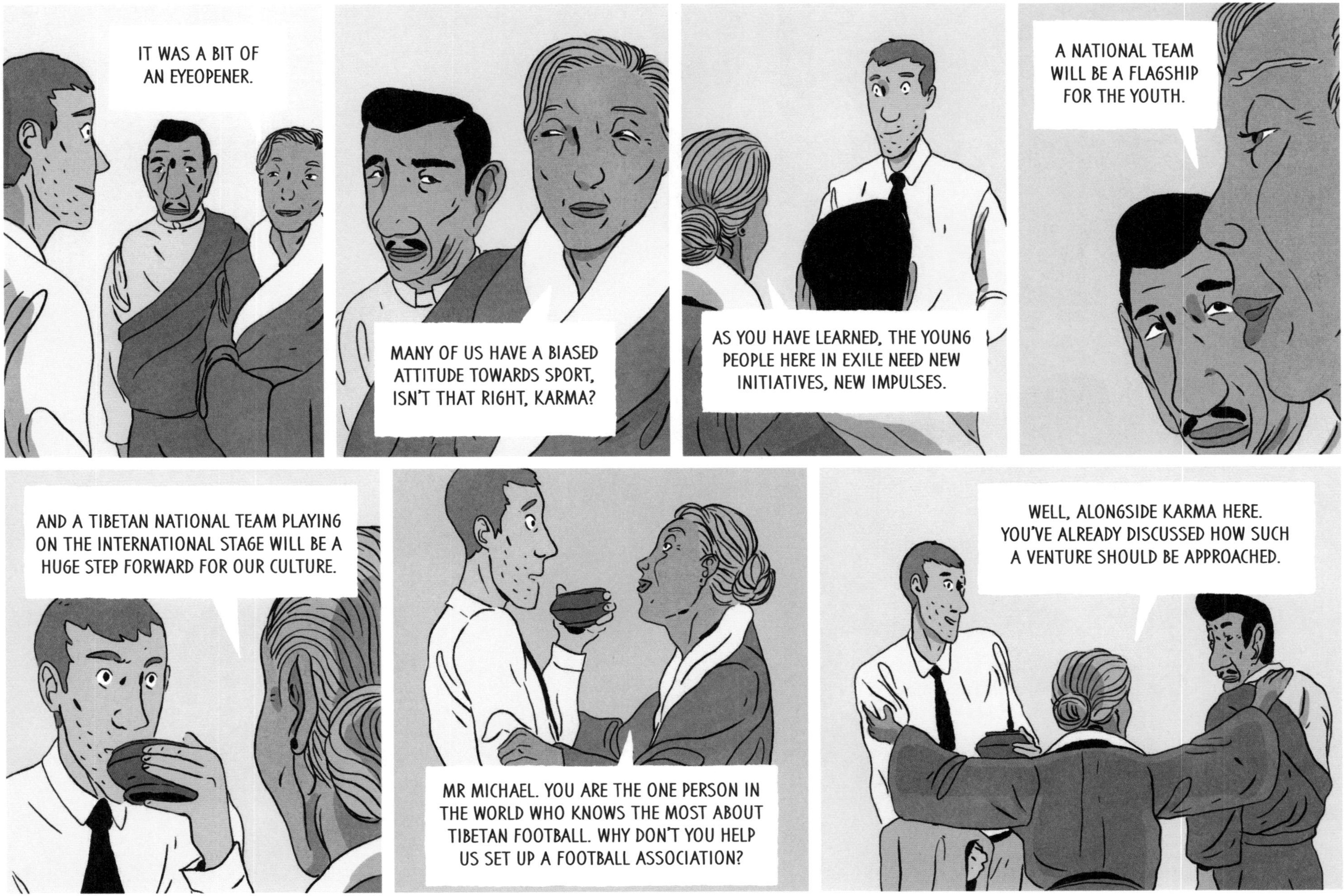
IT WAS A BIT OF AN EYEOPENER.
MANY OF US HAVE A BIASED ATTITUDE TOWARDS SPORT, ISN'T THAT RIGHT, KARMA?
AS YOU HAVE LEARNED, THE YOUNG PEOPLE HERE IN EXILE NEED NEW INITIATIVES, NEW IMPULSES.
A NATIONAL TEAM WILL BE A FLAGSHIP FOR THE YOUTH.
AND A TIBETAN NATIONAL TEAM PLAYING ON THE INTERNATIONAL STAGE WILL BE A HUGE STEP FORWARD FOR OUR CULTURE.
MR MICHAEL. YOU ARE THE ONE PERSON IN THE WORLD WHO KNOWS THE MOST ABOUT TIBETAN FOOTBALL. WHY DON'T YOU HELP US SET UP A FOOTBALL ASSOCIATION?
WELL, ALONGSIDE KARMA HERE. YOU'VE ALREADY DISCUSSED HOW SUCH A VENTURE SHOULD BE APPROACHED.

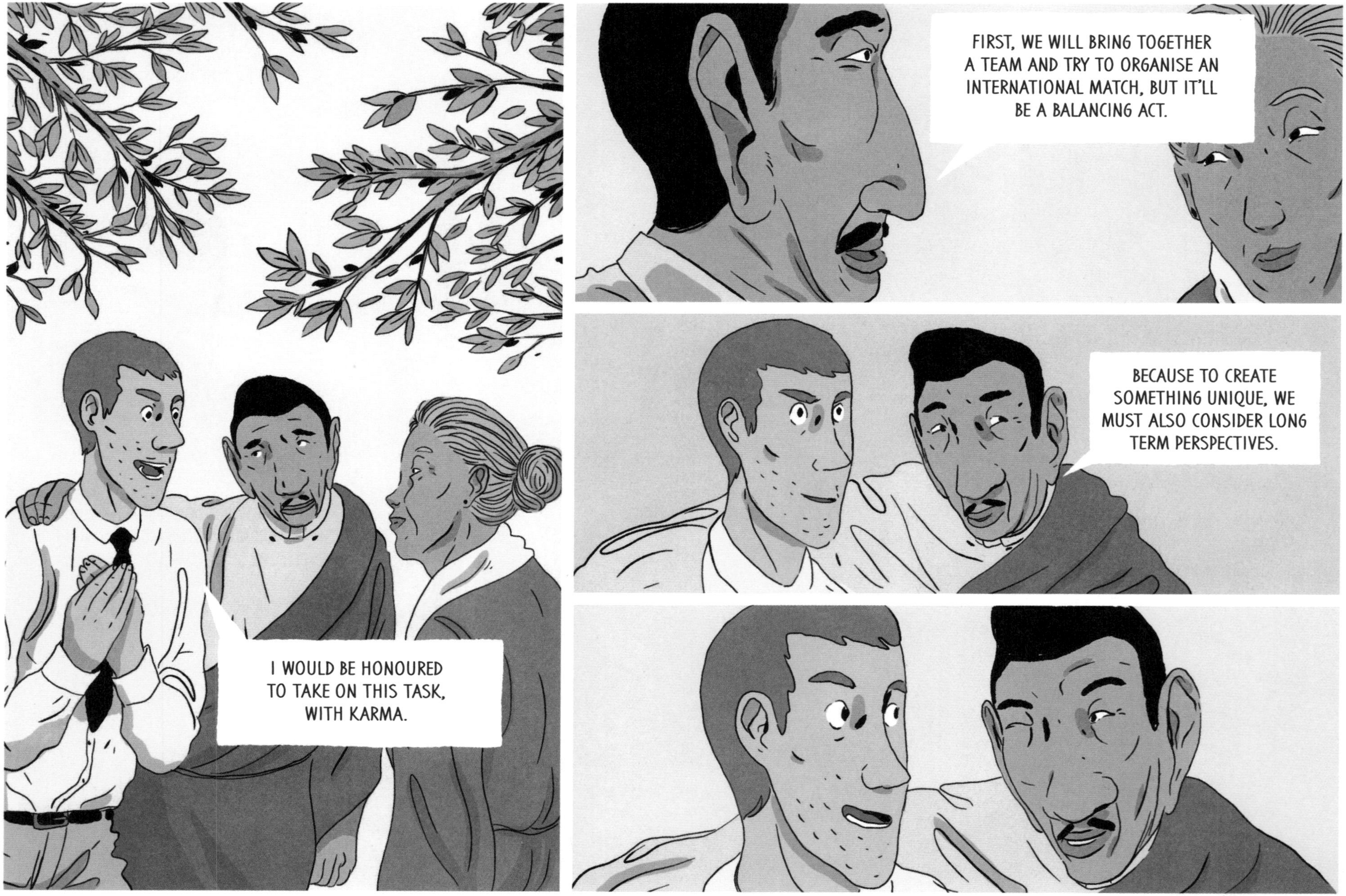
I WOULD BE HONOURED TO TAKE ON THIS TASK, WITH KARMA.
FIRST, WE WILL BRING TOGETHER A TEAM AND TRY TO ORGANISE AN INTERNATIONAL MATCH, BUT IT'LL BE A BALANCING ACT.
BECAUSE TO CREATE SOMETHING UNIQUE, WE MUST ALSO CONSIDER LONG TERM PERSPECTIVES.

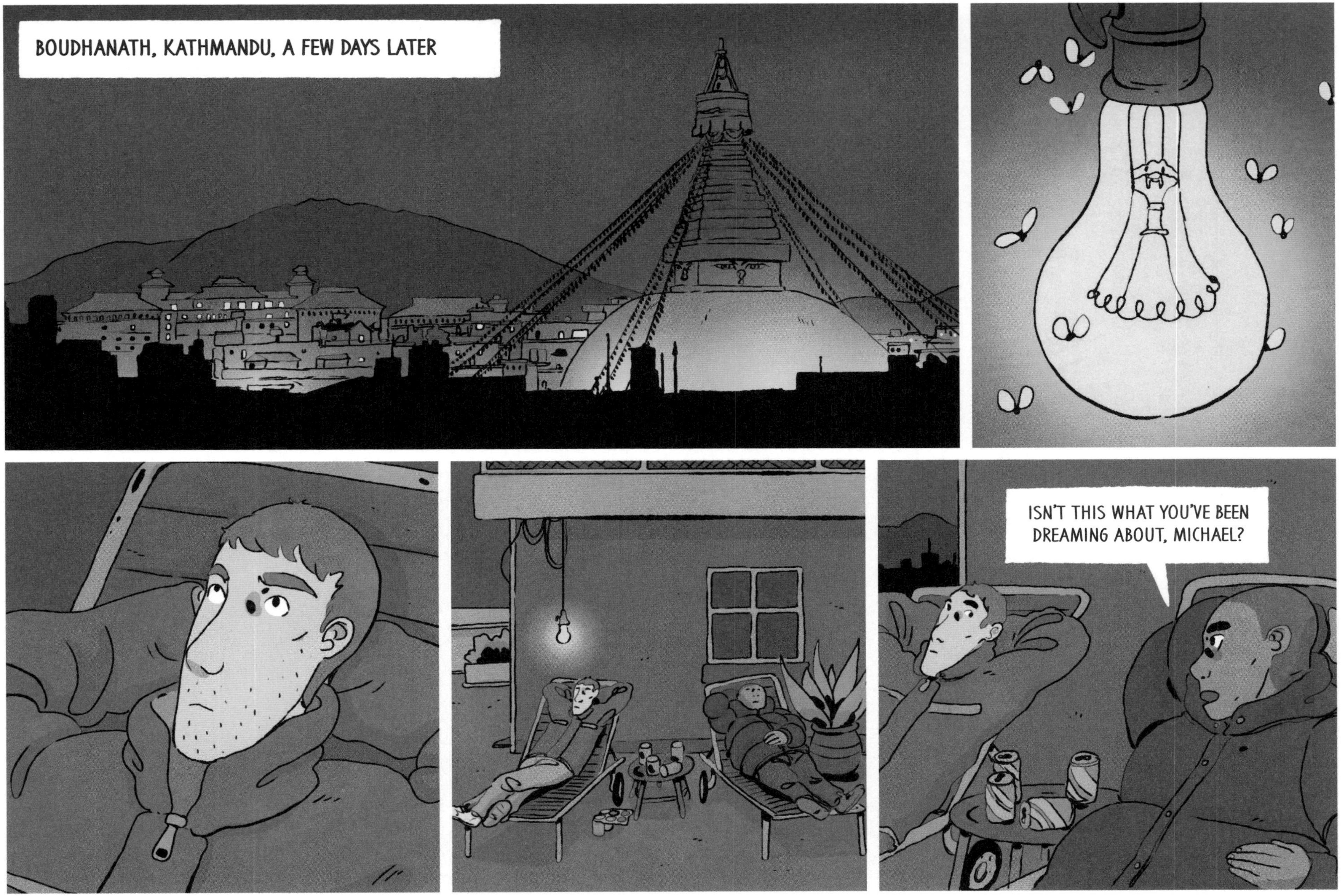
BOUDHANATH, KATHMANDU, A FEW DAYS LATER
ISN'T THIS WHAT YOU'VE BEEN DREAMING ABOUT, MICHAEL?

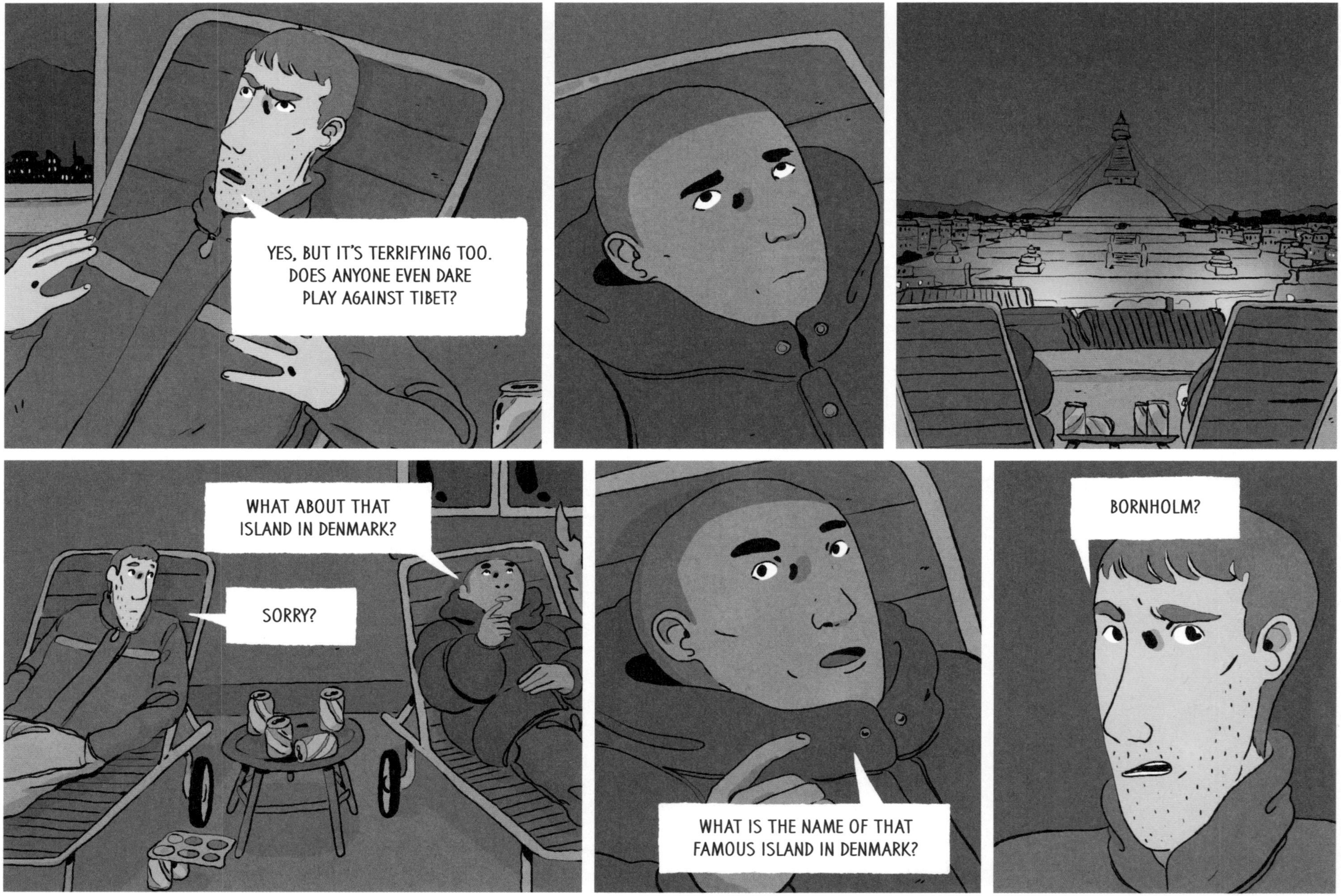
YES, BUT IT'S TERRIFYING TOO. DOES ANYONE EVEN DARE PLAY AGAINST TIBET?
WHAT ABOUT THAT ISLAND IN DENMARK?
SORRY?
WHAT IS THE NAME OF THAT FAMOUS ISLAND IN DENMARK?
BORNHOLM?

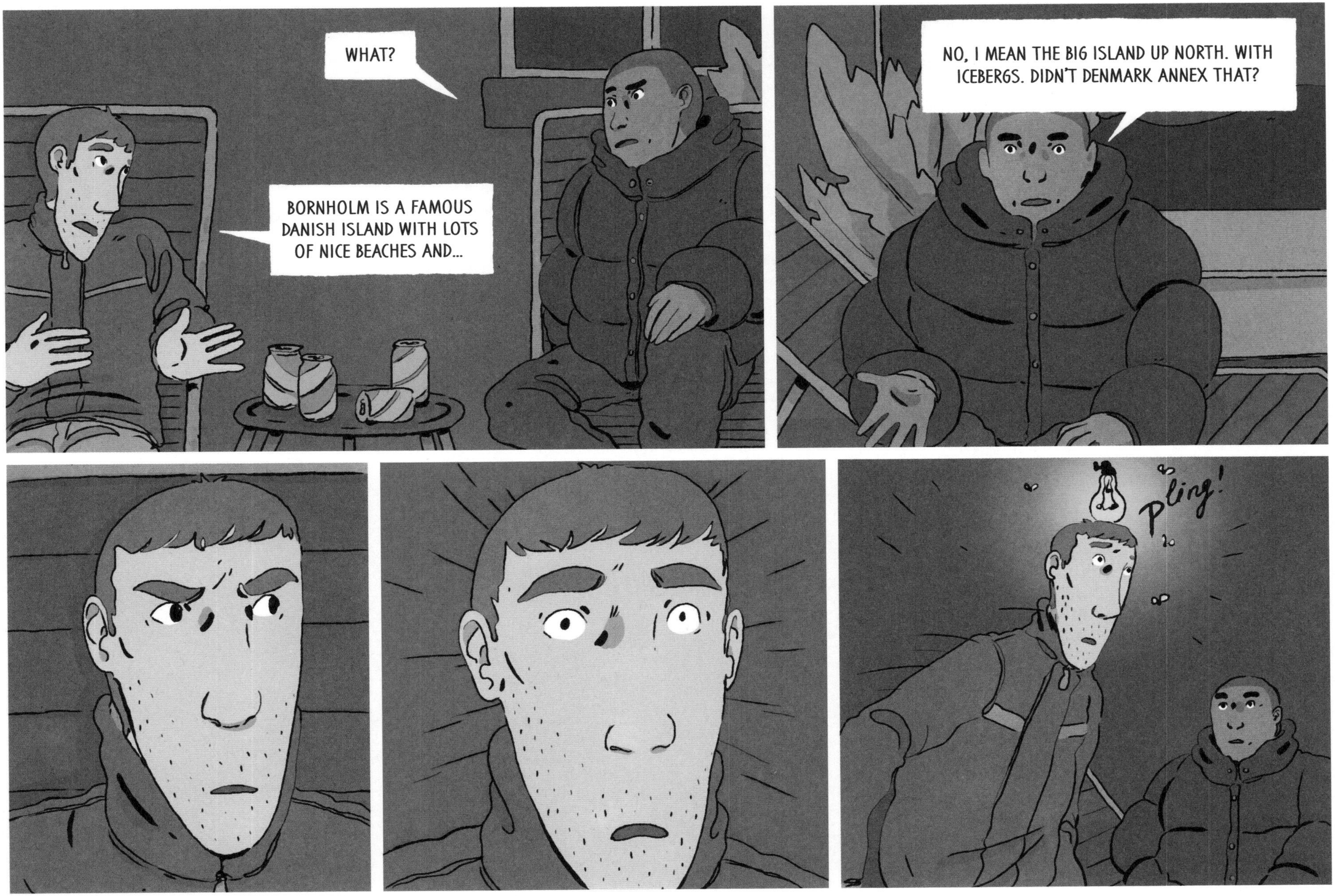
WHAT?
BORNHOLM IS A FAMOUS DANISH ISLAND WITH LOTS OF NICE BEACHES AND...
NO, I MEAN THE BIG ISLAND UP NORTH. WITH ICEBERGS. DIDN'T DENMARK ANNEX THAT?
Pling!

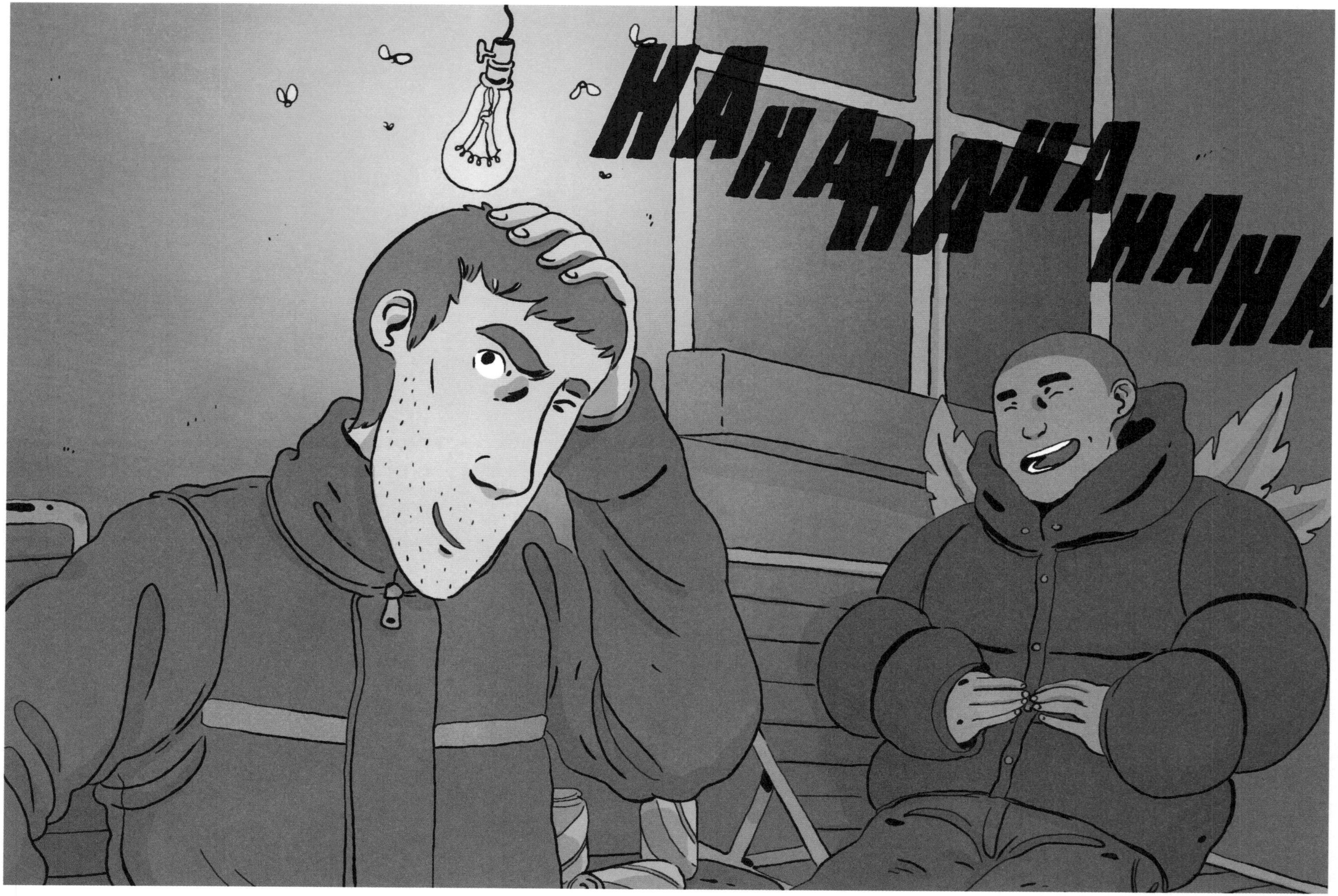
HAHAHAHAHAHAHAHAHA

CHAPTER 5
DHARMA PLAYER

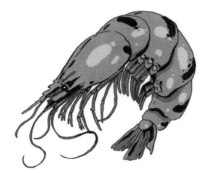

sport

GREENLAND VS TIBET

Dane behind the establishment of Tibetan national football team and its first match against Greenland, to be played the summer of 2001.

Twenty-nine-year-old Michael Nybrandt recently returned from a stay in Nepal and India, where he wrote his dissertation on Tibetan football. The Tibetans have neither a football association, nor a national team, but that may all change because Nybrandt was sent back home with a job. "When I presented my results to the Tibetan exile government, they kicked the ball back to me and asked if I would assist them in the development of a national team." He agreed, with the condition that it should be a sustainable organisation and not just a political weapon in the form of a national team with no fertile grounding in a football culture.

Sustainable dream

"All young Tibetans should be able to dream and have a chance to play on the national team through tourna-ments and matches," Michael Nybrandt emphasises. "My basic idea is to establish an organisation to manage the development of Tibetan football with coaching education, tournaments and a national team." In the eyes of many, this seems an unrealistic project due to the current Chinese occupation of Tibet, and their longtime status as a people in exile. But the organisation is based in Dharamsala, northern India, where the Tibetan leader Dalai Lama and the rest of the exile government reside, along with hundreds of thousands of Tibetan refugees. "I believe my study demonstrates that they have all the tools to implement this project, they have a budding football culture and organisational talent, but they have probably lacked the belief that it was possible, and someone to tie it all together. That's where I come in," Nybrandt laughs.

Tandem in Tibet

However, Nybrandt's Tibetan football adventure started earlier. Years ago he cycled through Tibet on a tandem bike, one night dreaming that he was the coach of the Tibetan football team. "I saw myself standing at the head of a Tibetan national football team – it was the ultimate job for me. After this vision, he left Copenhagen to apply for Kaospilot training in Aarhus. Michael set as the objective of his education that he should become Tibet's coach. "The study environment prepared me for this task. I was supported in my dream by fellow students and by the Principal of the school," he says of the unorthodox, but goal-oriented and strategic 3-year project management degree. In his time at the Kaospilots, Nybrandt interned with the Danish Football Association where he learned how an association works in practice, and he also helped set up football schools in war-torn areas in Bosnia, discovering how football could be used to unite a people and create an identity.

Greenland kicks off

Michael has already made contact with a future opponent, in the form of the Greenlandic national team. The idea of Greenland arrived somewhat coincidentally. "We discussed at length how we needed to kick off this project, and with an international friendly football match we would be sending a signal to young Tibetans, sponsors and partners about the seriousness and validity of our project."

"When Greenland became a potential opponent, things really lit up," says Nybrandt. "There are several layers in this match, because there are many similarities between the two

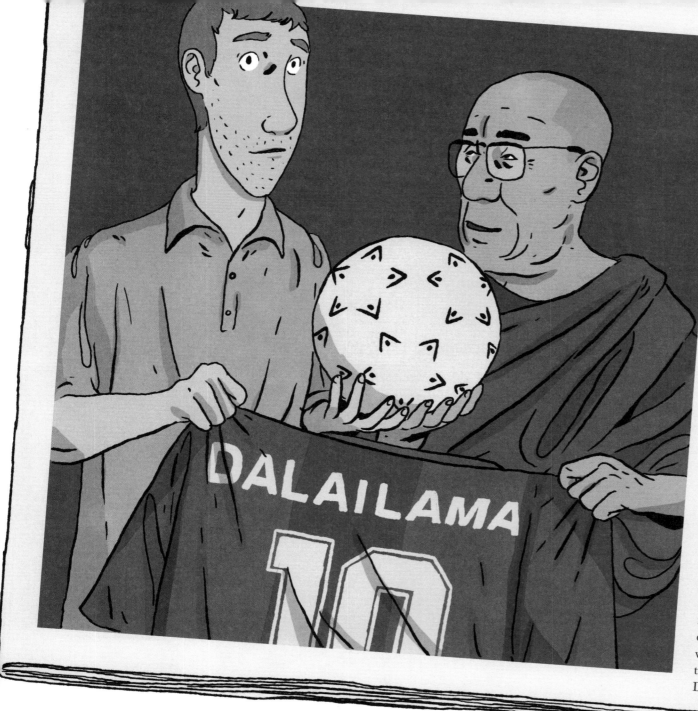

indigenous peoples – cultural, sporting and political. That's why, immediately when I came home from India, I called Sepp [Sepp Piontek, coach of the Greenland team], and he was on board," says Michael Nybrandt who also expects that there will be some turbulence when the match is announced. "It's always like that when Tibetans hoist their flag and draw attention to themselves, then the Chinese rattle their sabres. But it should not have any direct influence on the project or the match against Greenland", he says, revealing that he is well underway in negotiations with a sponsor who will provide the financial basis necessary for the match to go ahead.

"When Greenland became a potential opponent, things really lit up. There are several layers in this match, because there are many similarities between the two indigenous peoples."

The meeting with Dalai Lama

A few weeks ago the Tibetan religious leader visited Copenhagen. On that occasion, Nybrandt met with the charismatic figure and handed him a national team jersey. "It was overwhelming for me to meet him, and a milestone for the project. And it's just a good example of a picture being worth a thousand words," Nybrandt says smiling about the portrait that was taken when he presented the Dalai Lama with a football and a jersey.

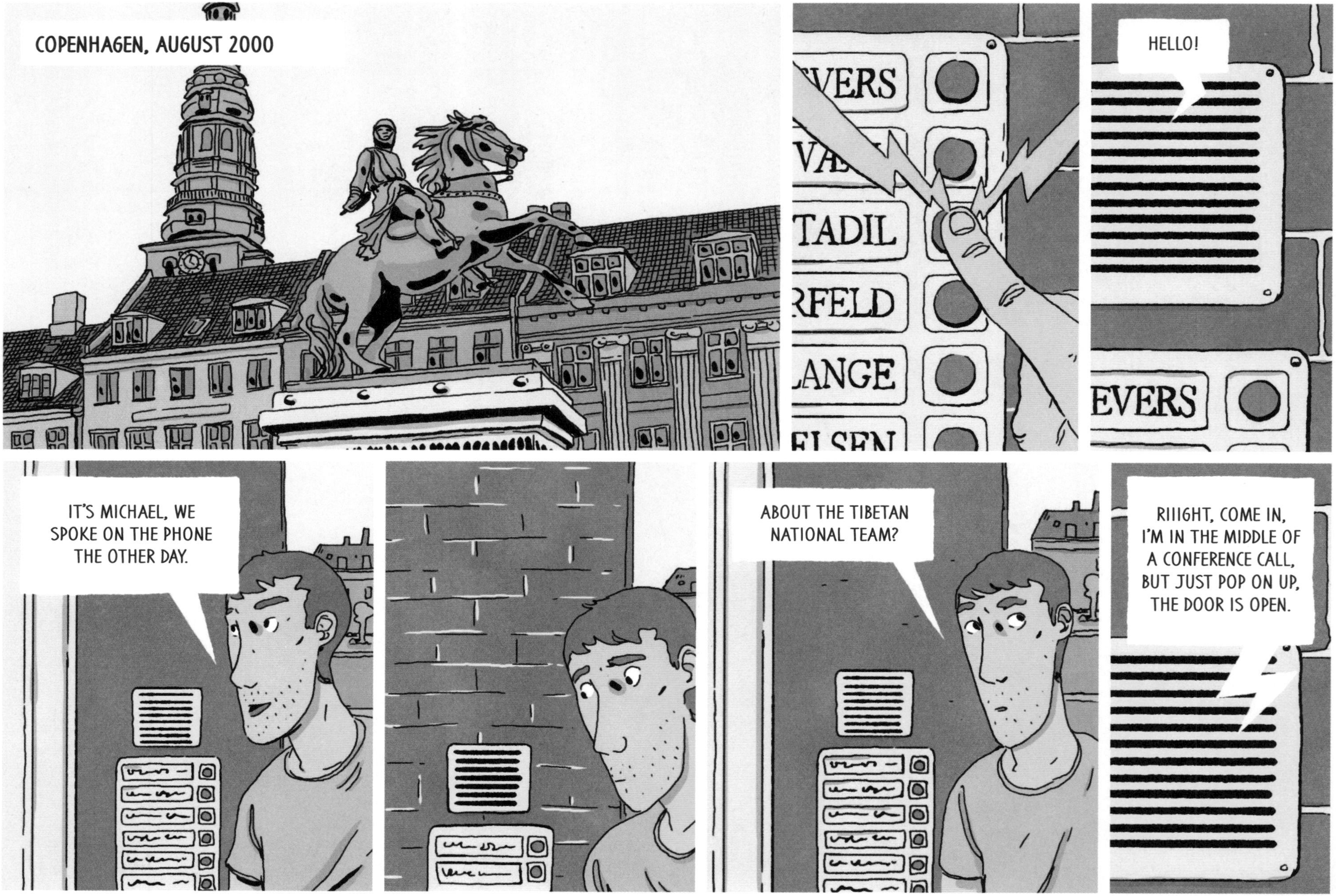
COPENHAGEN, AUGUST 2000
VERS
TADIL
RFELD
LANGE
HELLO!
EVERS
IT'S MICHAEL, WE SPOKE ON THE PHONE THE OTHER DAY.
ABOUT THE TIBETAN NATIONAL TEAM?
RIIIGHT, COME IN, I'M IN THE MIDDLE OF A CONFERENCE CALL, BUT JUST POP ON UP, THE DOOR IS OPEN.

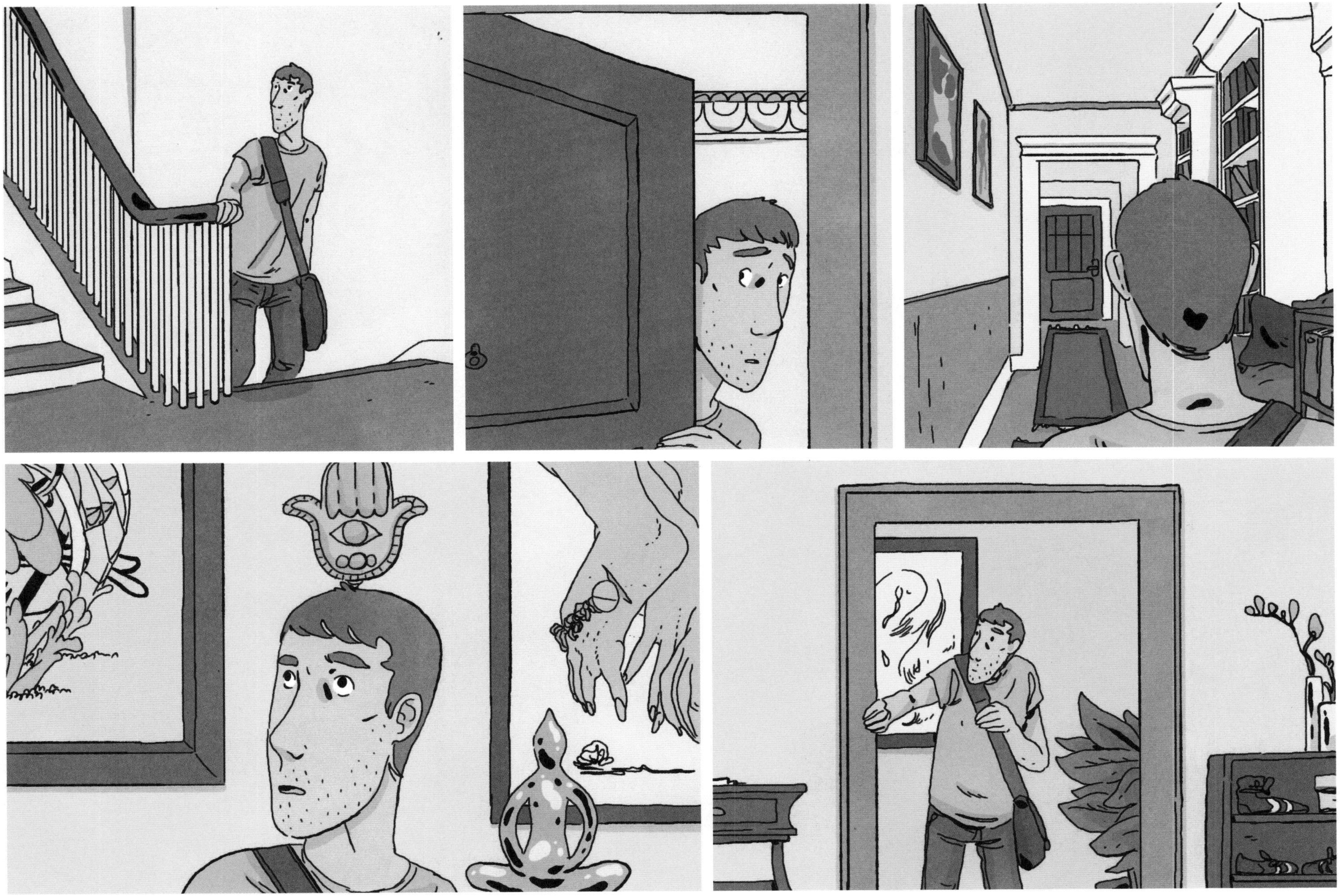

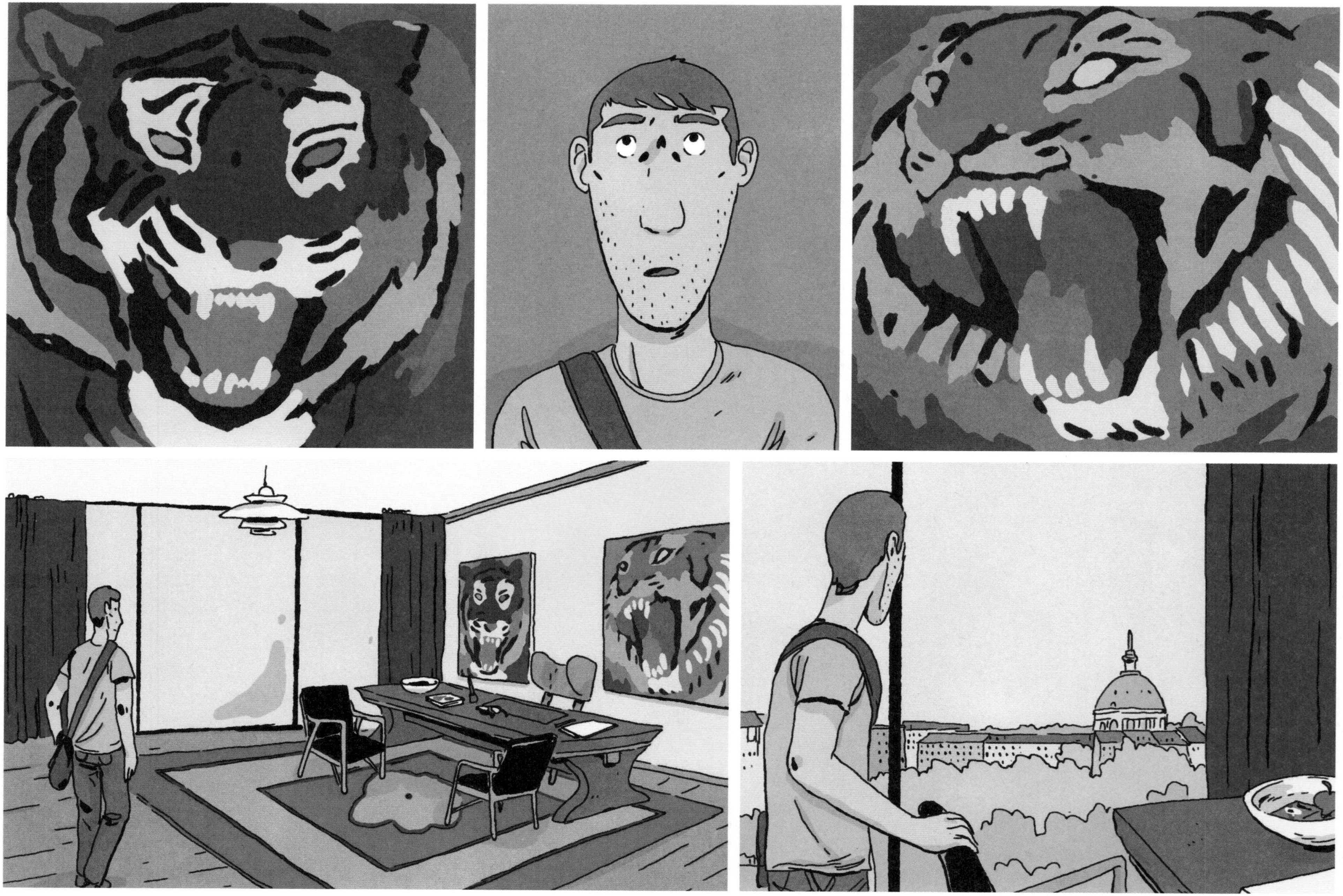

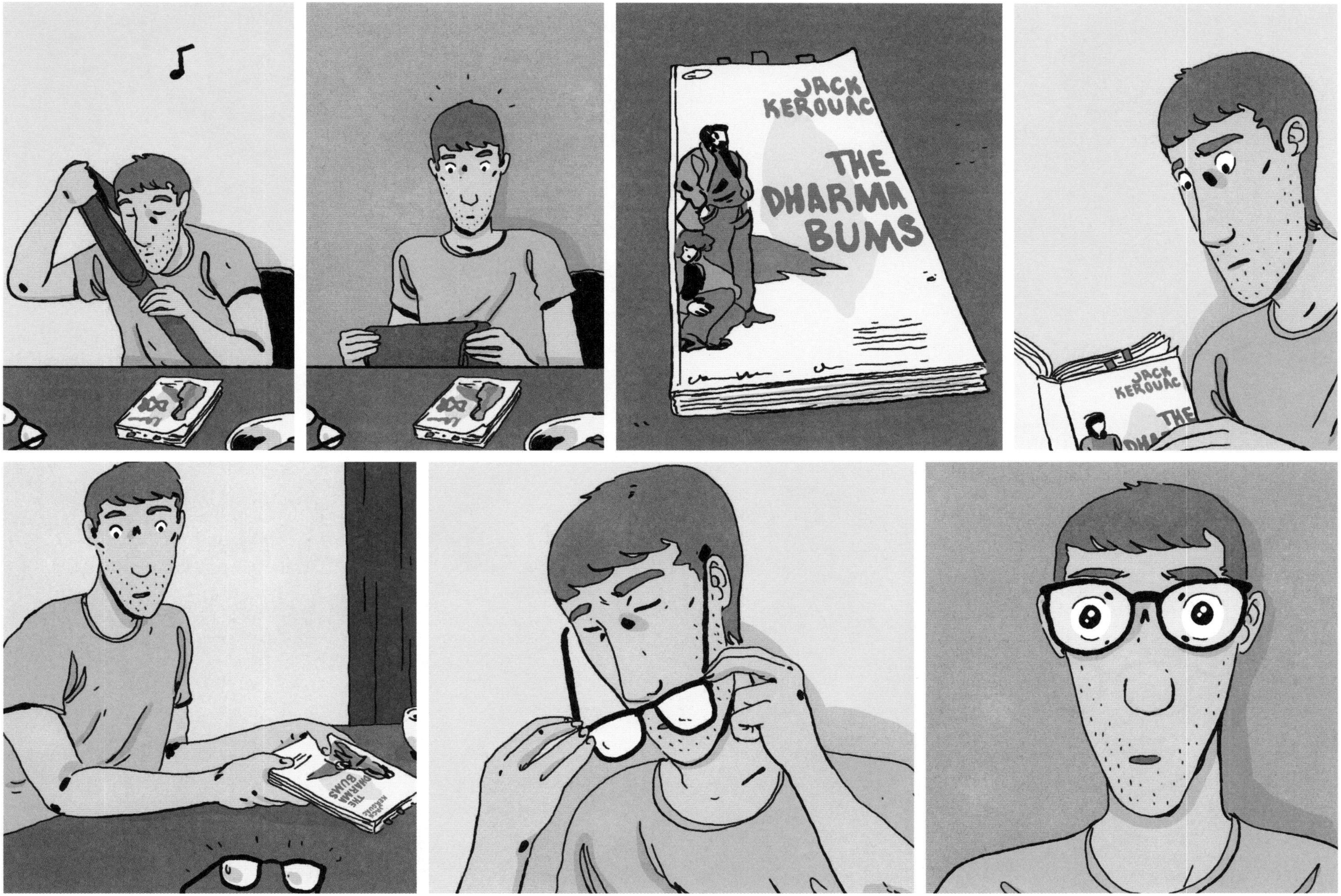
JACK
KEROUAC
THE
DHARMA
BUMS

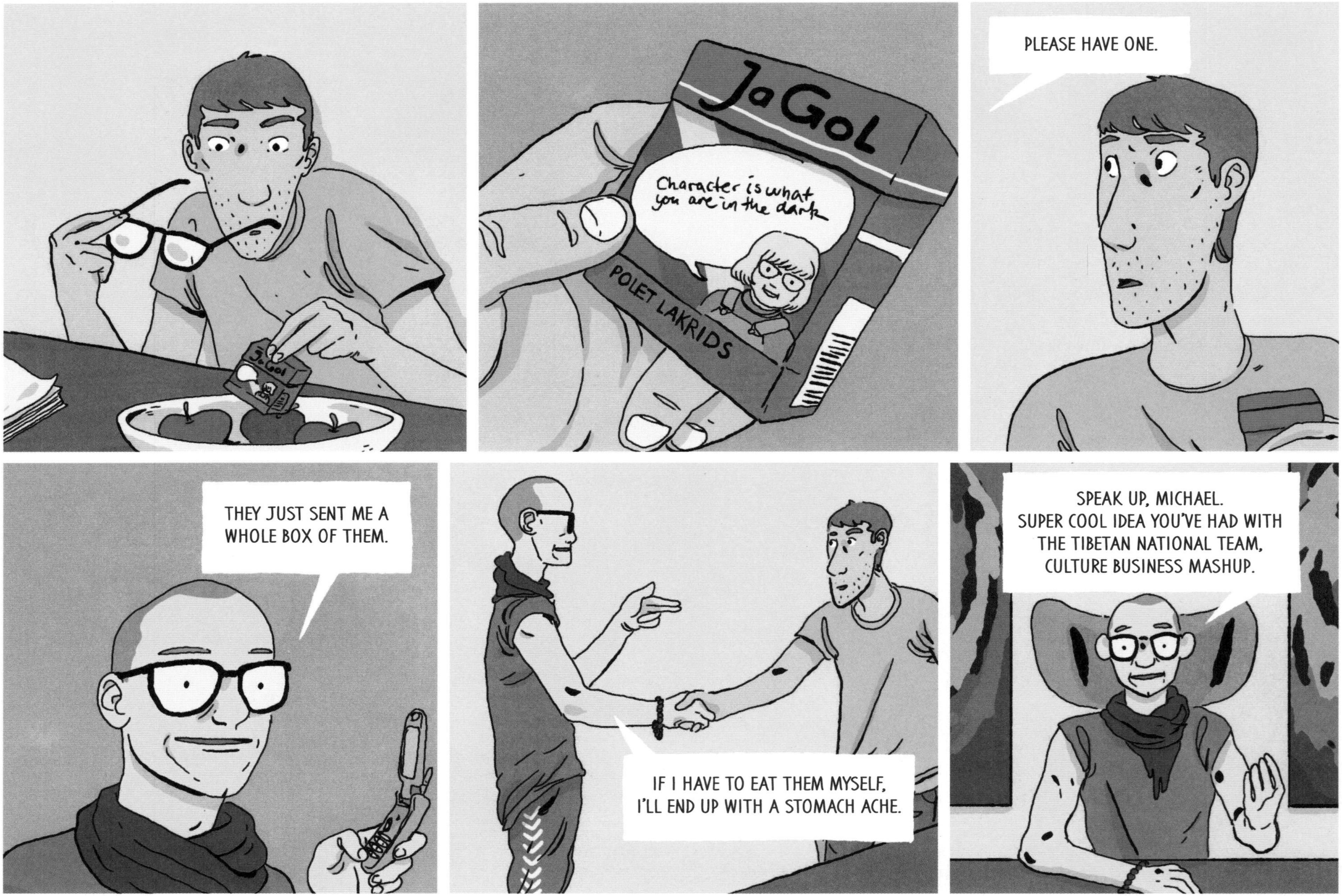
JaGoL
Character is what you are in the dark
POLET LAKRIDS
PLEASE HAVE ONE.
THEY JUST SENT ME A WHOLE BOX OF THEM.
IF I HAVE TO EAT THEM MYSELF, I'LL END UP WITH A STOMACH ACHE.
SPEAK UP, MICHAEL. SUPER COOL IDEA YOU'VE HAD WITH THE TIBETAN NATIONAL TEAM, CULTURE BUSINESS MASHUP.

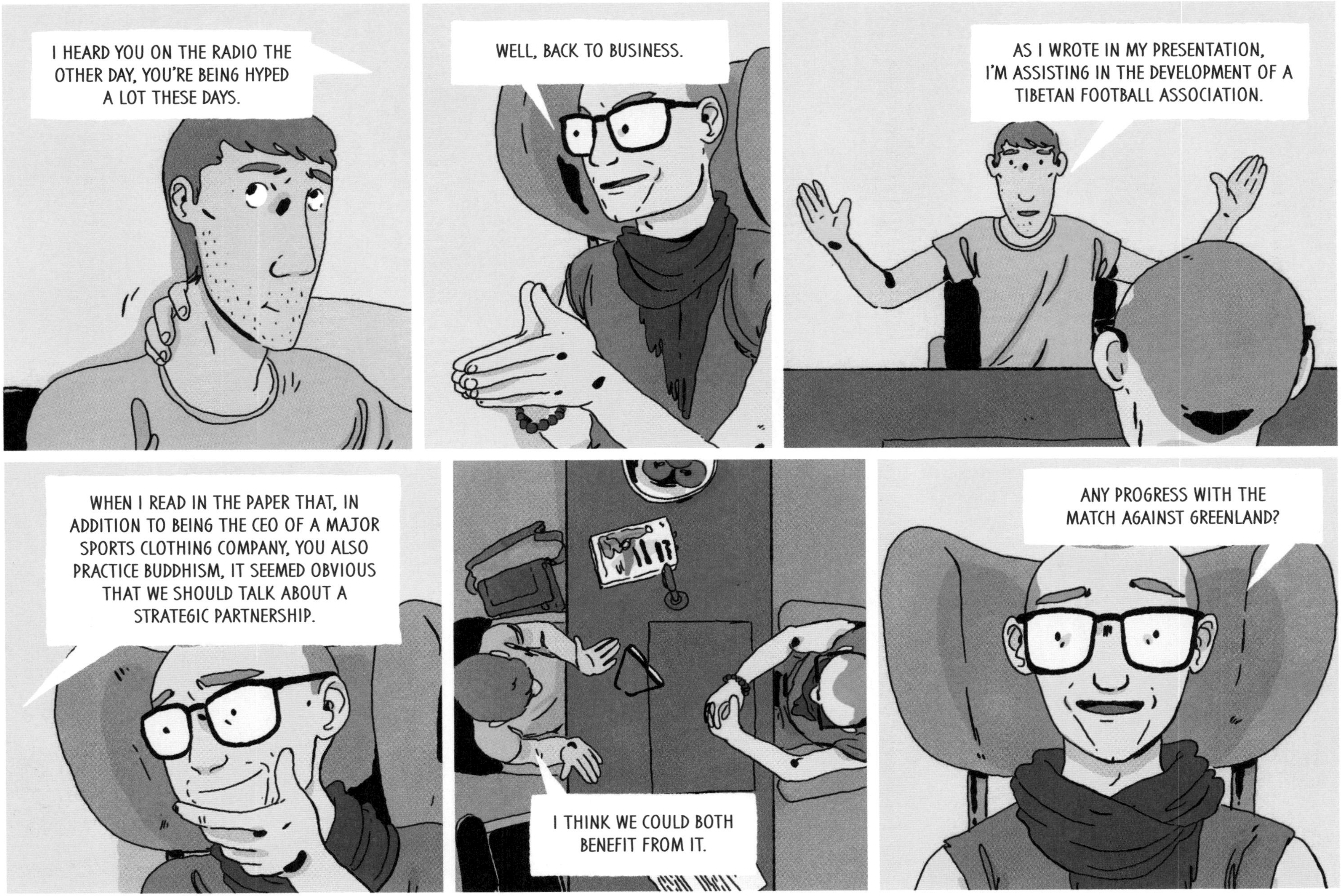
I HEARD YOU ON THE RADIO THE OTHER DAY, YOU'RE BEING HYPED A LOT THESE DAYS.
WELL, BACK TO BUSINESS.
AS I WROTE IN MY PRESENTATION, I'M ASSISTING IN THE DEVELOPMENT OF A TIBETAN FOOTBALL ASSOCIATION.
WHEN I READ IN THE PAPER THAT, IN ADDITION TO BEING THE CEO OF A MAJOR SPORTS CLOTHING COMPANY, YOU ALSO PRACTICE BUDDHISM, IT SEEMED OBVIOUS THAT WE SHOULD TALK ABOUT A STRATEGIC PARTNERSHIP.
I THINK WE COULD BOTH BENEFIT FROM IT.
ANY PROGRESS WITH THE MATCH AGAINST GREENLAND?

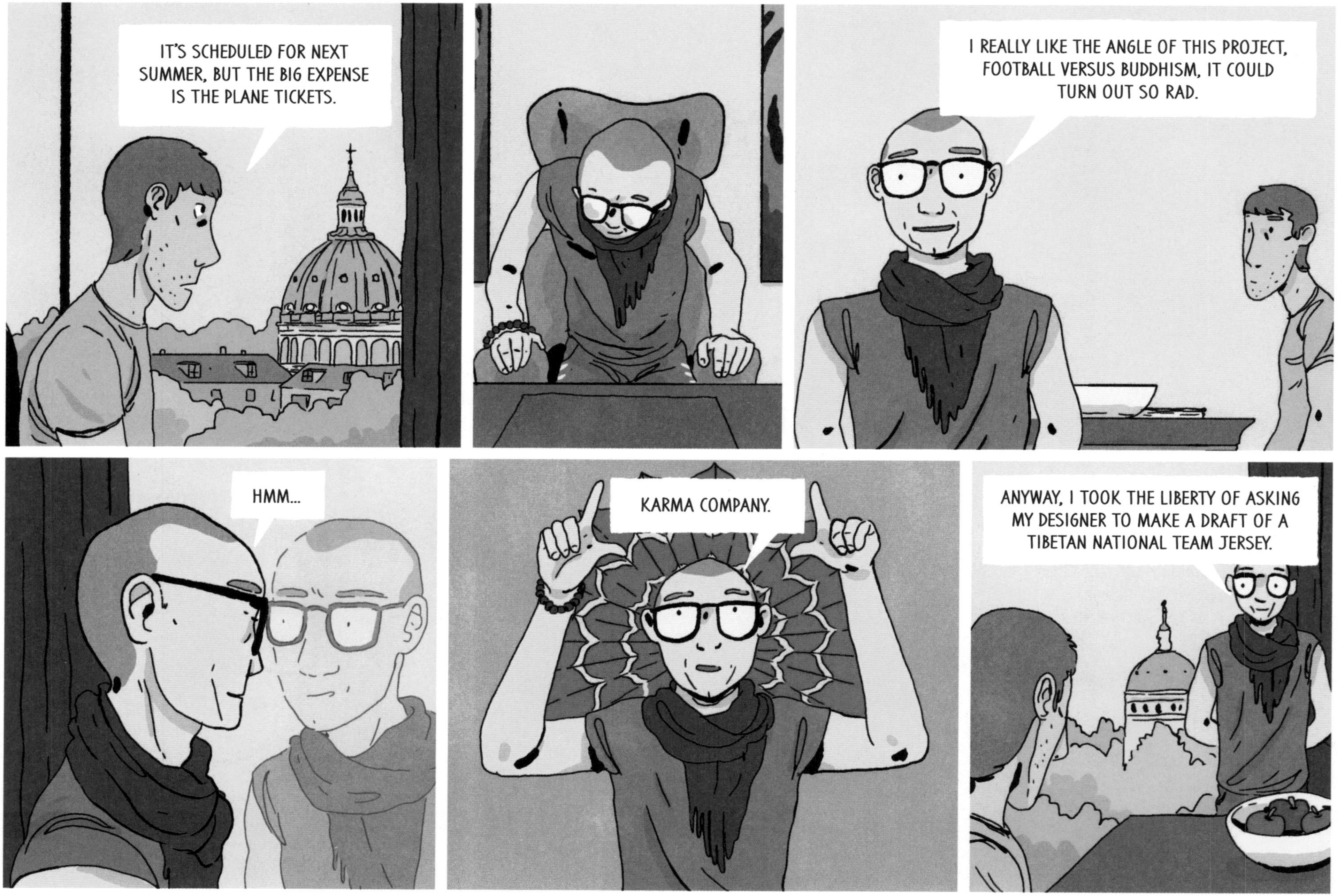
IT'S SCHEDULED FOR NEXT SUMMER, BUT THE BIG EXPENSE IS THE PLANE TICKETS.
I REALLY LIKE THE ANGLE OF THIS PROJECT, FOOTBALL VERSUS BUDDHISM, IT COULD TURN OUT SO RAD.
HMM...
KARMA COMPANY.
ANYWAY, I TOOK THE LIBERTY OF ASKING MY DESIGNER TO MAKE A DRAFT OF A TIBETAN NATIONAL TEAM JERSEY.

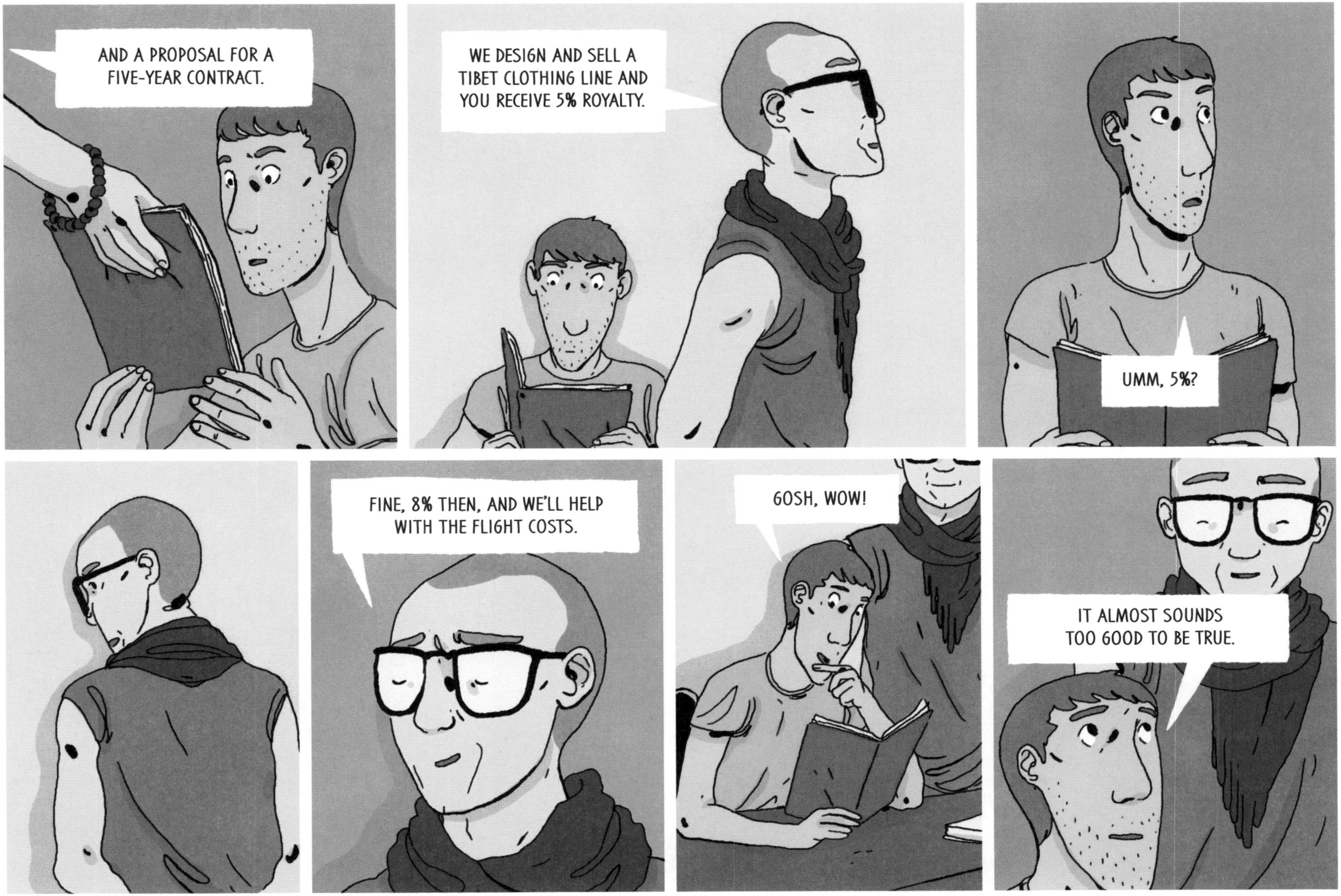
AND A PROPOSAL FOR A FIVE-YEAR CONTRACT.
WE DESIGN AND SELL A TIBET CLOTHING LINE AND YOU RECEIVE 5% ROYALTY.
UMM, 5%?
FINE, 8% THEN, AND WE'LL HELP WITH THE FLIGHT COSTS.
GOSH, WOW!
IT ALMOST SOUNDS TOO GOOD TO BE TRUE.

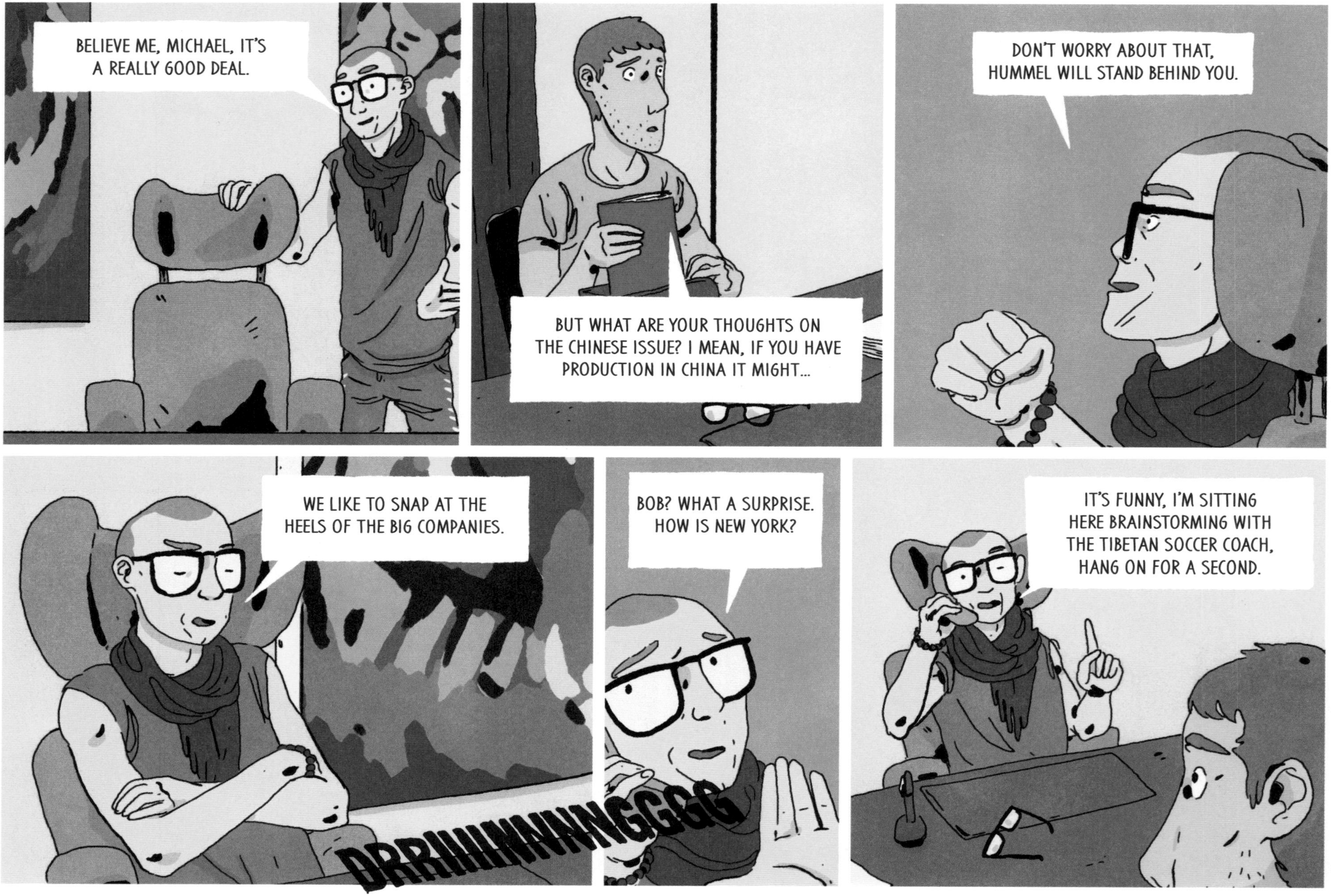
BELIEVE ME, MICHAEL, IT'S A REALLY GOOD DEAL.
BUT WHAT ARE YOUR THOUGHTS ON THE CHINESE ISSUE? I MEAN, IF YOU HAVE PRODUCTION IN CHINA IT MIGHT...
DON'T WORRY ABOUT THAT, HUMMEL WILL STAND BEHIND YOU.
WE LIKE TO SNAP AT THE HEELS OF THE BIG COMPANIES.
DRRIIIIINNNNGGGG
BOB? WHAT A SURPRISE. HOW IS NEW YORK?
IT'S FUNNY, I'M SITTING HERE BRAINSTORMING WITH THE TIBETAN SOCCER COACH, HANG ON FOR A SECOND.

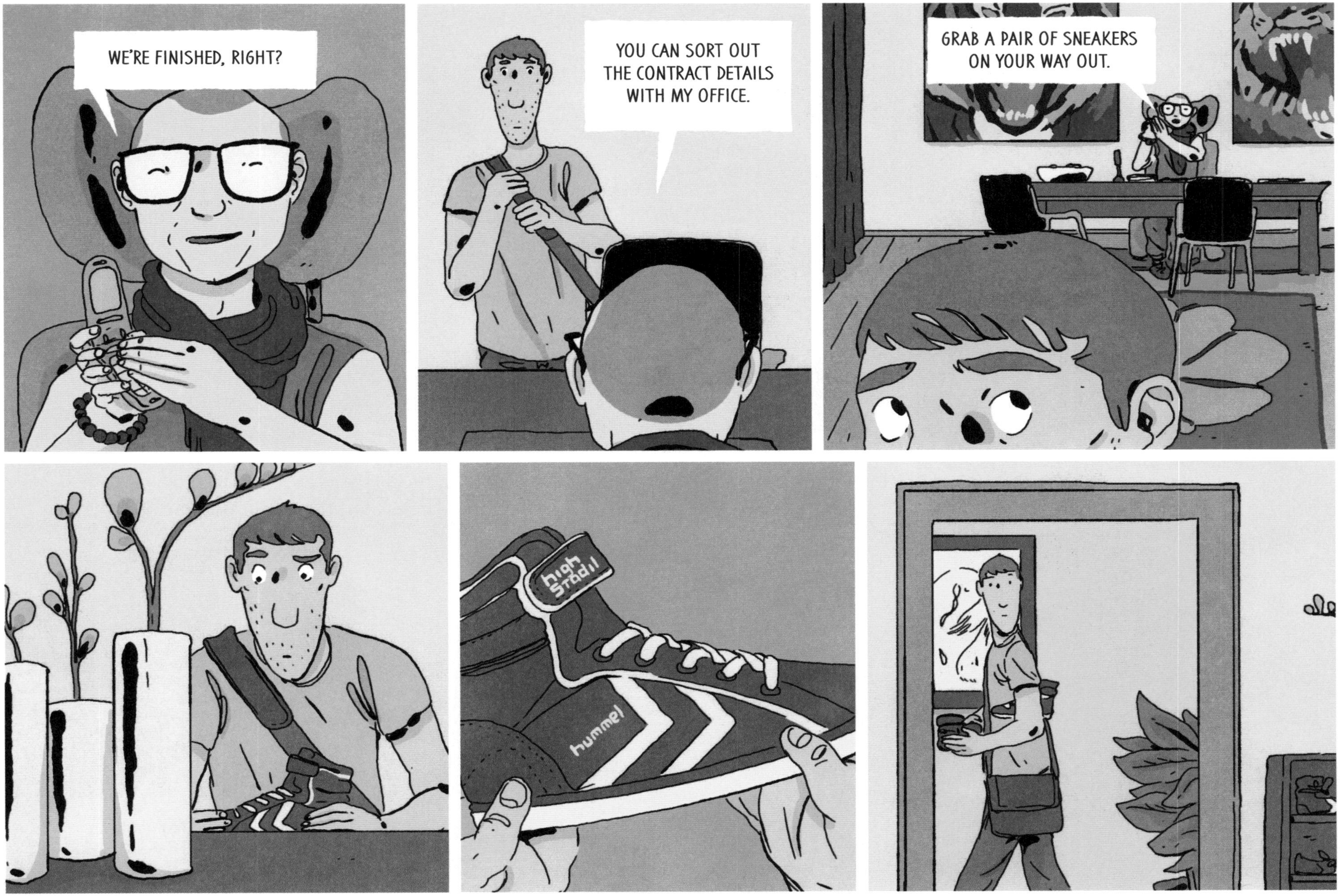
WE'RE FINISHED, RIGHT?
YOU CAN SORT OUT THE CONTRACT DETAILS WITH MY OFFICE.
GRAB A PAIR OF SNEAKERS ON YOUR WAY OUT.
high Stadil
hummel

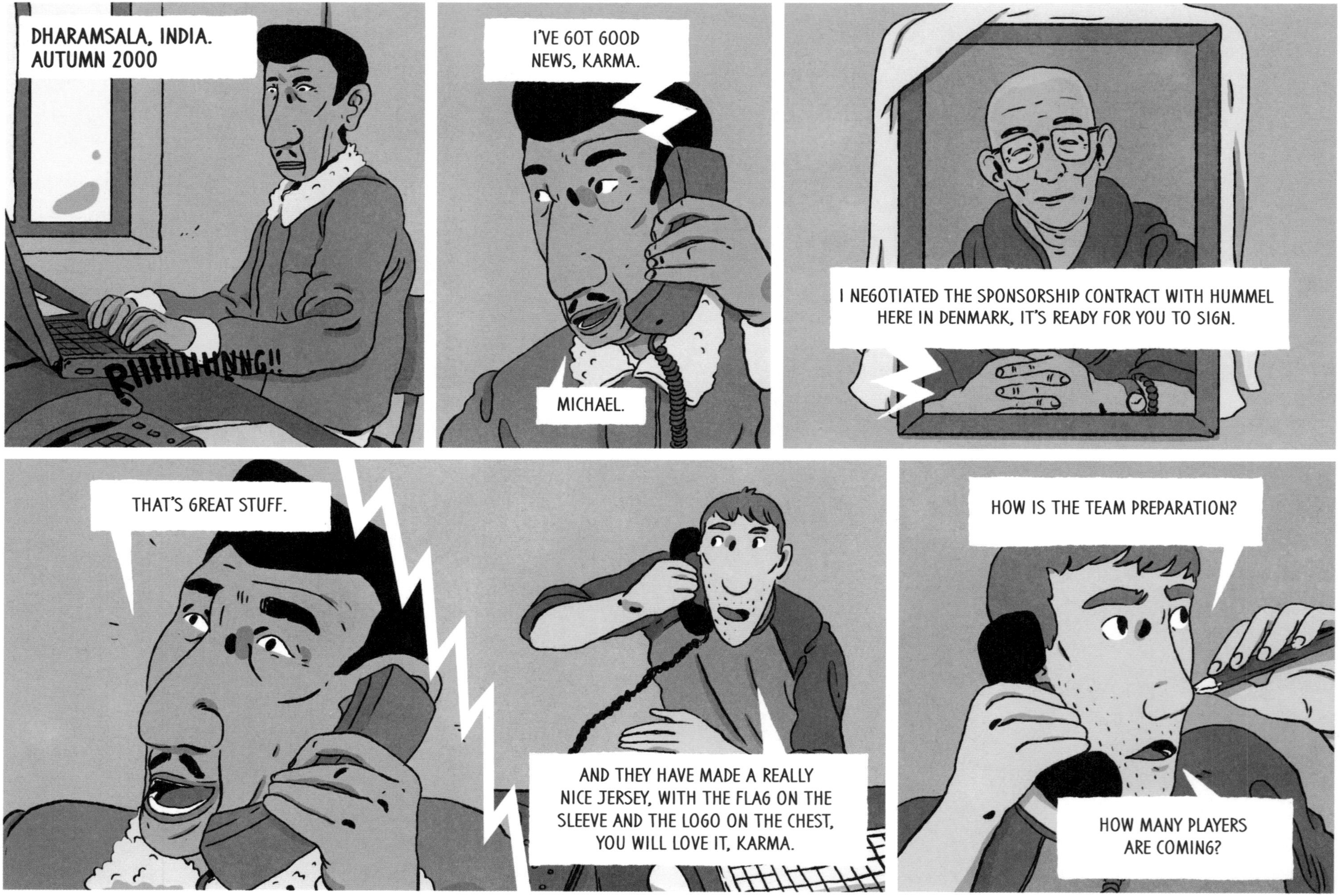
DHARAMSALA, INDIA.
AUTUMN 2000
RIIIIIINNNG!!
I'VE GOT GOOD NEWS, KARMA.
MICHAEL.
I NEGOTIATED THE SPONSORSHIP CONTRACT WITH HUMMEL HERE IN DENMARK, IT'S READY FOR YOU TO SIGN.
THAT'S GREAT STUFF.
AND THEY HAVE MADE A REALLY NICE JERSEY, WITH THE FLAG ON THE SLEEVE AND THE LOGO ON THE CHEST. YOU WILL LOVE IT, KARMA.
HOW IS THE TEAM PREPARATION?
HOW MANY PLAYERS ARE COMING?

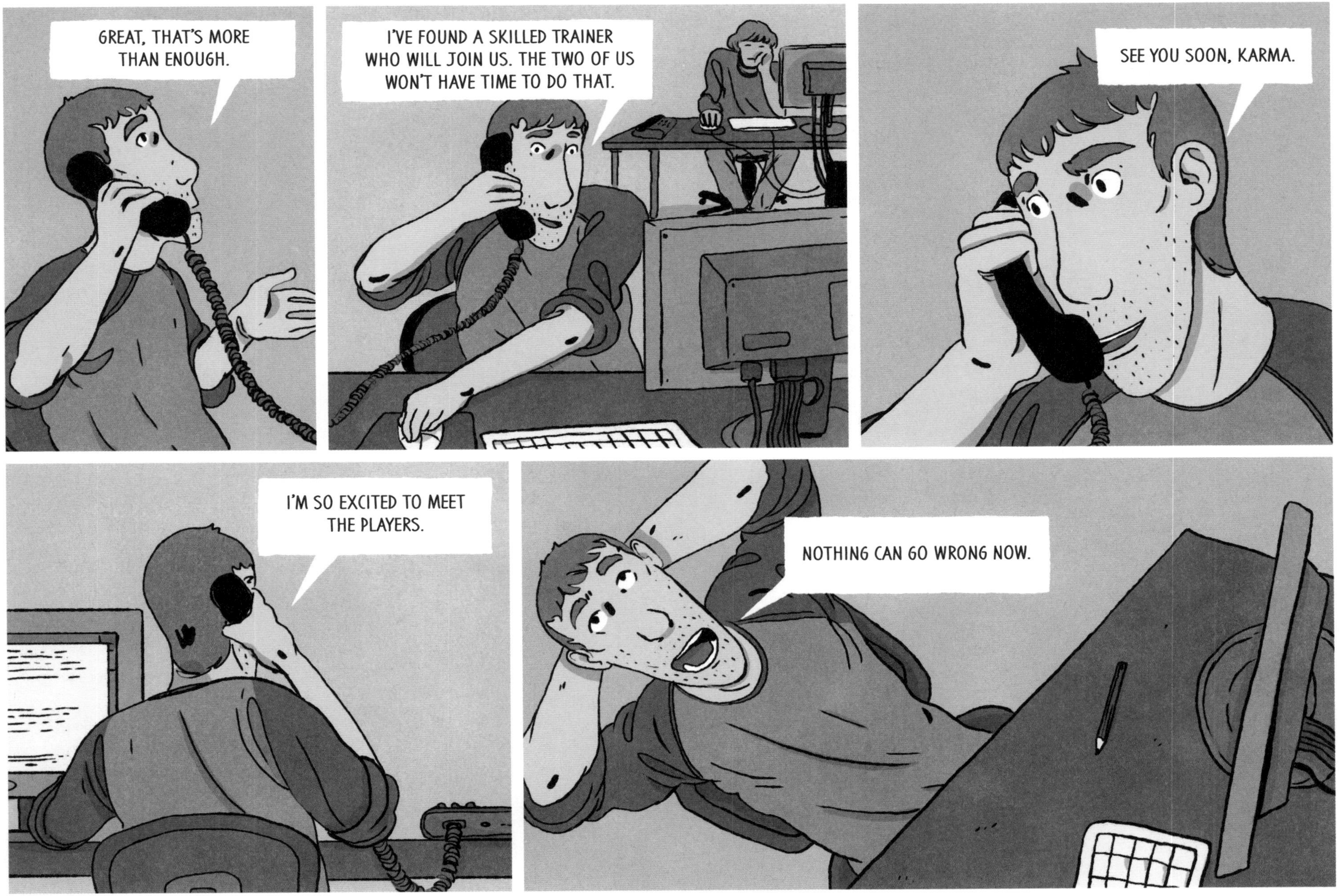
GREAT, THAT'S MORE THAN ENOUGH.
I'VE FOUND A SKILLED TRAINER WHO WILL JOIN US. THE TWO OF US WON'T HAVE TIME TO DO THAT.
SEE YOU SOON, KARMA.
I'M SO EXCITED TO MEET THE PLAYERS.
NOTHING CAN GO WRONG NOW.

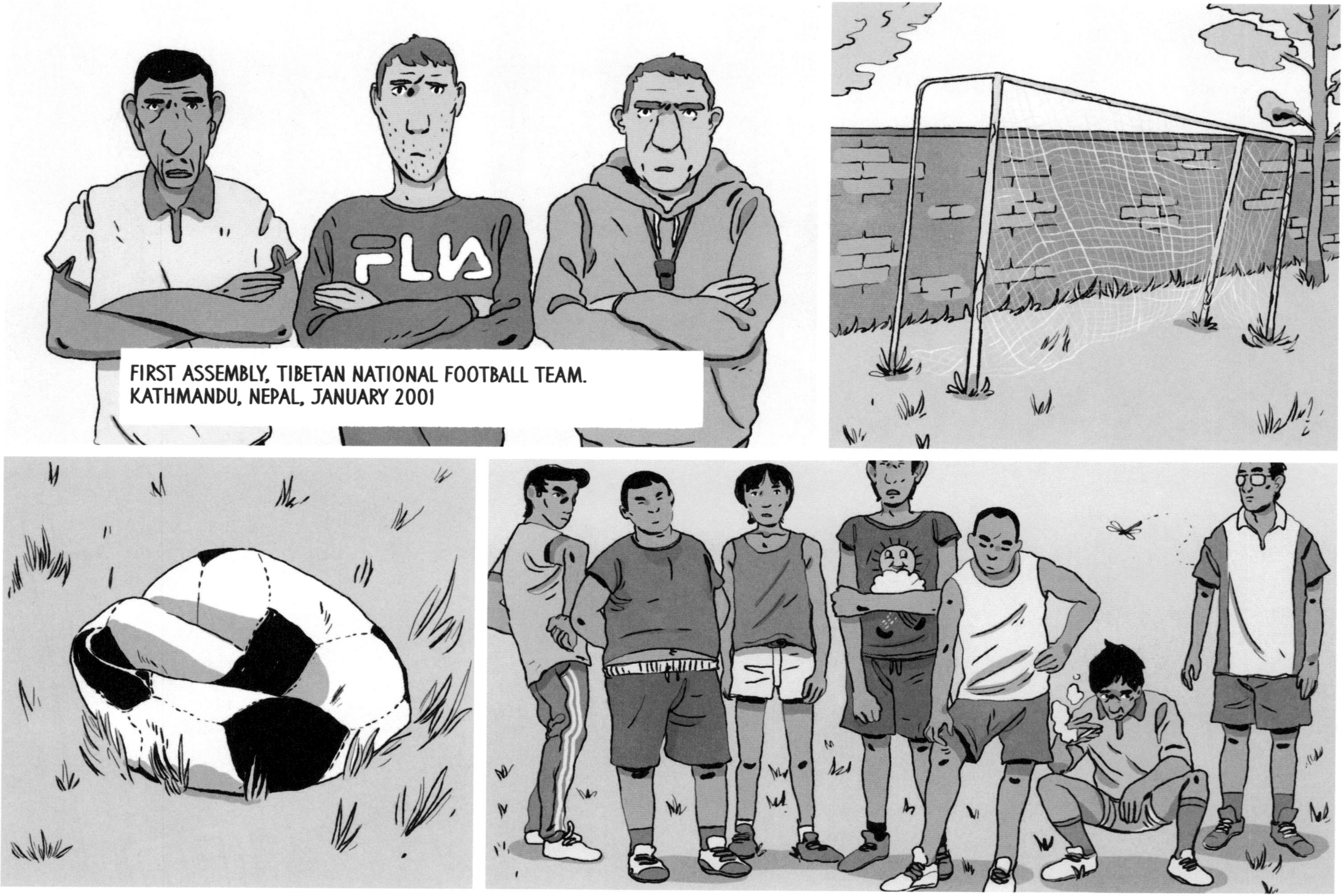
FIRST ASSEMBLY, TIBETAN NATIONAL FOOTBALL TEAM.
KATHMANDU, NEPAL, JANUARY 2001

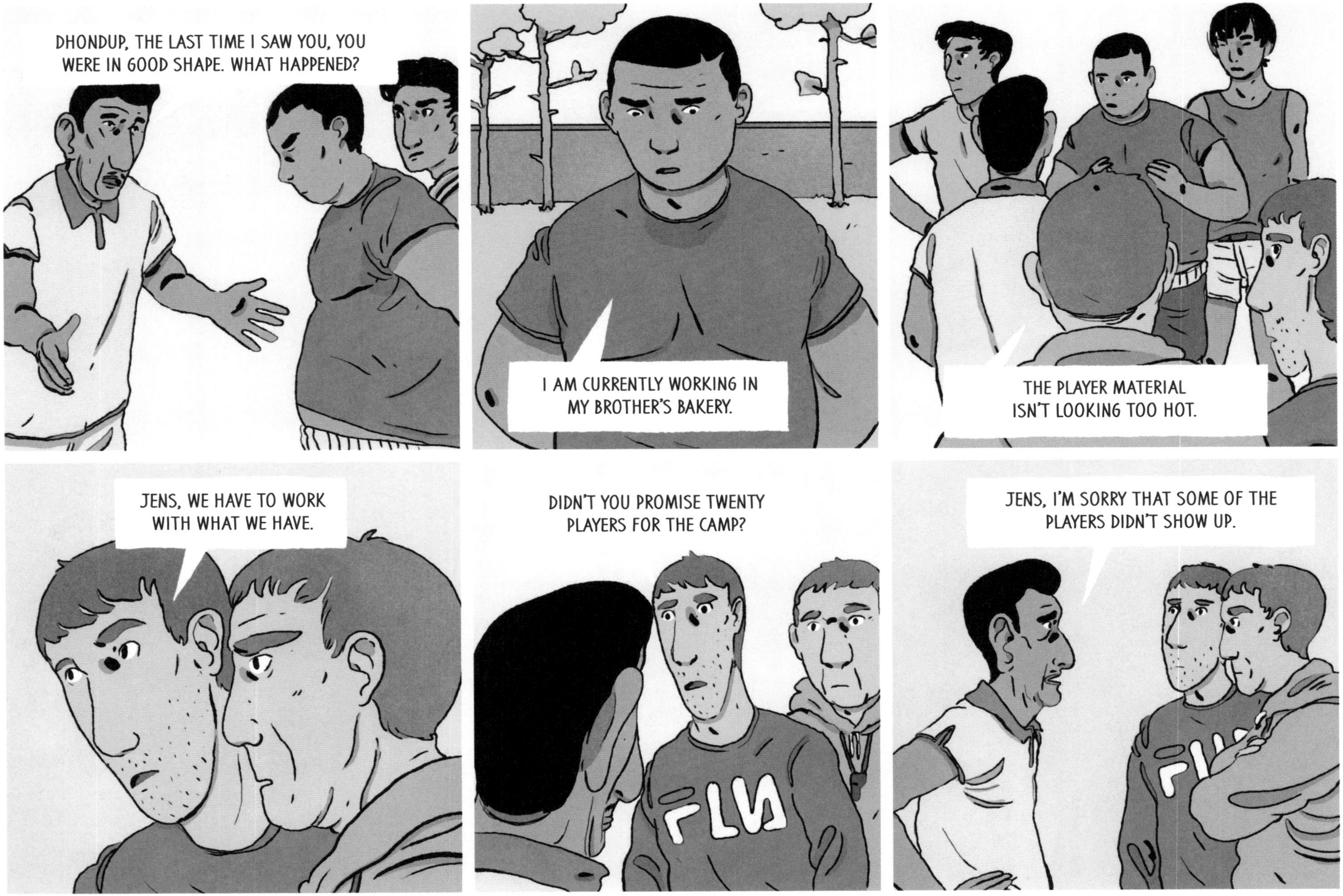
DHONDUP, THE LAST TIME I SAW YOU, YOU WERE IN GOOD SHAPE. WHAT HAPPENED?
I AM CURRENTLY WORKING IN MY BROTHER'S BAKERY.
THE PLAYER MATERIAL ISN'T LOOKING TOO HOT.
JENS, WE HAVE TO WORK WITH WHAT WE HAVE.
DIDN'T YOU PROMISE TWENTY PLAYERS FOR THE CAMP?
JENS, I'M SORRY THAT SOME OF THE PLAYERS DIDN'T SHOW UP.

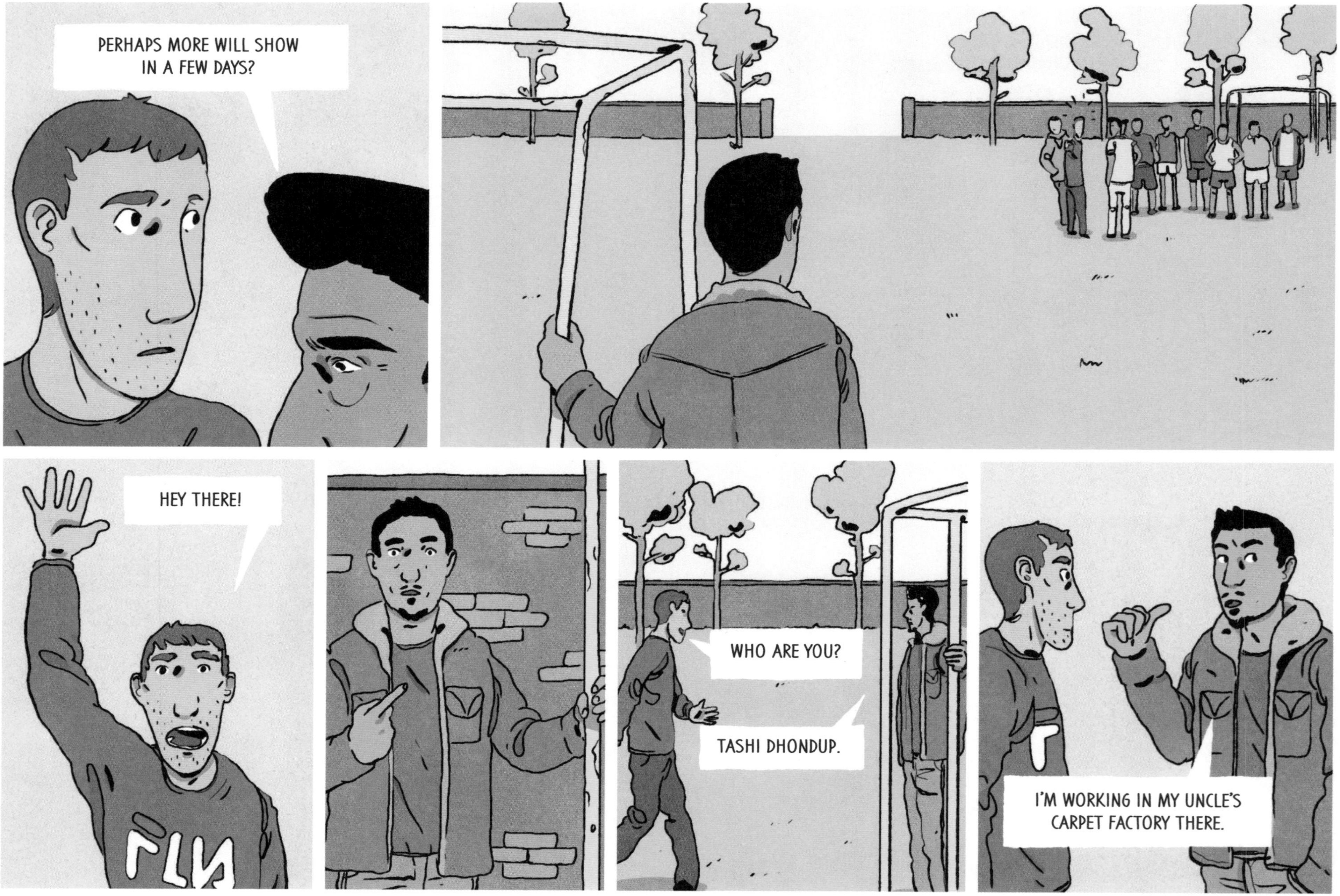
PERHAPS MORE WILL SHOW IN A FEW DAYS?
HEY THERE!
WHO ARE YOU?
TASHI DHONDUP.
I'M WORKING IN MY UNCLE'S CARPET FACTORY THERE.

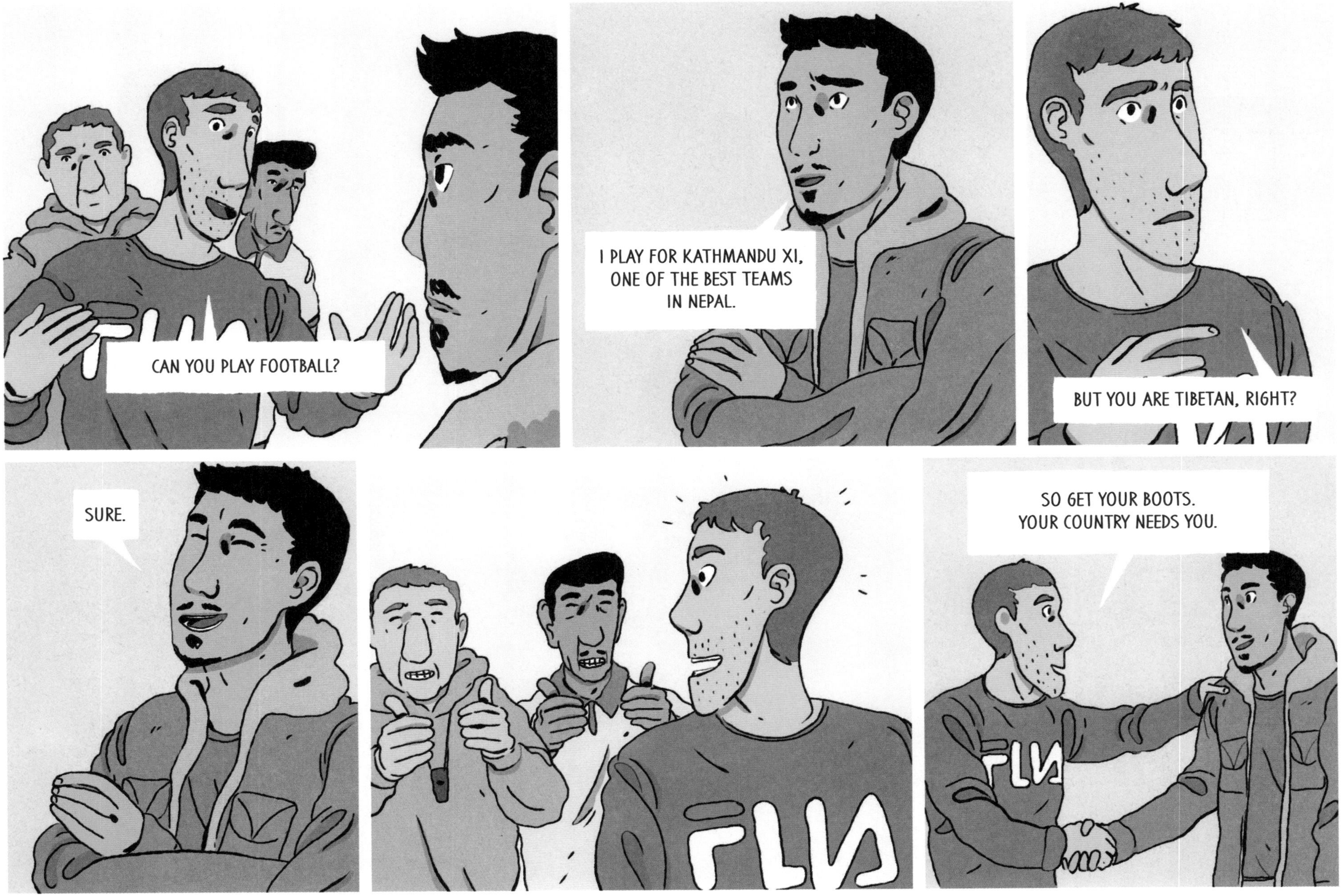
CAN YOU PLAY FOOTBALL?
I PLAY FOR KATHMANDU XI, ONE OF THE BEST TEAMS IN NEPAL.
BUT YOU ARE TIBETAN, RIGHT?
SURE.
SO GET YOUR BOOTS. YOUR COUNTRY NEEDS YOU.

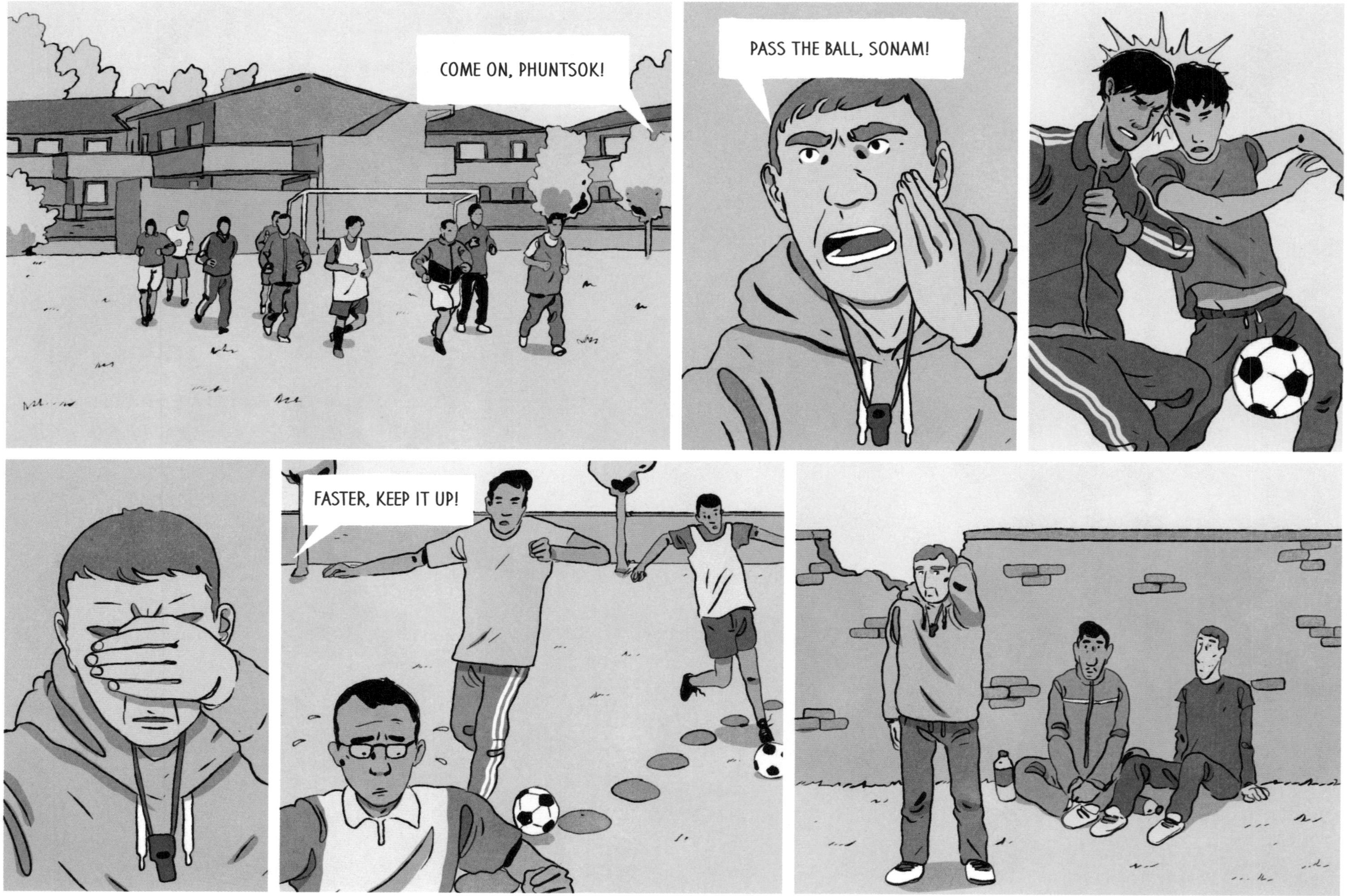
COME ON, PHUNTSOK!
PASS THE BALL, SONAM!
FASTER, KEEP IT UP!

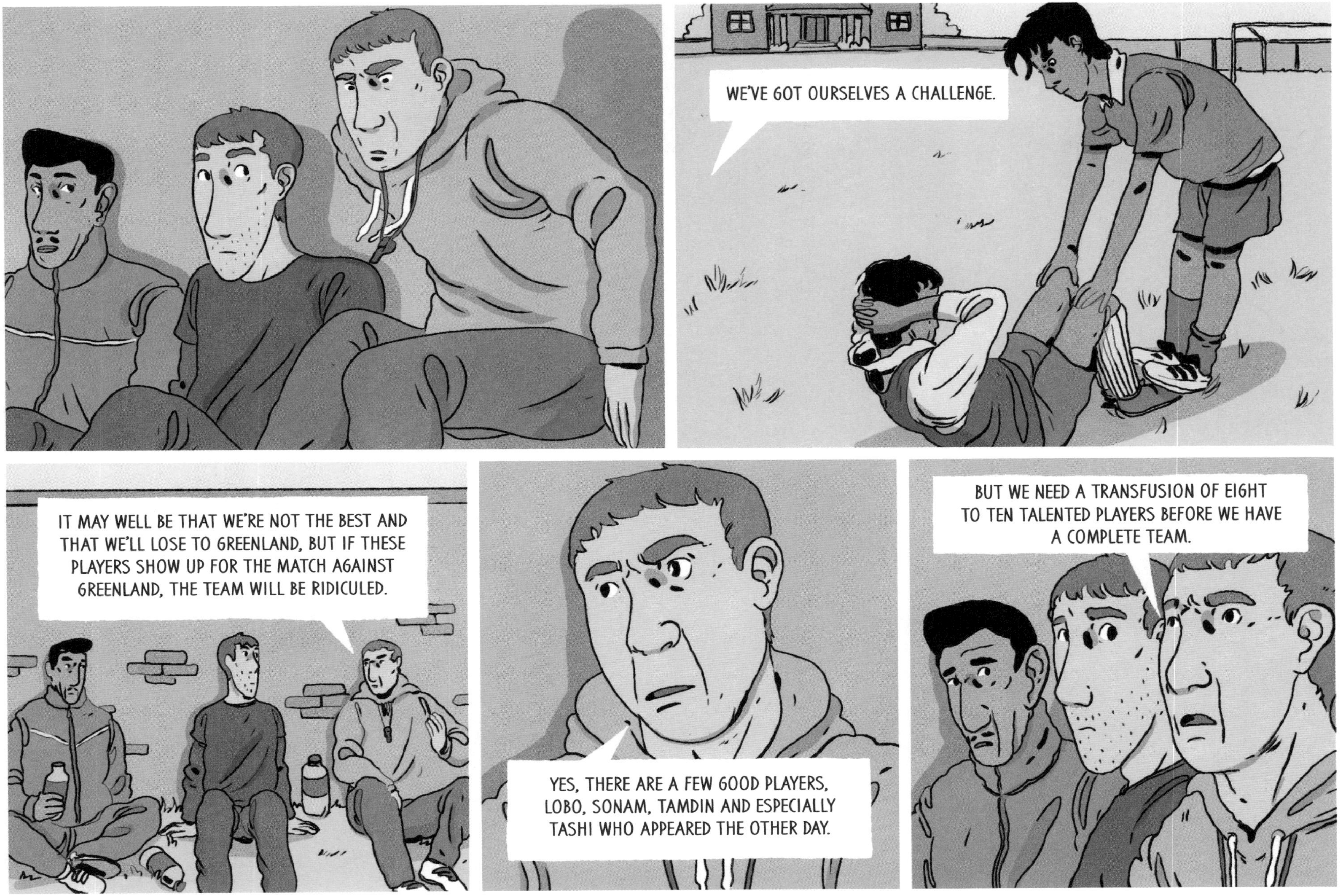
WE'VE GOT OURSELVES A CHALLENGE.
IT MAY WELL BE THAT WE'RE NOT THE BEST AND THAT WE'LL LOSE TO GREENLAND, BUT IF THESE PLAYERS SHOW UP FOR THE MATCH AGAINST GREENLAND, THE TEAM WILL BE RIDICULED.
YES, THERE ARE A FEW GOOD PLAYERS, LOBO, SONAM, TAMDIN AND ESPECIALLY TASHI WHO APPEARED THE OTHER DAY.
BUT WE NEED A TRANSFUSION OF EIGHT TO TEN TALENTED PLAYERS BEFORE WE HAVE A COMPLETE TEAM.

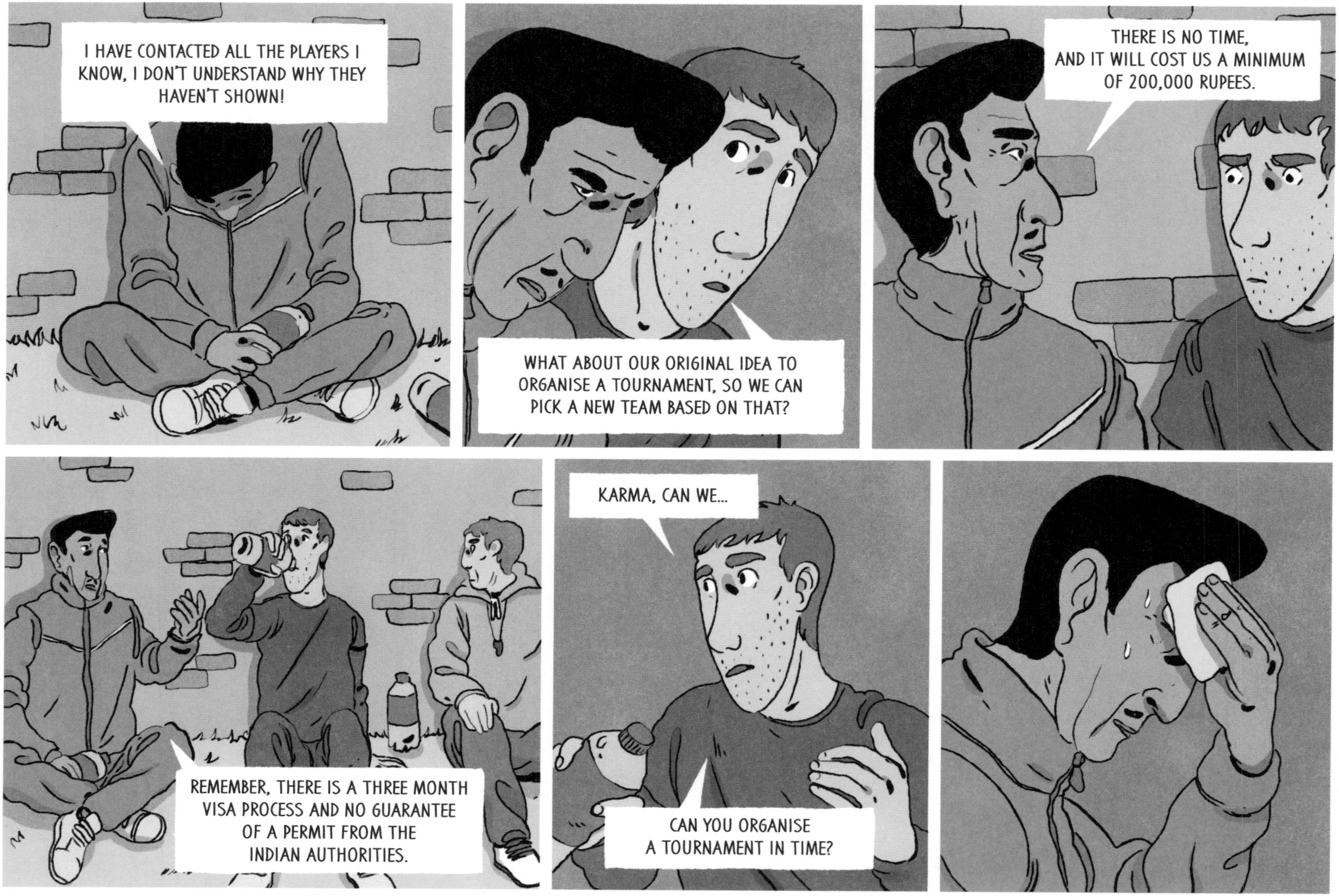
I HAVE CONTACTED ALL THE PLAYERS I KNOW, I DON'T UNDERSTAND WHY THEY HAVEN'T SHOWN!
WHAT ABOUT OUR ORIGINAL IDEA TO ORGANISE A TOURNAMENT, SO WE CAN PICK A NEW TEAM BASED ON THAT?
THERE IS NO TIME, AND IT WILL COST US A MINIMUM OF 200,000 RUPEES.
REMEMBER, THERE IS A THREE MONTH VISA PROCESS AND NO GUARANTEE OF A PERMIT FROM THE INDIAN AUTHORITIES.
KARMA, CAN WE...
CAN YOU ORGANISE A TOURNAMENT IN TIME?

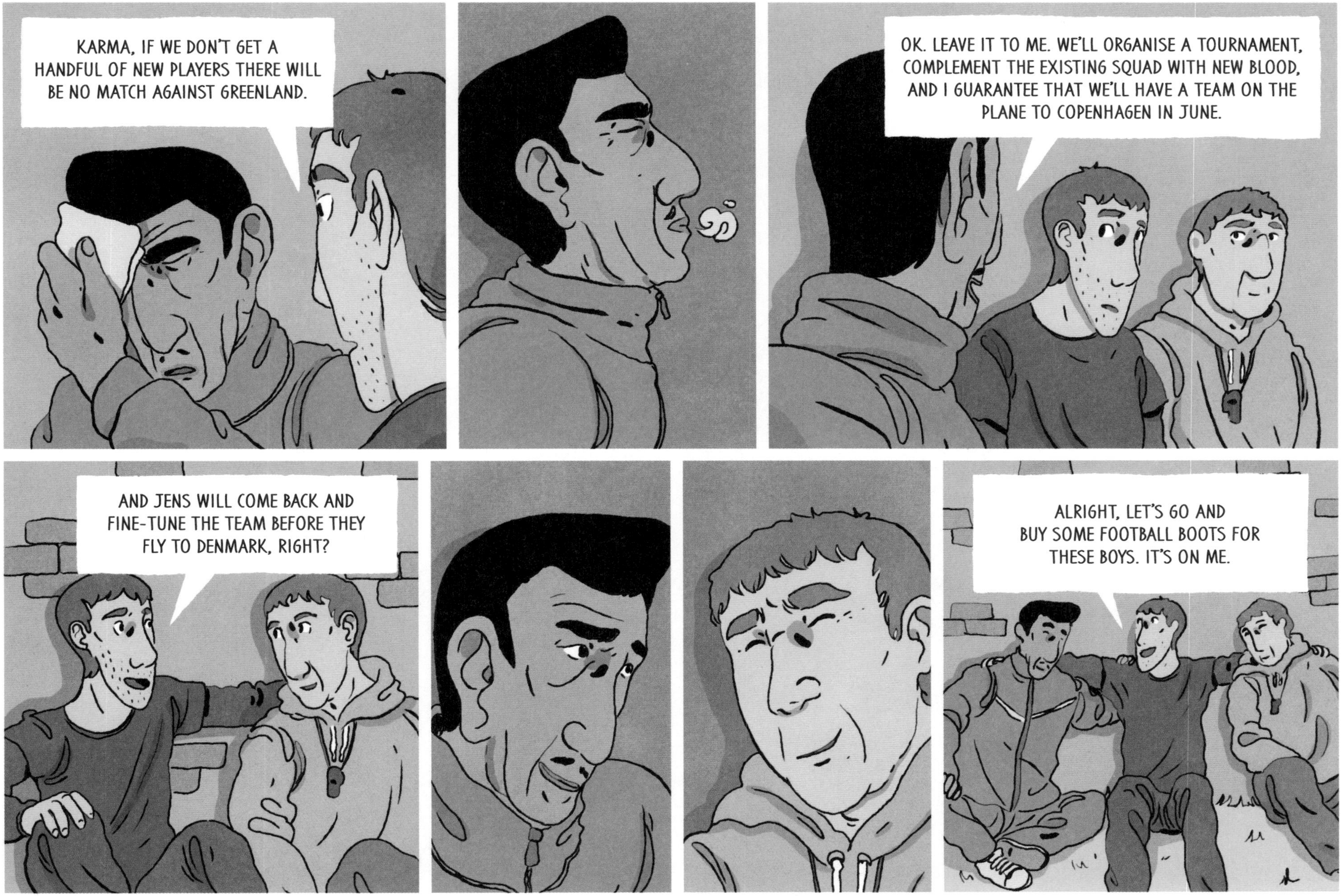
KARMA, IF WE DON'T GET A HANDFUL OF NEW PLAYERS THERE WILL BE NO MATCH AGAINST GREENLAND.
OK. LEAVE IT TO ME. WE'LL ORGANISE A TOURNAMENT, COMPLEMENT THE EXISTING SQUAD WITH NEW BLOOD, AND I GUARANTEE THAT WE'LL HAVE A TEAM ON THE PLANE TO COPENHAGEN IN JUNE.
AND JENS WILL COME BACK AND FINE-TUNE THE TEAM BEFORE THEY FLY TO DENMARK, RIGHT?
ALRIGHT, LET'S GO AND BUY SOME FOOTBALL BOOTS FOR THESE BOYS. IT'S ON ME.

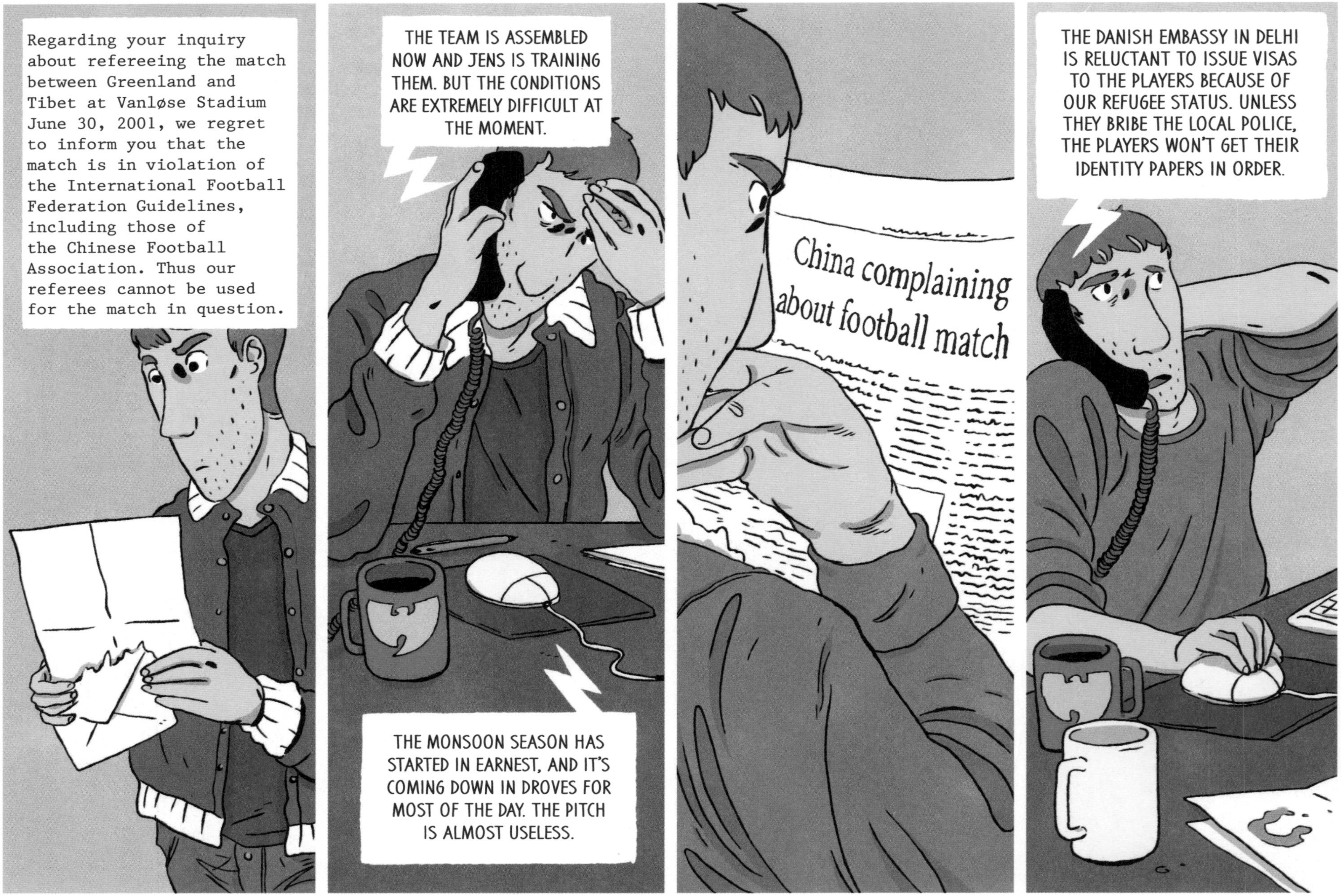
Regarding your inquiry about refereeing the match between Greenland and Tibet at Vanløse Stadium June 30, 2001, we regret to inform you that the match is in violation of the International Football Federation Guidelines, including those of the Chinese Football Association. Thus our referees cannot be used for the match in question.
THE TEAM IS ASSEMBLED NOW AND JENS IS TRAINING THEM. BUT THE CONDITIONS ARE EXTREMELY DIFFICULT AT THE MOMENT.
THE MONSOON SEASON HAS STARTED IN EARNEST, AND IT'S COMING DOWN IN DROVES FOR MOST OF THE DAY. THE PITCH IS ALMOST USELESS.
China complaining about football match
THE DANISH EMBASSY IN DELHI IS RELUCTANT TO ISSUE VISAS TO THE PLAYERS BECAUSE OF OUR REFUGEE STATUS. UNLESS THEY BRIBE THE LOCAL POLICE, THE PLAYERS WON'T GET THEIR IDENTITY PAPERS IN ORDER.

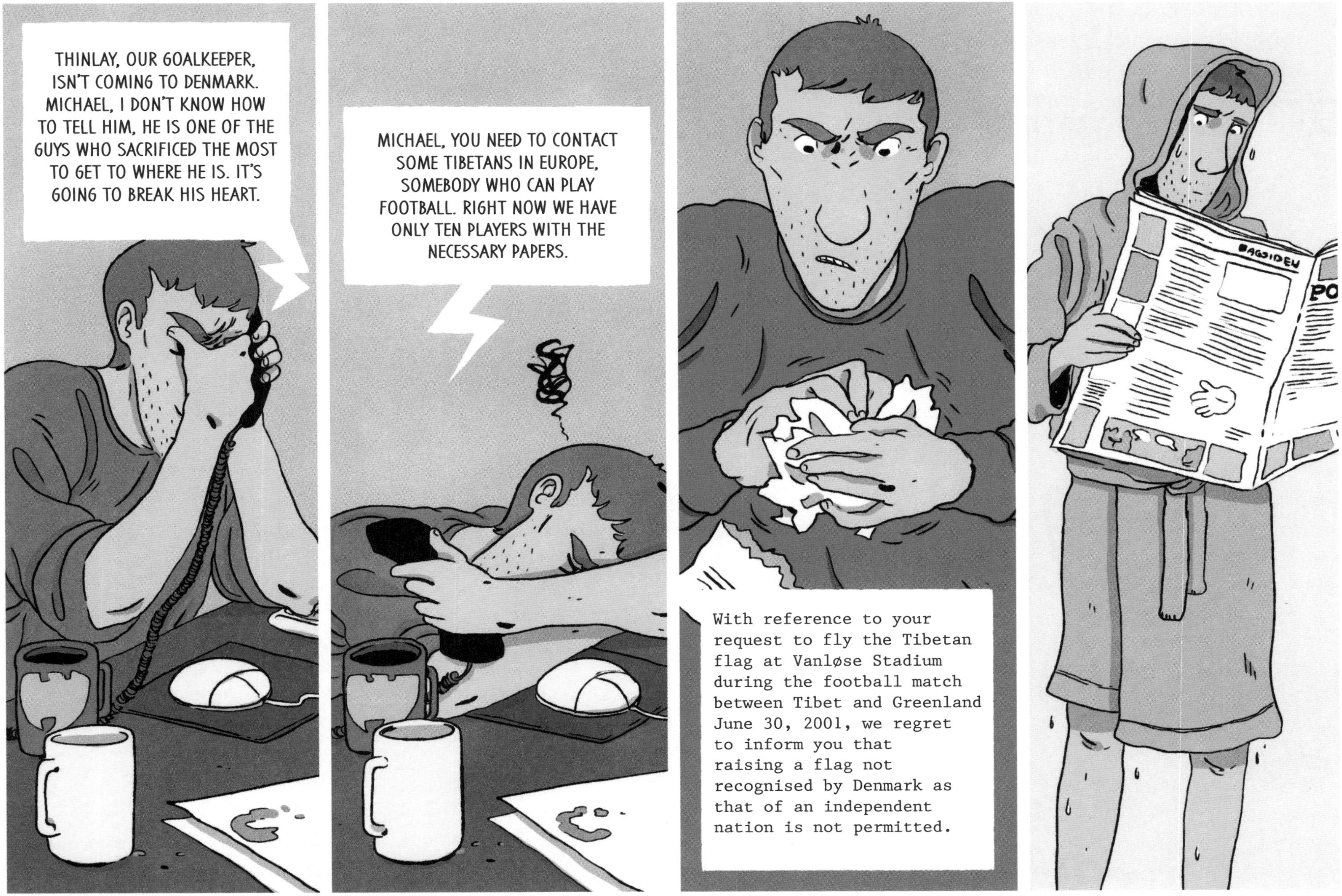
THINLAY, OUR GOALKEEPER, ISN'T COMING TO DENMARK. MICHAEL, I DON'T KNOW HOW TO TELL HIM, HE IS ONE OF THE GUYS WHO SACRIFICED THE MOST TO GET TO WHERE HE IS. IT'S GOING TO BREAK HIS HEART.
MICHAEL, YOU NEED TO CONTACT SOME TIBETANS IN EUROPE, SOMEBODY WHO CAN PLAY FOOTBALL. RIGHT NOW WE HAVE ONLY TEN PLAYERS WITH THE NECESSARY PAPERS.
With reference to your request to fly the Tibetan flag at Vanløse Stadium during the football match between Tibet and Greenland June 30, 2001, we regret to inform you that raising a flag not recognised by Denmark as that of an independent nation is not permitted.
BAGSIDEN

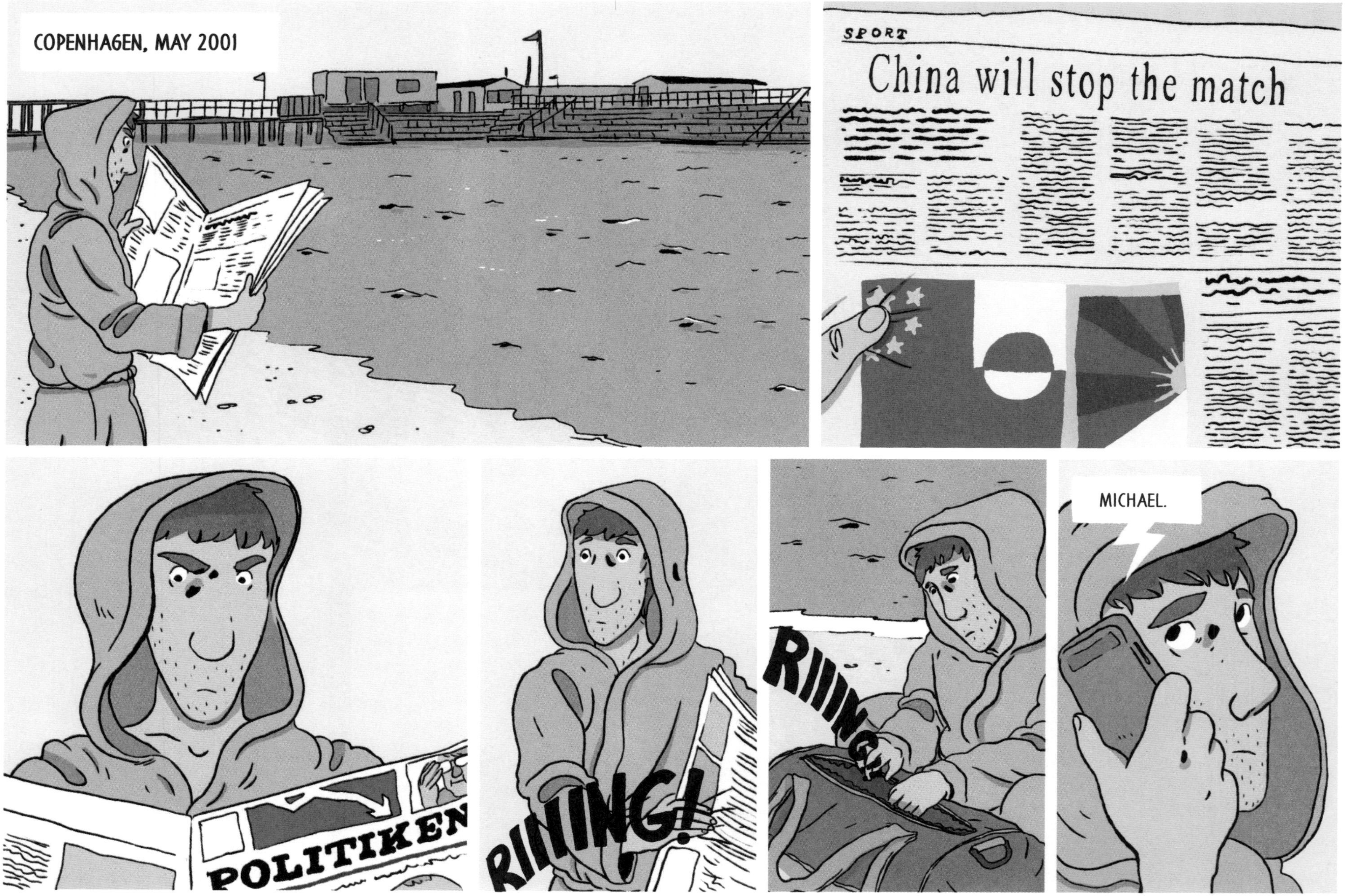
COPENHAGEN, MAY 2001
SPORT
China will stop the match
POLITIKEN
RIIIING!
RIIIING!
MICHAEL.

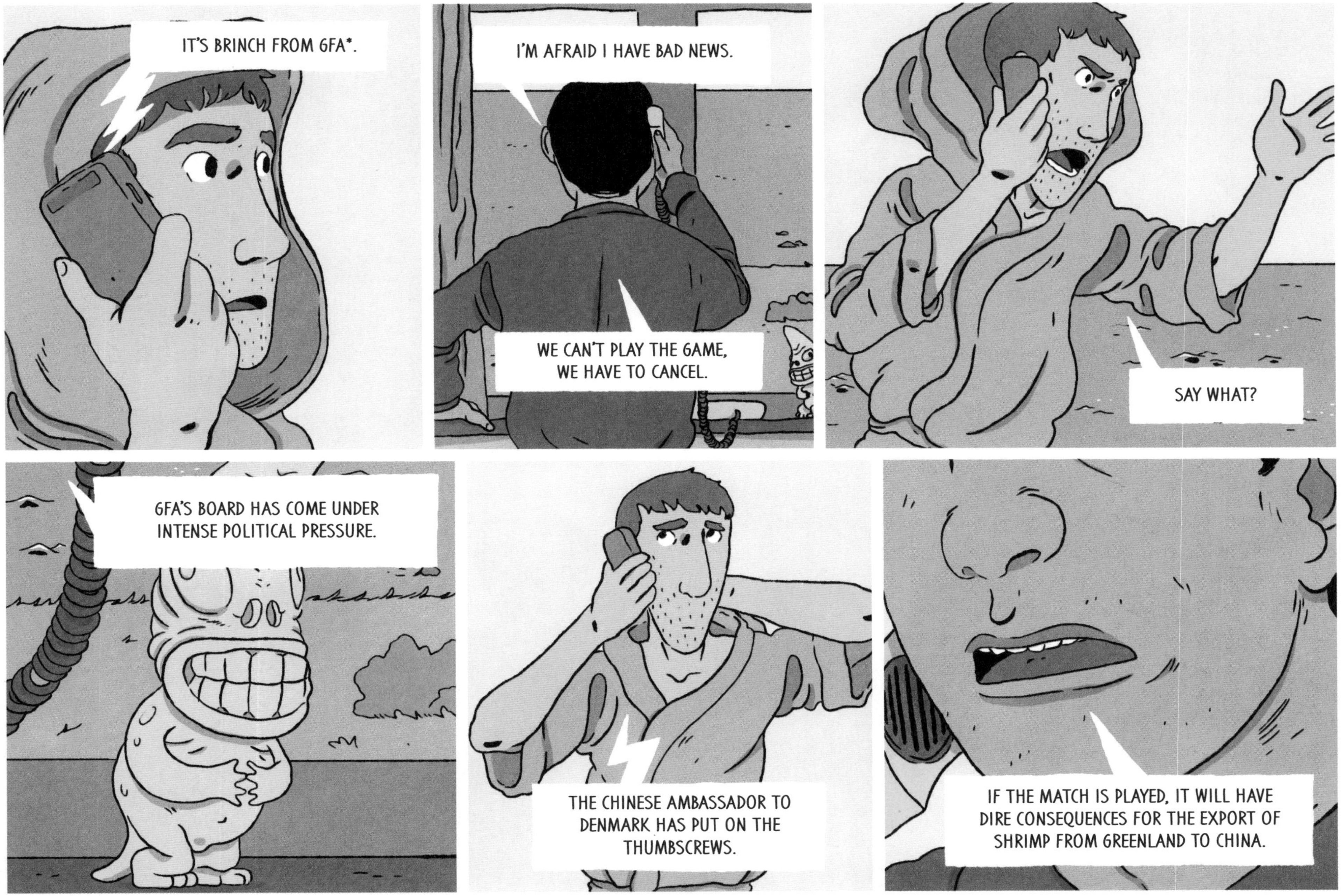
IT'S BRINCH FROM GFA*.
I'M AFRAID I HAVE BAD NEWS.
WE CAN'T PLAY THE GAME, WE HAVE TO CANCEL.
SAY WHAT?
GFA'S BOARD HAS COME UNDER INTENSE POLITICAL PRESSURE.
THE CHINESE AMBASSADOR TO DENMARK HAS PUT ON THE THUMBSCREWS.
IF THE MATCH IS PLAYED, IT WILL HAVE DIRE CONSEQUENCES FOR THE EXPORT OF SHRIMP FROM GREENLAND TO CHINA.

*GREENLAND'S FOOTBALL ASSOCIATION

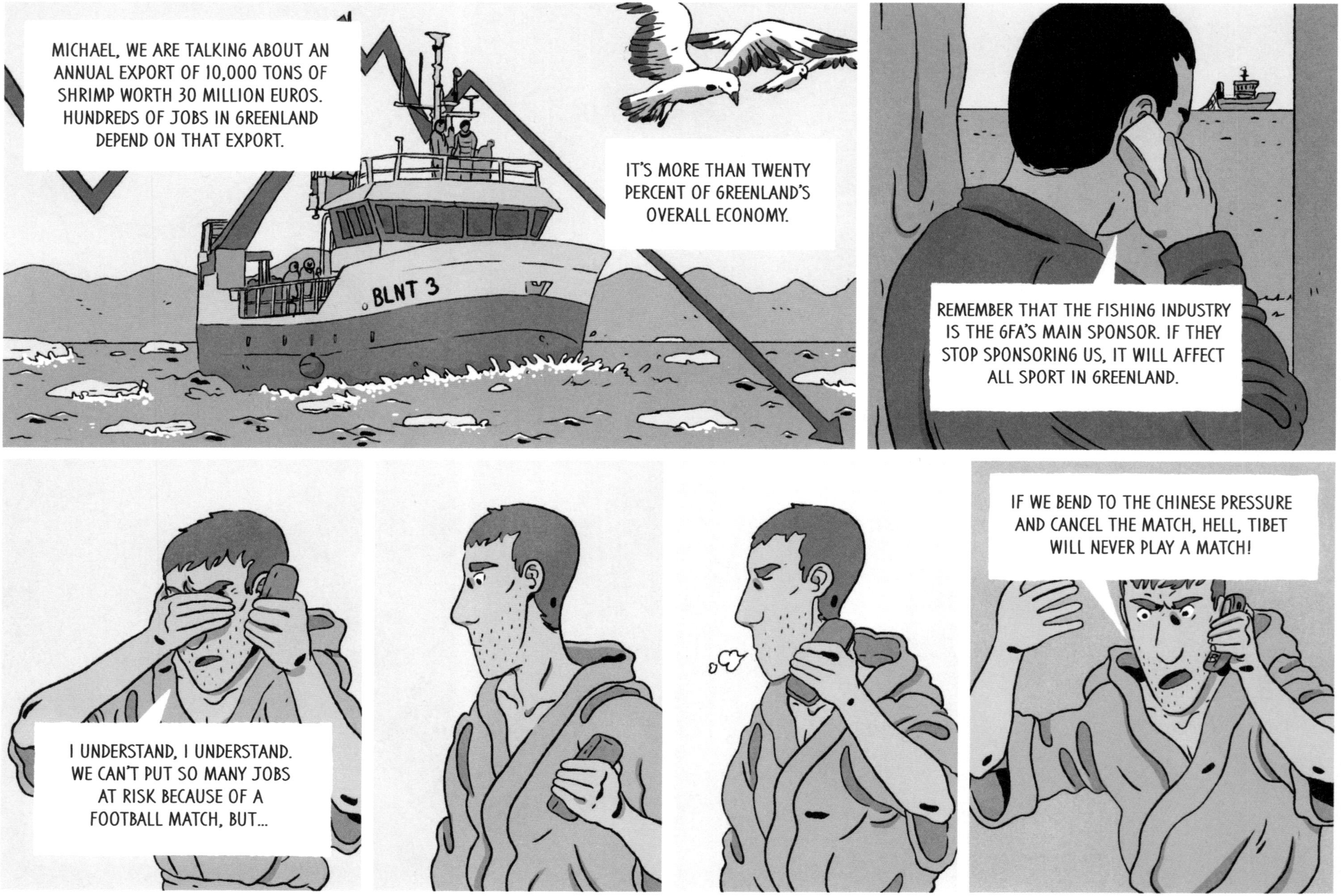
MICHAEL, WE ARE TALKING ABOUT AN ANNUAL EXPORT OF 10,000 TONS OF SHRIMP WORTH 30 MILLION EUROS. HUNDREDS OF JOBS IN GREENLAND DEPEND ON THAT EXPORT.
BLNT 3
IT'S MORE THAN TWENTY PERCENT OF GREENLAND'S OVERALL ECONOMY.
REMEMBER THAT THE FISHING INDUSTRY IS THE GFA'S MAIN SPONSOR. IF THEY STOP SPONSORING US, IT WILL AFFECT ALL SPORT IN GREENLAND.
I UNDERSTAND, I UNDERSTAND. WE CAN'T PUT SO MANY JOBS AT RISK BECAUSE OF A FOOTBALL MATCH, BUT...
IF WE BEND TO THE CHINESE PRESSURE AND CANCEL THE MATCH, HELL, TIBET WILL NEVER PLAY A MATCH!

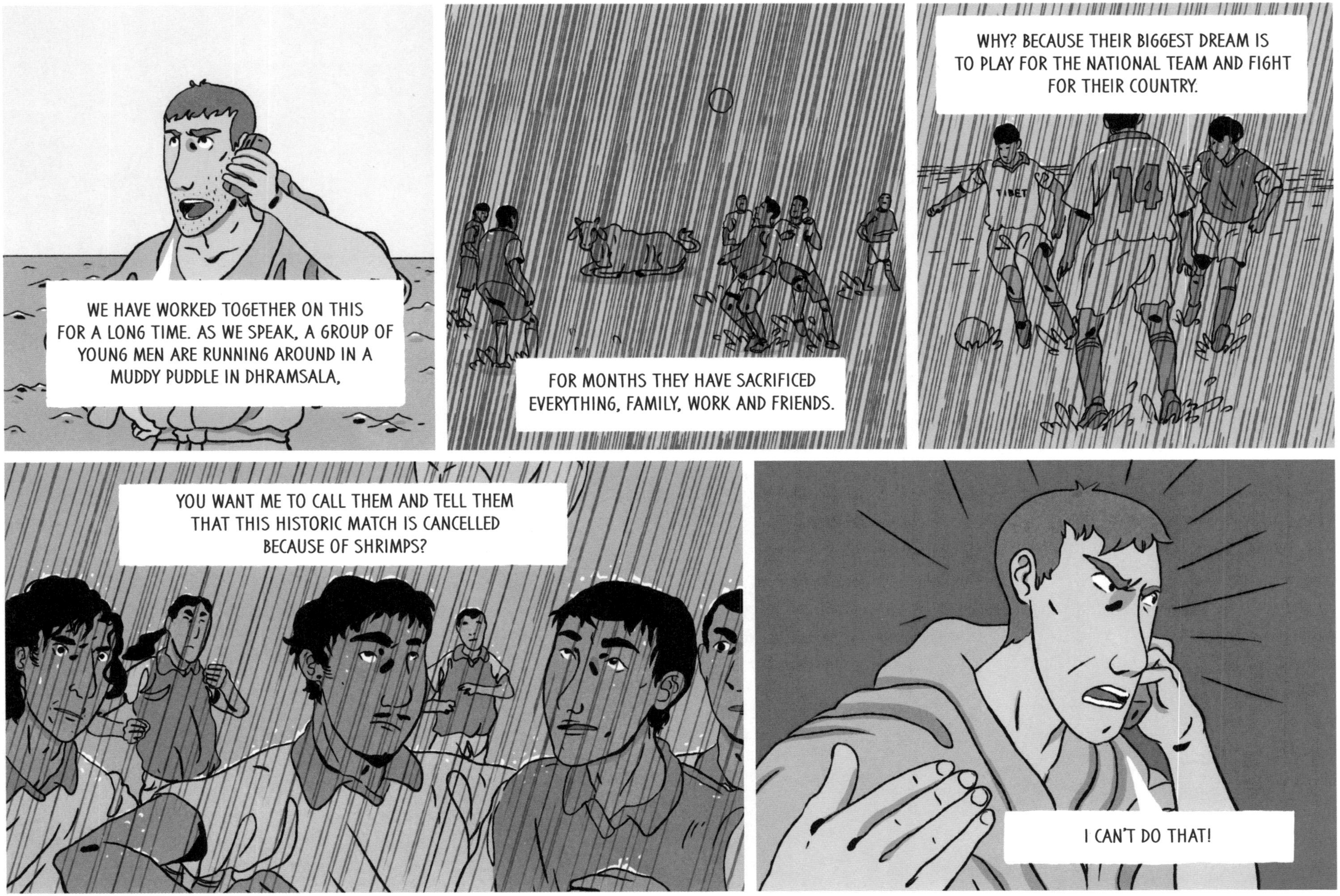
WE HAVE WORKED TOGETHER ON THIS FOR A LONG TIME. AS WE SPEAK, A GROUP OF YOUNG MEN ARE RUNNING AROUND IN A MUDDY PUDDLE IN DHRAMSALA,
FOR MONTHS THEY HAVE SACRIFICED EVERYTHING, FAMILY, WORK AND FRIENDS.
WHY? BECAUSE THEIR BIGGEST DREAM IS TO PLAY FOR THE NATIONAL TEAM AND FIGHT FOR THEIR COUNTRY.
TIBET
14
YOU WANT ME TO CALL THEM AND TELL THEM THAT THIS HISTORIC MATCH IS CANCELLED BECAUSE OF SHRIMPS?
I CAN'T DO THAT!

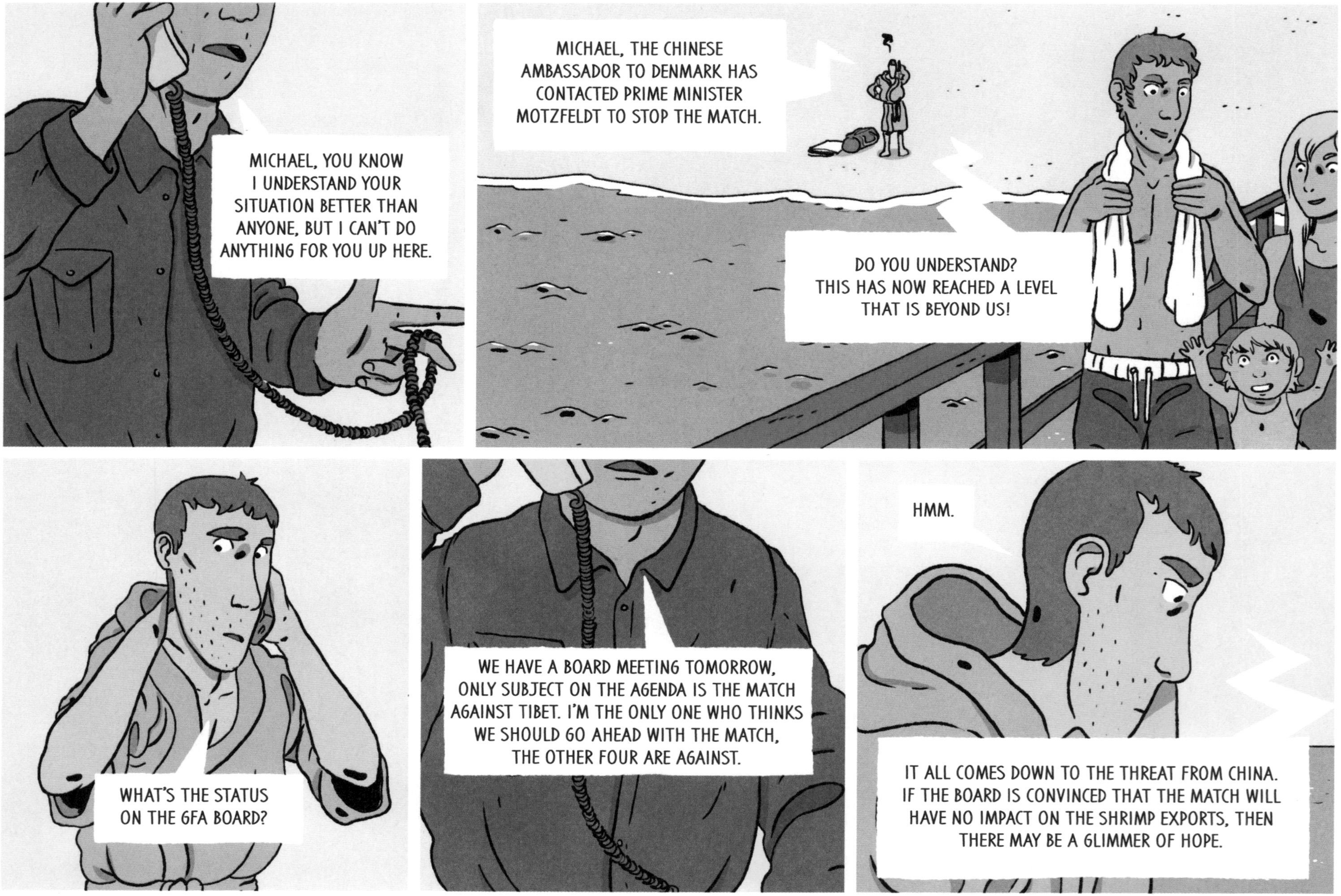
MICHAEL, YOU KNOW I UNDERSTAND YOUR SITUATION BETTER THAN ANYONE, BUT I CAN'T DO ANYTHING FOR YOU UP HERE.
MICHAEL, THE CHINESE AMBASSADOR TO DENMARK HAS CONTACTED PRIME MINISTER MOTZFELDT TO STOP THE MATCH.
DO YOU UNDERSTAND? THIS HAS NOW REACHED A LEVEL THAT IS BEYOND US!
WHAT'S THE STATUS ON THE GFA BOARD?
WE HAVE A BOARD MEETING TOMORROW, ONLY SUBJECT ON THE AGENDA IS THE MATCH AGAINST TIBET. I'M THE ONLY ONE WHO THINKS WE SHOULD GO AHEAD WITH THE MATCH, THE OTHER FOUR ARE AGAINST.
HMM.
IT ALL COMES DOWN TO THE THREAT FROM CHINA. IF THE BOARD IS CONVINCED THAT THE MATCH WILL HAVE NO IMPACT ON THE SHRIMP EXPORTS, THEN THERE MAY BE A GLIMMER OF HOPE.

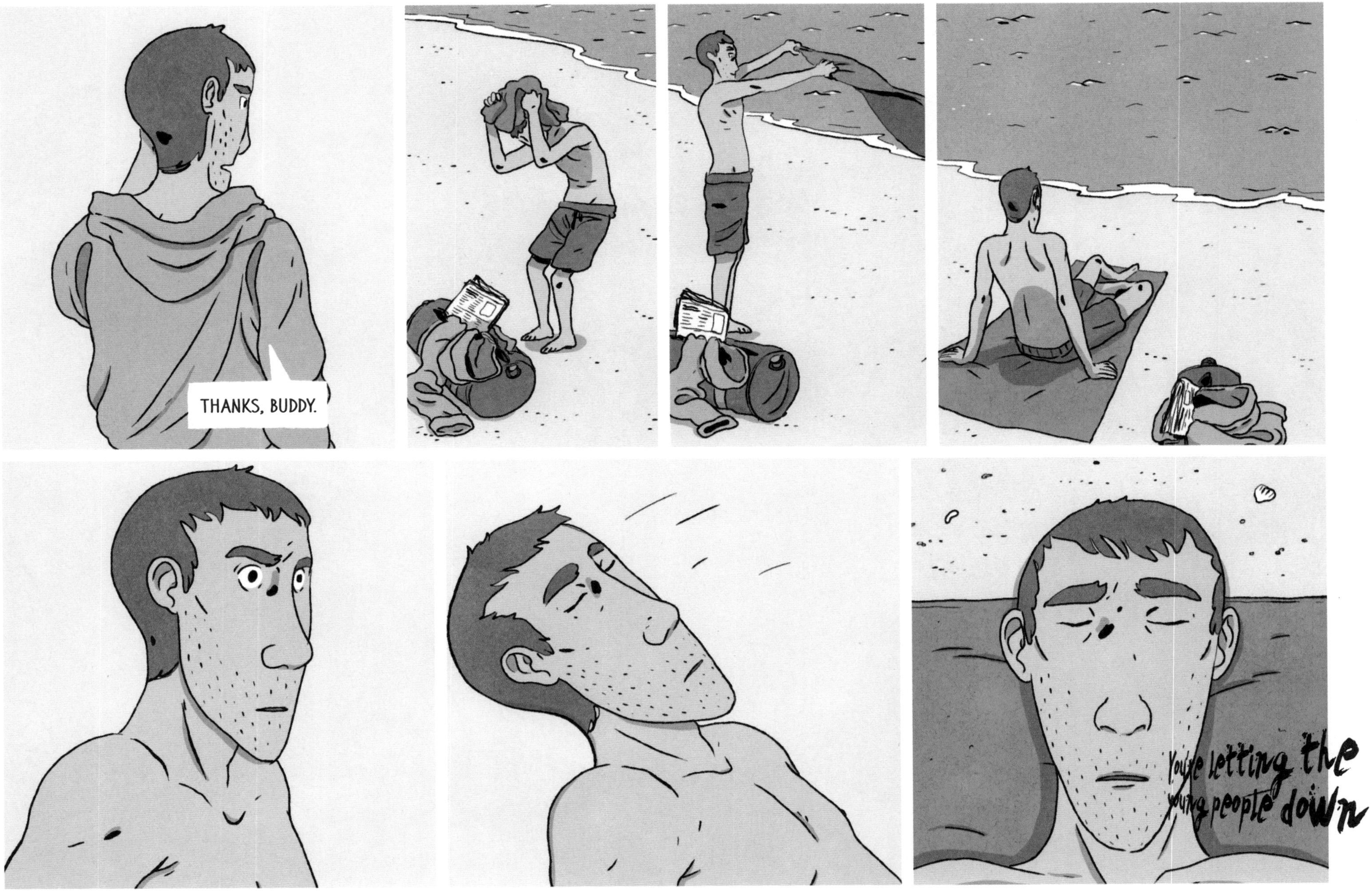
THANKS, BUDDY.
You're letting the young people down

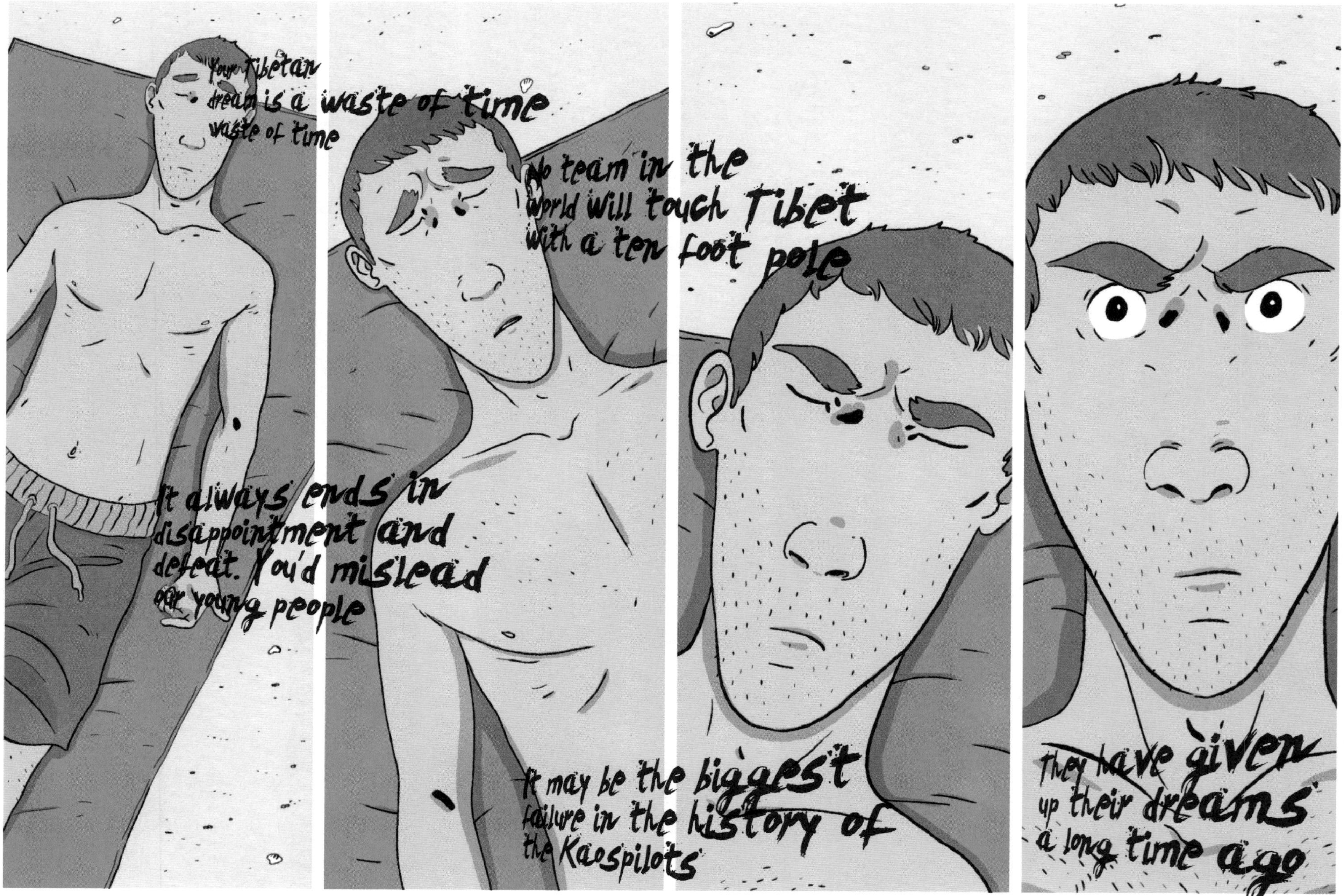
Your Tibetan dream is a waste of time waste of time
No team in the world will touch Tibet with a ten foot pole
It always ends in disappointment and defeat. You'd mislead our young people
It may be the biggest failure in the history of the Kaospilots
They have given up their dreams a long time ago

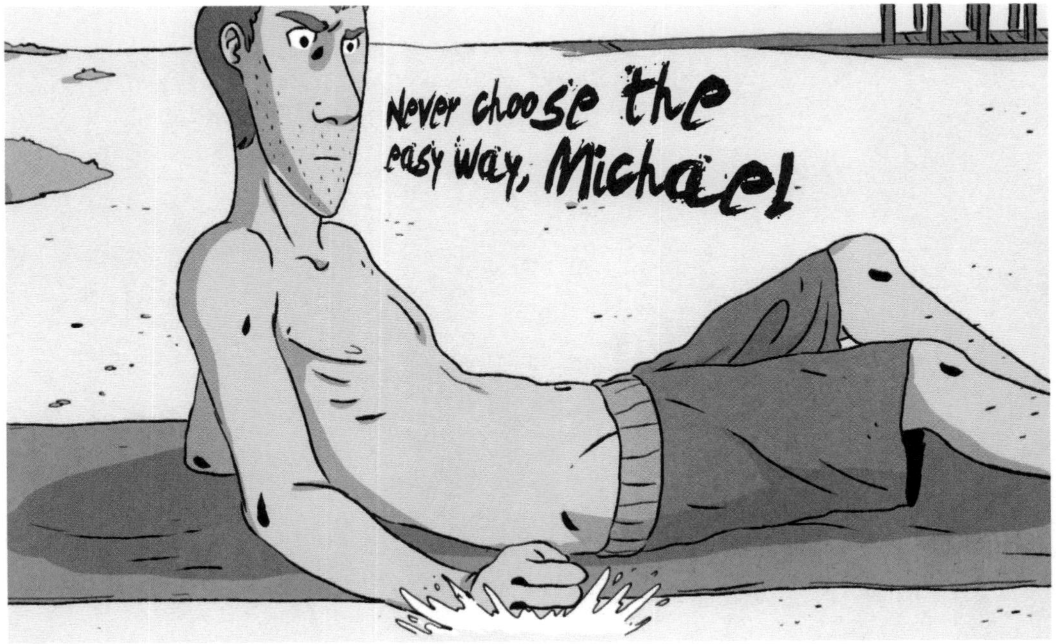
Never choose the easy way, Michael
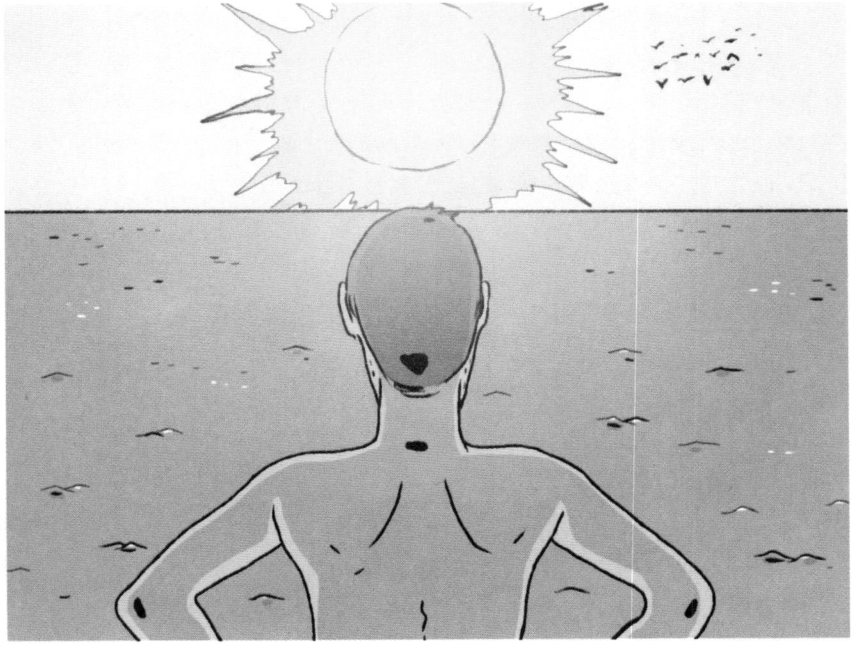
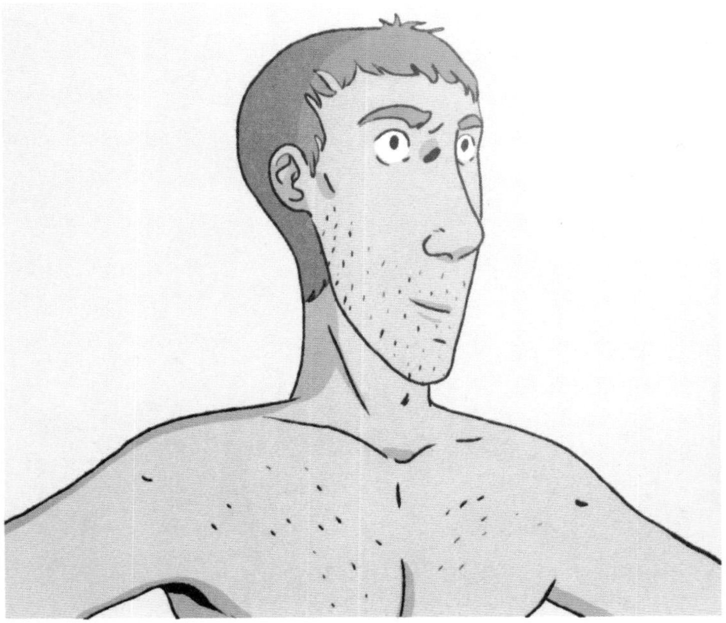
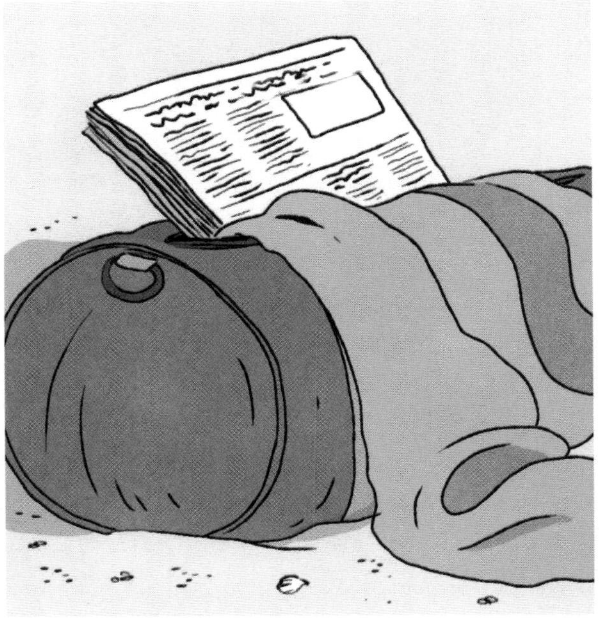
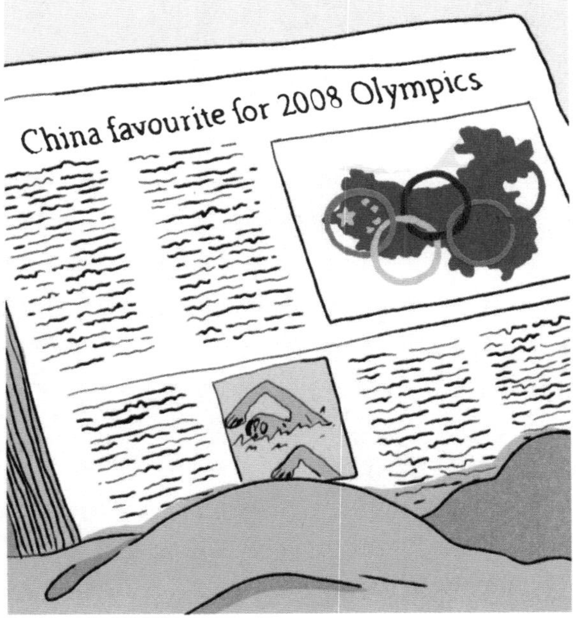
China favourite for 2008 Olympics

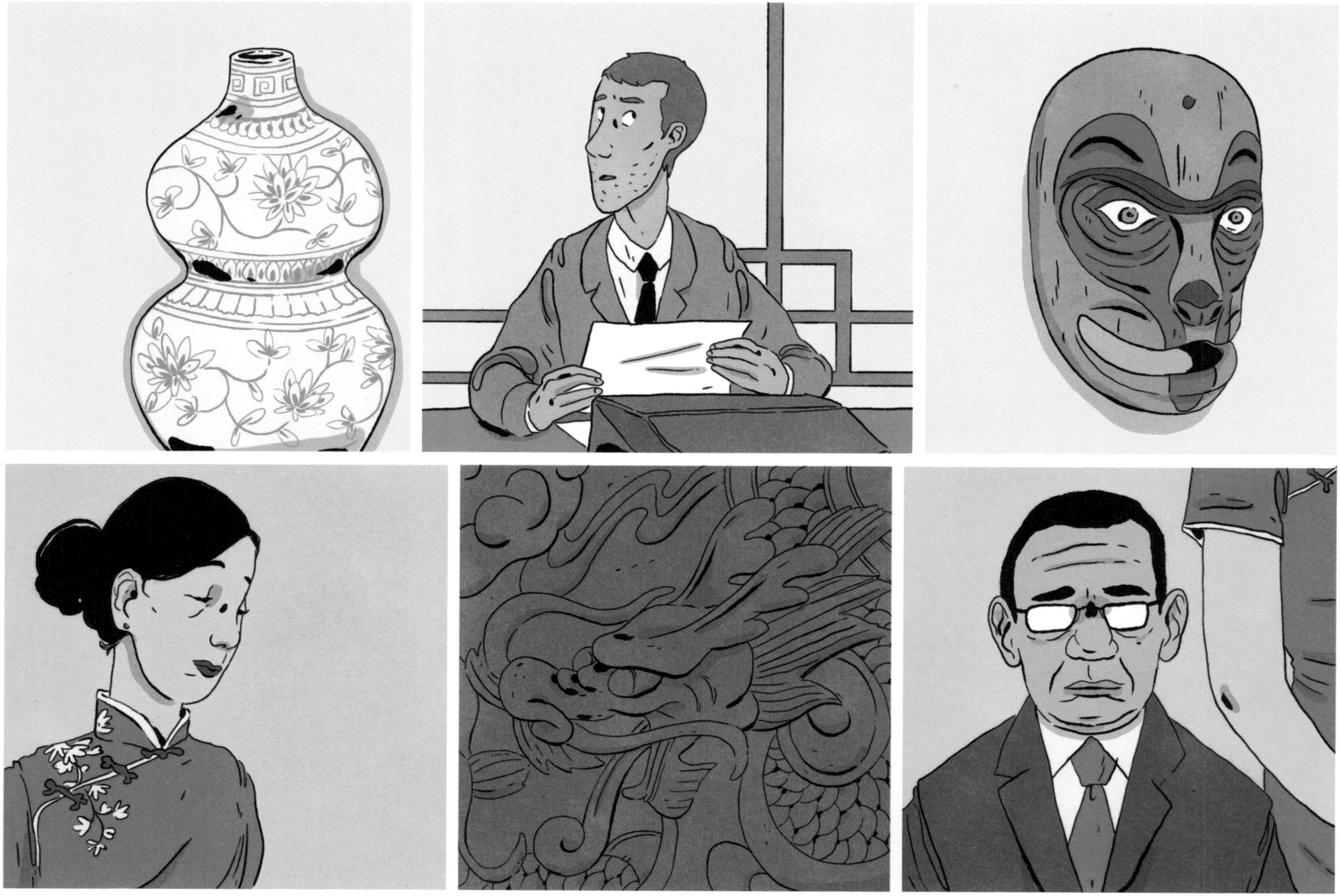

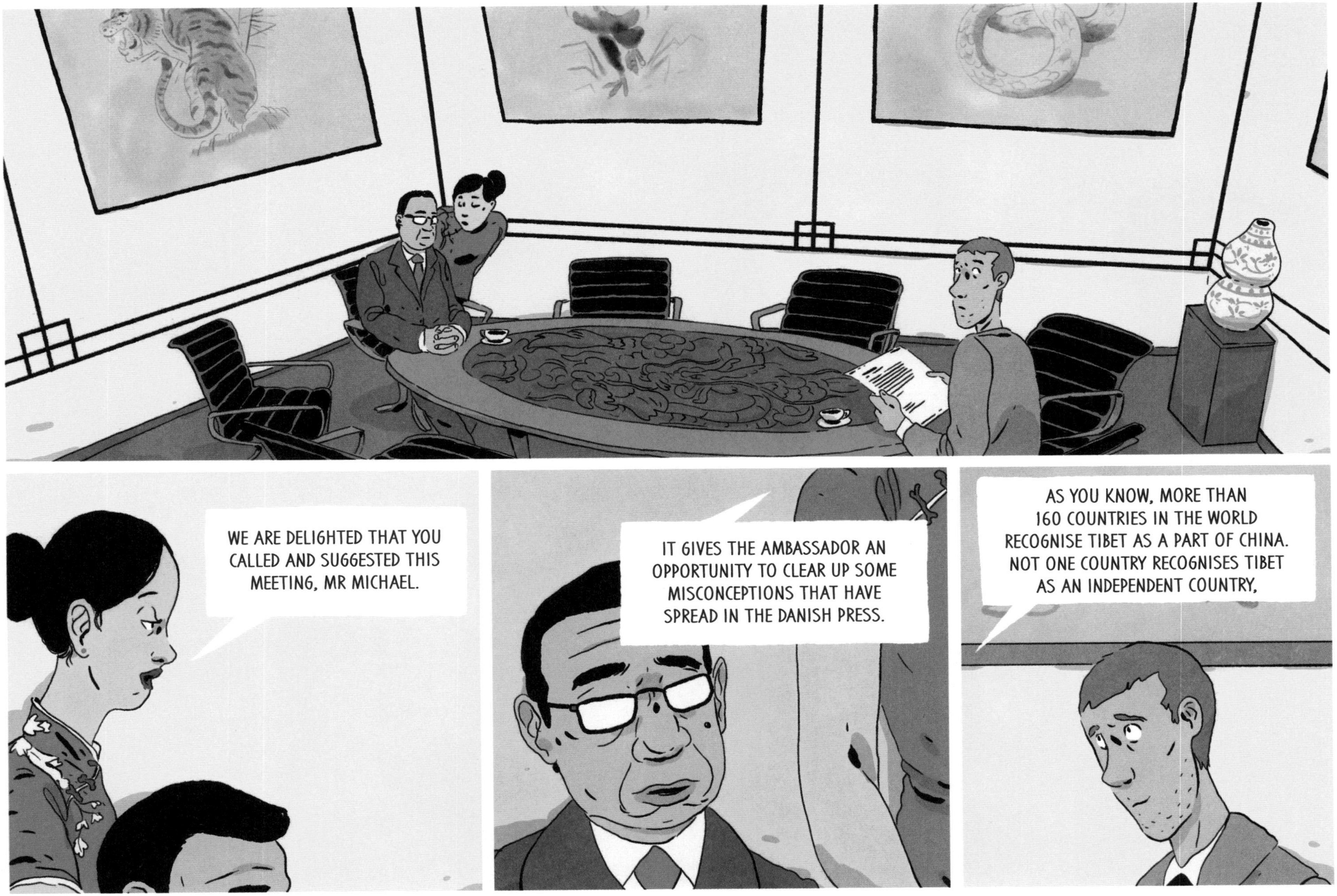
WE ARE DELIGHTED THAT YOU CALLED AND SUGGESTED THIS MEETING, MR MICHAEL.
IT GIVES THE AMBASSADOR AN OPPORTUNITY TO CLEAR UP SOME MISCONCEPTIONS THAT HAVE SPREAD IN THE DANISH PRESS.
AS YOU KNOW, MORE THAN 160 COUNTRIES IN THE WORLD RECOGNISE TIBET AS A PART OF CHINA. NOT ONE COUNTRY RECOGNISES TIBET AS AN INDEPENDENT COUNTRY,

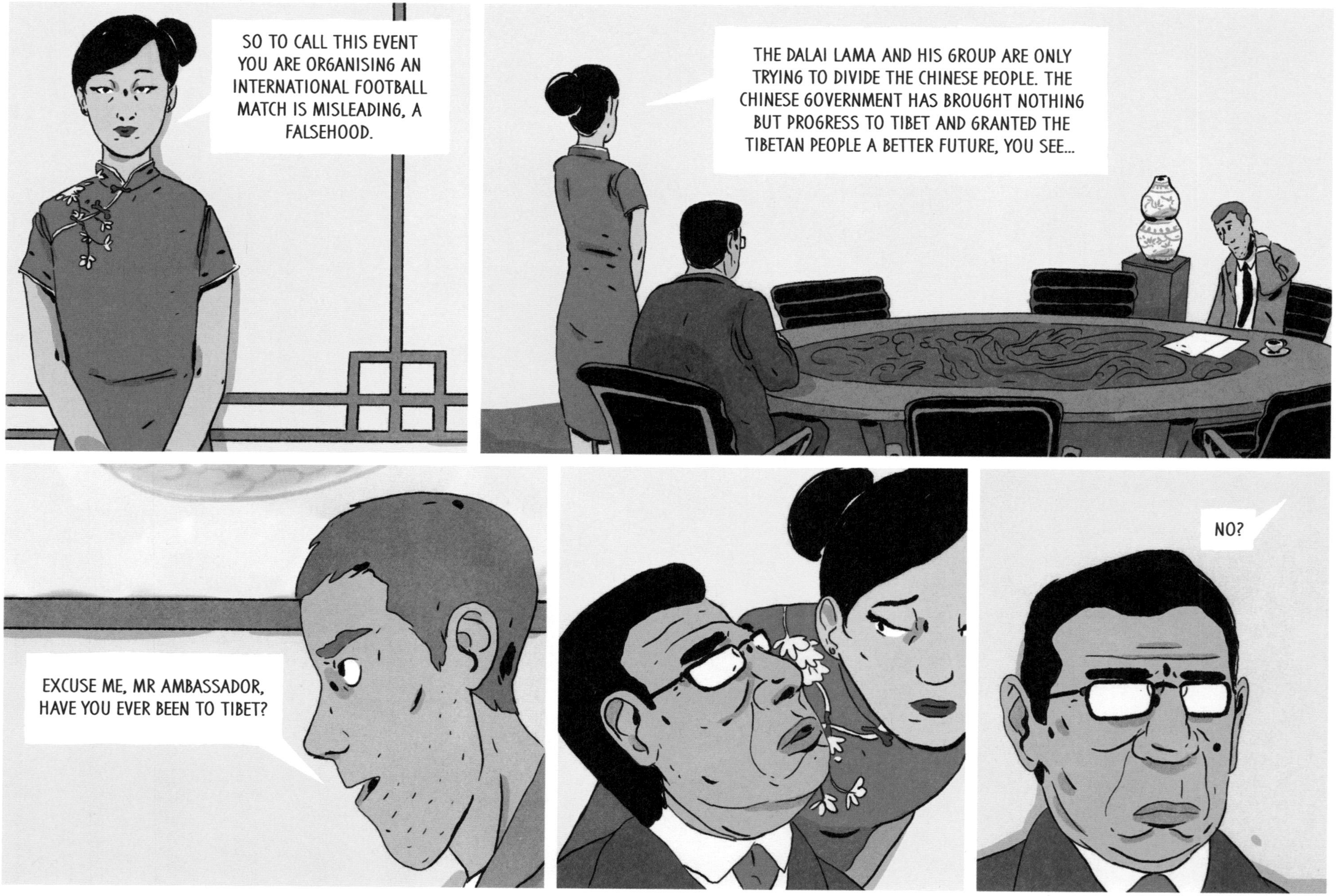

SO TO CALL THIS EVENT YOU ARE ORGANISING AN INTERNATIONAL FOOTBALL MATCH IS MISLEADING, A FALSEHOOD.
THE DALAI LAMA AND HIS GROUP ARE ONLY TRYING TO DIVIDE THE CHINESE PEOPLE. THE CHINESE GOVERNMENT HAS BROUGHT NOTHING BUT PROGRESS TO TIBET AND GRANTED THE TIBETAN PEOPLE A BETTER FUTURE, YOU SEE...
EXCUSE ME, MR AMBASSADOR, HAVE YOU EVER BEEN TO TIBET?
NO?

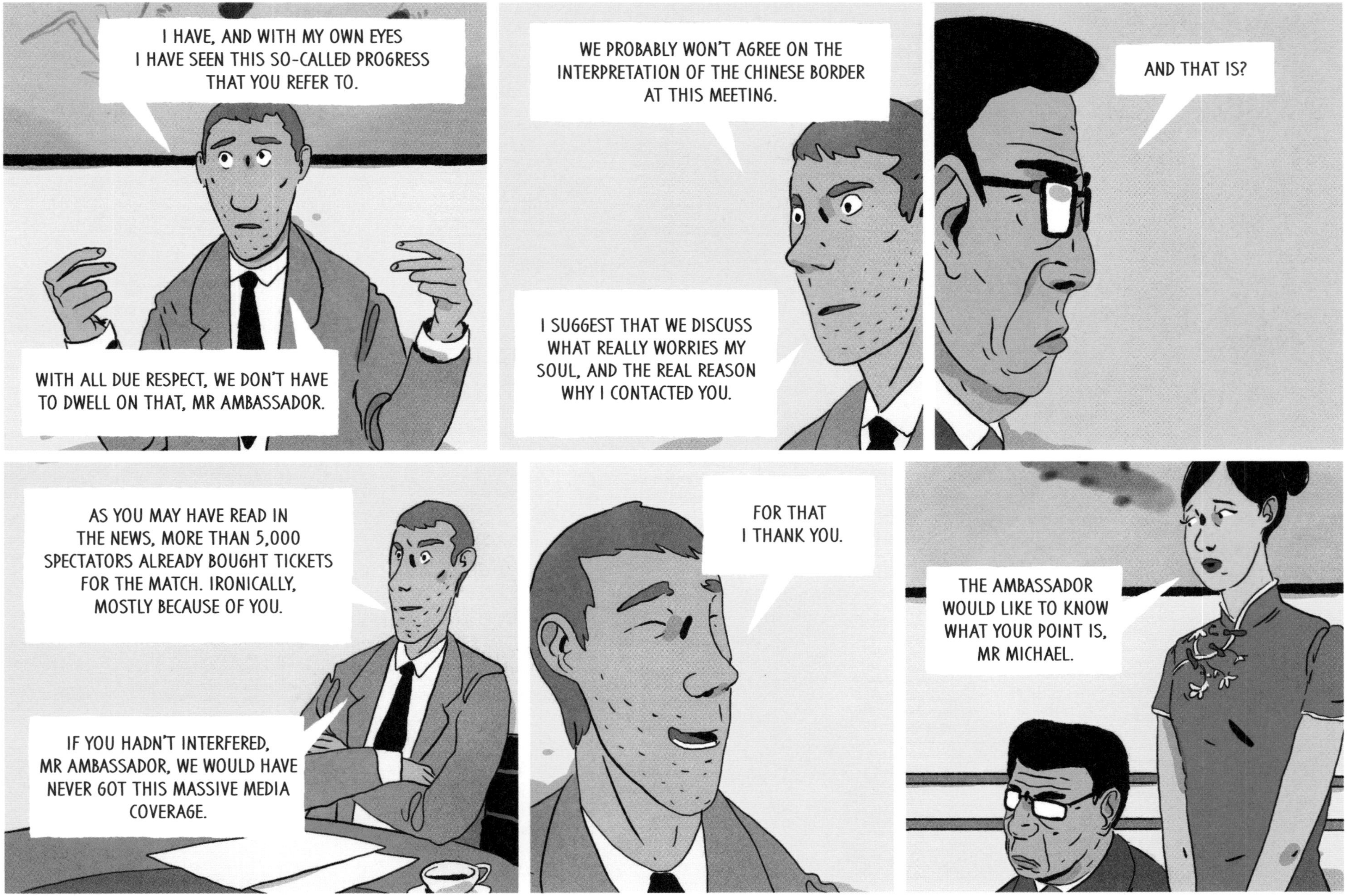
I HAVE, AND WITH MY OWN EYES I HAVE SEEN THIS SO-CALLED PROGRESS THAT YOU REFER TO.
WITH ALL DUE RESPECT, WE DON'T HAVE TO DWELL ON THAT, MR AMBASSADOR.
WE PROBABLY WON'T AGREE ON THE INTERPRETATION OF THE CHINESE BORDER AT THIS MEETING.
I SUGGEST THAT WE DISCUSS WHAT REALLY WORRIES MY SOUL, AND THE REAL REASON WHY I CONTACTED YOU.
AND THAT IS?
AS YOU MAY HAVE READ IN THE NEWS, MORE THAN 5,000 SPECTATORS ALREADY BOUGHT TICKETS FOR THE MATCH. IRONICALLY, MOSTLY BECAUSE OF YOU.
IF YOU HADN'T INTERFERED, MR AMBASSADOR, WE WOULD HAVE NEVER GOT THIS MASSIVE MEDIA COVERAGE.
FOR THAT I THANK YOU.
THE AMBASSADOR WOULD LIKE TO KNOW WHAT YOUR POINT IS, MR MICHAEL.

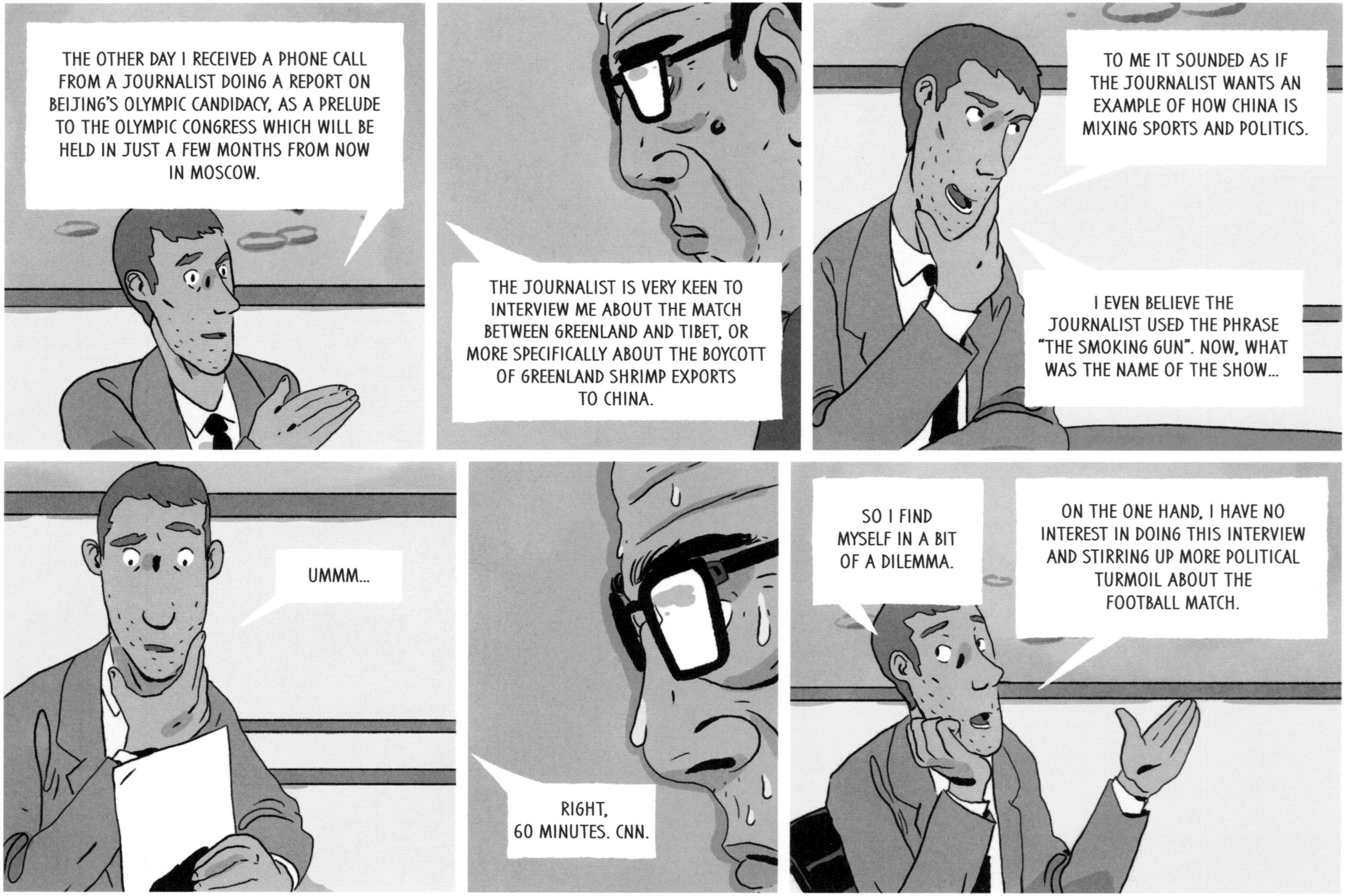
THE OTHER DAY I RECEIVED A PHONE CALL FROM A JOURNALIST DOING A REPORT ON BEIJING'S OLYMPIC CANDIDACY, AS A PRELUDE TO THE OLYMPIC CONGRESS WHICH WILL BE HELD IN JUST A FEW MONTHS FROM NOW IN MOSCOW.
THE JOURNALIST IS VERY KEEN TO INTERVIEW ME ABOUT THE MATCH BETWEEN GREENLAND AND TIBET, OR MORE SPECIFICALLY ABOUT THE BOYCOTT OF GREENLAND SHRIMP EXPORTS TO CHINA.
TO ME IT SOUNDED AS IF THE JOURNALIST WANTS AN EXAMPLE OF HOW CHINA IS MIXING SPORTS AND POLITICS.
I EVEN BELIEVE THE JOURNALIST USED THE PHRASE "THE SMOKING GUN". NOW, WHAT WAS THE NAME OF THE SHOW...
UMMM...
RIGHT, 60 MINUTES. CNN.
SO I FIND MYSELF IN A BIT OF A DILEMMA.
ON THE ONE HAND, I HAVE NO INTEREST IN DOING THIS INTERVIEW AND STIRRING UP MORE POLITICAL TURMOIL ABOUT THE FOOTBALL MATCH.

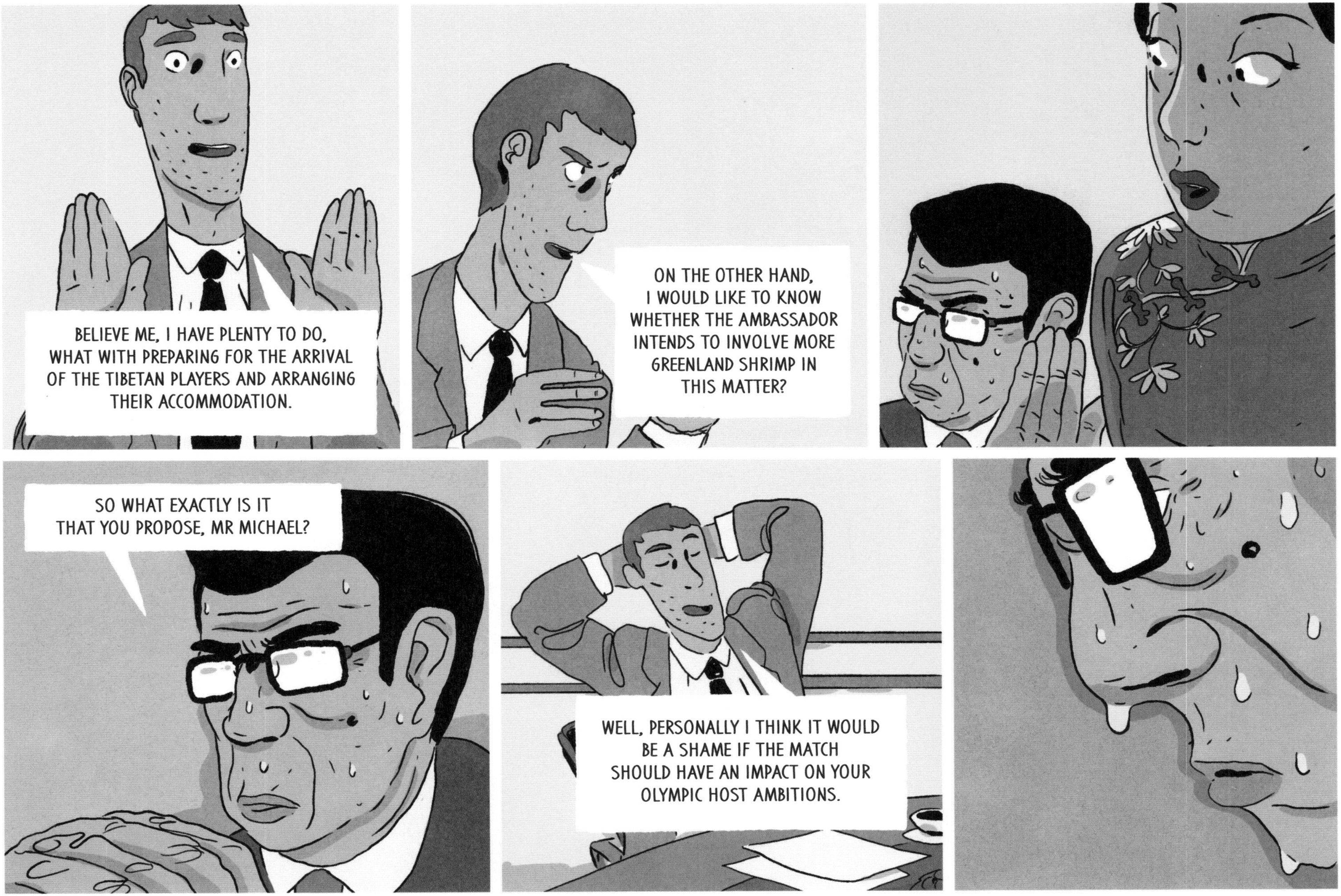
BELIEVE ME, I HAVE PLENTY TO DO, WHAT WITH PREPARING FOR THE ARRIVAL OF THE TIBETAN PLAYERS AND ARRANGING THEIR ACCOMMODATION.
ON THE OTHER HAND, I WOULD LIKE TO KNOW WHETHER THE AMBASSADOR INTENDS TO INVOLVE MORE GREENLAND SHRIMP IN THIS MATTER?
SO WHAT EXACTLY IS IT THAT YOU PROPOSE, MR MICHAEL?
WELL, PERSONALLY I THINK IT WOULD BE A SHAME IF THE MATCH SHOULD HAVE AN IMPACT ON YOUR OLYMPIC HOST AMBITIONS.

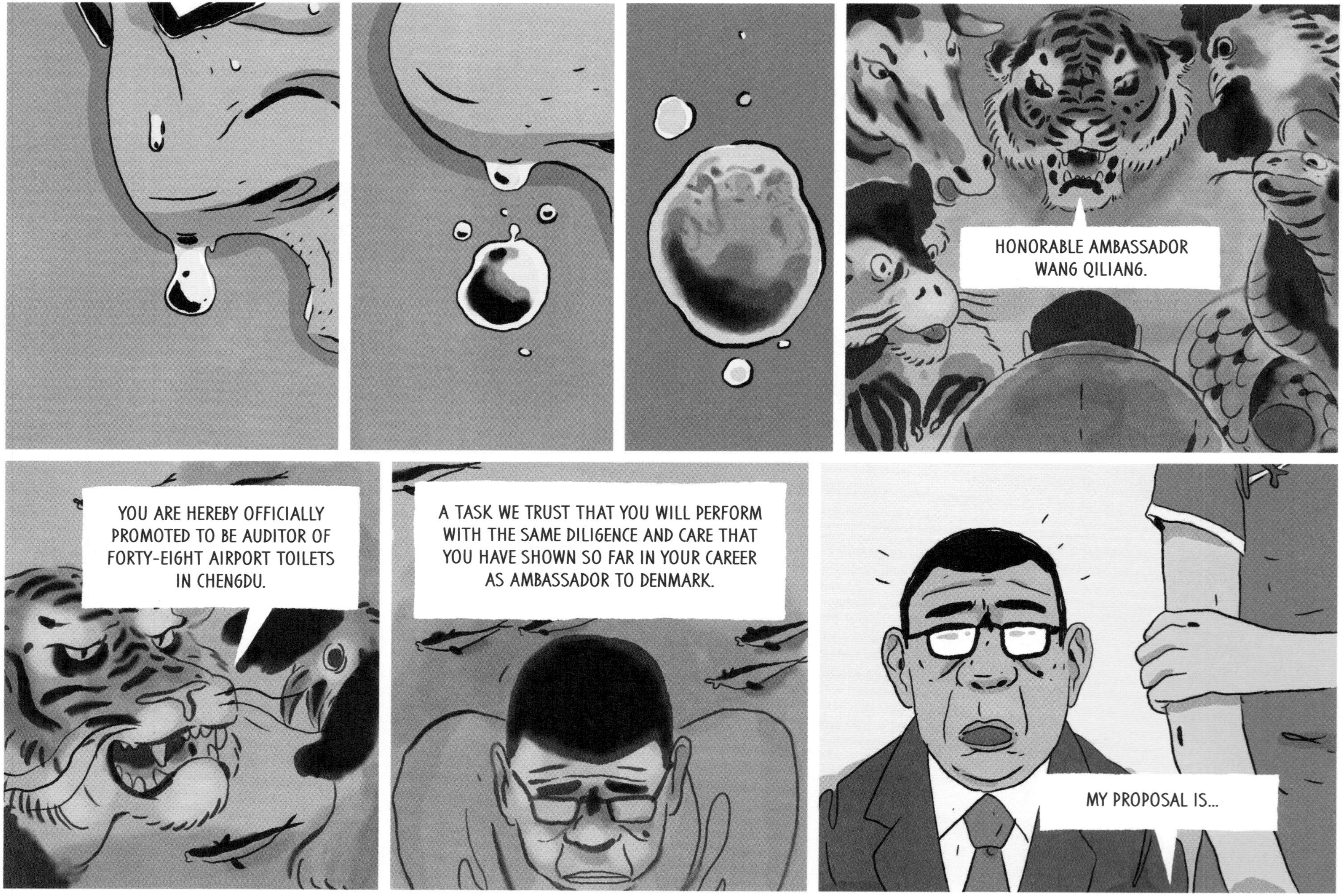
HONORABLE AMBASSADOR WANG QILIANG.
YOU ARE HEREBY OFFICIALLY PROMOTED TO BE AUDITOR OF FORTY-EIGHT AIRPORT TOILETS IN CHENGDU.
A TASK WE TRUST THAT YOU WILL PERFORM WITH THE SAME DILIGENCE AND CARE THAT YOU HAVE SHOWN SO FAR IN YOUR CAREER AS AMBASSADOR TO DENMARK.
MY PROPOSAL IS...

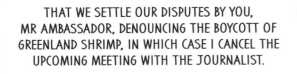

THAT WE SETTLE OUR DISPUTES BY YOU, MR AMBASSADOR, DENOUNCING THE BOYCOTT OF GREENLAND SHRIMP, IN WHICH CASE I CANCEL THE UPCOMING MEETING WITH THE JOURNALIST.

MR AMBASSADOR, AS A SHOW OF GOOD WILL, I PROMISE THAT WE WILL NOT RAISE THE TIBETAN FLAG OFFICIALLY ON THE MATCH DAY.

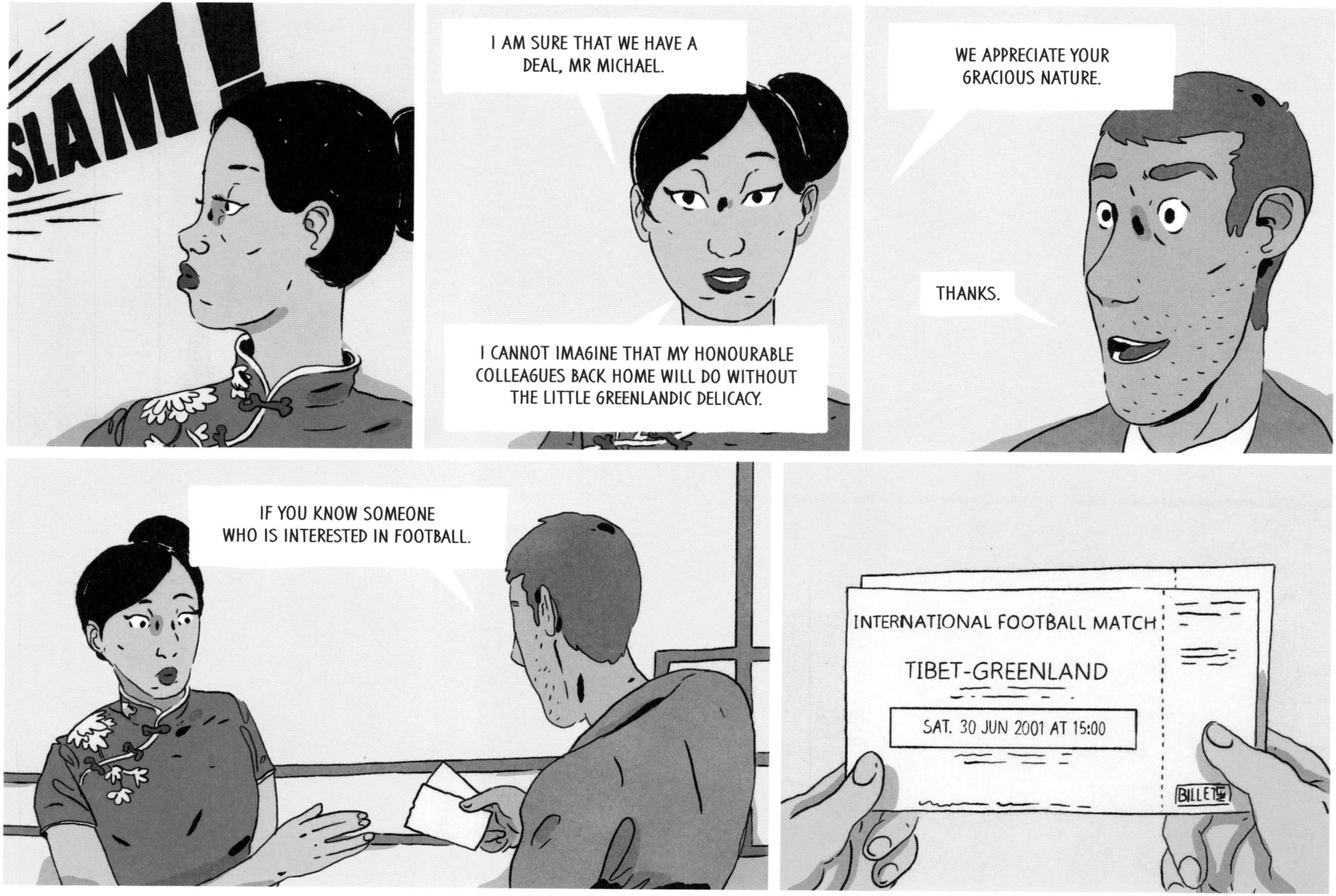
SLAM!
I AM SURE THAT WE HAVE A DEAL, MR MICHAEL.
I CANNOT IMAGINE THAT MY HONOURABLE COLLEAGUES BACK HOME WILL DO WITHOUT THE LITTLE GREENLANDIC DELICACY.
WE APPRECIATE YOUR GRACIOUS NATURE.
THANKS.
IF YOU KNOW SOMEONE WHO IS INTERESTED IN FOOTBALL.
INTERNATIONAL FOOTBALL MATCH
TIBET-GREENLAND
SAT. 30 JUN 2001 AT 15:00
BILLET

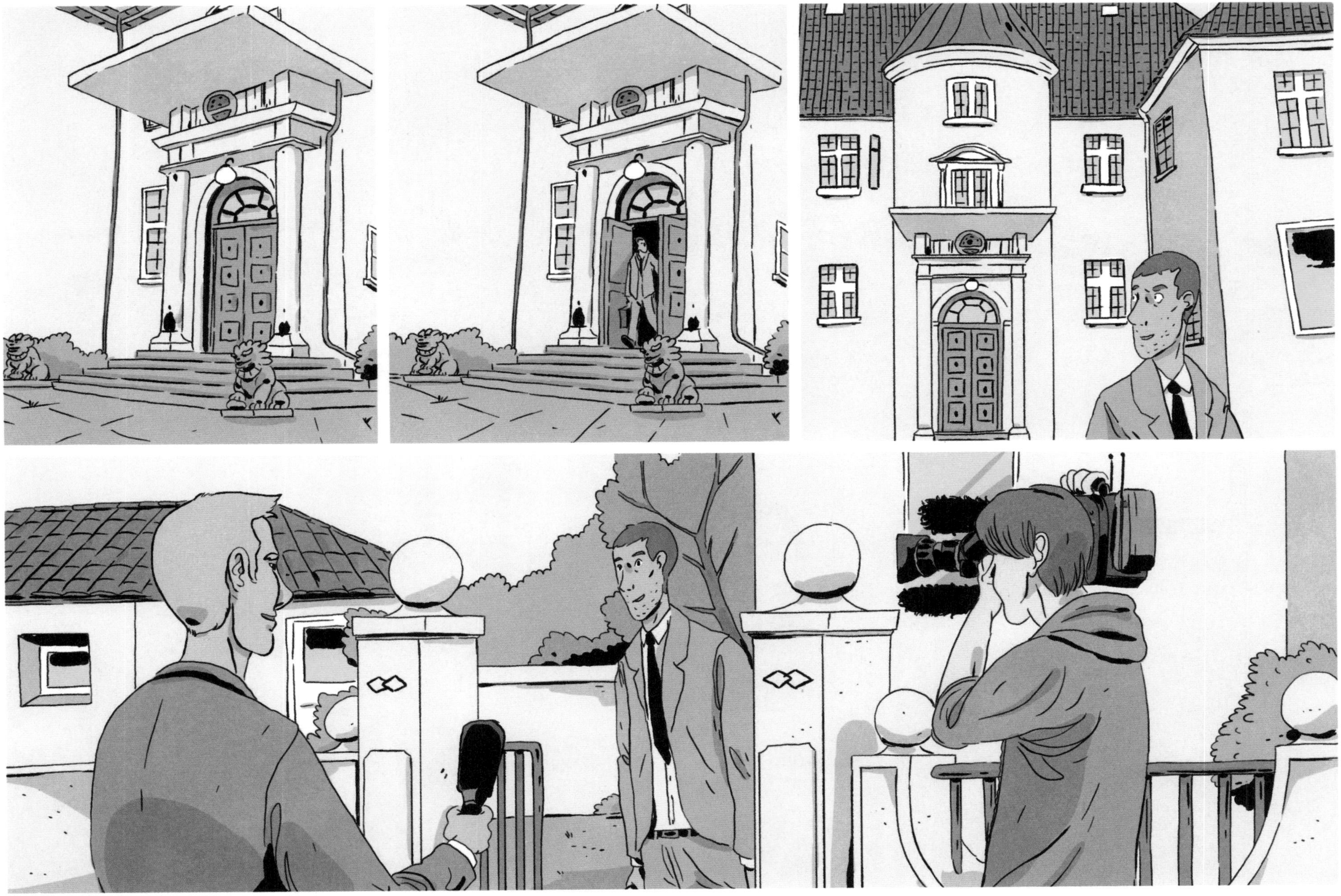

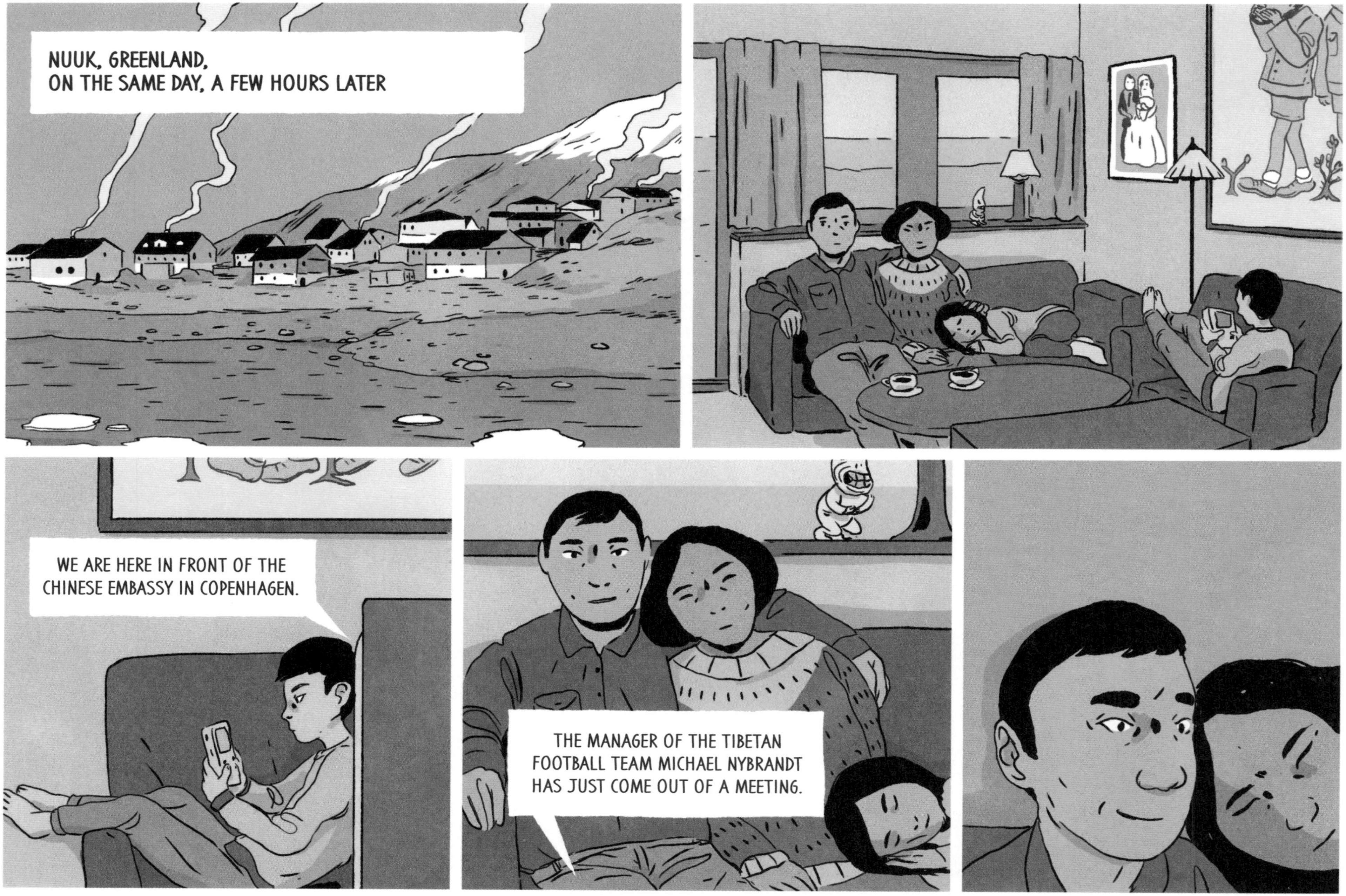

NUUK, GREENLAND,
ON THE SAME DAY, A FEW HOURS LATER
WE ARE HERE IN FRONT OF THE CHINESE EMBASSY IN COPENHAGEN.
THE MANAGER OF THE TIBETAN FOOTBALL TEAM MICHAEL NYBRANDT HAS JUST COME OUT OF A MEETING.

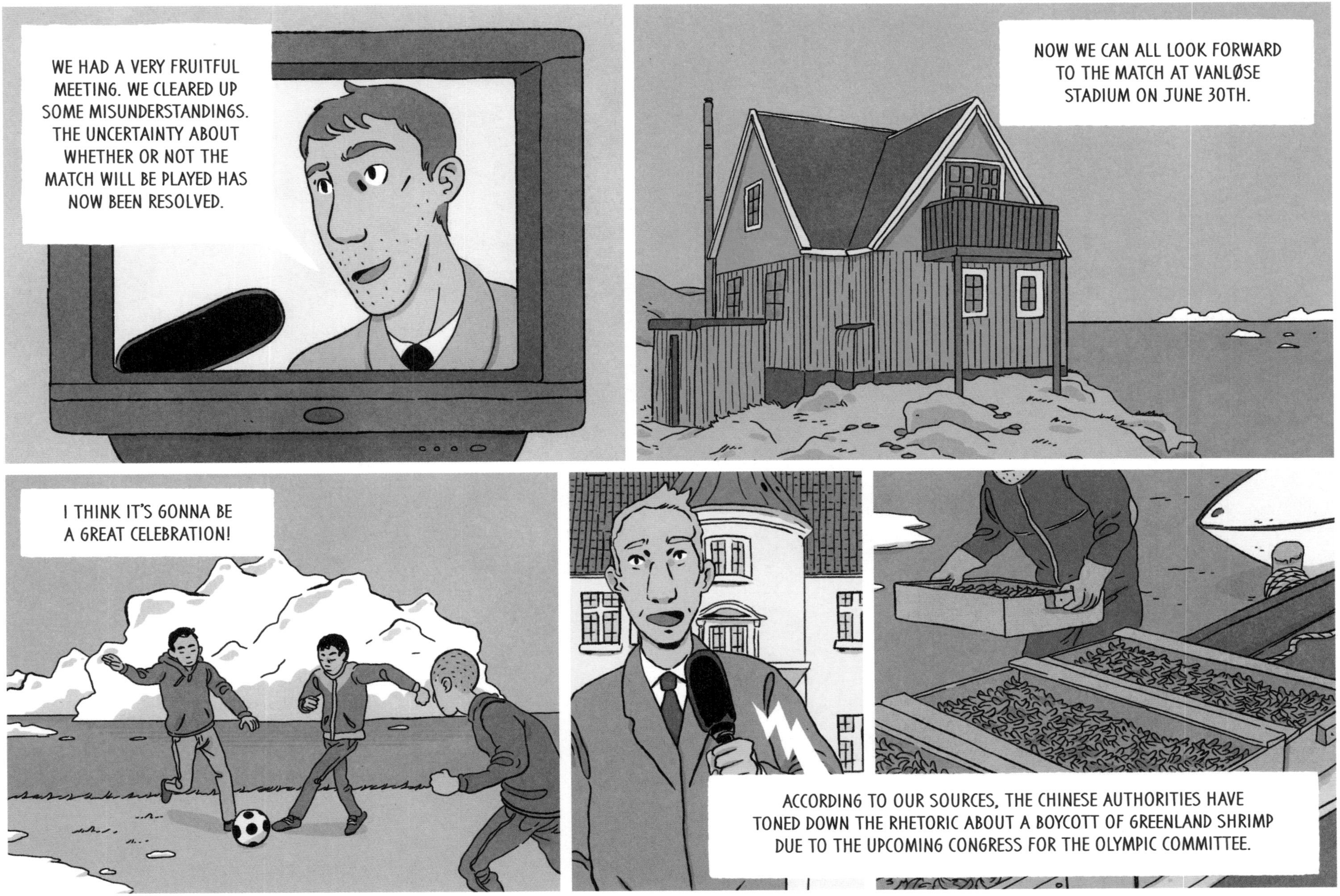
WE HAD A VERY FRUITFUL MEETING. WE CLEARED UP SOME MISUNDERSTANDINGS. THE UNCERTAINTY ABOUT WHETHER OR NOT THE MATCH WILL BE PLAYED HAS NOW BEEN RESOLVED.
NOW WE CAN ALL LOOK FORWARD TO THE MATCH AT VANLØSE STADIUM ON JUNE 30TH.
I THINK IT'S GONNA BE A GREAT CELEBRATION!
ACCORDING TO OUR SOURCES, THE CHINESE AUTHORITIES HAVE TONED DOWN THE RHETORIC ABOUT A BOYCOTT OF GREENLAND SHRIMP DUE TO THE UPCOMING CONGRESS FOR THE OLYMPIC COMMITTEE.

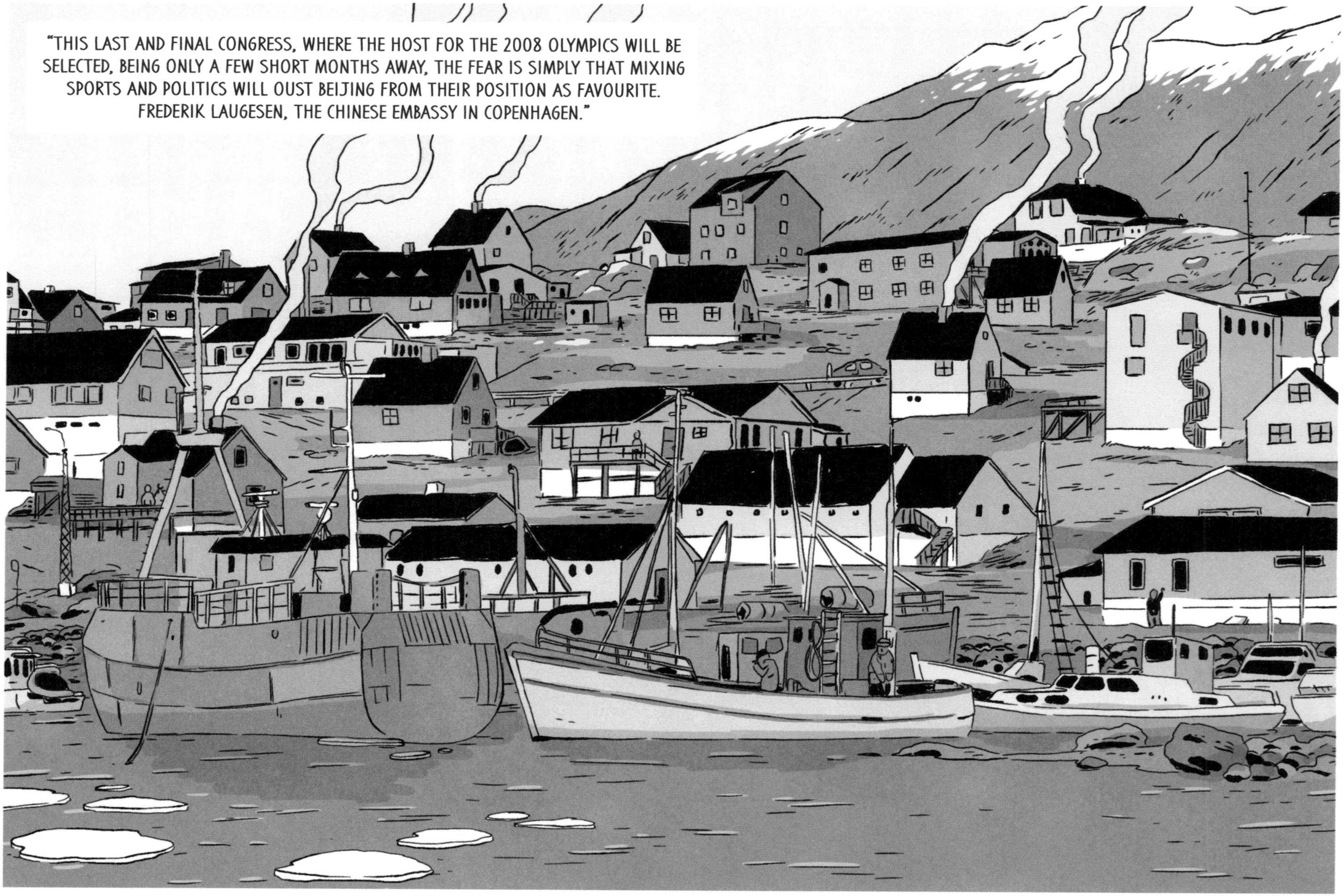
"THIS LAST AND FINAL CONGRESS, WHERE THE HOST FOR THE 2008 OLYMPICS WILL BE SELECTED, BEING ONLY A FEW SHORT MONTHS AWAY, THE FEAR IS SIMPLY THAT MIXING SPORTS AND POLITICS WILL OUST BEIJING FROM THEIR POSITION AS FAVOURITE. FREDERIK LAUGESEN, THE CHINESE EMBASSY IN COPENHAGEN."

CHAPTER 6

NINETY MINUTES OF RECOGNITION

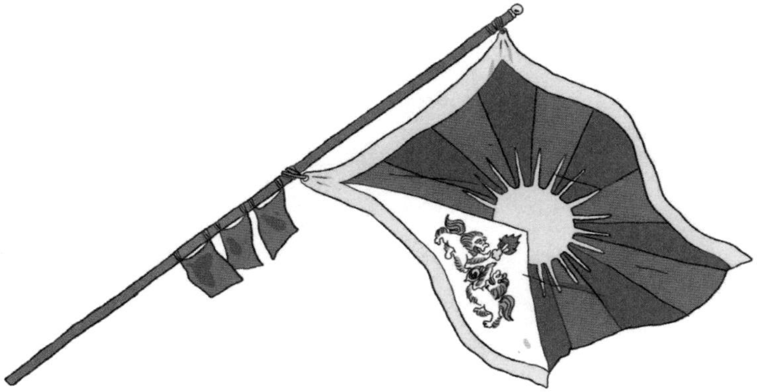

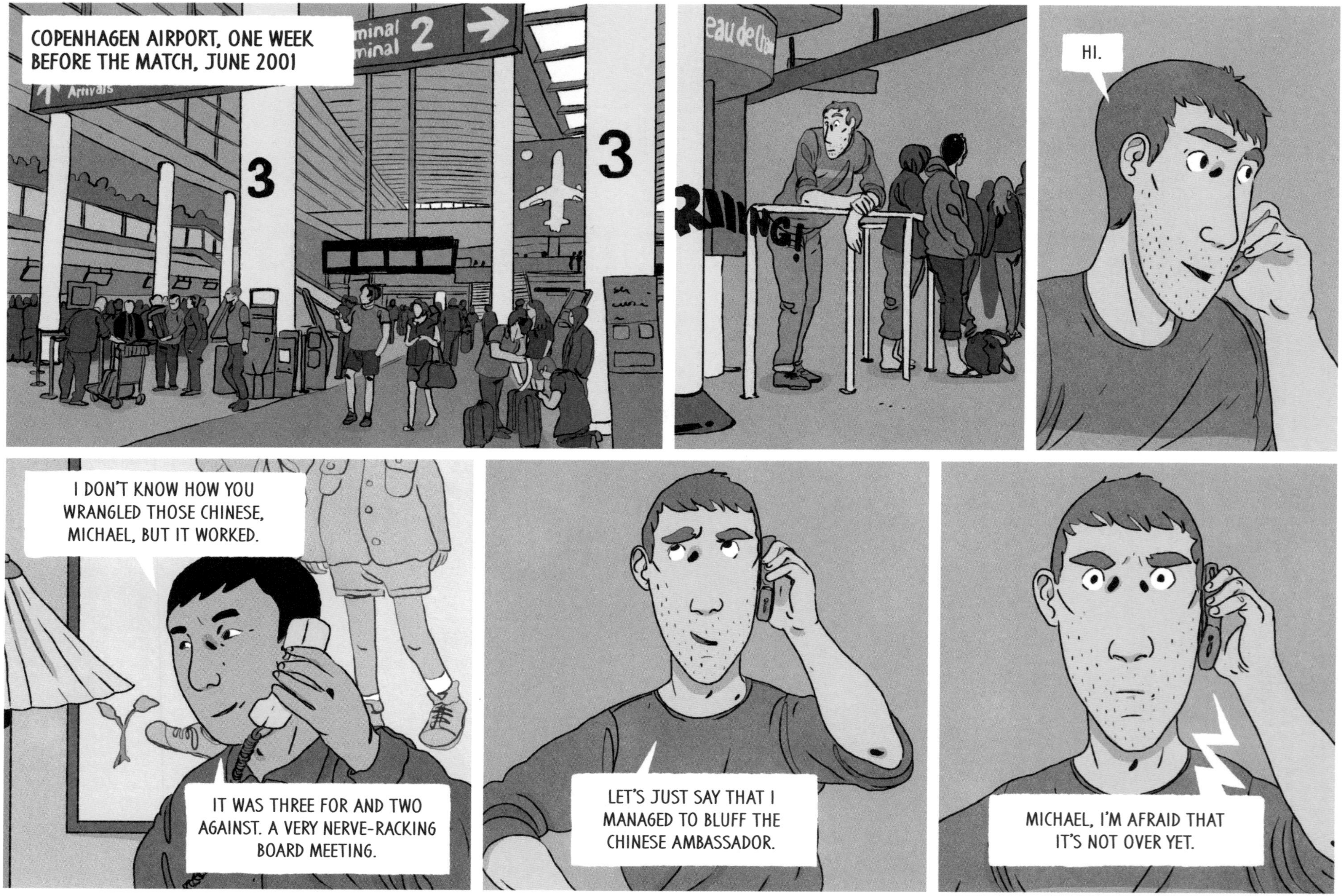
COPENHAGEN AIRPORT, ONE WEEK BEFORE THE MATCH, JUNE 2001
minal 2
minal
Arrivals
3
3
RIIING!
HI.
I DON'T KNOW HOW YOU WRANGLED THOSE CHINESE, MICHAEL, BUT IT WORKED.
IT WAS THREE FOR AND TWO AGAINST. A VERY NERVE-RACKING BOARD MEETING.
LET'S JUST SAY THAT I MANAGED TO BLUFF THE CHINESE AMBASSADOR.
MICHAEL, I'M AFRAID THAT IT'S NOT OVER YET.

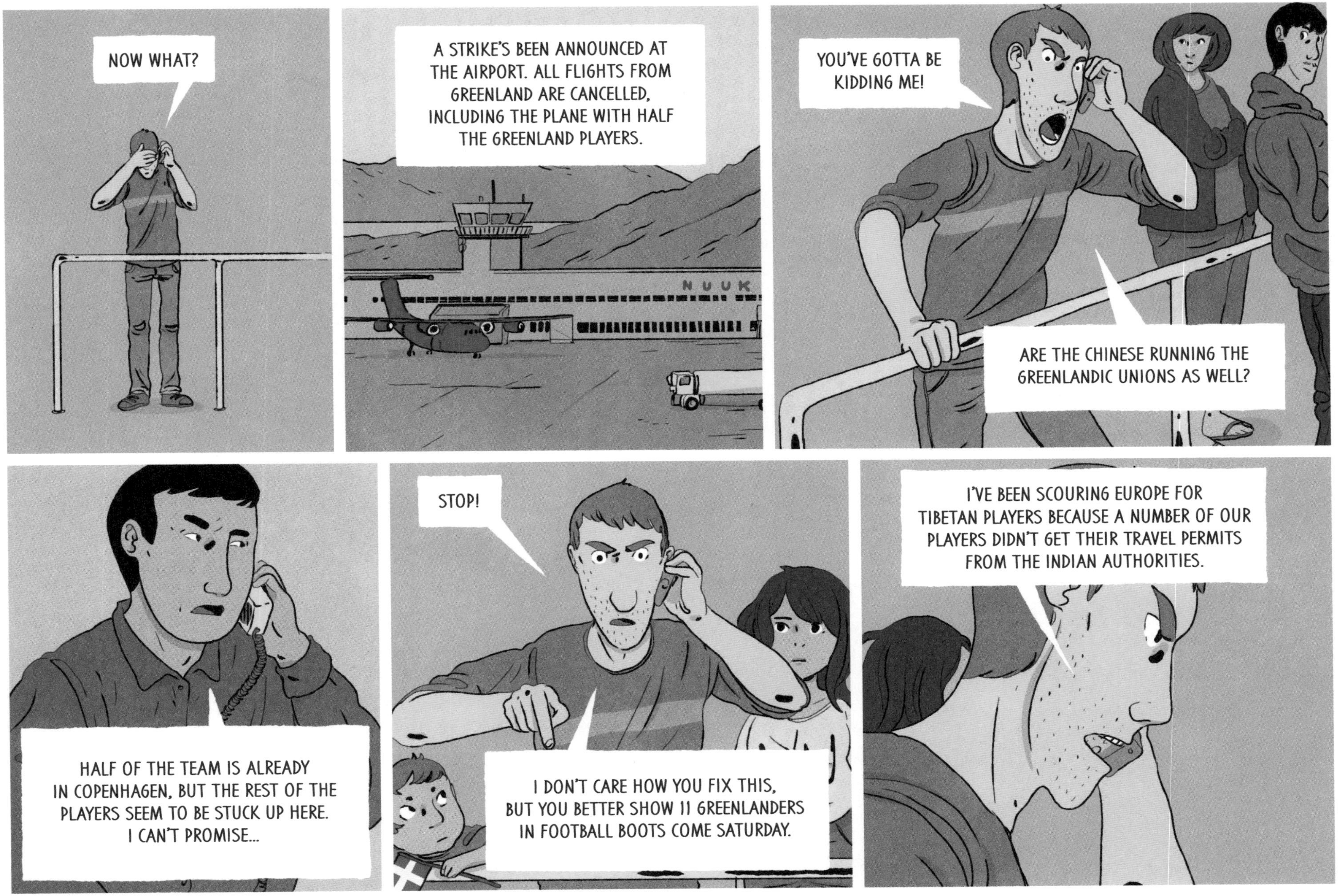
NOW WHAT?
A STRIKE'S BEEN ANNOUNCED AT THE AIRPORT. ALL FLIGHTS FROM GREENLAND ARE CANCELLED, INCLUDING THE PLANE WITH HALF THE GREENLAND PLAYERS.
NUUK
YOU'VE GOTTA BE KIDDING ME!
ARE THE CHINESE RUNNING THE GREENLANDIC UNIONS AS WELL?
HALF OF THE TEAM IS ALREADY IN COPENHAGEN, BUT THE REST OF THE PLAYERS SEEM TO BE STUCK UP HERE. I CAN'T PROMISE...
STOP!
I DON'T CARE HOW YOU FIX THIS, BUT YOU BETTER SHOW 11 GREENLANDERS IN FOOTBALL BOOTS COME SATURDAY.
I'VE BEEN SCOURING EUROPE FOR TIBETAN PLAYERS BECAUSE A NUMBER OF OUR PLAYERS DIDN'T GET THEIR TRAVEL PERMITS FROM THE INDIAN AUTHORITIES.

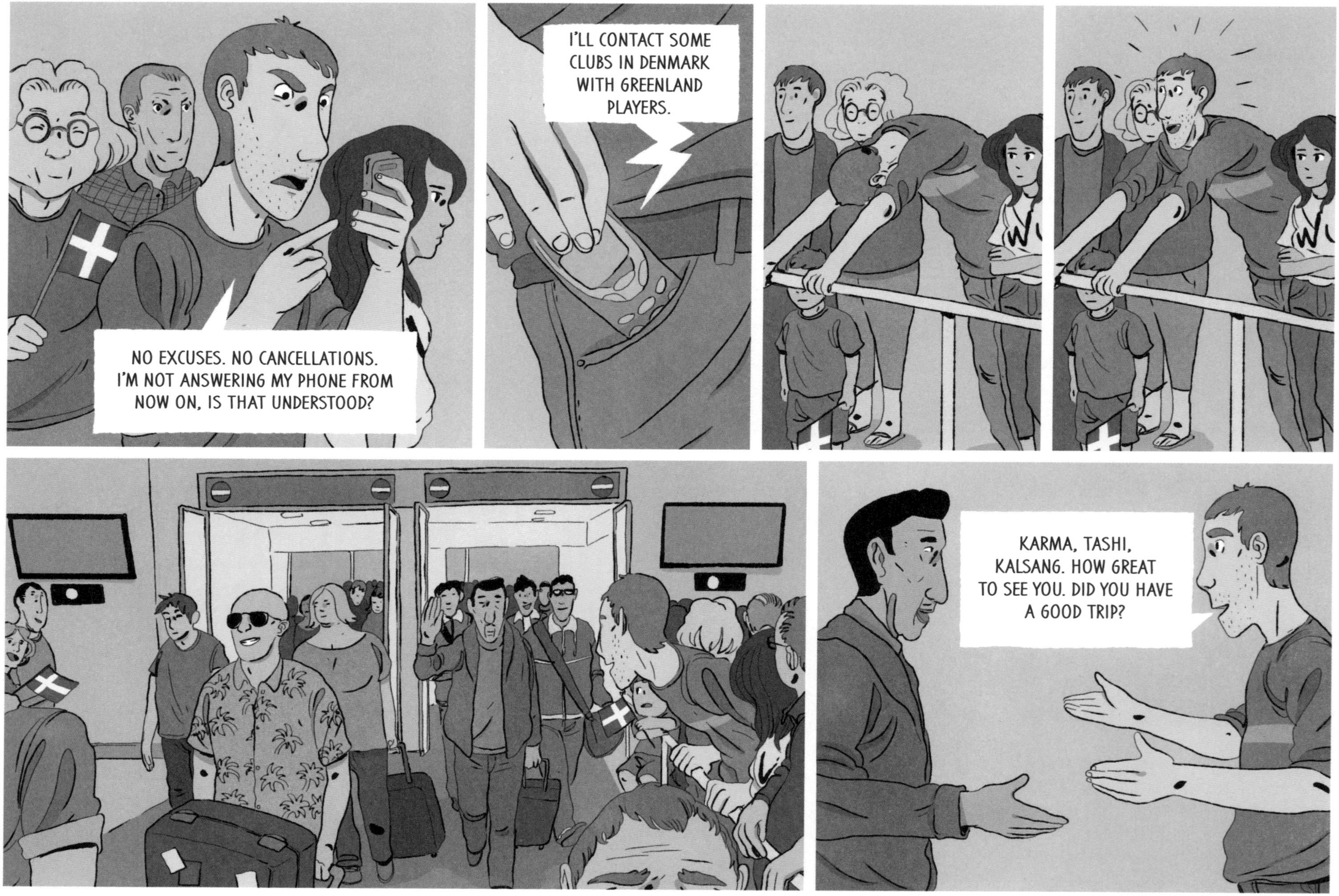
NO EXCUSES. NO CANCELLATIONS. I'M NOT ANSWERING MY PHONE FROM NOW ON, IS THAT UNDERSTOOD?
I'LL CONTACT SOME CLUBS IN DENMARK WITH GREENLAND PLAYERS.
KARMA, TASHI, KALSANG. HOW GREAT TO SEE YOU. DID YOU HAVE A GOOD TRIP?

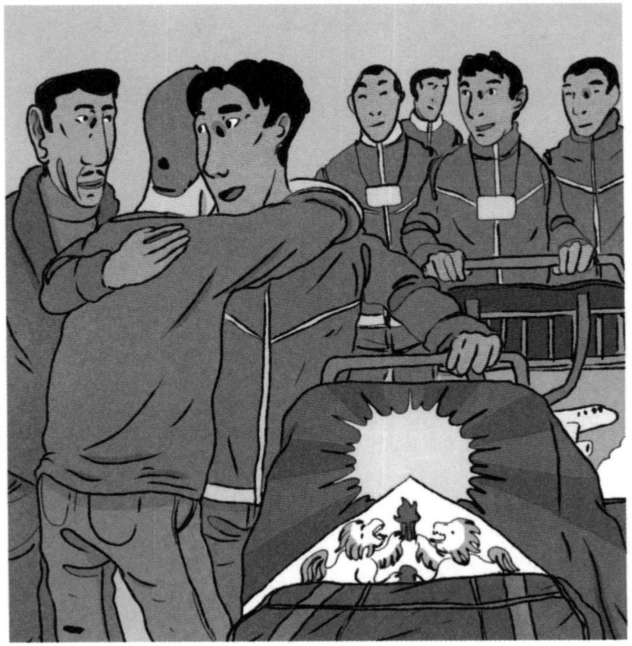

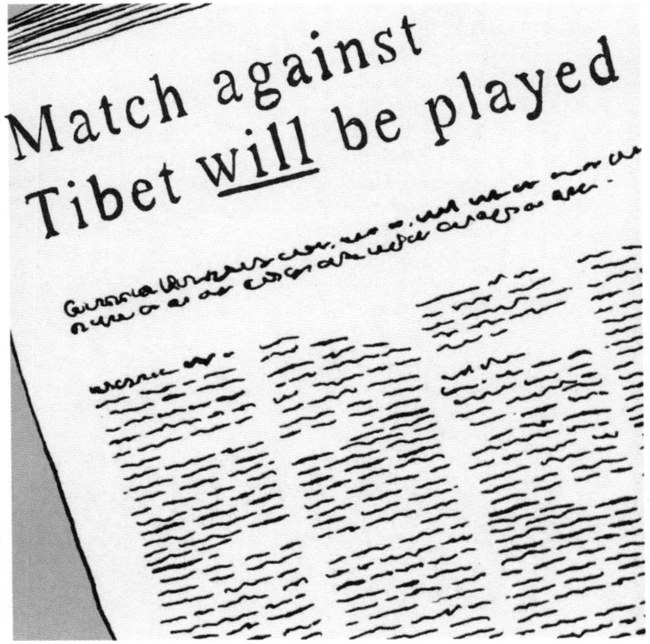
Match against
Tibet will be played

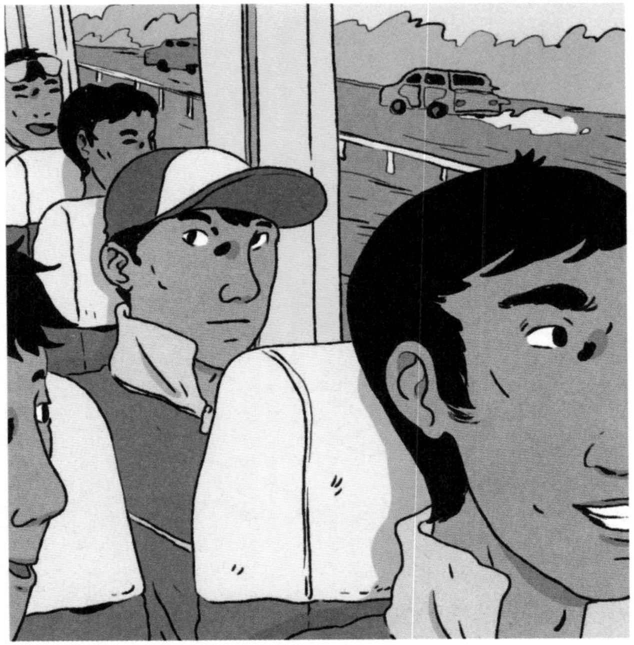

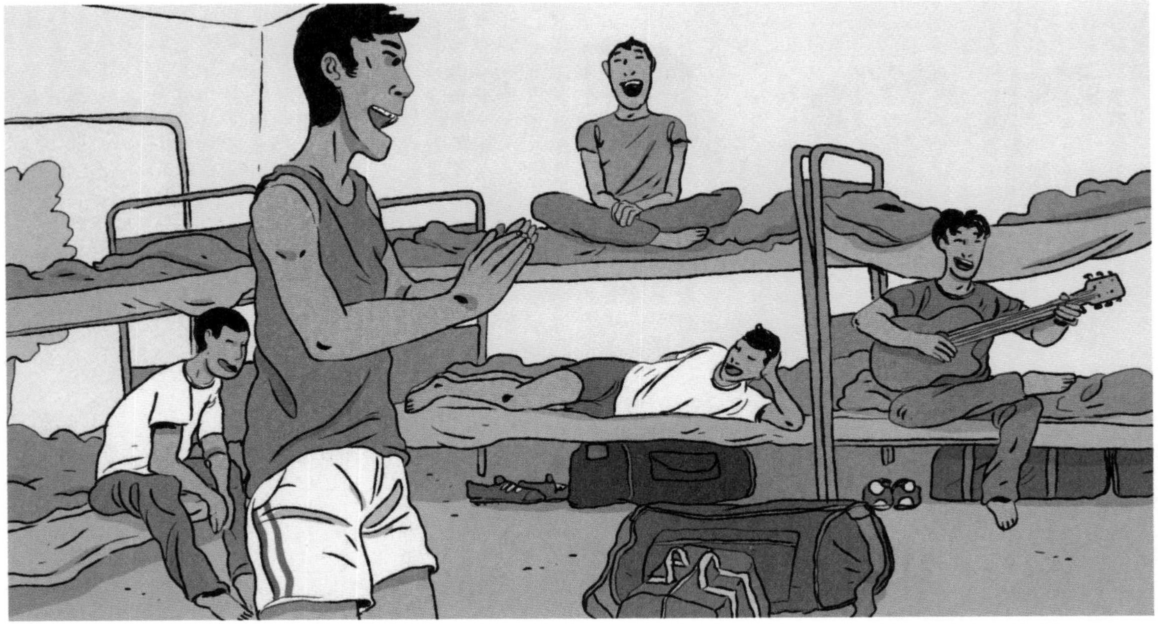

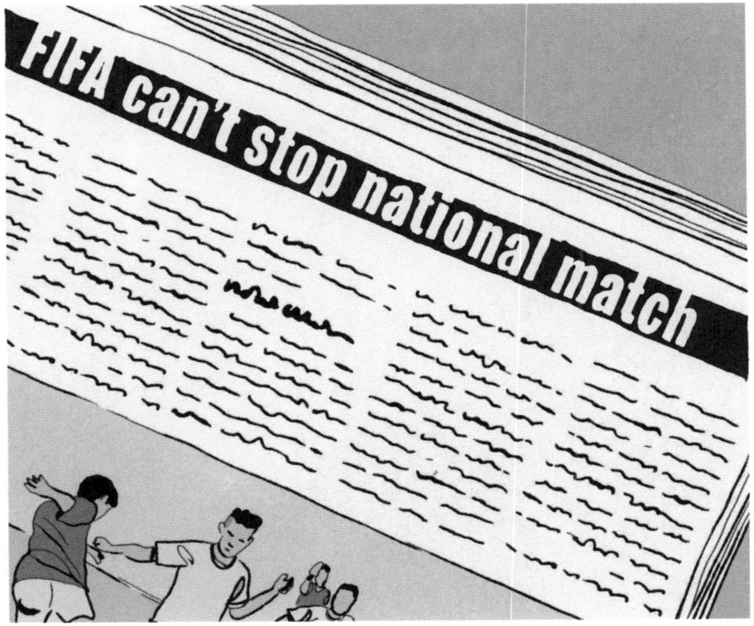
FIFA can't stop national match

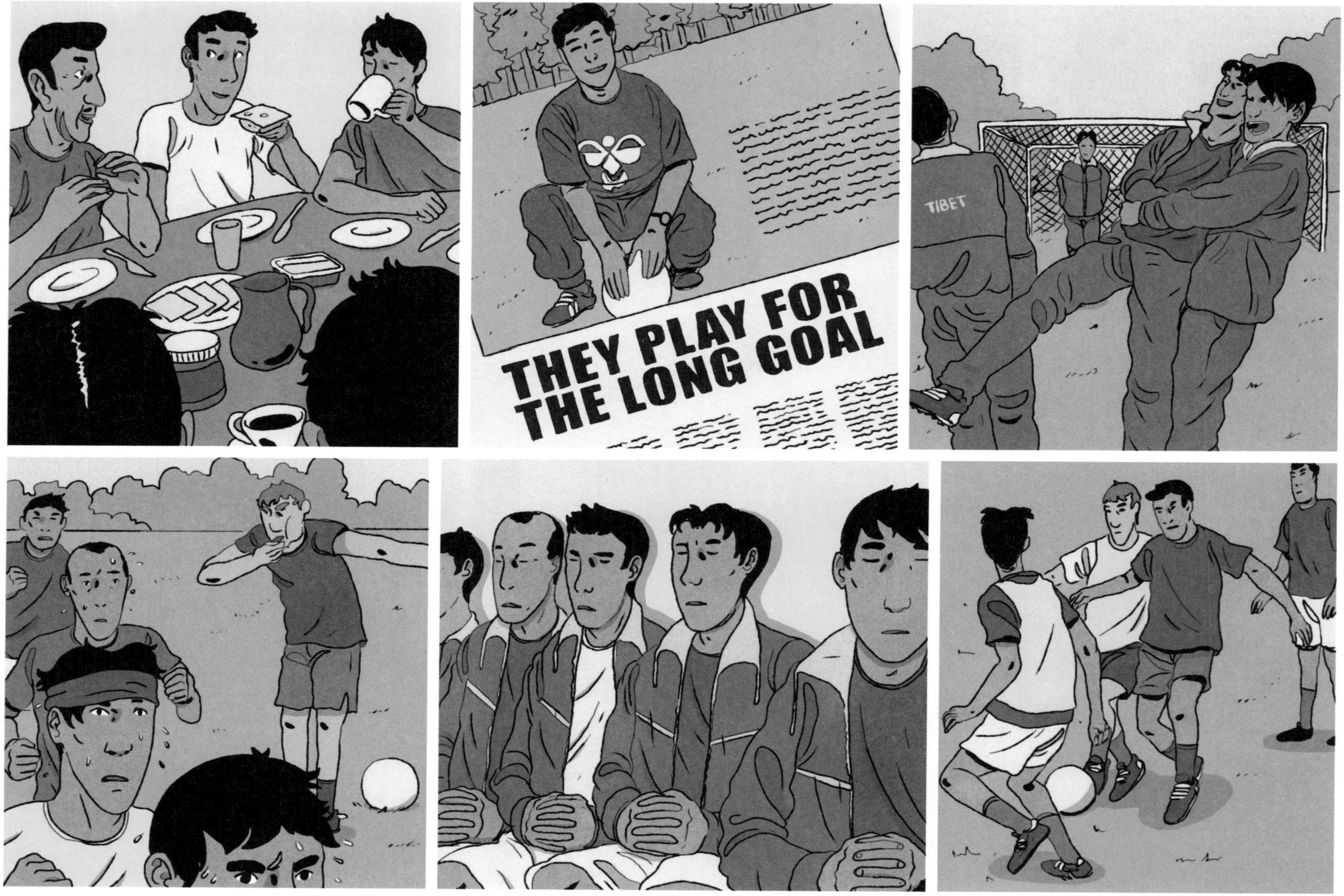
THEY PLAY FOR
THE LONG GOAL
TIBET

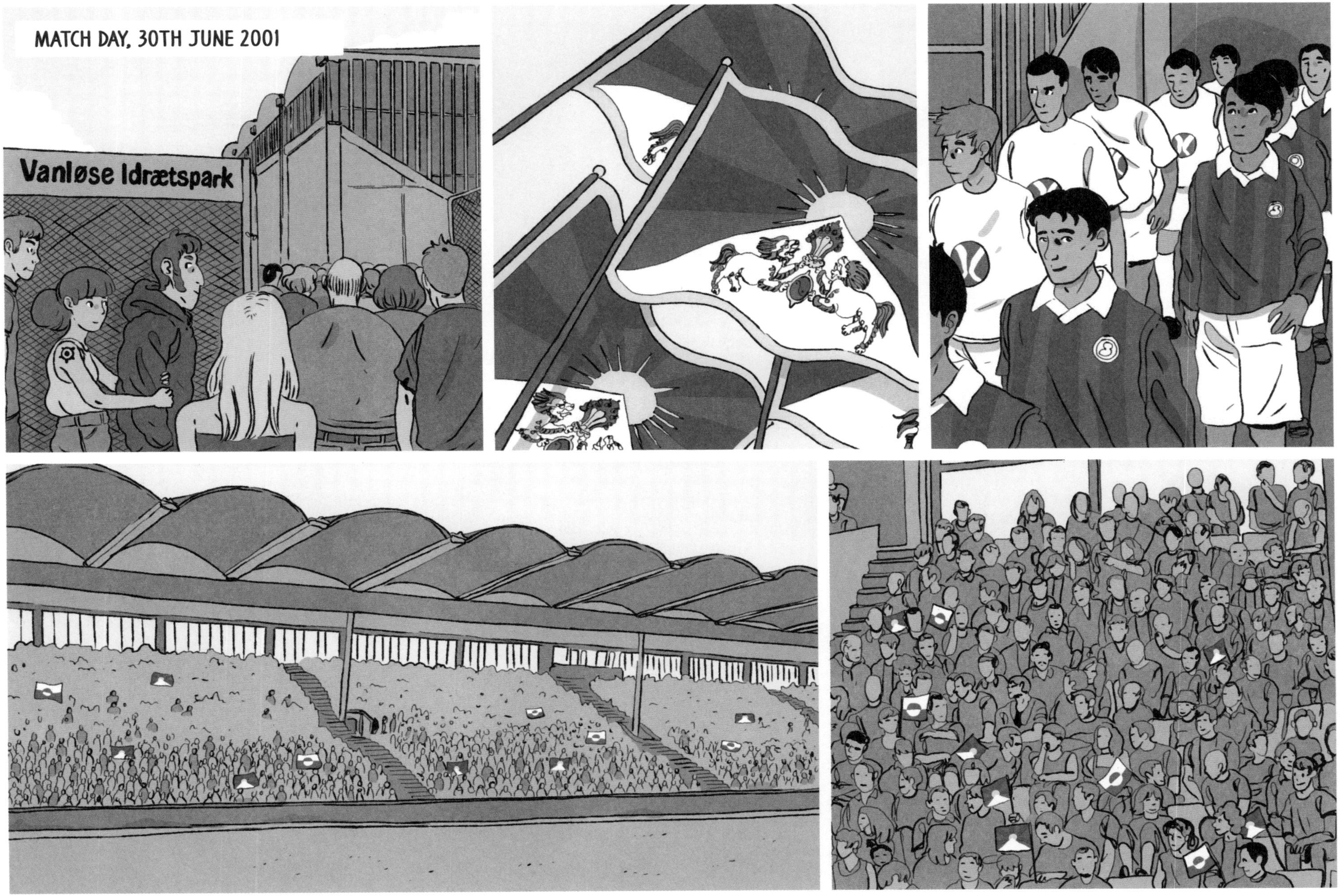
MATCH DAY, 30TH JUNE 2001
Vanløse Idrætspark

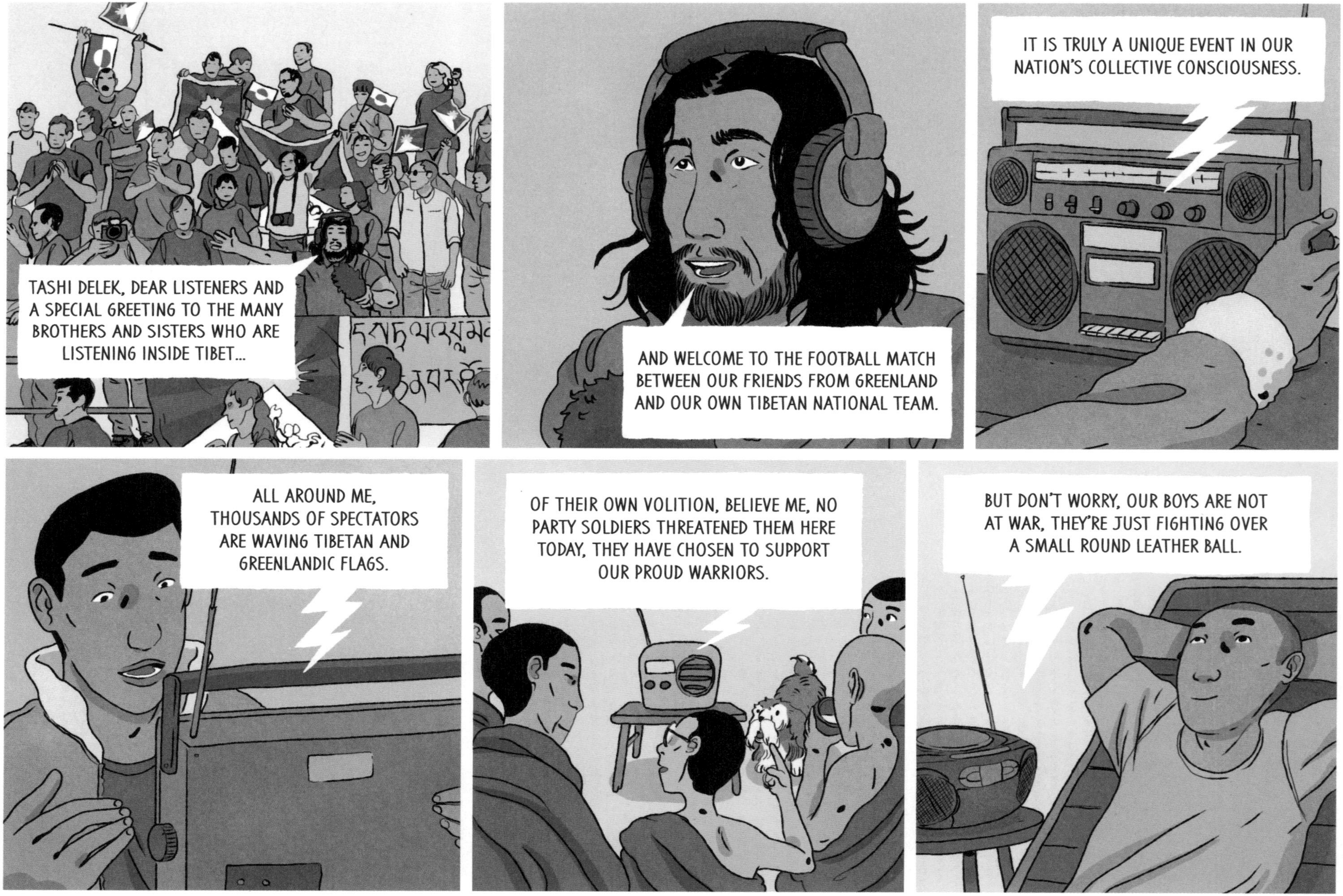
TASHI DELEK, DEAR LISTENERS AND A SPECIAL GREETING TO THE MANY BROTHERS AND SISTERS WHO ARE LISTENING INSIDE TIBET...
AND WELCOME TO THE FOOTBALL MATCH BETWEEN OUR FRIENDS FROM GREENLAND AND OUR OWN TIBETAN NATIONAL TEAM.
IT IS TRULY A UNIQUE EVENT IN OUR NATION'S COLLECTIVE CONSCIOUSNESS.
ALL AROUND ME, THOUSANDS OF SPECTATORS ARE WAVING TIBETAN AND GREENLANDIC FLAGS.
OF THEIR OWN VOLITION, BELIEVE ME, NO PARTY SOLDIERS THREATENED THEM HERE TODAY, THEY HAVE CHOSEN TO SUPPORT OUR PROUD WARRIORS.
BUT DON'T WORRY, OUR BOYS ARE NOT AT WAR, THEY'RE JUST FIGHTING OVER A SMALL ROUND LEATHER BALL.

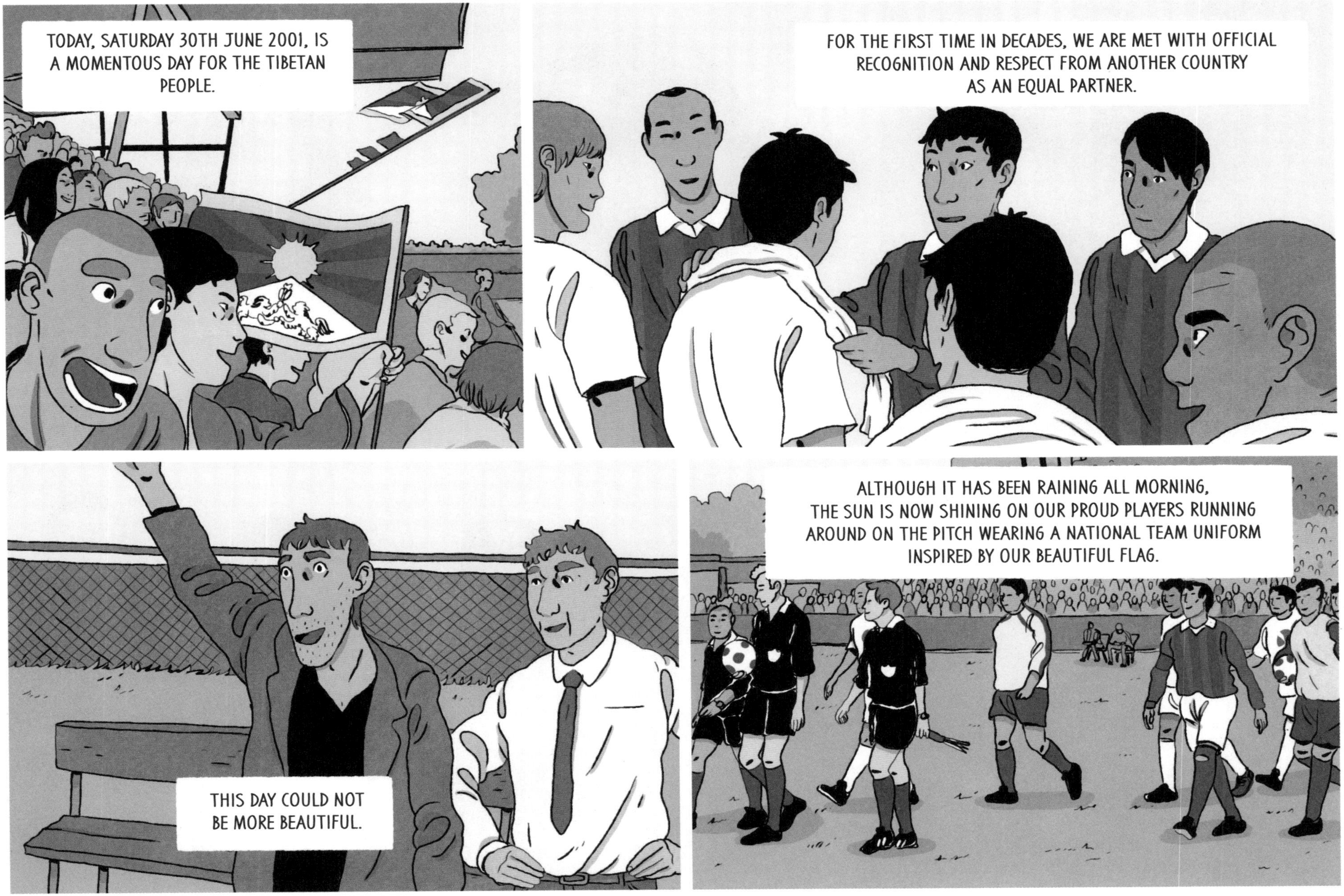
TODAY, SATURDAY 30TH JUNE 2001, IS A MOMENTOUS DAY FOR THE TIBETAN PEOPLE.
FOR THE FIRST TIME IN DECADES, WE ARE MET WITH OFFICIAL RECOGNITION AND RESPECT FROM ANOTHER COUNTRY AS AN EQUAL PARTNER.
THIS DAY COULD NOT BE MORE BEAUTIFUL.
ALTHOUGH IT HAS BEEN RAINING ALL MORNING, THE SUN IS NOW SHINING ON OUR PROUD PLAYERS RUNNING AROUND ON THE PITCH WEARING A NATIONAL TEAM UNIFORM INSPIRED BY OUR BEAUTIFUL FLAG.

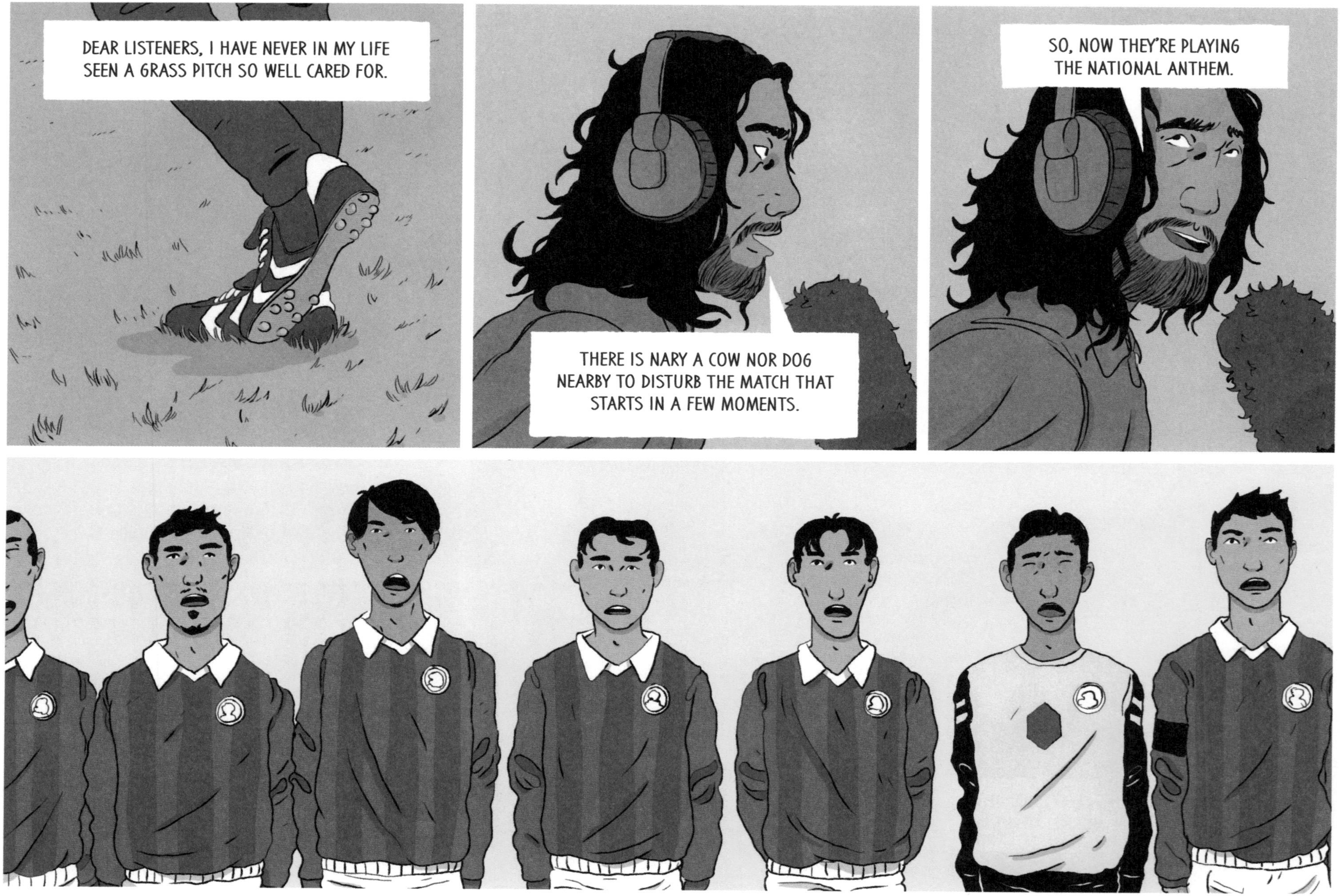
DEAR LISTENERS, I HAVE NEVER IN MY LIFE SEEN A GRASS PITCH SO WELL CARED FOR.
THERE IS NARY A COW NOR DOG NEARBY TO DISTURB THE MATCH THAT STARTS IN A FEW MOMENTS.
SO, NOW THEY'RE PLAYING THE NATIONAL ANTHEM.

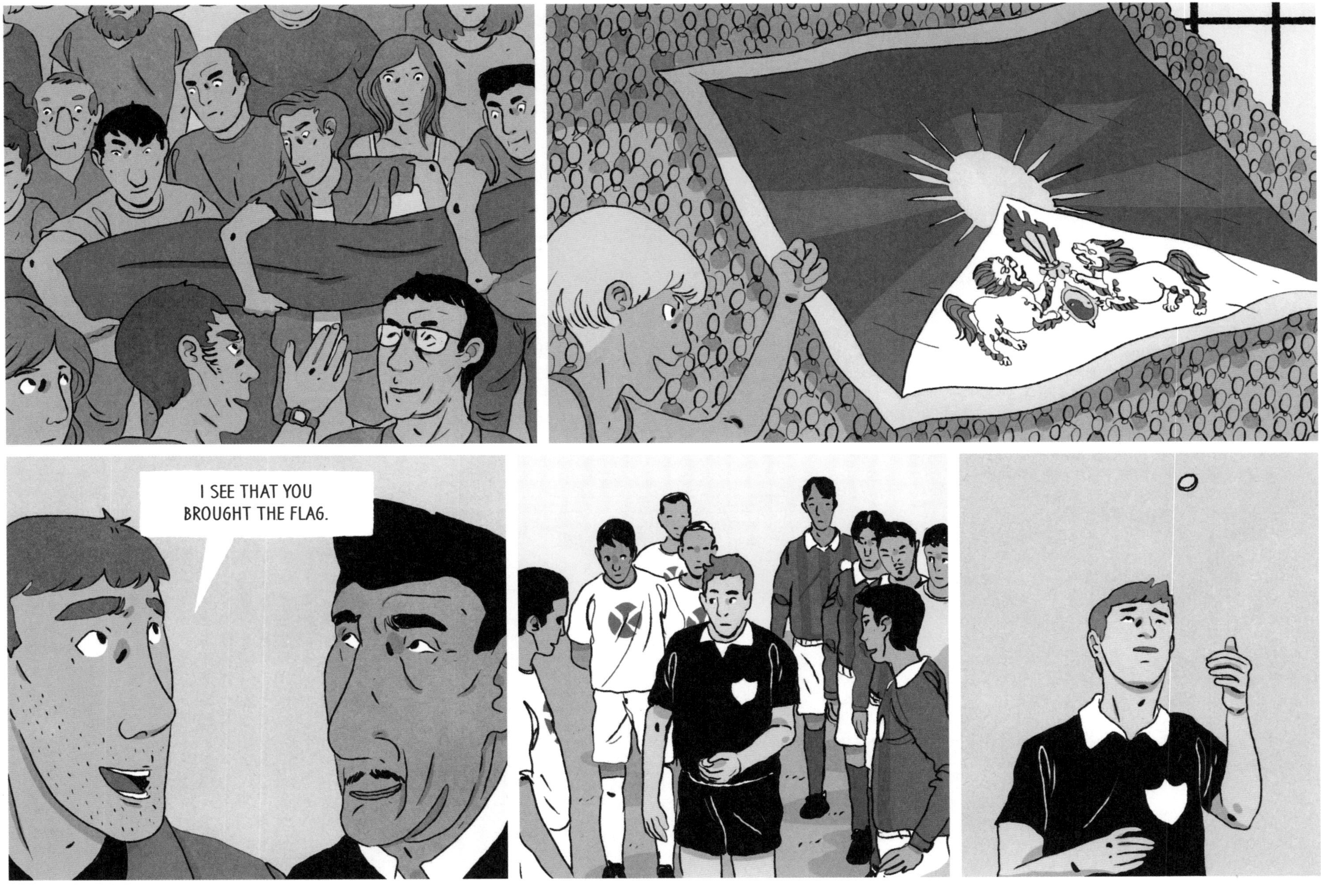
I SEE THAT YOU
BROUGHT THE FLAG.

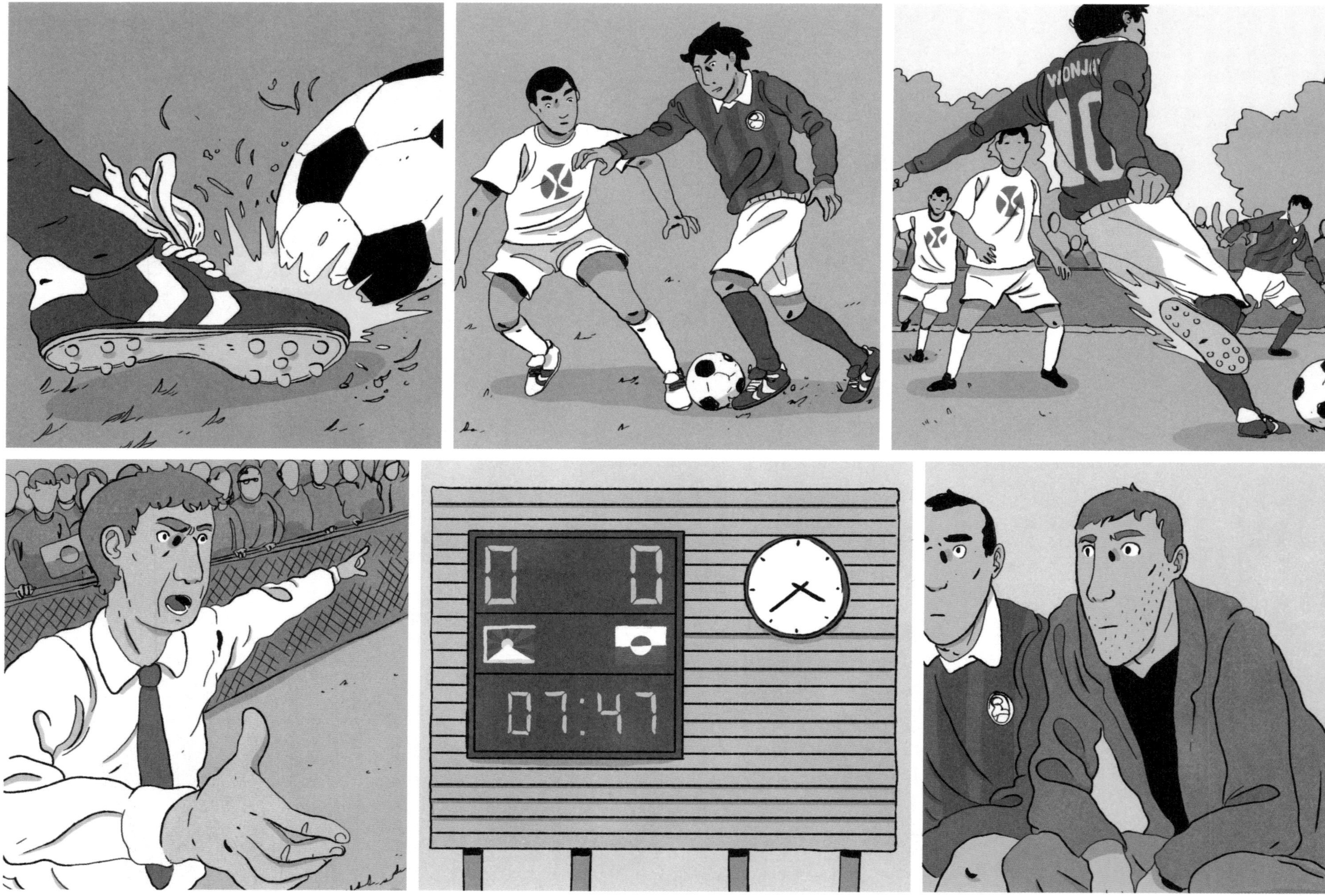
10
0
0
07:47

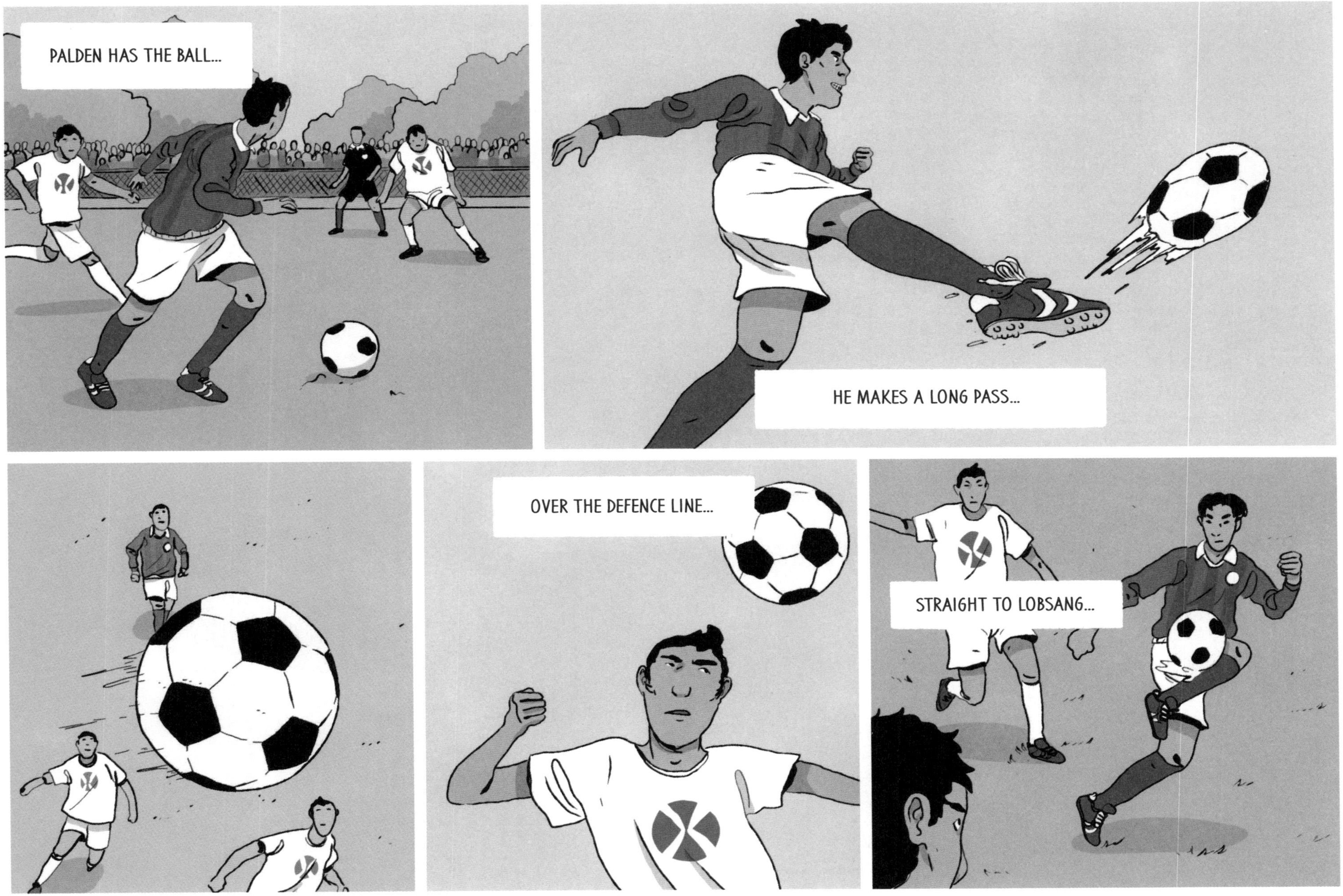
PALDEN HAS THE BALL...
HE MAKES A LONG PASS...
OVER THE DEFENCE LINE...
STRAIGHT TO LOBSANG...

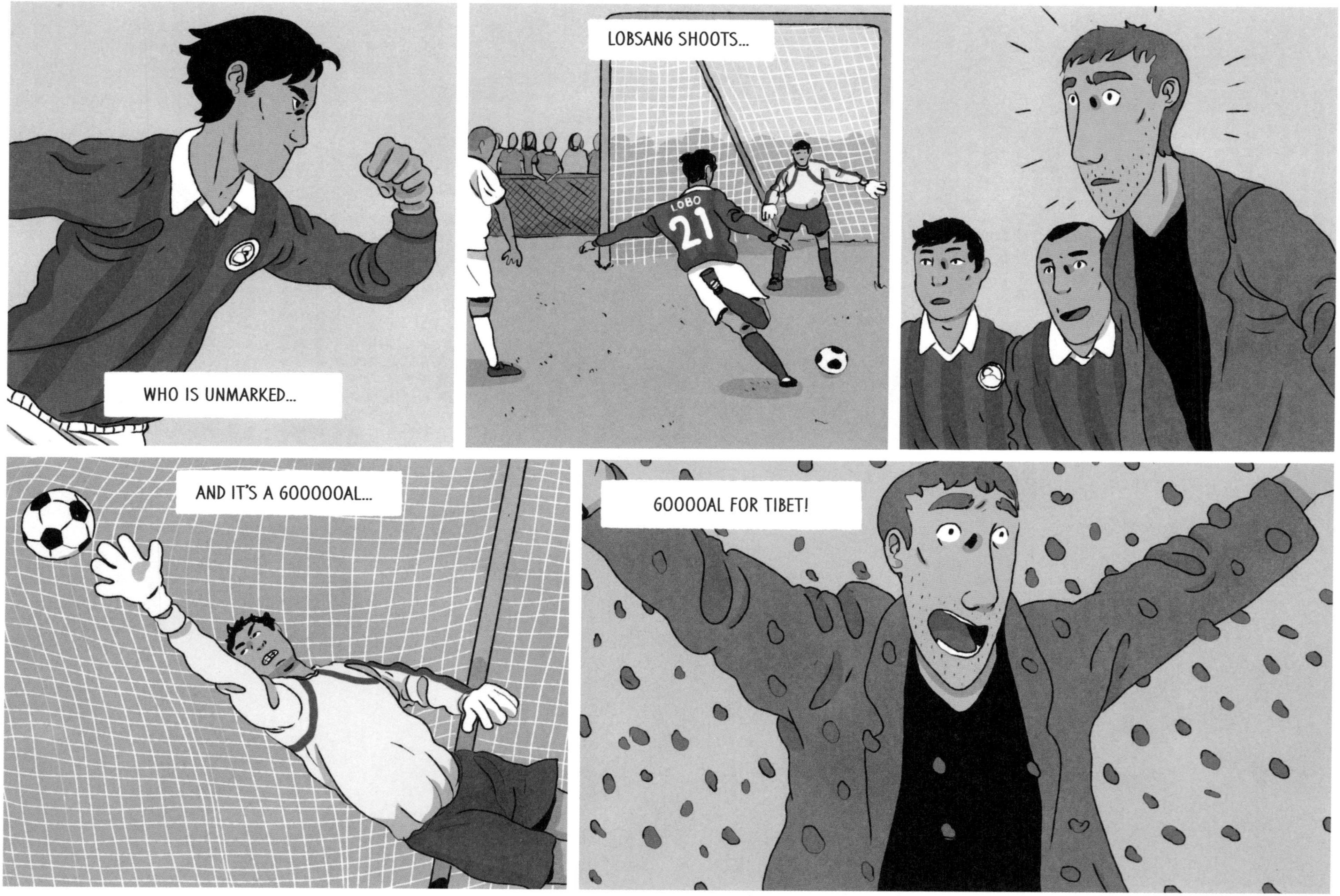
WHO IS UNMARKED...
LOBSANG SHOOTS...
LOBO
21
AND IT'S A GOOOOOAL...
GOOOOAL FOR TIBET!

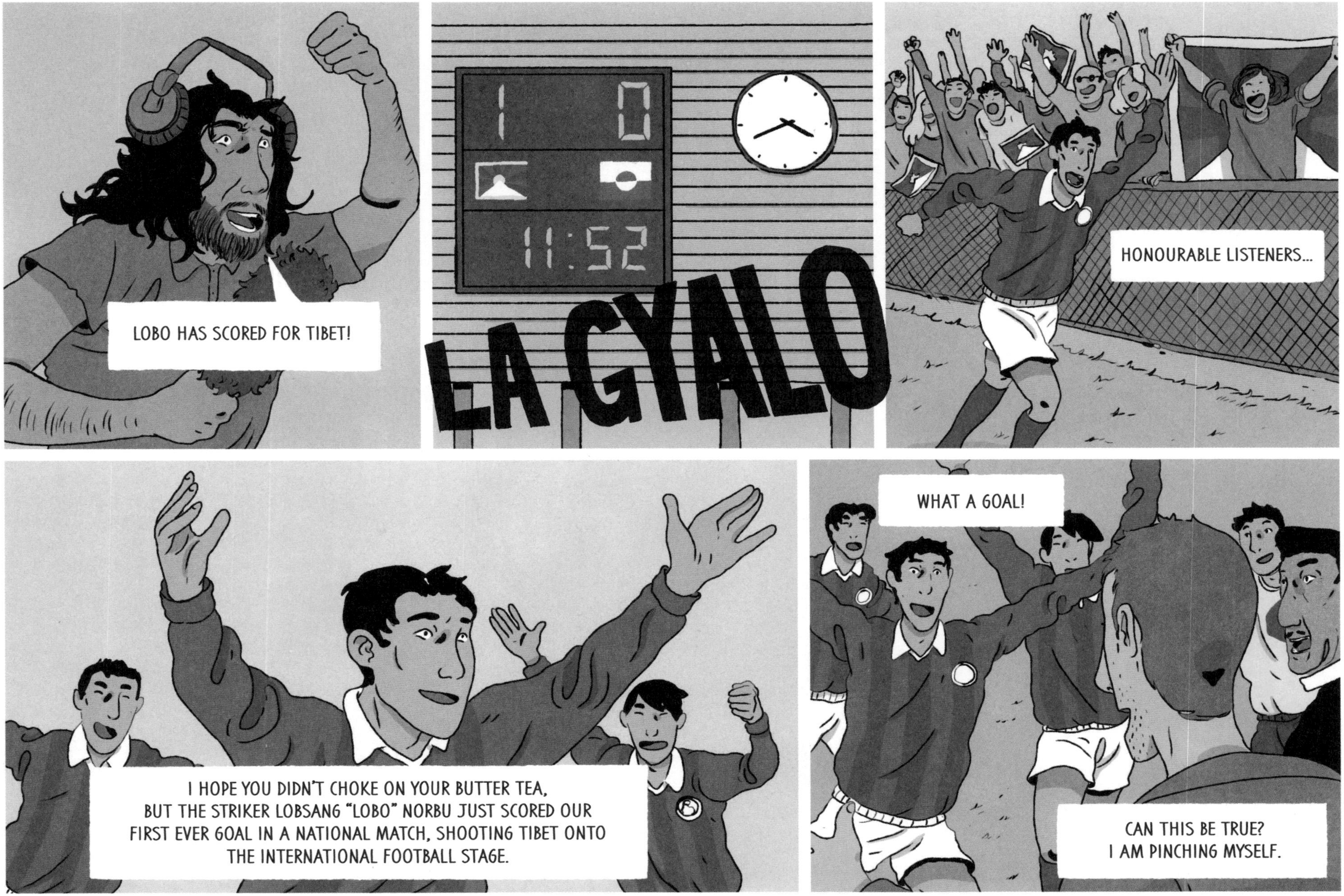
LOBO HAS SCORED FOR TIBET!
1 0
11:52
LA GYALO
HONOURABLE LISTENERS...
I HOPE YOU DIDN'T CHOKE ON YOUR BUTTER TEA, BUT THE STRIKER LOBSANG "LOBO" NORBU JUST SCORED OUR FIRST EVER GOAL IN A NATIONAL MATCH, SHOOTING TIBET ONTO THE INTERNATIONAL FOOTBALL STAGE.
WHAT A GOAL!
CAN THIS BE TRUE? I AM PINCHING MYSELF.

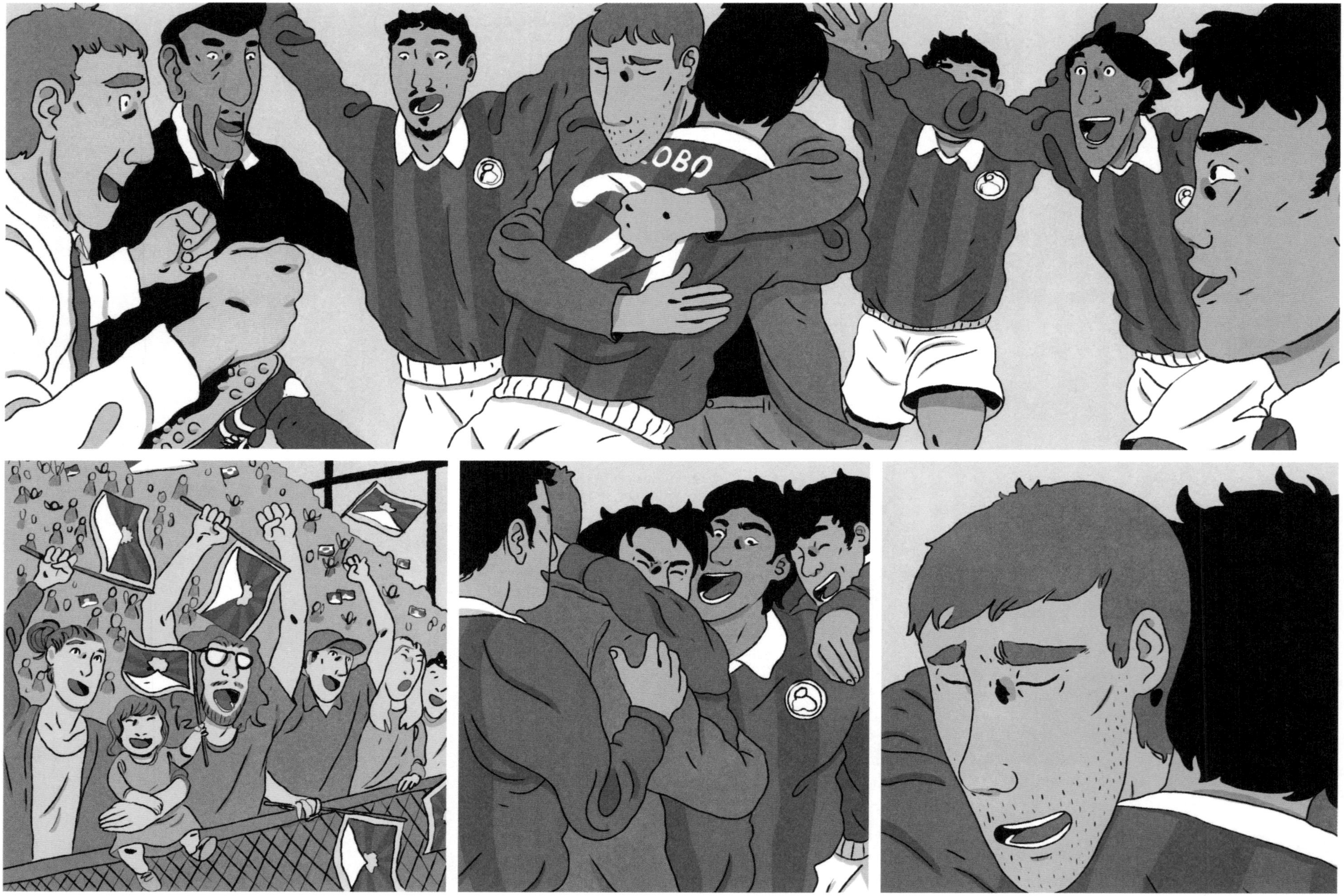

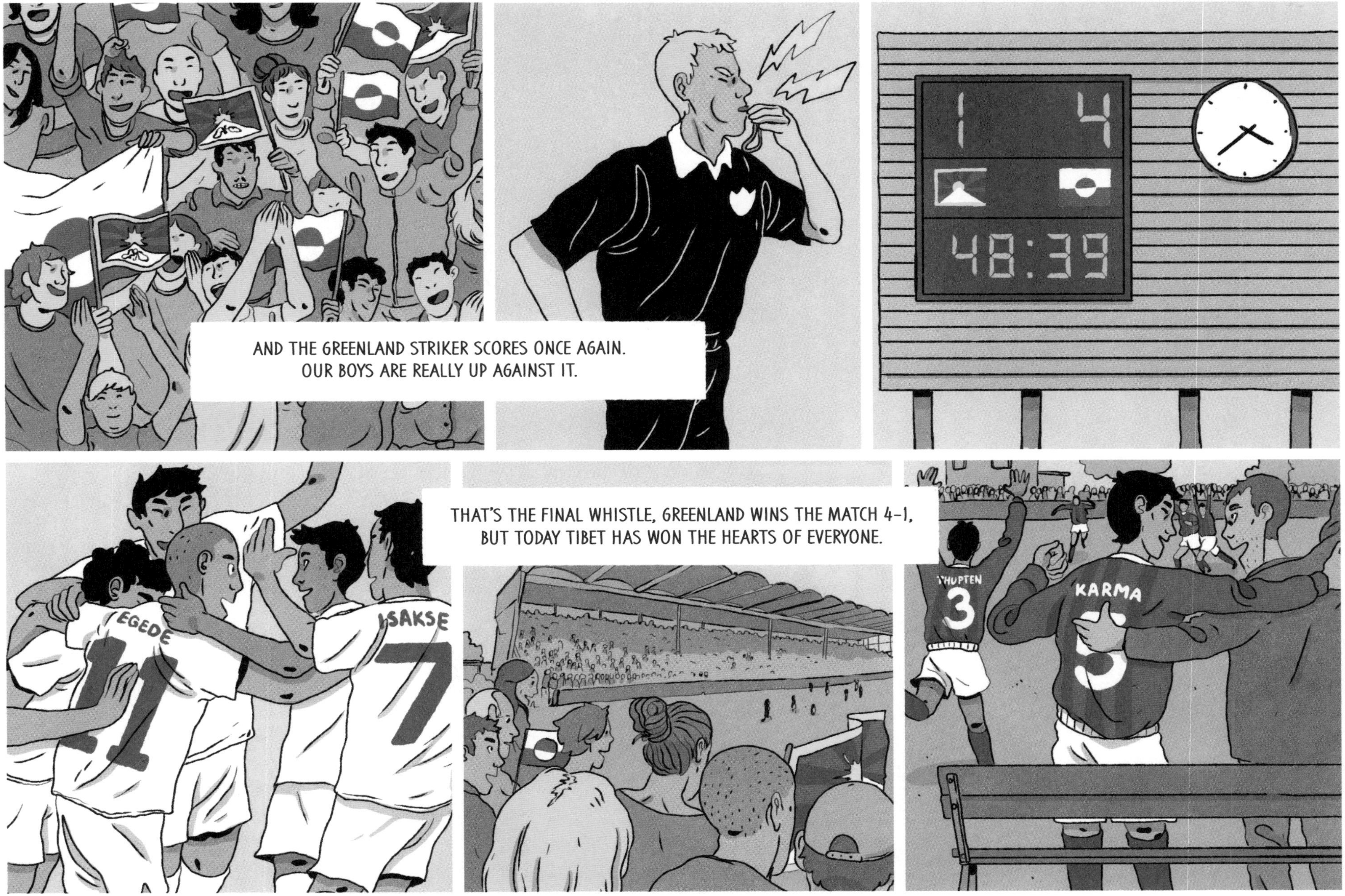
AND THE GREENLAND STRIKER SCORES ONCE AGAIN.
OUR BOYS ARE REALLY UP AGAINST IT.
1 4
48:39
EGEDE
11
7
THAT'S THE FINAL WHISTLE, GREENLAND WINS THE MATCH 4-1,
BUT TODAY TIBET HAS WON THE HEARTS OF EVERYONE.
3
KARMA
5

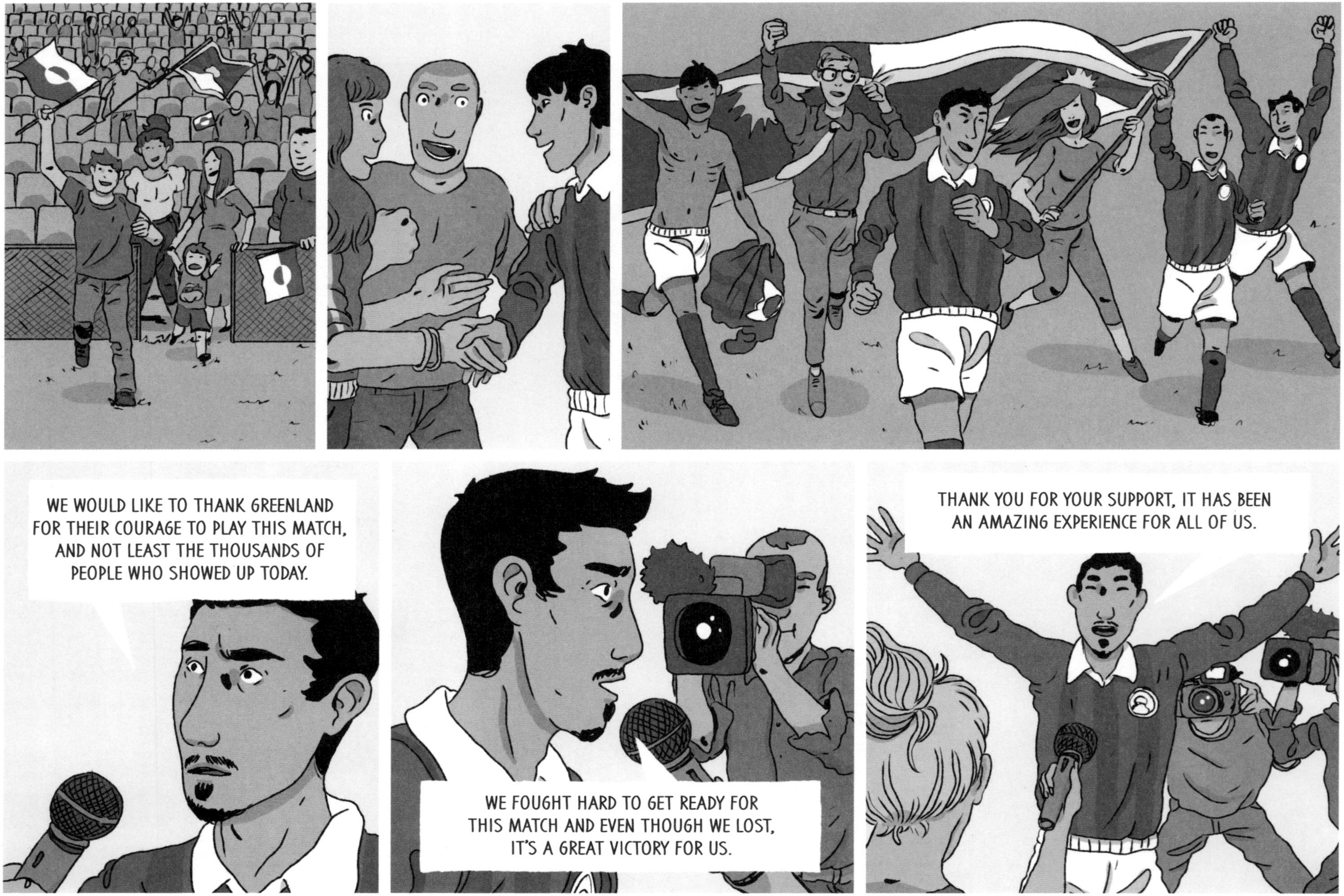
WE WOULD LIKE TO THANK GREENLAND FOR THEIR COURAGE TO PLAY THIS MATCH, AND NOT LEAST THE THOUSANDS OF PEOPLE WHO SHOWED UP TODAY.
WE FOUGHT HARD TO GET READY FOR THIS MATCH AND EVEN THOUGH WE LOST, IT'S A GREAT VICTORY FOR US.
THANK YOU FOR YOUR SUPPORT, IT HAS BEEN AN AMAZING EXPERIENCE FOR ALL OF US.

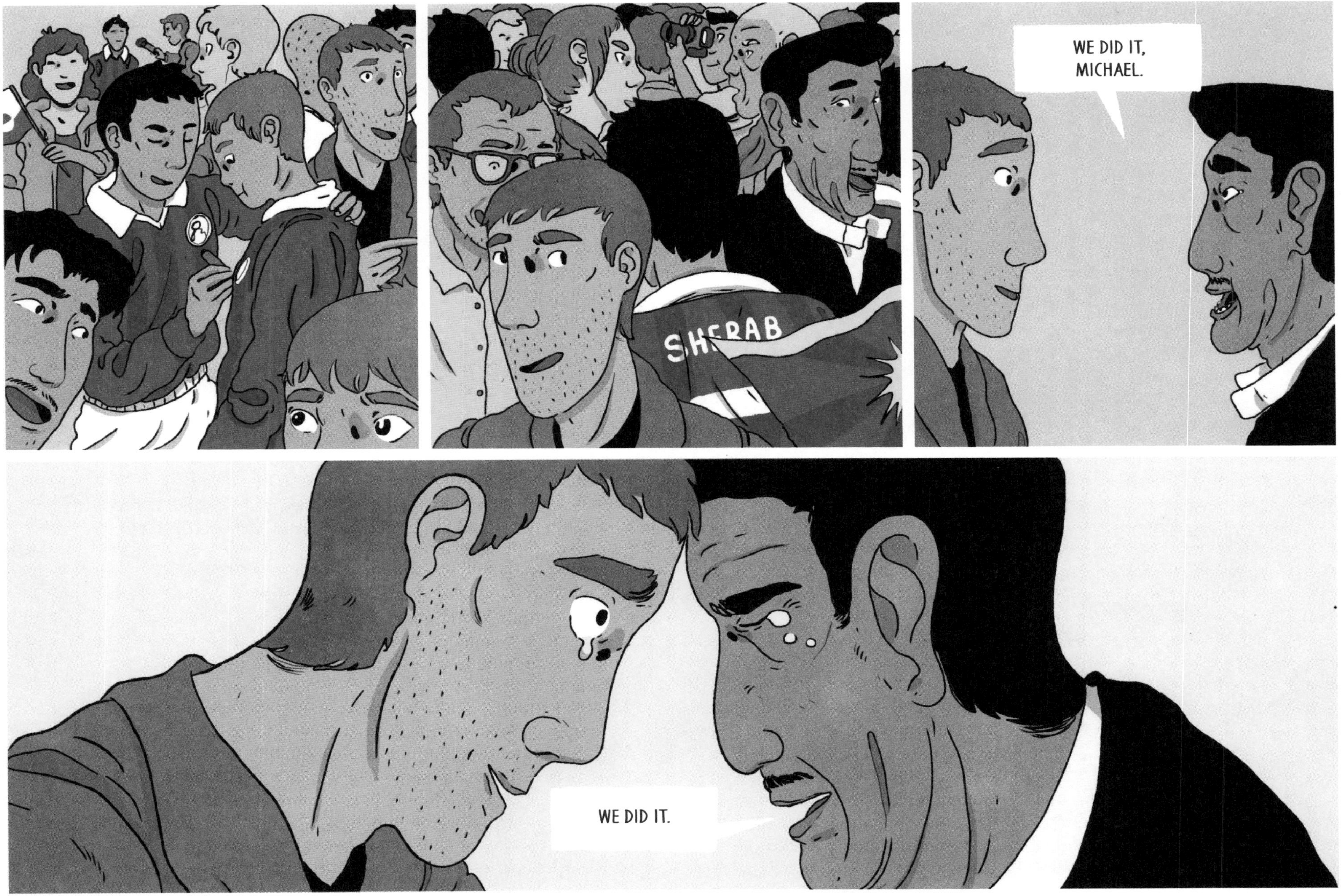
SHERAB
WE DID IT, MICHAEL.
WE DID IT.

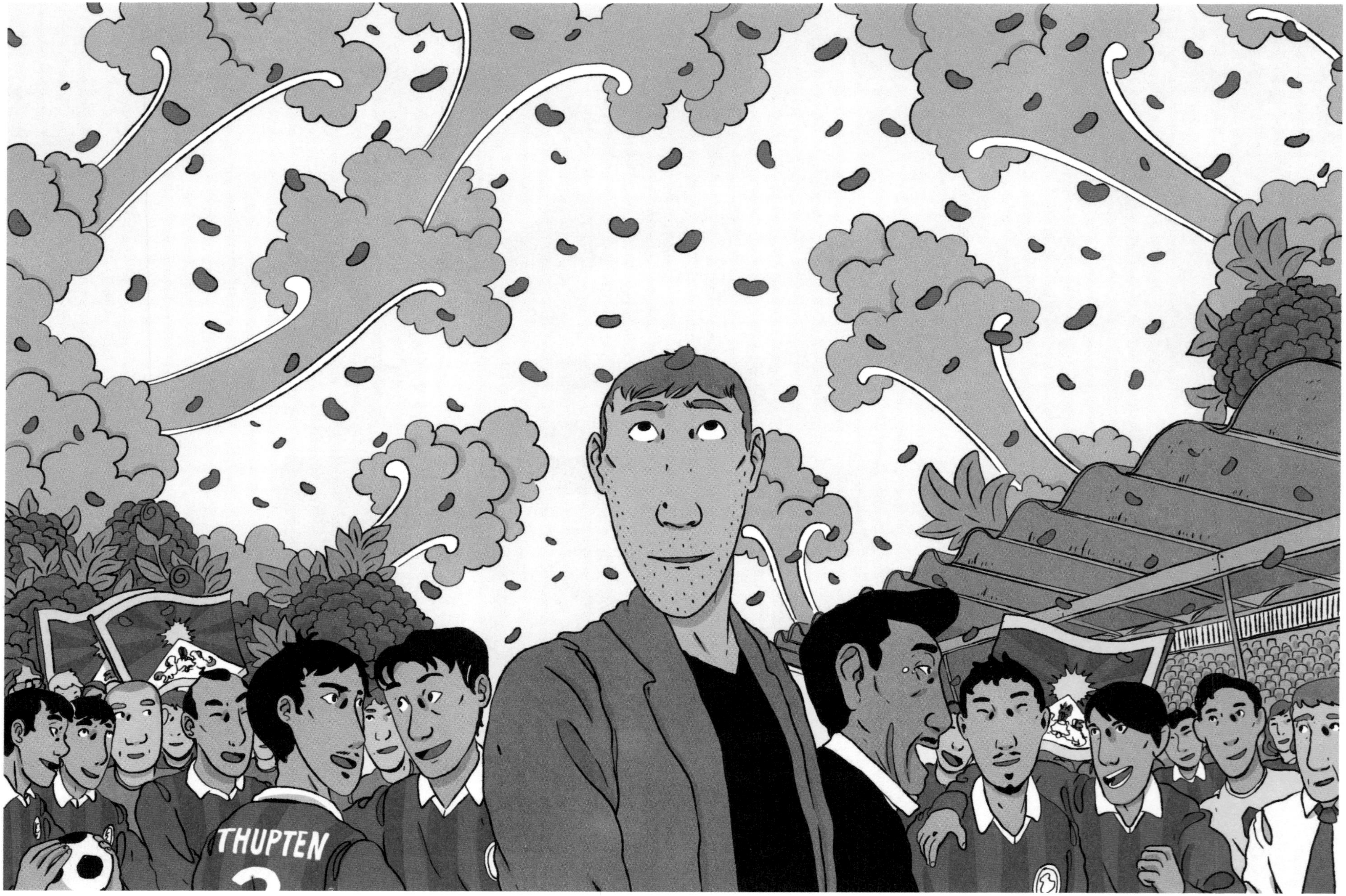
THUPTEN

EPILOGUE
BY THE AUTHOR

This book was written as a tribute to Tibetan football and the fight for an independent Tibet. From the many amazing experiences I've had with Tibetan football over the past sixteen years, I have communicated my story as it happened through memories, diary notes and old newspaper articles, however, I have taken the liberty of changing some events and characters. The book is developed in close collaboration with Thomas Engelbrecht Mikkelsen, an eminent illustrator, who put a lot of hard work into this book. I owe him and my Tibetan friends, on and off the pitch, a big thank you for their inspiration and fighting spirit which kept me going over the five years it took to create this book.

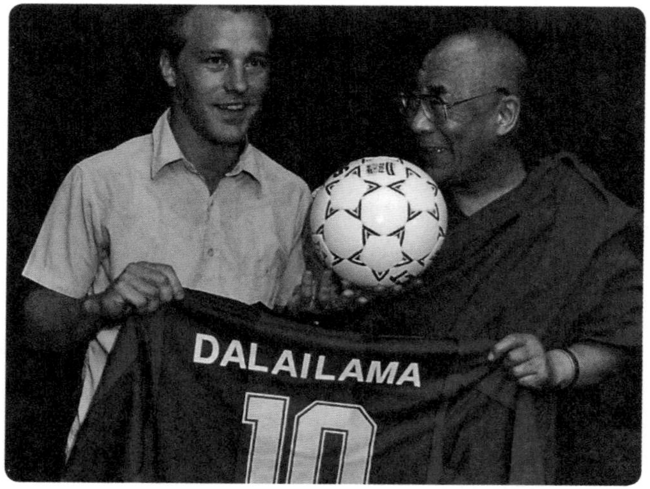
DALAILAMA
10

The players who represented the team against Greenland do not play on the national team anymore, but several of them are involved with sports and have helped to develop the football culture among Tibetans. Since the match against Greenland, Tibetan football has undergone rapid development. Several clubs have emerged, the national team has played more international matches. The annual Tibetan championship (a tournament that is also streamed online) has been a huge success in terms of teams and spectators. And Tibetan football is, moreover, not only for boys. Girls are currently developing their football talent as well. Football and sport generally has become a respected part of the Tibetan exile community.

Not everything in the development of the Tibetan Football Association has been positive. Sponsors have disappeared because of the potential loss of Chinese export opportunities, and there has been resistance from the Chinese authorities who, at every opportunity, have tried to hamper the team. Many people mistakenly believe that the suffering inflicted by the Chinese authorities in Tibet is a closed chapter, but every day Tibetans are imprisoned and abused by the Chinese regime. The struggle for Tibet is far from over. The Tibetan national football team appears in this context as an important ambassador when it plays matches on the international stage, becoming a voice for the many thousands of Tibetans living in exile. It is my humble hope that this book will create more awareness about the Tibetan (football) culture and that the Tibetan football players get more opportunities to travel around the world and share their football passion with others.

I am sure that Tibetan football has a bright future. Who knows, maybe one day Tibet will play a match against the Vatican State or participate in the Olympic Games? Everybody has the right to dream.

Michael Magnus Nybrandt, Copenhagen, July 2016

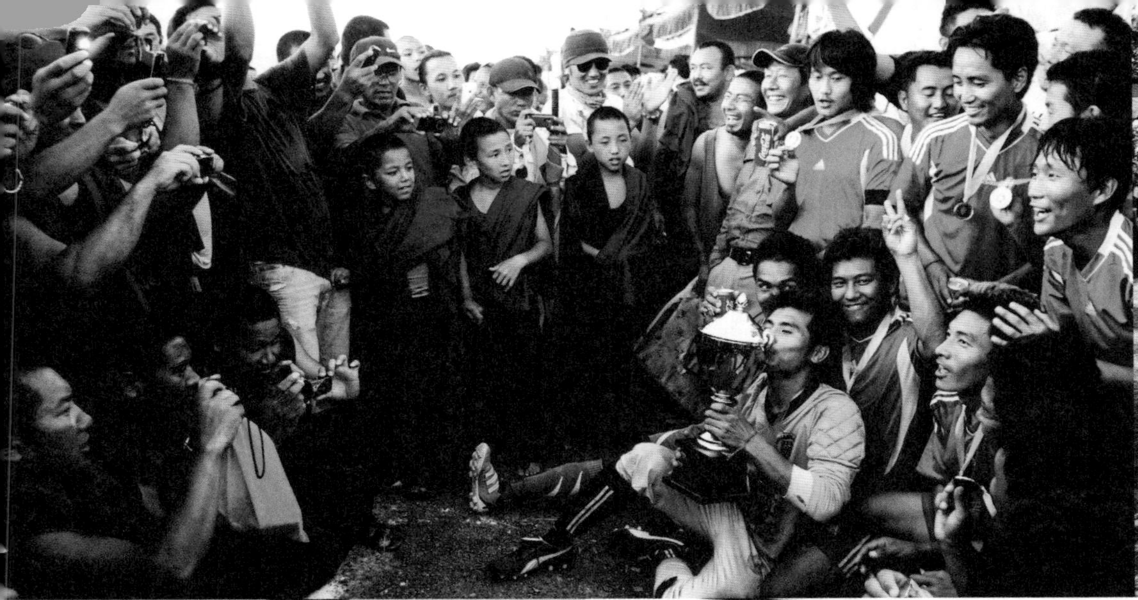
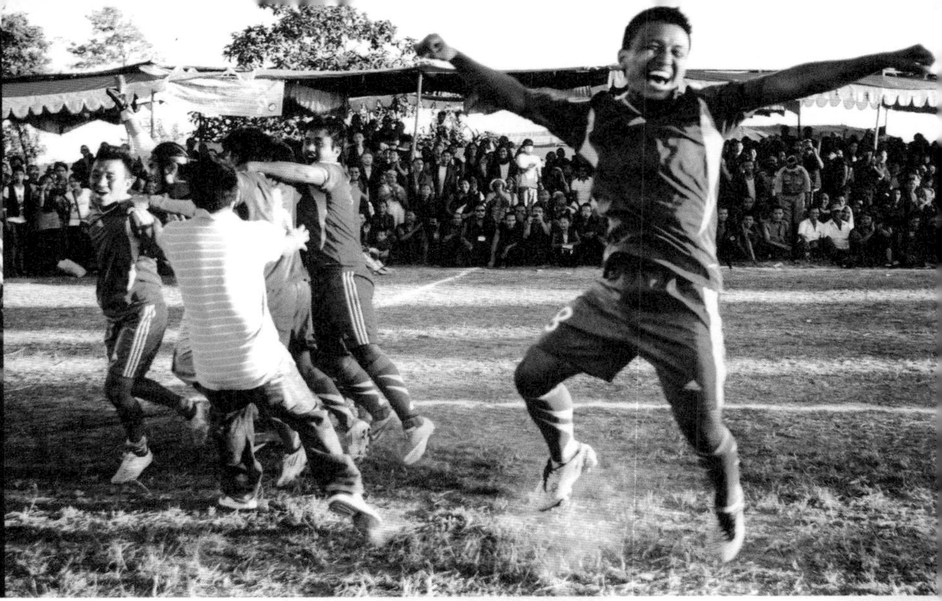
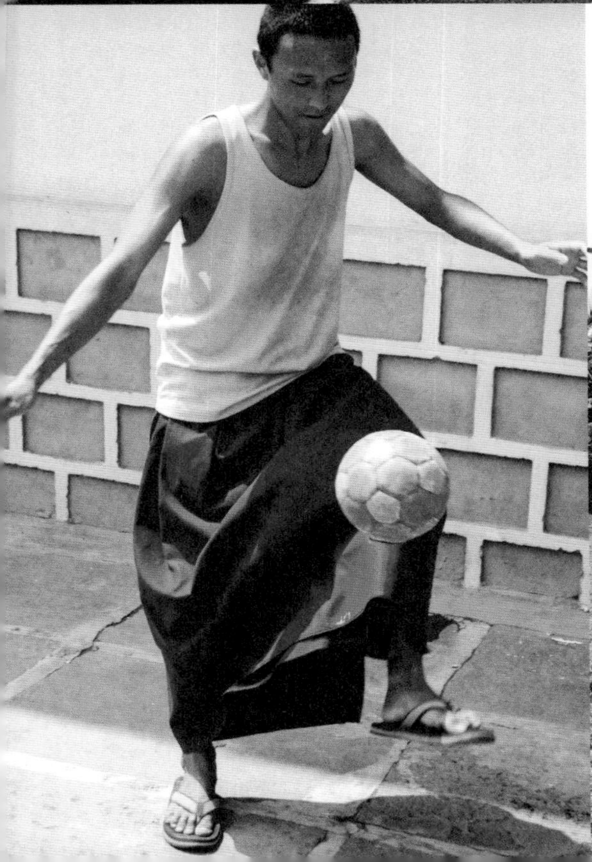
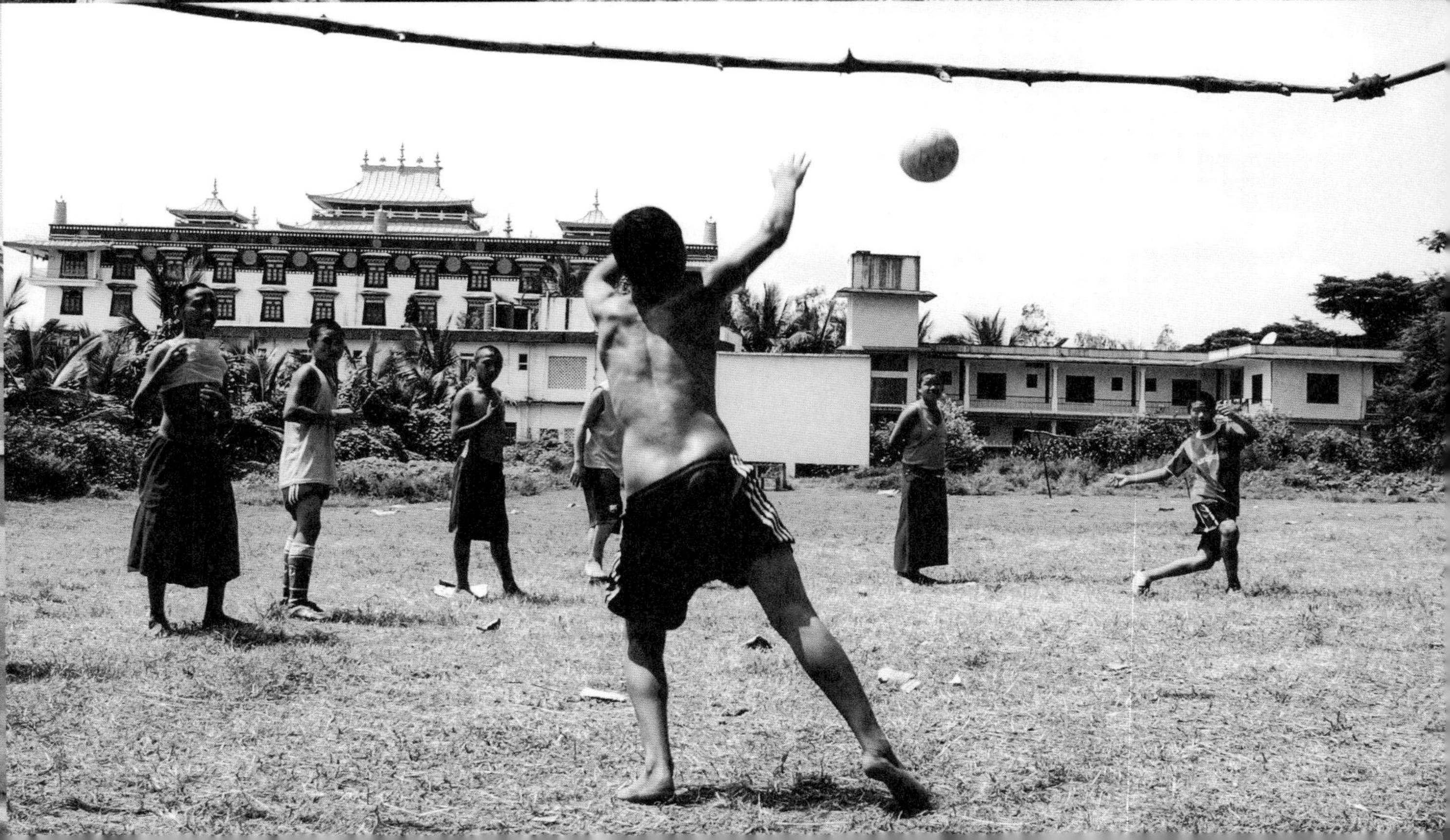

ACKNOWLEDGEMENT

To family and friends. Thanks to Kulkælderen, Serieskolan, Danish Arts Foundation, Danish Writers Association and especially our Danish publisher Forlaget Forlaens. Thanks to all comic colleagues who have helped in one way or another in the making of this book. Finally a huge thank you to Michael and Nadja for your tremendous support and patience during the project.

Thomas Engelbrecht Mikkelsen

For Julie, Louis and Joelle, family and friends. My Tibetan friends and footballers. A special thank you to Thomas, Karma, Kalsang & Tashi, Jens, Rasmus, Arnold, Danish Tibetan Cultural Society and Attention Film. The Kaospilots, Uffe and Karin, Rene and Henrik, Torben, Bo, Steffen, Thorhauge, KB, Mikkel, Cees, Wilfried, Grethe, Vincent, Gert, Christian Peulicke, Magnus, Nils, Minna Haddar, Rune Bachs and Obersten.

Michael Magnus Nybrandt

A special thanks to all the crowdfunders who supported the making of this book.

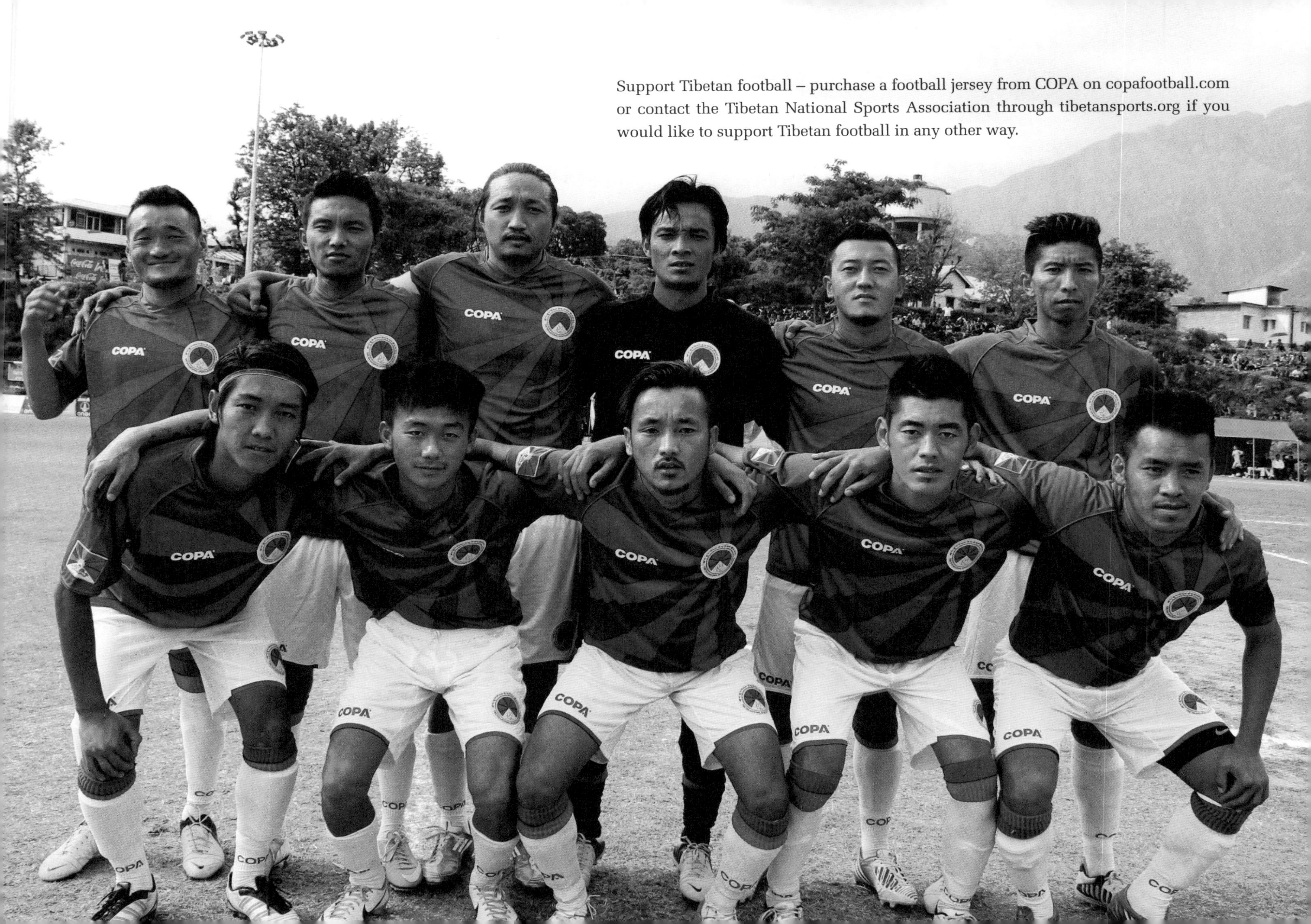
COPA

Support Tibetan football – purchase a football jersey from COPA on copafootball.com or contact the Tibetan National Sports Association through tibetansports.org if you would like to support Tibetan football in any other way.

This book is dedicated to Jamphel Yeshi and the thousands of
Tibetans who have lost their lives as a result of the Chinese occupation,
and to the many who still yearn for freedom.
La Gyalo!

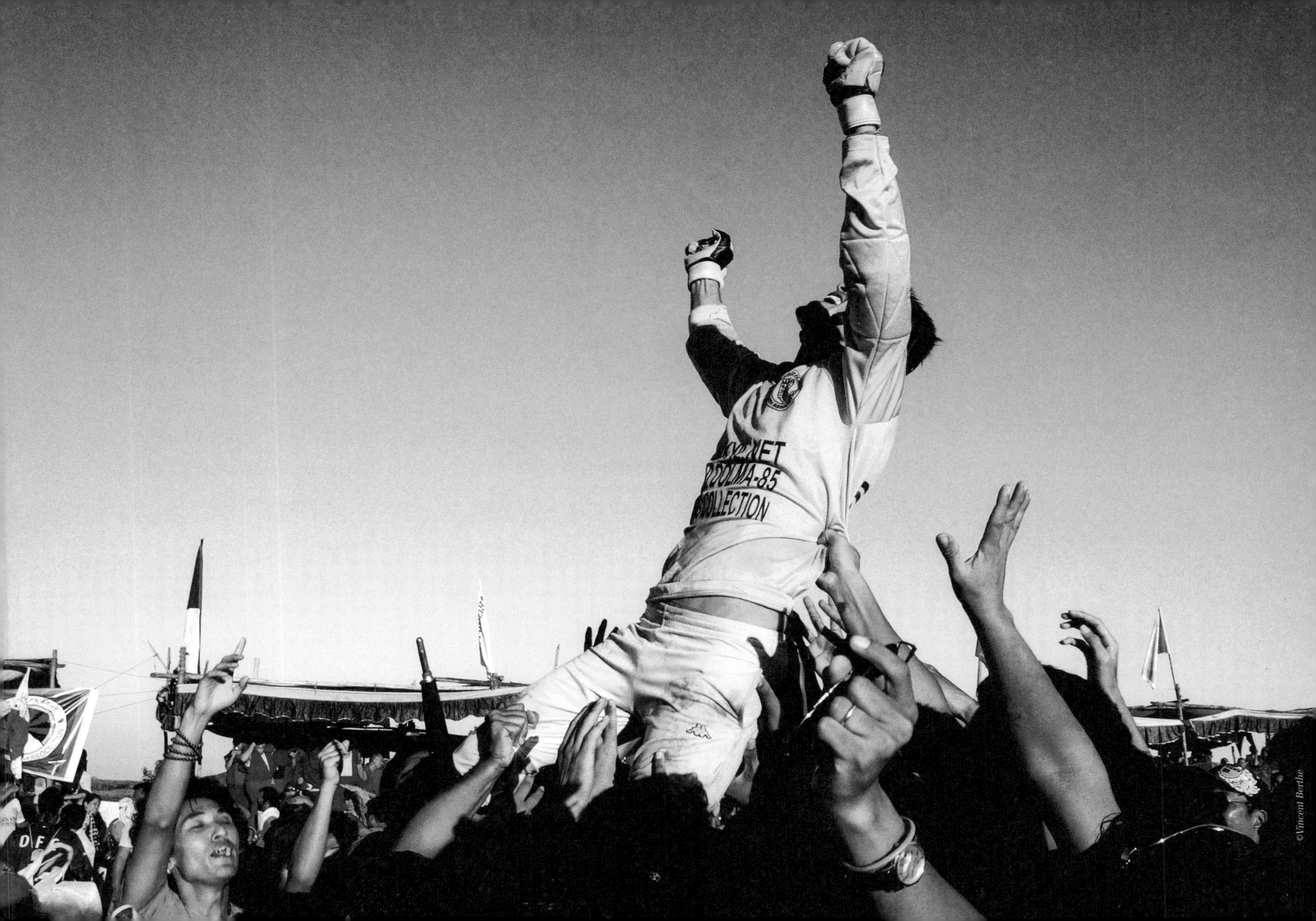

©Vincent Berthe

DREAMS IN THIN AIR

The book was originally supported by The Danish Writers Association and Danish Arts Foundation

DANISH ARTS FOUNDATION

Printed in Latvia
ISBN: 978-1-77262-010-8
Translated by: Steffen Rayburn-Maarup
Editors: Minna Haddar and Torben Hansen
Layout: Michael Magnus Nybrandt and Torben Hansen
Photos: Vincent Berthe

Conundrum Press wishes to acknowledge the Canada Council for the Arts and the province of Nova Scotia and the Creative Industries Fund for financial support

www.conundrumpress.com

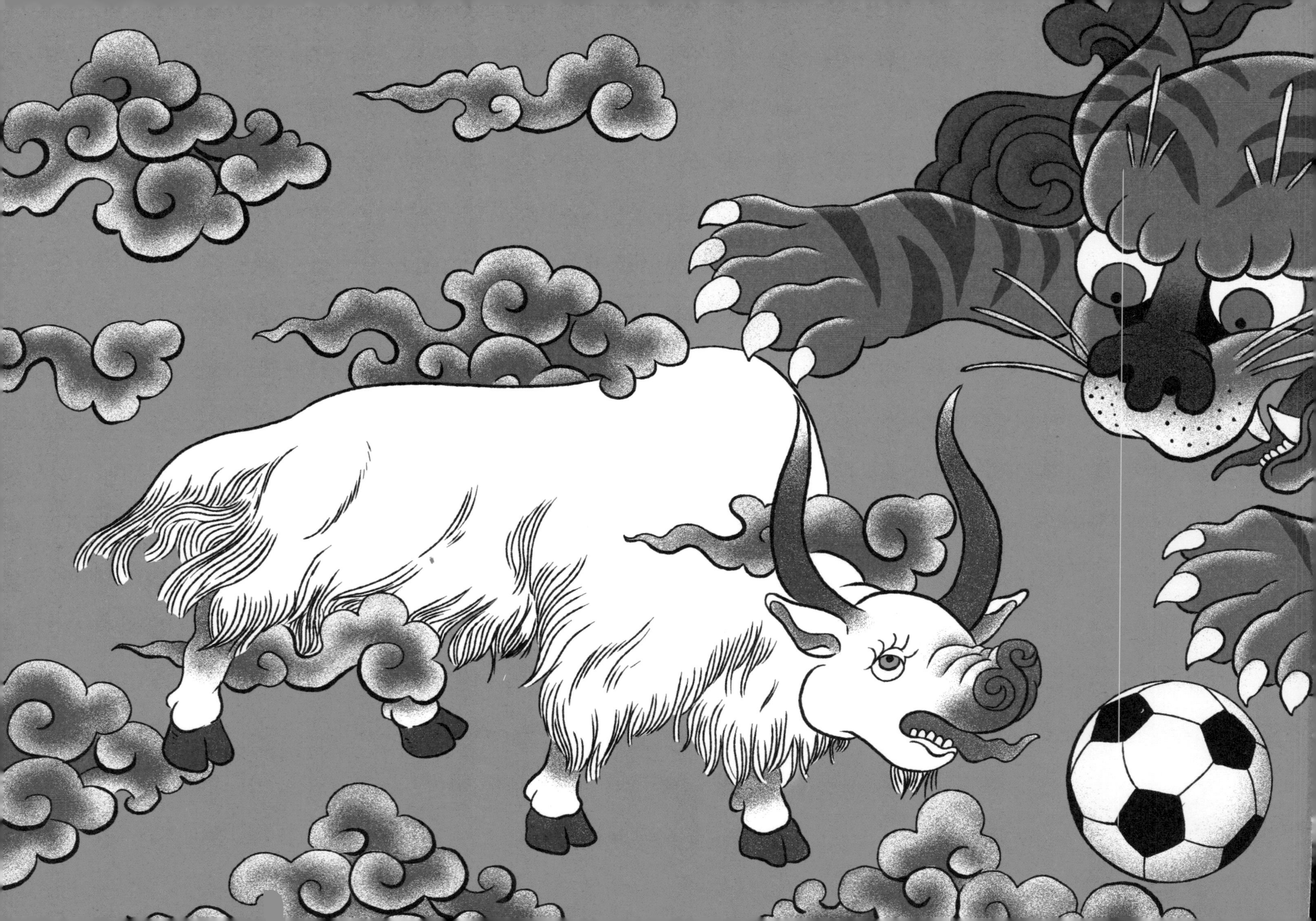